Paying the Piper

THE ECONOMICS OF EDUCATION

Paying the Piper: Productivity, Incentives, and Financing in U.S. Higher Education, by Michael S. McPherson, Morton Owen Schapiro, and Gordon C. Winston

Paying the Piper

Productivity, Incentives, and Financing in U.S. Higher Education

Michael S. McPherson, Morton Owen Schapiro, and Gordon C. Winston

Ann Arbor

THE UNIVERSITY OF MICHIGAN PRESS

Copyright © by the University of Michigan 1993
All rights reserved
Published in the United States of America by
The University of Michigan Press
Manufactured in the United States of America

1997   1996   1995   4   3   2

Library of Congress Cataloging-in-Publication Data

McPherson, Michael S.
    Paying the piper : productivity, incentives, and financing in U.S. higher
education / Michael S. McPherson, Morton Owen Schapiro,
and Gordon C. Winston.
        p.   cm. — (The Economics of education)
    Includes bibliographical references (p.) and index.
    ISBN 0-472-10404-7
    1. Education, Higher—United States—Finance.   2. Student aid—United
States.   3. Universities and colleges—United States—Administration.
I. Schapiro, Morton Owen.   II. Winston, Gordon C.   III. Title.   IV. Series.
LB2342.M375   1994
378'.02'0973—dc20   93-33322
                                                                            CIP

B
34 2
1 25
9 3

Contents

Part 1
Background

CHAPTER 1

Introduction

*Michael S. McPherson, Morton Owen Schapiro,
and Gordon C. Winston*

Higher education is under assault. The combination of revenue shortfalls and expenditure pressures along with a variety of well-publicized controversies involving political correctness, the neglect of teaching, the misuse of government research funding, and similar public relations disasters have led to a sharp reduction in trust between colleges and universities and the public.

All too easily lost in the rhetoric is a careful examination of the many successes of U.S. higher education, the identification of real problems, and a careful analysis of potential solutions. This volume is intended to help fill this void.

Many of the complaints about higher education relate to wasteful spending and nebulous educational outcomes. The productivity concerns voiced over the past decade are an attempt to link explicitly the various types of expenditures with particular outputs. While the precise measure of these variables—especially on the output side—is a matter of contention, the effort to identify cost-effective educational methods and organizations is laudable. Productivity increases, after all, are the key to economic growth for the nation. For colleges and universities, they could very well be the difference between a thriving higher education industry in the 1990s and beyond and a declining industry, outmoded and noncompetitive.

Productivity measures and concerns are quite appealing to economists. As educators, however, we quickly recognize the need to avoid simple-minded attempts to quantify phenomena that are multidimensional and abstract. Are there useful output measures? Is it possible to do a better job measuring both educational inputs and outputs without losing sight of the broader purposes of education? We believe progress on this front is possible. As our ability to measure educational outputs gradually improves, the natural next question is how to influence the higher education system to produce more of the desired outputs. Economists can contribute here mainly through the study of incentives. What outputs do the existing set of incentives facing students and institutions encourage them to produce? Can we change the

3

incentive system to encourage productivity growth? Of course, an important part of this system involves the basic financing of U.S. higher education. By deciding who pays the bill, our financing system creates a set of incentives that ultimately plays a large part in determining how productive our higher education industry is. It gets back to the old proposition that whoever pays the piper calls the tune. While financial incentives are far from the whole story in higher education, they do take us some distance in explaining the system we end up with. If we seek to change this system—to get greater output for our inputs—a different financing scheme could alter incentives and affect student and institutional behavior in a positive way.

Over the past few years we have written a number of articles about productivity, incentives, and financing in U.S. higher education. Several are reprinted here along with some new work. The chapters tend to rely on similar data sets and often represent different angles on particular topics. Our view is that the combination of chapters in this volume is valuable beyond the contribution of any single chapter.

Chapter 2, "Trends in Revenues and Expenditures in U.S. Higher Education: Where Does the Money Come From? Where Does It Go?" sets the stage for what follows. It is a new study of the financial situation of different types of colleges and universities. While there has been much recent speculation about revenues and expenditures in higher education, there have been relatively few careful examinations of the relevant data. We have assembled a data set consisting of financial and other information on individual colleges and universities during the period 1978–79 to 1988–89, and, in summarizing these data, we disaggregate institutions by type (university, four-year college, or two-year college) and control (public or private).

It is no surprise that these data document rapid growth in tuition and in per student spending at private universities in the 1980s. Perhaps the most striking finding is the spectacular growth in spending on new plant and equipment at private universities, especially in the latter half of the 1980s. A finding that is perhaps less to be expected is that the revenue squeeze that has hit public higher education so hard in the 1990s was already underway by the mid-1980s, as very slow growth in state support for public universities led to low rates of spending growth and rates of tuition increase that matched those in the private sector. Thus, for universities, growth in tuition in the private sector in the 1980s was part of a general period of expansion in revenues and expenditures on a wide front, while for the publics, the 1980s saw tuition increases being used to try to preserve programs in the face of lagging growth in state support. This gradual change in the relative competitive positions of public and private universities has of course become much sharper and more visible in the early 1990s. As chapter 2 shows, similar but more muted changes in the relative position of public and private four-year colleges and two-year colleges occurred in the 1980s. Student aid has become an increasingly important competitive tool for all types of private institutions in the 1980s. While federal student aid per student actually declined in real terms for private universities and four-year colleges in the 1980s, this decline was more than made up by increases in the discounting of tuition through institutional student aid over the period. In fact, net of student aid, public four-year colleges actually raised prices faster than private four-year colleges over the 1978–79 to 1988–89 period.

The contribution of tuition to total revenue also dramatically increased during this period at public four-year and two-year colleges. Tuition revenues grew in importance at public universities as well, making up for the drop in the role of federal research funding. The decline in the relative contribution of federal research support at public universities was modest compared to the experience at private universities, who were able to compensate with a major increase in the role of gift and endowment earnings.

The analysis of changes in the composition of revenues and expenditures raises serious worries about the financial health of U.S. higher education, especially in the public sector. Public institutions are highly reliant on state and local appropriations. In fact, public four-year and two-year colleges have become more dependent on state and local appropriations over time. Yet these operating subsidies grew only slightly in real terms from 1978–79 to 1988–89 at all types of public institutions, especially at community colleges. Since then, subsidies have actually dropped in many states, making pressures on funding even more severe.

Chapter 2 provides much more detail on the trends briefly summarized here, as well as on patterns of change in individual spending and revenue categories, such as instruction and administrative expenditures. This close examination of levels and trends in expenditures and revenues serves as the foundation for the chapters that follow. Expenditure increases are closely linked to the productivity and organization discussions in chapters 3, 4, and 5. Changes in gross tuition, institutional and federal financial aid, and net price are the core of the student finance analyses presented in chapters 6, 7, 8, and 9. Finally, while chapter 2 focuses on describing levels and trends in revenue and expenditure data, chapters 10 and 11 contain a more ambitious causal analysis of links between revenues and expenditures and take a much closer look at the proper measurement of institutional finance variables.

Chapter 2 cautiously avoids any attempt to link expenditure categories to proxies for institutional excellence. No doubt many readers will be particularly interested in the share of operating expenditures going to instruction and self-supported research as opposed to the administration categories. But we avoid the mention of productivity—the ratio of output to expenditures— given the difficulty in using our aggregate data to measure educational output.

While it may very well be true that the link between instructional spending and educational output is stronger than, say, the link between educational output and institutional support, we leave for chapter 3 a detailed discussion of whether we can in fact ever hope to measure educational output in a meaningful way.

"The Concept of Productivity As Applied to U.S. Higher Education" was prepared in 1987 for an international conference on productivity in higher education. The goal was to review the state of research on how productivity measures can be developed and applied in U.S. higher education. Chapter 3 begins with a brief description of the "assessment movement" in this country and continues with a discussion of the general concept of productivity.

The most basic output measure, used extensively over the years by a variety of economists and other researchers, is simply the number of students or, for an individual, the number of years of schooling. Although obviously crude, measures of the numbers of students served or numbers of degrees produced are certainly of interest. Indeed, an important recent volume on graduate education by William Bowen and Neil Rudenstine, *In Pursuit of the Ph.D.* (Princeton, NJ: Princeton University Press, 1992) leans heavily and effectively on degree production as a measure of effectiveness of graduate education. One way of refining "headcount" measures is through examining test scores. There already exists an impressive range of tests that go to great lengths to assess cognitive achievement and processes. Such tests can of course be abused: no test can measure all the things education aims to achieve, and a misplaced emphasis on tests alone in evaluating educational output could distort incentives for institutions and faculty. Still, the combination of data on the average increase in test scores while in college plus appropriate control variables could provide at least partial measures of the value added by college. Probably the best way to improve these measures is to use them thoughtfully, and to discuss their implications and their limitations openly.

Measuring inputs into the educational process is far easier than measuring outputs. In fact, many of the expenditure categories used in chapter 2 are prime candidates. However, systematic study of the relationship between output and input, even when the output measure is very simple, is quite rare. Exceptions are noted, but we are a long way from understanding how different inputs affect educational outcomes. Without this information, our ability to increase productivity in higher education is severely limited.

The next chapter, "The Economics of Cost, Price, and Quality in U.S. Higher Education," originally prepared for a conference at the Aspen Institute on American education, also considers our success in measuring educational outcomes and argues that it is our inability to measure school quality in an easy and convincing way that leads to some of the expenditure growth documented in chapter 2. This essay includes a review of the economic literature on markets in which information about the quality of products is scarce, unreliable, and costly. When the provision of direct information about product quality is inadequate, buyers seek and producers provide indirect or symbolic indicators of product quality. College education is clearly a service whose quality is hard for the inexperienced consumer to judge. One result is that colleges try to offer signals of high quality to prospective consumers.

These signals take the form of both image advertising and certain types of expenditures. Colleges have devoted increasing resources to improving the presentation of materials they mail to prospective customers (note the levels and changes in the student services category in the data presented in chapter 2, especially in the private sector). They have also paid close attention to those on-campus investments that signal that the school has the confidence and the wherewithal to put substantial resources behind those aspects of the enterprise that most attract students. It is hard for a prospective student to monitor changes in instructional expenditures, but it is easy to tour the campus and admire architecturally striking new buildings devoted to activities whose benefits students can readily grasp. Theaters, athletic facilities, computer centers, museums, and the like rank high on a list of such facilities. The staggering increases in capital spending highlighted in chapter 2 document in a vivid way the decision of college and university administrators to signal their quality through bricks and mortar. One theme of chapter 4 is that colleges and universities, when they engage in these kinds of conspicuous expenditure are not simply being irrational or profligate: they are responding in understandable ways to their market situation. If changing this behavior is socially desirable (as we believe it is), it is probably more productive (although perhaps less fun) to change the incentives and the market situation of these institutions than to scold them. In fact, the recession and the increasing cost consciousness of education consumers may already be having this effect.

Some observers would likely point out that the data in chapter 2 show that the largest part of expenditures goes to the instruction category. Most of the spending here is for faculty salaries. Perhaps it is the basic organization of work relations in higher education—namely the tenure system—that lies at the root of our inability to control costs. Few economists have taken a serious look at the unusual contracting system found at the vast majority of our colleges and universities. One exception, "The Economics of Academic Tenure: A Relational Perspective," is reprinted as chapter 5.

This chapter applies work in analytical labor economics showing the value of stable long-term employment relationships. While many observers defend the tenure system in terms of academic freedom and similar noneconomic benefits, it is argued here that, independently of those considerations, there are good economic reasons underlying academic tenure. These relate to the difficulty of monitoring faculty work performance and the highly specific character of faculty jobs and job training. An alternative to the academic tenure system, term contracting, is then examined and found to be lacking on economic grounds. In sum, while some may view academic tenure as an expensive luxury that should be reconsidered in these times of financial stringency, this paper defends the tenure system on economic efficiency grounds. While the criteria for tenure, the specificity of faculty training, and other aspects of employment relations in higher education are certainly worthy of scrutiny, the increasingly common practice of blaming the academic tenure system for perceived stagnation or decline in productivity may very well be misguided.

In all, these chapters on productivity and organization offer two principal lessons. On one hand, there is good reason to lean against the claim by some in higher education that their work is somehow beyond the reach of systematic quantitative analysis. On the other hand, it is important to recognize that both the mission and the organizational structure of colleges and universities make them distinctive enterprises, whose institutional complexities analysts must recognize.

We turn next to a group of papers that fall under the heading "Student Finance." Chapter 2 documented the recent history of tuition charges, federal aid, and institutional aid at different types of schools. Chapters 6 to 9 access various aspects of the student finance system in more detail, examining its purposes and its effects.

The section begins with a paper titled "How Can We Tell If Federal Student Aid Is Working?" Originally prepared at the request of the College Board as a means of broadening the discussion of student aid beyond the relatively narrow focus of many Washington discussions of the subject, the paper identifies three fundamental questions: has federal aid encouraged the enrollment and broadened the educational choices of disadvantaged students? has federal student aid made the distribution of higher education's benefits, and the sharing of its costs, fairer? and has federal student aid made higher education institutions work better, by making them financially more secure and educationally more effective?

The answer to the first question—the one that has occupied center stage in most policy discussions—is quite controversial. The literature includes a number of attempts to estimate the impact of federal aid on enrollment rates and there is a well-known disagreement about the answer. Our own study, which attempts to reconcile differences in the literature and to present new empirical results, is described below (chapter 8). Despite the importance of this question of enrollment effects, a major theme of chapter 6 is that issues of fairness and institutional impact are also vital aspects of policy discussion of student aid. Indeed, as the recent reauthorization of the Higher Education

Act shows, Congress is motivated at least as much by concerns about the perceived fairness in treatment of different groups of aid recipients as about the overall efficiency of the aid programs in promoting enrollment. Thus, for example, Congress's decision to eliminate home equity from the calculation of family ability to pay for college is a way of moving some aid dollars toward middle-income families who feel aggrieved. The legislative history of federal student aid makes clear that the impact of aid on the well-being of higher education institutions has also been on the Congress's mind, with student aid being viewed partly as a strategy for bolstering the finances of institutions enrolling large numbers of needy students. Unfortunately, empirical work on institutional impacts of aid is, if anything, more difficult than work on the impacts of aid on student choice. Once again, our own empirical study of this problem is described below (chapter 10).

Chapter 7, "Federal Student Aid Policy: Can We Learn from Experience?," presents a more detailed description of federal aid programs and options. This chapter, prepared originally as a lecture in the Rockefeller Institute's series on public policy, attempts to embed policy disputes about student aid in a historical context. While it is easy to show that the existing student financing system is far short of what anyone would call ideal, it may be more instructive to ask whether Congress and the president, at decisive moments in the history of federal student aid, made good or bad choices among politically realistic alternatives. When the record is viewed in this way, the governmental processes shaping student aid look pretty good. Even the decision in the late 1970s to uncap subsidized student loans, thereby providing an unjustified bonanza to affluent families, seems forgivable when it is seen as a means of heading off a move for providing tax benefits for families' spending on higher education. The tax expenditure alternative would have been worse distributionally and probably harder to reverse than the student loan giveaway proved to be. There is always the risk that in reviewing the historical choices Congress made one will back into the position that "to understand all is to forgive all," failing then to criticize existing programs because the alternatives were worse. Yet while it is important to stop short of that fatalistic position, a reminder of the political-economic constraints within which the policy process operates may contribute to more realistic policy discussion.

As mentioned above, one central criterion for evaluating the efficacy of the federal aid programs is their effect on the enrollment of low-income students. Chapter 8, "Measuring the Effects of Federal Student Aid: An Assessment of Some Methodological and Empirical Problems," examines this topic in detail. The chapter, originally developed in the context of a Department of Education initiative to examine the effects of student aid, follows up the previous two in paying special attention to the seeming conflict between empirical findings based on cross-sectional econometric results that tend to find large effects of aid and the actual historical experience in which these effects are not readily discernible in the aggregate data. New results are presented that go some distance toward reconciling these various findings. A properly controlled econometric analysis of time-series data for white students shows significant effects of aid on enrollment for students from low-income families.

This finding is very important—it provides an economic foundation for the considerable investments in financial aid the federal government and institutions made that were documented in chapter 2. Specifically, our results indicate that increases in net cost over time lead to decreases in enrollment rates for low-income students. The magnitude of the coefficient on net cost implies that for lower-income students a $100 net cost increase, expressed in 1982–83 dollars, results in a 1.6 percent decline in enrollment for that income group. A consensus in the econometric literature based on cross-sectional studies is that a $100 increase in net cost reduces enrollment rates by 1.8 percent. Our result is thus broadly consistent with typical cross-sectional findings and thus helps to ease the worry that the historical evidence of the time-series studies is at odds with the best econometric work in the cross section.

We view this work as an important first step in resolving a long-standing controversy in the literature. These results derive from our having systematically related changes in net cost to changes in enrollment rather than simply looking at enrollment levels at two points in time. It is important to appreciate that these findings for low-income students would be obscured in an analysis that aggregated over income groups, since our evidence suggests (in line with the findings of cross-sectional studies) that the behavior of these income groups is quite different.

In particular, we found no evidence that increases in net cost inhibited enrollment for more affluent students. Thus, policies that call for cross-subsidization of students—affluent students paying a substantial share of educational and general costs with these revenues supporting discounts for low-income students—makes sense from the viewpoint of economic efficiency. But are these policies "fair"? The student finance section concludes with a brief analytical essay addressing this question, "Robin Hood in the Forests of Academe."

It is common to refer to the practice of making wealthier families pay much more and less wealthy families pay much less as Robin Hooding. This term carries the suggestion that wealthier families are being forcibly subjected to a policy that is basically unfair. But an economist would view differential payments by affluent and poor families as simple price discrimination, charging different prices on the basis of differences in willingness and ability to pay, a mainstay of a capitalist system. Few observers, for example, accuse the airlines of Robin Hooding when they charge more to business travelers on full fare than to vacationers on excursion fares. One thing that distinguishes price discrimination in higher education from that in for-profit industries is that colleges charge different prices not to maximize profit but to ensure that able students can have access to an excellent education regardless of family income (and, as the previous chapters argue, these policies are in fact very effective in raising enrollment rates for low-income students).

Not only is the purpose of cross-subsidization policies a socially desirable one, it is important to note that students from wealthy families enter into these arrangements voluntarily. Moreover, even the richest student gets some educational subsidy, a fact documented in chapter 2 by the comparison between operating expenditures per student and gross tuition (and the difference would be even more striking if capital costs were accounted for). The case for need-based aid originally developed in this essay in the mid-1980s has gained a surprising legal relevance in the last several years, as the Justice Department has alleged antitrust violations against Ivy League institutions for agreeing together to follow the kinds of Robin Hood policies we defend.

We turn finally to the section titled "Institutional Finance." A central implication of the analyses presented in the preceding section is that federal student aid, as long as it lowers the net price faced by low-income students, has a significant positive effect on enrollment. An important policy issue, however, is whether changes in federal aid in fact wind up changing net cost. Just as farm subsidies may do more to bolster farmers' incomes than to lower food prices, it is conceivable that colleges, rather than students, wind up capturing most of the benefits of federal student aid. Chapter 10, "The Effect of Government Financing on the Behavior of Colleges and Universities," contains an empirical study of this question.

The chapter presents an econometric model in which changes over time in tuition charges, institution-specific financial aid, and instructional expenditures are explained in terms of changes over time in levels of federal student aid, federal grants and contracts, state support, and other variables. Hence, this chapter not only ties government policy to college affordability, it also links various of the expenditure and revenue categories examined separately in chapter 2.

A number of results provide insight into the multiple effects of government funds on institutions of higher learning. At private four-year schools, increases in federal student aid do not induce increases in gross tuition. Interestingly, however, increases in federal financial aid do lead to higher tuition at public four-year institutions. Federal grants and contracts not only affect tuition, they also affect institutional scholarships and instructional expenditures throughout higher education. Our results indicate that cutbacks in that important revenue source would lead to higher tuition at private four-year and public two-year schools, lower institutional financial aid at four-year private and both four- and two-year public institutions, and lower instructional expenditures for all three groups. Finally, increases in state and local appropriations significantly increase instructional spending in all three of the institutional categories examined.

Understanding these relationships is important to lessen the chances that changes in government policy will have unanticipated, undesirable effects on the educational sector. It also goes quite far in making sense of the various trends in institutional finance variables documented in chapter 2.

Most of the quantitative work in this volume has been content to rely on the standard list of expenditure and revenue categories enshrined in the survey instruments the federal government employs in gathering financial data from institutions. These survey forms, in turn, embody a set of accounting conventions for nonprofit institutions referred to as fund accounting. But that data limitations compel us to rely on these types of data does not imply that we agree that the best way to examine finance issues is to arrange the data in the usual manner. In fact, in a number of these studies we rearranged the figures from the Higher Education General Information Survey (HEGIS) and the Integrated Postsecondary Education Data System (IPEDS) to compute our own categories, the best example of which is the gift and endowment income measure used extensively in chapters 2 and 10.

Chapter 11, "Total College Income: An Economic Overview of Williams College 1956–57 to 1986–87," and Chapter 12, "The Necessary Revolution in Financial Accounting," can be taken together. They present an alternative way to organize the financial data of colleges and universities and an alternative way to describe their economic performance. The total income approach described in chapter 11, with an application to Williams College, provides a basis for the comprehensive or global accounting of a college's economic activity that is needed to overcome the restrictions on perspective and information imposed by fund accounting. Many of those restrictions arise from the fact that fund accounting describes a college in a way that is simply very difficult to understand. So an objective of global accounting has been to illuminate simple and fundamental questions like, All things considered, did the year's activities leave the college better off or worse off? Chapter 12 then spells out in some detail how that simpler and more global description is produced. When implemented, administrators, governing boards, and educational researchers have access to indicators that much more accurately represent the economic realities facing colleges and universities. This way of organizing the data focuses attention on the opportunities and trade-offs a nonprofit institution faces. A forthcoming study by Gordon Winston and Duncan Mann shows that these data can be developed for institutions that differ considerably in scale and scope from the relatively simple environment of an institution like Williams.

The issues raised by this alternative outlook on financial data impinge on the analysis of higher education costs as well as revenues. Chapter 13 explores an important dimension of costs that colleges and universities as well as other nonprofit organizations handled poorly: the cost of capital. This chapter explains that capital costs are largely neglected in nonprofit organizations because the standard treatment of capital costs in business commingle opportunity costs of capital with profits. However, the absence of consistent treatment of the cost to universities of the capital they own can lead to significant distortions in decision making, for example, by misrepresenting the relative costs of renting and owning capital equipment. The essay includes constructive suggestions for treating capital costs more rationally in a comprehensive economic picture of university costs and revenues.

The chapters in this book differ substantially in style and analytical approach. But they all demonstrate our view that the application of basic economic principles and the combination of both descriptive and econometric analyses can illuminate a number of pressing issues. Questions concerning productivity, incentives, and financing in U.S. higher education are becoming more and more important as the situation of the higher educational industry becomes increasingly tenuous. We hope that our readers agree that our use of economic concepts and tools has provided insight into these pressing questions by helping us understand the recent past, anticipate the future, and develop policies that can influence the future in a desirable way. The concluding chapter offers some thoughts on future issues and future directions for economic research on the higher education enterprise.

CHAPTER 2

Trends in Revenues and Expenditures in U.S. Higher Education: Where Does the Money Come From? Where Does It Go?

Scott W. Blasdell, Michael S. McPherson, and Morton Owen Schapiro

Over the past decade or so there has been a great deal of speculation concerning the course of revenues and expenditures in U.S. higher education. However, presumably due to data limitations, there have been few attempts to analyze the recent history of higher education finances at the national level. This chapter seeks to fill this void by asking two simple questions for different groups of colleges and universities: Where does the money come from? Where does it go?

The first section describes the data set employed in our analysis. The second section presents a detailed look at the recent behavior of higher education institutions in the nation. The third section looks explicitly at changes over time in the composition of expenditures and revenues. The fourth section concludes.

The Data

Our data set consists of financial and other information on individual colleges and universities from 1978–79 to 1988–89. It was constructed by merging three smaller data sets. One, the Financial Statistics report from HEGIS for the period up to 1985–86 and IPEDS for the more recent period, describes the basic financial accounts of almost all public and private nonprofit postsecondary institutions in the United States. The second, the Fiscal-Operations Report and Application to Participate (FISAP) data base, provides more detailed information on student aid spending and revenues and on the aided population at colleges and universities who apply for federal assistance under any of the so-called campus-based programs (direct loans, Supplementary Educational Opportunity Grants (SEOGs), and college work study). The third, the HEGIS and IPEDS Enrollment Survey, reports full- and part-time enrollment for all institutions, allowing us to construct estimates of full-time-equivalent (FTE) enrollment, which we use to express all the financial data on a per FTE enrollment basis. We have these merged data sets for the majority of private nonprofit and public colleges and universities and concentrate here on three academic years: 1978–79 (referred to as 1979 in the tables and text that follow), 1985–86 (referred to as 1986), and 1988–89 (referred to as 1989). All our numbers are adjusted for inflation and are presented in 1990–91 dollars. The data set has been constructed as a panel, so that only those schools with data for all three observation years are included. Painstaking efforts have been made to clean the final data set of reporting and recording errors.

In the tables summarizing these data, we disaggregate institutions by type (university, four-year college, and two-year college) and control (public and private). Table 1 presents data on university expenditures, while table 2 presents analogous data on university revenues. Tables 3 and 4 examine four-year colleges, while tables 5 and 6 examine two-year colleges.

All our expenditure and revenue categories are explained in detail in the glossary at the end of this chapter. Briefly, expenditure categories include total per FTE spending net of student aid (NETSPEND),[1] which is then broken down into spending on instruction and self-supported research (INSTRUCT), externally supported research (RESEARCH), public service (PUBSERV), academic support other than library expenditures (ACADSUPP), library expenditures (LIBRARY), student services (STUDSERV), institutional support (INSTSUPP), operation and maintenance (OPMNEXP), and a residual category (OTHER). Restricted scholarships (SCLREST), unrestricted scholarships (SCLUNRES), and plant additions (PLANTADD) complete the list of expenditures. Revenue categories include per FTE values of gross tuition and fees (TANDF), federal grants and contracts (FEDGRCN), state and local grants and contracts (SLGRCN), state and local appropriations (SLAPP), resources from gifts and endowment earnings (GIFT&END), tuition and fee revenue net of institutional aid (NETTANDF), total scholarship aid from institutional funds (TOTSCH), and federal financial aid (FEDFNAID).

A number of these variables are related to each other. Net spending equals the sum of all expenditure variables except for scholarships and plant additions. Unrestricted scholarships plus restricted scholarships less federal financial aid equals total scholarship aid from institutional funds. Finally, gross tuition and fees less scholarship aid from institutional funds equals net tuition and fee revenues.

---

1. We have netted out student aid spending because part of this spending is directly passed through from federal student aid and the rest is best seen as foregone institutional revenue rather than as spending on educational programs.

TABLE 1. University Expenditure Levels in 1979, 1986, and 1989 and Annual Rates of Change (in 1990–91 dollars)

Expenditure Category	N	1979	Annual % Change 1979 to 1986	1986	Annual % Change 1986 to 1989	1989	Annual % Change 1979 to 1989
NETSPEND							
Public	71	12,012.22	1.54%	13,379.01	2.48%	14,411.66	1.82%
Private	52	18,796.30	2.76%	22,797.44	4.76%	26,300.51	3.36%
INSTRUCT							
Public	71	4,972.55	1.17%	5,397.21	1.72%	5,683.58	1.34%
Private	52	7,315.68	3.14%	9,117.13	4.99%	10,589.53	3.70%
RESEARCH							
Public	71	2,195.37	1.99%	2,522.93	4.99%	2,930.72	2.89%
Private	52	4,553.42	1.01%	4,887.43	4.75%	5,635.38	2.13%
PUBSERV							
Public	71	1,060.11	0.96%	1,133.94	2.53%	1,223.25	1.43%
Private	52	508.65	3.91%	668.95	13.89%	1,014.89	6.91%
ACADSUPP							
Public	71	731.27	2.34%	861.47	4.07%	973.49	2.86%
Private	52	909.84	3.97%	1,200.98	7.71%	1,513.62	5.09%
LIBRARY							
Public	71	414.59	1.80%	470.11	−0.03%	469.73	1.25%
Private	52	846.18	0.90%	901.41	1.55%	944.24	1.10%
STUDSERV							
Public	71	478.65	1.67%	538.03	2.14%	573.74	1.81%
Private	52	703.12	4.68%	975.64	3.02%	1,068.02	4.18%
INSTSUPP							
Public	71	898.86	3.10%	1,116.69	2.20%	1,193.00	2.83%
Private	52	1,855.31	4.93%	2,619.34	4.36%	2,985.72	4.76%
OPMNEXP							
Public	71	1,136.94	0.82%	1,203.99	−0.76%	1,176.68	0.34%
Private	52	1,833.10	1.98%	2,105.47	0.49%	2,136.60	1.53%
OTHER							
Public	71	123.93	1.18%	134.62	11.03%	187.43	4.14%
Private	52	270.81	2.44%	321.15	8.35%	412.62	4.21%
SCLREST							
Public	71	493.13	2.25%	577.35	2.09%	614.79	2.21%
Private	52	997.91	0.47%	1,031.12	5.30%	1,208.67	1.92%
SCLUNRES							
Public	71	167.90	4.68%	233.05	9.04%	305.66	5.99%
Private	52	812.59	7.98%	1,420.32	5.78%	1,689.23	7.32%
PLANTADD							
Public	71	1,387.49	8.22%	2,466.85	−1.34%	2,369.39	5.35%
Private	52	1,445.46	11.10%	3,143.76	14.54%	4,862.44	12.13%

Expenditures and Revenues: Levels and Trends

Table 1 shows that net spending per student at private universities in 1989 was almost twice that in the public sector ($26,301 versus $14,412, in 1990–91 academic year dollars) and that the difference grew over time (net spending increased at an annual real growth rate of 3.36 percent at private universities versus 1.82 percent at public universities). While some public sector expenditures are "off budget" and are therefore not included in these financial data, it is undoubtedly the case that expenditures per student are strikingly different between sectors and that this difference has grown over the past decade.[2] The disparity in levels of spending is apparent in the important category of instruction and self-supported research, as well as in every expenditure category with the exception of public service where public universities spend slightly more per student than do their private counterparts. Moreover, most categories grew faster in the private sector, suggesting the gap in spending in these areas will widen further. While all but the last expenditure category relates to the operating budget, the final category, plant additions, relates to the capital budget. In 1979, additions to plant and equipment were almost identical in the public and private sectors, with additions of about $1,400 per FTE student during that academic year. By 1989, however, plant additions were twice as large per student at private universities than at public universities. This reflects an enormous acceleration in building at private universities, especially between 1986 and 1989, when the annual real growth rate was 14.54 percent. Hence, the building boom from 1979 to 1986 at private universities reached even higher levels after 1986.

While the above paragraph highlights some of the most notable information in table 1, there is a plethora of information of likely interest to particular readers. In terms of the financial aid budget, for example, the annual rate of increase in scholarships from unrestricted funds at private universities slowed after 1986 (from 7.98 percent from 1979 to 1986 to 5.78 percent from 1986 to 1989), although the real increase continues to be very high. While the recent rate of increase in unrestricted aid at private universities is lower than earlier, the increase in restricted aid has accelerated (from .47 percent to 5.30 percent).

Turning to other expenditure categories, real growth in operation and maintenance expenditures at private universities has almost ceased after 1986 (going from 1.98 percent per year to .49 percent), while expenditure growth in institutional support and in student services has slowed modestly (going

---

2. An example of an off-budget item is that, in some states, certain parts of employee benefits (such as pension plans) appear on state government budgets rather than institutional budgets. The underestimation of public expenditures may be especially important in analyzing capital spending, where significant plant additions may be off-budget.

from 4.93 percent to 4.36 percent, and from 4.68 percent to 3.02 percent). On the other hand, the rate of increase in academic support spending has increased substantially (from 3.97 percent to 7.71 percent). Real library spending has been increasing somewhat more rapidly of late (the annual real increase rose from .90 percent to 1.55 percent), although such increases are still rather small. Research expenditures have accelerated considerably at private universities (1.01 percent to 4.75 percent), with a similar change taking place in the public sector (1.99 percent to 4.99 percent). Finally, the rate of increase in instruction and self-supported research rose at both private and public universities (3.14 percent to 4.99 percent and 1.17 percent to 1.72 percent).

Table 2 shows that, while gross tuition and fees (sometimes called the sticker price) are far greater at private universities than at public universities ($11,735 versus $3,014), annual real growth rates over the entire period were quite similar (4.07 percent in the private sector versus 3.68 percent in the public sector). Note that from 1986 to 1989, private tuition increased at a slower rate than public tuition, reversing the trend from 1979 to 1986. While both federal grants and contracts and state and local grants and contracts are also much larger at private universities ($6,435 versus $2,139, and $1,120 versus $379), federal grants and contracts mirror the pattern for tuition and fees, with the rate of growth from 1986 to 1989 being higher at public universities than in the private sector. As expected, state and local appropriations for public universities are very important, although the figure grew only slightly in real terms from 1979 to 1989. Revenues from gifts and endowment earnings, while a bit more than twice as high at private universities in 1979, was almost four times as high in 1989. Net tuition revenues, on the other hand, have increased at about the same rate over the period in the two sectors (with an annual real increase of roughly 3.6 percent), although the rate of increase from 1986 to 1989 was higher in the public sector (3.70 percent) than in the private sector (3.24 percent). Total scholarships from institutional sources increased more rapidly at private universities over the period while federal financial aid increased modestly at public universities as opposed to private universities, where it failed to keep pace with inflation.

To examine the average net price faced by students, as opposed to net tuition revenues received by schools, we subtract federal financial aid contributions from net tuition and fees. Thus, the average private university has a sticker price of $11,735, provides $2,664 in institutional aid, and therefore receives net tuition revenues of $9,071 per student. The average student attending a private university also receives $234 in federal aid, making the average net price faced by students equal to $8,837. The comparable price to attend a public university is $2,094. The ratio of the average net price at a private university to the average net price at a public university is 4.2, exactly the same as the value in 1979. Hence, the real decline in federal financial aid

TABLE 2.   University Revenue Levels in 1979, 1986, and 1989 and Annual Rates of Change (in 1990–91 dollars)

Revenue Category	N	1979	Annual % Change 1979 to 1986	1986	Annual % Change 1986 to 1989	1989	Annual % Change 1979 to 1989
TANDF							
Public	71	2,086.14	3.44%	2,653.50	4.25%	3,014.01	3.68%
Private	52	7,807.83	4.13%	10,423.59	3.95%	11,735.18	4.07%
FEDGRCN							
Public	71	1,972.92	−0.31%	1,930.01	3.43%	2,139.22	0.81%
Private	52	5,642.34	0.61%	5,890.23	2.95%	6,434.60	1.31%
SLGRCN							
Public	71	304.00	−0.88%	285.82	9.41%	379.01	2.21%
Private	52	415.05	2.84%	506.44	26.45%	1,119.84	9.93%
SLAPP							
Public	71	6,707.22	1.25%	7,321.22	0.35%	7,397.52	0.98%
Private	52	300.62	−0.34%	293.50	−4.01%	260.27	−1.44%
GIFT&END							
Public	71	2,355.85	4.69%	3,272.23	−4.01%	3,216.35	3.11%
Private	52	5,297.30	11.71%	12,025.96	1.63%	12,629.82	8.69%
NETTANDF							
Public	71	1,701.85	3.53%	2,179.38	3.70%	2,435.59	3.58%
Private	52	6,256.76	3.92%	8,231.71	3.24%	9,071.06	3.71%
TOTSCH							
Public	71	384.30	3.00%	474.08	6.63%	578.46	−1.44%
Private	52	1,551.02	4.94%	2,191.86	6.50%	2,664.06	5.41%
FEDFNAID							
Public	71	276.72	2.79%	336.33	0.56%	341.99	2.12%
Private	52	259.47	0.01%	259.58	−3.48%	233.84	−1.04%

for students attending private universities and the higher rate of increase in gross tuition were compensated for by the relatively high rate of increase in institutional aid.

Let's step back for a minute to reflect on the most important findings of this discussion of universities. The most striking part of the expenditure analysis is probably the extraordinary building boom in the private sector, with expenditures per student in 1989 ($4,862) substantially higher than in any other category with the exception of research expenditures ($5,635) and expenditures on instruction and self-supported research ($10,590). Capital expenditures in the public sector are much more modest ($2,369), although here too this figure exceeds spending in all categories with the exception of research and instruction. On the revenue side, it will surprise some to find out that real annual percentage increases in net tuition and fee revenues over the entire period were virtually identical in the two sectors, with rates of increase from 1986 to 1989 being higher in the public sector. The largest revenue source for private universities, resources from gifts and endowment earnings, rose at a very rapid annual rate over the entire period (8.69 percent)[3], as did the second most important revenue source, net tuition and fees (which increased at a rate of 3.71 percent per year). However, the third most important revenue source, federal grants and contracts, increased by only 1.31 percent annually. From 1986 to 1989, increased resources from gifts and endowment earnings rose much more slowly (1.63 percent per year), net tuition revenues increased at a slightly lower rate than in the longer period (3.24 percent), while federal grants and contracts did relatively well (increasing at a real rate of 2.95 percent per year).

The situation for public universities is far more precarious. The principal revenue source, state and local appropriations, increased by about 1 percent per year after adjusting for inflation (.98 percent), while—going in the order of budgetary importance—gifts and endowment earnings rose by 3.11 percent annually, net tuition and fee revenues rose by 3.58 percent, and federal grants and contracts increased at a rate of only .81 percent per year. The single most worrying fact is that public universities rely much more on state and local appropriations than on any other revenue source. (The ratio of state and local appropriations to net tuition and fees, for example, equals 3.0.) The minuscule real increase in these appropriations, particularly over the most recent period (where the annual increase in state and local appropriations from 1986 to 1989 was .35 percent), and the well-known budgetary crises in states throughout the nation imply that these universities are going to have to gain an increased share of their revenues from other sources. While gifts and endowment earnings as well as federal grants and contracts are two possibilities, revenue from tuition and fees is the most likely candidate to take up the slack from reductions in state and local appropriations, thereby continuing the recent trend in which public universities have become more tuition dependent and costs to their students have rapidly risen.

Tables 3 and 4 provide expenditure and revenue data for four-year colleges and tell a slightly different story. While private four-year colleges spend more than public four-year colleges ($10,142 per FTE student in 1989 versus $8,174 for NETSPEND), the difference is much smaller than for universities ($26,301 versus $14,412), especially in the important instruction and self-supported research category ($4,081 versus $3,956 at four-year colleges; $10,590 versus

---

3. Of course, this revenue source varies year to year by a significant amount depending largely on the performance of the stock market and the existence of major capital campaigns. For example, the Dow Jones Industrial Average increased by only 2.6 percent in 1978–79 (while the CPI rose by 9.2 percent) but increased by 42.4 percent in 1985–86 (while the CPI rose by 2.7 percent).

TABLE 3. Four-Year College Expenditure Levels in 1979, 1986, and 1989 and Annual Rates of Change (in 1990–91 dollars)

Expenditure Category	N	1979	Annual % Change 1979 to 1986	1986	Annual % Change 1986 to 1989	1989	Annual % Change 1979 to 1989
NETSPEND							
Public	276	7,318.21	1.26%	7,992.82	0.75%	8,173.78	1.11%
Private	753	7,843.05	2.52%	9,358.55	2.68%	10,141.54	2.57%
INSTRUCT							
Public	276	3,598.75	0.84%	3,817.92	1.19%	3,956.38	0.95%
Private	753	3,348.83	1.88%	3,820.39	2.20%	4,081.49	1.98%
RESEARCH							
Public	276	309.95	3.62%	399.32	8.09%	509.07	4.96%
Private	753	238.08	1.40%	262.52	1.79%	276.98	1.51%
PUBSERV							
Public	276	167.55	3.23%	209.99	2.98%	229.62	3.15%
Private	753	148.38	5.78%	222.43	6.28%	268.51	5.93%
ACADSUPP							
Public	276	406.99	1.14%	440.95	6.01%	528.12	2.61%
Private	753	332.80	3.62%	428.76	10.61%	589.49	5.72%
LIBRARY							
Public	276	327.29	−0.00%	327.20	−3.77%	292.26	−1.13%
Private	753	343.95	1.32%	377.27	−3.37%	341.03	−0.09%
STUDSERV							
Public	276	531.40	1.24%	579.70	−0.60%	569.43	0.69%
Private	753	737.63	4.12%	984.06	4.23%	1,117.21	4.15%
INSTSUPP							
Public	276	834.91	4.21%	1,121.29	−2.27%	1,047.45	2.27%
Private	753	1,478.03	3.49%	1,886.37	2.97%	2,062.76	3.33%
OPMNEXP							
Public	276	926.21	−0.39%	901.31	−1.05%	873.41	−0.59%
Private	753	1,000.21	1.74%	1,130.05	0.56%	1,149.36	1.39%
OTHER							
Public	276	215.17	−1.40%	195.14	−4.99%	168.04	−2.47%
Private	753	215.14	1.93%	246.21	1.13%	254.72	1.69%
SCLREST							
Public	276	501.34	1.30%	549.76	3.32%	607.29	1.91%
Private	753	848.36	1.50%	942.16	3.05%	1,032.48	1.96%
SCLUNRES							
Public	276	80.37	5.81%	120.72	4.70%	139.01	5.48%
Private	753	474.96	8.20%	843.07	9.23%	1,111.99	8.51%
PLANTADD							
Public	276	963.34	0.61%	1,005.67	1.71%	1,058.54	0.94%
Private	753	944.30	4.92%	1,332.67	7.05%	1,646.59	5.56%

TABLE 4.   Four-Year College Revenue Levels in 1979, 1986, and 1989 and Annual Rates of Change (in 1990–91 dollars)

Revenue Category	N	1979	Annual % Change 1979 to 1986	1986	Annual % Change 1986 to 1989	1989	Annual % Change 1979 to 1989
TANDF							
Public	276	1,391.75	3.96%	1,836.62	2.64%	1,987.92	3.57%
Private	753	5,745.87	3.28%	7,226.59	4.33%	8,228.06	3.59%
FEDGRCN							
Public	276	600.12	−3.27%	477.35	1.37%	497.41	−1.88%
Private	753	647.32	−4.62%	468.45	−2.84%	430.14	−4.09%
SLGRCN							
Public	276	155.59	2.50%	185.37	9.27%	244.83	4.53%
Private	753	182.08	5.88%	274.79	13.44%	411.29	8.15%
SLAPP							
Public	276	5,132.82	0.75%	5,407.71	0.74%	5,528.73	0.74%
Private	753	118.90	−0.10%	118.06	0.68%	120.48	0.13%
GIFT&END							
Public	276	1,484.48	1.50%	1,649.19	−20.64%	887.98	−5.14%
Private	753	2,597.02	8.21%	4,614.76	2.19%	4,320.78	5.09%
NETTANDF							
Public	276	1,209.91	4.29%	1,633.19	1.89%	1,728.66	3.57%
Private	753	4,959.11	2.66%	5,975.16	3.20%	6,577.74	2.82%
TOTSCH							
Public	276	181.85	1.60%	203.43	8.08%	259.25	3.55%
Private	753	786.78	6.63%	1,251.45	9.22%	1,650.31	7.41%
FEDFNAID							
Public	276	400.36	2.20%	467.06	1.40%	487.04	1.96%
Private	753	536.56	0.07%	533.79	−2.57%	494.15	−0.82%

$5,684 at universities). While, again, plant additions have been considerable, especially in the private sector (where they equalled $1,647), the levels and rates of change are far more modest than in the earlier case.

It is interesting to note that, in comparing recent expenditure trends at private four-year colleges versus private universities, the colleges have had a more modest increase in instruction and institutional support, while having a small absolute decline in real library spending.[4] On the other hand, they have closed some of the gap in academic support and, from 1986 to 1989, increased their lead in student services. It is important to keep in mind, how-

---

4. Note that comparisons between colleges and universities should be made with caution because we are unable to separate undergraduate from graduate and professional school expenditures at universities.

ever, the very different structures and academic missions of these two types of institutions that in part drive these different patterns.

Net tuition revenues are the most important revenue source at four-year private colleges ($6,578), although gifts and endowment earnings ($4,321) again figure prominently (although not nearly as prominently as in the case of private universities where the FTE value was almost three times as large as the figure for private four-year colleges, and gifts and endowment earnings were more important than net tuition revenues).[5] Federal and state and local grants and contracts are relatively unimportant for four-year colleges. Real rates of increase in gifts and endowment earnings (5.09 percent) and in net tuition revenues (2.82 percent) are below those at private universities (8.69 percent and 3.71 percent), but nonetheless represent substantial growth over the period. The two major revenue sources for public four-year colleges—state and local appropriations and net tuition revenues (the ratio of state and local appropriations to net tuition and fees is even higher at public four-year colleges (3.2) than at public universities (3.0))—increased at a rate approximately equal to that for public universities (.74 percent and 3.57 percent versus .98 percent and 3.58 percent). However, the third most important revenue source, increased resources from gifts and endowment earnings, actually declined in real terms for public four-year colleges. Hence, these schools are even more vulnerable to cuts in state operating subsidies than are public universities, a fact that will be discussed in greater detail in the third section.

Lastly, we can again use the information in the table to compute the average net price faced by students attending four-year colleges—$6,084 in the private sector and $1,242 in the public sector (a ratio of 4.9). These numbers can be contrasted with $4,422 and $810 in 1979 (a ratio of 5.5). It is clear that, despite the real decline in federal financial aid for students attending private colleges, high rates of increase in institutional aid at private colleges, along with virtually identical increases in sticker prices, have decreased the net price of attending private colleges relative to their public counterparts.

Finally, Tables 5 and 6 present expenditure and revenue data for two-year colleges. An obvious change from the earlier discussion is that the difference in spending between private and public two-year colleges is only $991 per student, in contrast to $11,890 for universities and $1,968 for four-year colleges. It is interesting to note that spending on instruction and self-supported

---

5. The degree to which these differentials in gifts and endowment earnings are directly attributable to the particular development activities and endowment funds of the professional schools at the universities cannot be determined through these data.

TABLE 5. Two-Year College Expenditure Levels in 1979, 1986, and 1989 and Annual Rates of Change (in 1990–91 dollars)

Expenditure Category	N	1979	Annual % Change 1979 to 1986	1986	Annual % Change 1986 to 1989	1989	Annual % Change 1979 to 1989
NETSPEND							
Public	624	4,819.58	0.99%	5,166.18	0.63%	5,264.50	0.88%
Private	94	4,751.25	2.83%	5,793.73	2.56%	6,256.32	2.75%
INSTRUCT							
Public	624	2,467.53	0.88%	2,624.36	0.46%	2,660.93	0.75%
Private	94	1,785.64	2.04%	2,059.63	2.21%	2,200.96	2.09%
RESEARCH							
Public	624	8.57	−9.37%	4.45	11.28%	6.24	−3.18%
Private	94	2.36	−11.59%	1.05	29.36%	2.53	0.69%
PUBSERV							
Public	624	92.78	2.21%	108.27	7.68%	136.31	3.85%
Private	94	29.81	1.11%	32.22	4.25%	36.60	2.05%
ACADSUPP							
Public	624	237.30	3.08%	294.45	5.95%	351.96	3.94%
Private	94	215.85	3.59%	277.47	4.44%	317.01	3.84%
LIBRARY							
Public	624	166.52	−1.30%	152.05	−7.57%	121.16	−3.18%
Private	94	165.06	0.53%	171.24	0.33%	172.94	0.47%
STUDSERV							
Public	624	424.87	1.84%	483.11	1.90%	511.45	1.85%
Private	94	611.82	4.08%	814.30	4.38%	928.60	4.17%
INSTSUPP							
Public	624	731.94	1.28%	800.42	1.41%	835.04	1.32%
Private	94	1,137.83	3.71%	1,475.01	2.67%	1,598.09	3.40%
OPMNEXP							
Public	624	568.44	1.34%	624.43	−1.40%	598.83	0.52%
Private	94	645.02	2.54%	770.34	0.85%	790.15	2.03%
OTHER							
Public	624	121.63	−7.07%	74.14	−18.53%	42.52	−10.51%
Private	94	157.87	2.83%	192.49	2.81%	209.43	2.83%
SCLREST							
Public	624	349.36	2.90%	427.98	2.78%	465.19	2.86%
Private	94	1,289.93	−1.15%	1,190.37	−0.94%	1,157.13	−1.09%
SCLUNRES							
Public	624	25.36	1.20%	27.58	−1.03%	26.75	0.53%
Private	94	192.86	7.45%	324.30	13.07%	480.69	9.13%
PLANTADD							
Public	624	662.13	−3.07%	534.18	−0.60%	524.60	−2.33%
Private	94	624.95	1.80%	709.10	9.36%	939.08	4.07%

TABLE 6. Two-Year College Revenue Levels in 1979, 1986, and 1989 and Annual Rates of Change (in 1990–91 dollars)

Revenue Category	N	1979	Annual % Change 1979 to 1986	1986	Annual % Change 1986 to 1989	1989	Annual % Change 1979 to 1989
TANDF							
Public	624	776.36	3.14%	967.16	2.75%	1,050.46	3.02%
Private	94	3,545.06	3.22%	4,440.87	4.18%	5,033.91	3.51%
FEDGRCN							
Public	624	284.91	−2.69%	236.00	−2.85%	216.67	−2.74%
Private	94	197.50	−1.04%	183.68	3.15%	201.36	0.22%
SLGRCN							
Public	624	122.36	6.52%	193.19	17.27%	324.36	9.75%
Private	94	99.89	7.14%	164.68	13.62%	247.80	9.09%
SLAPP							
Public	624	3,614.90	0.60%	3,769.06	−0.41%	3,722.80	0.29%
Private	94	64.26	−7.11%	39.07	20.57%	72.43	1.20%
GIFT&END							
Public	624	698.41	−1.68%	620.74	−21.55%	325.22	−7.64%
Private	94	1,695.06	3.06%	2,100.41	−4.60%	1,829.80	0.76%
NETTANDF							
Public	624	695.15	3.25%	872.66	2.37%	936.85	2.98%
Private	94	3,188.93	4.50%	4,369.23	−1.22%	4,212.10	2.78%
TOTSCH							
Public	624	81.20	2.17%	94.51	6.13%	133.60	3.36%
Private	94	356.13	−22.91%	71.65	81.33%	821.81	8.36%
FEDFNAID							
Public	624	293.51	2.96%	361.04	1.56%	378.34	2.54%
Private	94	1,126.67	3.54%	1,443.53	−19.01%	816.00	−3.23%

research is actually higher at public two-year colleges than at private two-year colleges ($2,661 versus $2,201).[6]

A comparison between expenditure levels and trends at public four-year colleges versus public two-year colleges shows that the advantage in net spending at four-year colleges ($8,174 in 1989 versus $5,265) has basically been holding steady in recent years (from 1979 to 1989 net spending rose by 1.11 percent and .88 percent at public four-year colleges and public two-year colleges, respectively). For academic support and student services, however, public two-year colleges have narrowed the gap (with growth rates of 3.94 percent and 1.85 percent versus 2.61 percent and .69 percent). Public two-

---

6. That net spending is higher at private two-year colleges than at public two-year colleges despite relatively low spending on instruction and self-supported research results mainly from relatively high spending on student services and institutional support.

year colleges have also increased restricted scholarship spending at a faster rate (2.86 percent) than public four-year colleges (1.91 percent).

As was the case for private four-year colleges, net tuition revenues are the most important revenue source at private two-year colleges ($4,212), although gifts and endowment earnings ($1,830) are again important. Real rates of increase in gifts and endowment earnings (.76 percent) have been quite modest while growth in net tuition revenues (2.78 percent) closely track the growth in net tuition revenues at private four-year colleges. Net tuition revenues at public two-year colleges ($937) also increased at a healthy real rate (2.98 percent) although the major revenue source for public two-year colleges, state and local appropriations ($3,723), was basically stagnant in real terms (with an increase of .29 percent). Even more worrying is that state and local appropriations for public two-year colleges failed to keep pace with inflation from 1986 to 1989 (with an annual decline of .41 percent). Thus, while state and local appropriations grew only slightly from 1979 to 1989 for all types of public institutions (with growth rates of .98 percent, .74 percent, and .29 percent at public universities, four-year colleges, and two-year colleges), the growth rate was lowest at community colleges. Over the more recent period, 1986 to 1989, the real decline in state and local appropriations at public two-year colleges can be contrasted with small increases at public universities (.35 percent) and at public four-year colleges (.74 percent).

Lastly, the average net price faced by students attending two-year colleges—$3,396 in the private sector in 1989 and $558 in the public sector (a ratio of 6.1)   can be contrasted with $2,062 and $401 in 1979 (a ratio of 5.1). The rapid increase in institutional aid at private two-year colleges was not enough to maintain the net price to students relative to public two-year colleges given the decline in federal financial aid and the relatively large increase in sticker prices at the private schools.

Expenditures and Revenues: Changes in Composition

Tables 7 and 8 present the expenditure and revenue data in a different manner. Table 7 shows the share of operating expenditures going to each expenditure category in 1979 and 1989 for each type of institution.

The most striking finding in terms of the important category of instruction and self-supported research is that two institutional groups—public four-year colleges and public two-year colleges—allocate an unusually large percentage of their operating expenditures. This category accounts for about half of the expenditures for these groups, both in 1979 and in 1989. On the other hand, for both years, instruction and self-supported research accounts for only about 40 percent of operating expenditures at universities (public and private) and at private two-year and four-year colleges. The relatively small allocation

TABLE 7. Composition of Expenditures: 1979 and 1989

	Universities		Four-Year Colleges		Two-Year Colleges	
	Public	Private	Public	Private	Public	Private
			1979			
INSTRUCT	41.8%	39.5%	50.7%	43.9%	52.5%	38.9%
RESEARCH	18.5	24.6	4.4	3.1	0.2	0.0
PUBSERV	8.9	2.7	2.4	1.9	2.0	0.7
ACADSUPP	6.1	4.9	5.7	4.4	5.0	4.7
LIBRARY	3.5	4.6	4.6	4.5	3.6	3.6
STUDSERV	4.0	3.8	7.5	9.7	9.0	13.3
INSTSUPP	7.6	10.0	11.8	19.4	15.6	24.8
OPMNEXP	9.6	9.9	13.0	13.1	12.1	14.0
			1989			
INSTRUCT	40.0%	40.9%	49.4%	41.3%	51.0%	36.4%
RESEARCH	20.6	21.8	6.4	2.8	0.1	0.0
PUBSERV	8.6	3.9	2.9	2.7	2.6	0.6
ACADSUPP	6.8	5.8	6.6	6.0	6.7	5.2
LIBRARY	3.3	3.6	3.6	3.4	2.3	2.9
STUDSERV	4.0	4.1	7.1	11.3	9.8	15.4
INSTSUPP	8.4	11.5	13.1	20.9	16.0	26.4
OPMNEXP	8.3	8.3	10.9	11.6	11.5	13.1

to the instruction category for universities is explained by the large role that funded research plays in both the public and private sectors; for private two-year and four-year colleges it is institutional support and student services that take an unusual percentage of operating expenditures.

The role of institutional support has been growing for all institutional types and now accounts for a substantial percentage of operating expenditures, particularly, as mentioned above, at private four-year (20.9 percent) and two-year (26.4 percent) colleges. Academic support has also garnered an increasing percentage of spending over time while both library and operations and maintenance account for smaller percentages of operating expenditures in 1989 than in 1979 at all six institutional types.

We turn now to revenues. Given the various uncertainties relating to revenue sources in the future, it is worth asking if certain types of institutions are more diversified in terms of revenue sources than others. Taking total revenue as the sum of federal grants and contracts, state and local grants and contracts, state and local appropriations, gift and endowment income, and net tuition revenue, we find the distribution of revenues in 1979 and 1989 shown in table 8.

All institutional groups reduced their reliance on federal grants and contracts over the period, with a particularly large change taking place at private universities (where federal grants and contracts fell from 31.5 percent of revenues in 1979 to 21.8 percent of revenues in 1989). State and local grants and contracts, on the other hand, increased their contribution to total revenues, although their role remains small in all cases.

Public institutions remain highly reliant on state and local appropriations, although there have been some interesting changes over the past decade. Modest increases in the contribution of both gift and endowment earnings and net tuition revenues have compensated for the four-percentage-point decline in the contribution of state and local appropriations at public universities. At public four-year and two-year colleges, gift and endowment earnings have become much less important over time. These institutions have instead become more reliant on state and local appropriations while experiencing considerable increases in the role of net tuition revenues. Hence, net tuition revenues play a larger role in 1989 than in 1979 for all types of public institutions, although the degree of change is far greater at four-year colleges (14.1 percent to 19.5 percent) and at two-year colleges (12.8 percent to 17.0 percent) than at universities (13.1 percent to 15.6 percent).

TABLE 8. Composition of Revenues: 1979 and 1989

	Universities		Four-Year Colleges		Two-Year Colleges	
	Public	Private	Public	Private	Public	Private
			1979			
FEDGRCN	15.1%	31.5%	7.0%	7.6%	5.3%	3.8%
SLGRCN	2.3	2.3	1.8	2.1	2.3	1.9
SLAPP	51.4	1.7	59.8	1.4	66.8	1.2
GIFT&END	18.1	29.6	17.3	30.5	12.9	32.3
NETTANDF	13.1	34.9	14.1	58.3	12.8	60.8
			1989			
FEDGRCN	13.7%	21.8%	5.6%	3.6%	3.9%	3.1%
SLGRCN	2.4	3.8	2.8	3.5	5.9	3.8
SLAPP	47.5	0.9	62.2	1.0	67.4	1.1
GIFT&END	20.7	42.8	10.0	36.4	5.9	27.9
NETTANDF	15.6	30.7	19.5	55.5	17.0	64.2

The contribution of net tuition revenues, on the other hand, has declined at private universities (34.9 percent to 30.7 percent) and private four-year colleges (58.3 percent to 55.5 percent), although net tuition revenues became more important at private two-year colleges (60.8 percent to 64.2 percent). This presumably reflects the rapid growth in the role of gift and endowment earnings at private universities (29.6 percent to 42.8 percent) and at private four-year colleges (30.5 percent to 36.4 percent).

To summarize the revenue figures, the most dramatic change over the decade was the large decline in the role of federal grants and contracts that took place at private universities (a ten-percentage-point fall) and the compensating increase in gift and endowment earnings (a thirteen-percentage-point increase). Gift and endowment earnings also allowed private four-year colleges (where their contribution to revenues rose by six percentage points) to compensate for the decreasing role of federal grants and contracts (a four-percentage-point fall). Rises in the importance of net tuition revenues at public four-year and two-year colleges (averaging about five percentage points) helped reduce the shortfall due to the decline in the contribution of gift and endowment earnings (about seven percentage points). Finally, the revenue patterns at public universities and private two-year colleges were relatively stable over time.

Conclusion

The aim of this chapter is to provide an empirical basis for answering questions about levels and trends in expenditures and revenues in U.S. higher education. At the university level, expenditures per student are strikingly different between the public and private sectors, with the private university advantage growing over the past decade. The most prominent example of this divergence is in additions to plant and equipment, which were almost identical in the public and private sectors in 1979 but, by 1989, were twice as large per student at private universities than at public universities.

While both gross tuition and fees (sticker prices) and net tuition revenues are far greater at private universities than at public universities, annual real growth rates from 1979 to 1989 were quite similar. From 1986 to 1989, private tuition (gross and net) increased at a slower rate than public tuition, reversing the trend from 1979 to 1986.

The single most important revenue source for private universities, resources from gifts and endowment earnings, rose at a very rapid annual rate from 1979 to 1989, as did the second most important revenue source, net tuition and fees. However, the third most important revenue source, federal grants and contracts, increased only modestly.

The principal revenue source at public universities, state and local appropriations, increased only slightly after adjusting for inflation. Given the budgetary situation in most states, it is quite likely that these universities are going to have to gain an increased share of their revenues from other sources.

Turning to the nation's colleges, private four-year colleges spend more than public four-year colleges, although the difference is much smaller than for universities. Plant additions have once again been considerable but are modest relative to universities. At two-year colleges, differences in spending between private and public schools are quite small compared to differences in spending at four-year colleges and at universities. In fact, spending on instruction and self-supported research is higher at public two-year colleges than at private two-year colleges. Comparing expenditures at public four-year colleges and public two-year colleges shows stability in the net spending advantage at four-year colleges. An examination of the net price faced by students attending four-year colleges shows that the high rate of increase in institutional aid in the private sector has led to a decrease in the cost of attending private four-year colleges relative to their public counterparts.

Real rates of increase in gift and endowment earnings and in net tuition revenues are lower at private four-year colleges than at private universities, but nonetheless represent substantial growth from 1979 to 1989. Net tuition revenues at both private and public two-year colleges also increased at a healthy real rate although the major revenue source for public two-year colleges, state and local appropriations, barely increased in real terms over the entire period and failed to keep pace with inflation from 1986 to 1989. Finally, despite the rapid increase in institutional aid at private two-year colleges, the net price to students at such institutions increased relative to public two-year colleges.

Our comparison of changes in the composition of revenues and expenditures uncovered substantial changes in revenue sources for private universities, public four-year and two-year colleges, and private four-year colleges. At private universities, there was a large decline in the role of federal grants and contracts. Gift and endowment earnings more than compensated for this decline and also allowed private four-year colleges to make up for the decreasing role of federal grants and contracts. Declines in the contribution of gift and endowment earnings at public four-year and two-year colleges were offset in part by rises in the importance of net tuition revenues.

In terms of expenditures, public four-year colleges and public two-year colleges allocate unusually large percentages to instruction and self-supported research compared with other classes of institutions. At both public and private universities, funded research plays a substantial role while, at private two-year and four-year colleges, institutional support and student services absorb relatively high percentages of operating expenditures. The role of institutional support has been growing for all institutional types, as has academic support. However, for all groups, both library and operations and maintenance expenditures account for smaller percentages of operating expenditures in 1989 than in 1979.

The bottom line is that higher education expenditures and revenues have substantially changed in recent years. But different institutional groups have generally had very different experiences. Unless we recognize the degree of heterogeneity in U.S. higher education, we cannot hope to understand the factors affecting recent history and anticipate the course of the decade ahead.

GLOSSARY OF EXPENDITURE AND REVENUE CATEGORIES

Expenditures

ACADSUPP: academic support per FTE student. Expenditures for the support services that are an integral part of the institution's primary missions of instruction, research, or public service are included. Expenditures for museums, galleries, audiovisual services, academic computing support, ancillary support, academic administration, personnel development, and course and curriculum development are examples. We have taken out library expenditures and treated it as a separate category.

INSTRUCT: instruction and self-supported research per FTE student. Expenditures of the colleges, schools, departments, and other instructional divisions of the institution and expenditures for departmental research and public service that are not separately budgeted are included. Expenditures for academic administration for which the primary function is administration (e.g., academic deans) are excluded.

INSTSUPP: institutional support per FTE student. Included are expenditures for the day-to-day operational support of the institution, excluding expenditures for physical plant operations. Examples are general administrative services, executive direction and planning, legal and fiscal operations, and community relations.

LIBRARY: library spending per FTE student. Expenditures on libraries are included.

NETSPEND: net spending per FTE student. We compute this number as the average per-FTE-student value of educational and general spending net of student aid. We have netted out student aid spending because part of this spending is directly passed through from federal student aid and the rest is best seen as foregone institutional revenue, rather than as spending on educational programs.

OPMNEXP: operation and maintenance per FTE student. This category includes all expenditures for operations established to provide service and maintenance related to campus grounds and facilities used for educational and general purposes. Expenditures made from institutional plant funds accounts are excluded.

OTHER: other spending per FTE student. This is our residual category, equal to the difference between netspend and the sum of the eight components.

PLANTADD: plant additions per FTE student. We compute this number by summing over the three categories of physical plant additions during the year—land, buildings, and equipment. Additions during the year are additions to plant made through purchase, by gifts-in-kind from donors, and from other additions. Construction in progress and plant expenditures that represent capital fund investments in real estate are excluded.

PUBSERV: public service per FTE student. This category includes all funds budgeted specifically for public service and expended for activities established primarily to provide noninstructional services beneficial to groups external to the institution. Examples are seminars and projects provided to particular sectors of the community, community services, and cooperative extension projects.

RESEARCH: research per FTE student. All funds expended for activities specifically organized to produce research outcomes and either commissioned by an agency external to the institution or separately budgeted by an organizational unit within the institution are included.

SCLREST: scholarships from restricted funds per FTE student. Included are scholarships and fellowships awarded from restricted funds, including Pell grants.

SCLUNRES: scholarships from unrestricted funds per FTE student. Included are scholarships and fellowships awarded from unrestricted funds. This category, as well as the one above, applies only to moneys given in the form of outright grants and trainee stipends to individuals enrolled in formal coursework, either for credit or not. Aid to students in the form of tuition or fee remissions are included (except those remissions granted because of faculty or staff status). College work study program expenses are reported where the student served, not in either of the scholarship categories.

STUDSERV: student services per FTE student. This category includes funds expended for admissions, registrar activities, and activities whose primary purpose is to contribute to students' emotional and physical well-being and to their intellectual, cultural, and social development outside the context of the formal instruction program. Examples are career guidance, counseling, financial aid administration, student health services (except when operated as a self-supporting auxiliary enterprise), and the administrative allowance for Pell grants.

Revenues

FEDFNAID: the sum of Pell and SEOG grants disbursed per FTE student. Administrative expenses are included for SEOG.

FEDGRCN: federal grants and contracts per FTE student less Pell and SEOG amounts. Examples are research projects, training programs, and similar activities for which amounts are received or expenditures are reimbursable under the terms of a government grant or contract.

GIFT&END: gift and endowment income per FTE student. The sum of gifts to the endowment, gifts to the operating budget, realized and unrealized capital gains, interest, and dividends.

NETTANDF: net tuition and fee revenue per FTE student. We subtract the total amount of scholarship aid from institutional funds (TOTSCH) from gross tuition and fees (TANDF) to calculate this net revenue figure.

SLAPP: state and local appropriations per FTE student. This category includes all amounts received or made available to an institution through acts of a legislative body, except grants or contracts. These funds are for meeting current operating expenses and not for specific projects or programs.

SLGRCN: state and local grants and contracts per FTE student.

TANDF: gross tuition and fee revenue per FTE student. The convention followed by academic institutions is to calculate this amount by assuming that every student pays the sticker or list price; hence, this variable is gross of financial aid. Charges for room, board, and other services rendered by auxiliary enterprises are excluded.

TOTSCH: total scholarship aid from institutional funds per FTE student. We add scholarships and fellowships awarded from unrestricted (SCLUNRES) and restricted (SCLREST) funds and then subtract the financial aid contribution of the federal government (FEDFNAID) that is made in the form of Pell and SEOG grants.

Part 2
Productivity and Organization

CHAPTER 3

The Concept of Productivity As Applied to U.S. Higher Education

Morton Owen Schapiro

Productivity is defined as output per unit of input. It is commonly used to evaluate changes in economic efficiency over time and variation in efficiency at a particular time. It has proved to be a valuable concept in studies of economic growth and interindustry as well as intraindustry analyses.

The recent explosion in interest in measuring the "value" of education has led to the treatment of the "industry of education" along the lines of other industries. Hence, it is not surprising that the tools of industrial analysis are increasingly being applied to education. One such tool, naturally, is the concept of productivity.

There are a number of reasons for the growing concern with evaluating the costs and benefits of U.S. higher education. Enrollments have risen, test scores have fallen, costs have skyrocketed, and slower economic growth has forced the government to make increasingly difficult choices concerning priorities.[1] Education has traditionally been defended on economic grounds as improving the quality of the labor force, but in these days of cost consciousness, it is not surprising that some difficult questions are being raised. These include, How productive is the industry of education in the United States?

This chapter appeared in *The Concept of Productivity in Institutions of Higher Education* (Sainte-Foy, Quebec: University of Quebec Press, 1988). Used by permission.

Prepared under contract to the U.S. Department of Education for presentation at an OECD conference on "The Concept of Productivity in Institutions of Higher Education," May 25–27, 1987, Quebec, Canada. The views expressed in this paper do not necessarily reflect those of the Department of Education.

I would like to thank Michael S. McPherson and Laura Wefing for many helpful comments and suggestions and Lee B. Dalzell, Reference Librarian at the Williams College Library, for her indispensible assistance in collecting source material.

1. Roughly half of all high school graduates in the United States enroll in postsecondary institutions, bringing the number to about 18 million. Total spending by these institutions is rapidly approaching the $100 billion mark, with federal, state, and local governments accounting for almost half of this total. For a discussion of test scores, see Adelman 1985 and Congressional Budget Office 1986.

Which academic institutions are more productive than others? And how can productivity in higher education be enhanced?

Who is asking questions about the effectiveness of higher education? There is no single group, although public institutions are certainly in the forefront of what can be called the "assessment movement" in this country.[2] The National Governors Association has called for careful evaluation of the output of education, and an increasing number of states (presently over a dozen) have instituted value-added analysis—where students are tested upon entering and tested again before graduation in order to determine what they have learned.[3] Assessing output is only half of a productivity analysis, but it is a necessary condition for properly measuring a more important variable— output per unit of input. Thus far most of the interest has been in the output measure, and some states have gone so far as to link budget allocations explicitly to the results of a value-added appraisal. The states of Tennessee (with its Performance Funding Program) and Missouri are leaders in this movement, but the indications are that other states will soon follow a similar path.[4]

While it is natural that institutions relying extensively on government funds are most involved in the assessment issue, private colleges and universities, perhaps spurred by the rising concern of accreditation organizations with measuring educational output, have not been completely left behind. Scores of private institutions are quite serious about this topic and have been experimenting with a variety of evaluation methods—some of which began well before the recent increase in interest.[5]

Along with the concern expressed by state governments and specific institutions, and in some cases, preceding it, has been a growing interest on the part of academic organizations and the federal government. Secretary of Education William J. Bennett has been a vocal advocate of the need for evaluation, and the Department of Education has supported a variety of efforts in this direction. The Carnegie Foundation for the Advancement of Teaching and the Association of American Colleges are among several organizations

---

2. The popular press has chronicled this movement and may be contributing to its growth. See, for example, the recent front-page article in the Sunday issue of the *New York Times*, January 18, 1987 (Fiske 1987).

3. National Governors Association 1986 contains the text of the section of their report on college quality.

4. Banta 1985 reports that the potential value of Tennessee's academic performance award equals 5 percent of the instructional budget.

5. See Pace 1985 and Hanson 1986 for a partial list of these institutions. El-Khawas 1986 reports that a recent survey found considerable support among college and university administrators for continued efforts at assessment, particularly where it is linked to improving instruction.

concerned with academic issues that have released major reports highlighting problems with undergraduate education.[6]

The attention to quality issues in U.S. higher education could be expected. There has been a great deal of recent work on primary and secondary school education, and it was only a matter of time before postsecondary institutions fell under the same scrutiny.[7] However, there are relevant concerns that have been voiced about the "costs" of assessment, particularly at the postsecondary level, and monetary costs are only a small part of this anxiety.

Some critics question whether it is possible to measure accurately some of the more important outcomes of education such as increases in leadership potential, certain cognitive skills, and moral integrity. Others point to the problem of simple tests and the natural inclination to "teach to the test"— especially when funding is linked to test performance. Finally, there is the important question of determining the optimal curriculum. How much should be dictated by a common, centrally determined subject matter, and how much should be left to particular institutions and to their instructors? This question has obvious and important implications for the U.S. tradition of academic freedom and respect for the competence of individual institutions.

Yet proponents quickly point out that some type of assessment or productivity measurement is the norm in industry as well as in government. Why should education be different? Perhaps it shouldn't be, although the proper application of the concept of productivity necessitates particularly careful efforts at measuring the output of education as well as the inputs.

A simple look at productivity for General Motors, for example, may examine the number of cars (standardized for quality) produced per dollar of expenditures or, in the case of labor productivity, per man-hour. There is no analog for education that is similarly basic. In fact, there is no simple measure of the output of education. Perhaps the number of students who graduate, or their improvement in test scores, or maybe, in the case of higher education, the number of articles faculty members publish as well, can give a very crude idea of the output, although some of the more qualitative outcomes mentioned above are obviously more difficult to measure. For inputs, the task is a bit easier. There are the faculty, the staff, the administrators, the library, the students themselves, etc. But, even here, there is the question of how these disparate factors should be aggregated.

---

6. Reports include Boyer 1987, Association of American Colleges 1985, Southern Regional Education Board 1985, Study Group on the Conditions of Excellence in American Higher Education 1984, and Bennett 1984, among others.

7. See, for example, Boyer 1983, Twentieth Century Fund 1983, National Commission on Excellence in Education 1983, Education Commission of the States 1983, Task Force on Teaching as a Profession 1986, and U.S. Department of Education 1984 and 1986.

Supposing that the proper output and inputs could be ascertained, is the concept of productivity really appropriate to education? There are some factors that are often cited in arguing that education is different in nature from many other industries. These include, among others, the complexity of the production process, the long time period needed before the output can be fully identified, the difficulty in controlling for the effects of outside factors, and the inability to derive detailed policy implications from the usual type of empirical analysis.[8]

In short, are there special problems with education that make it hard or even impossible to apply the concept of productivity? If so, this would be unfortunate, for understanding and measuring productivity provides us with a useful evaluative tool. Higher efficiency can be encouraged, and low efficiency can be used as a signal for change. After all, productivity is a key to allocative efficiency in the private noneducational sector, where, in a competitive market, the efficient prosper and the inefficient decline. Proper measurement of productivity in education would allow the more efficient institutions to be rewarded, say with public and private funds or with positive publicity, and less efficient institutions could theoretically benefit by recognizing their shortcomings.[9]

The question of productivity in education necessarily gets us into a number of sticky issues. What educational institutions actually do is clearly related to what they should do. Issues like this one are addressed below, but the primary task is not to discuss such grand topics but instead to ask the questions, Is productivity a useful concept for education? What are the problems involved in its application? How have people attempted to deal with these problems? How successful have they been? and, finally, Is the expected payoff from this line of inquiry high enough to warrant our time and effort in the future?

This chapter narrows the field from the start. The concern here is postsecondary education (although some of the theoretical analysis relates to earlier years of education as well) and is limited to research on the United States (although, once again, the theoretical analysis should be applicable elsewhere). The format is as follows: the first part contains a brief discussion

---

8. The latter point is argued in Hanushek 1986, a comprehensive review of the literature on the economics of education and an important background source for this paper.

9. Ewell 1985 lists a number of productive ways in which an institution could put assessment results to use. McClain and Krueger 1985 describe how one university, Northeast Missouri State, has constructively used the results of its extensive assessment efforts, while Mentkowski and Loacker 1985 discuss how the leader in assessment, Alverno College, makes assessment a teaching tool. Kinnick 1985 describes how assessment feedback could be used more productively, and Heywood 1977 provides an interesting look at the relationship between assessment and learning.

of the concept of productivity as used by economists; the second part deals with measuring the output of education; the third part concerns the measurement of the inputs into the educational process; the fourth part reviews a variety of relevant studies that have been done in the United States; and the fifth part presents conclusions and suggestions for further research. The aim is to look at where we are and to suggest a path for the future.

The Concept of Productivity

Economists have been interested in the notion of productivity as far back as the start of modern economics—Adam Smith's *Wealth of Nations* in 1776.[10] Much of the more recent interest has involved aggregate studies, either of a particular country over time or across countries at a given time. It has been much less common to see either interindustry analyses or microstudies of firm-specific productivity.

The fascination with macrostudies most likely relates to our concern with understanding growth rates for different countries or changes in the growth rate for a particular country. A popular exercise among economists in the United States has involved an examination of economic growth and its attribution to different sources.[11] Simply put, growth in output must be the result of either an increase in the quantity of inputs (for example, more labor, capital, or land), an enhancement in the quality of inputs (such as a better educated labor force), or an improvement in the technology that transforms inputs into output. In order to do this exercise, the concept of the production function is crucial.

The production function provides a mathematical expression that defines the maximum output achievable with any given set of inputs and is determined by the state of technical knowledge.[12] The production function provides a valuable growth accounting framework. Analysis of the production function has allowed economists to say, for example, that 40 percent of the growth in output is attributable to the growth in labor, 25 percent is attributable to capital, etc. However, the sum of the different contributions may be less than 100 percent.

In fact, for decades economists have been concerned that this residual (the difference between 100 percent and the sum of the factor contributions) has been large—indicating that a substantial portion of economic growth has

---

10. Modern economists would interpret chapter 1 as dealing with productivity growth and technological change.

11. Solow 1970 and Binswanger and Ruttan 1978 review the theoretical literature while Nelson 1981 summarizes the state of the art and suggests new directions for research.

12. Early studies include Denison 1962, 1967, and 1974; Kendrick 1961 and 1973; Griliches 1960; and Jorgenson and Griliches 1967.

resulted from factors other than the growth of inputs. The missing element is technological progress, which, by improving the methods of production, means that greater output accompanies a given amount of inputs. However, assuming that everything that is not explained by input growth must be attributable to a particular unobserved factor—improvements in technology—is quite problematic since at least part of the residual probably reflects specification and other statistical errors. Thus, a great deal of effort has gone into understanding what is in the residual—"the measure of our ignorance." Examples of this work include attempts to better measure labor and capital inputs (by disaggregating the number of workers into workers of different age and sex with differing levels of educational attainment and by distinguishing between machinery of different vintage) along with the addition of other important inputs (such as natural resources and energy).[13]

Attention has also been paid to the interrelationships among the various sources of economic growth. It appears that factors such as a growing capital stock, technological progress, and increasing levels of educational attainment are complementary.[14] Improvements in technology raise the return to education and to physical investment. Advances in technology, in turn, are encouraged by a better educated labor force and a rapid growth in the capital stock.

The link between education and technological change is of obvious importance given the role attributed to technological progress in fostering economic growth. There are a number of studies showing that the adoption rate of new technologies is positively related to levels of education.[15] A plausible explanation for this is that higher education leads to greater flexibility as well as an increased facility to learn quickly how to implement new techniques and to use new products. This familiar argument in support of higher education will be returned to below.

A popular exercise of late has been to attempt to explain the slowdown in productivity growth during the post-1973 period. This audience would be particularly interested in the role attributed to educational factors, especially when comparing relative declines in productivity growth rates among different nations.[16] However, despite all this macro- or aggregate-level work, relatively little effort has gone into examining productivity differences among firms or industries.[17]

---

13. See Nadiri 1970, Hahn and Matthews 1967, Denison 1979, and Kendrick and Grossman 1980 for surveys of this literature.

14. See Nelson 1981.

15. These include Ryan and Gross 1943; Coleman, Katz, and Menzel 1957; Nelson and Phelps 1966; and Welch 1970.

16. Pavitt 1980 examines the impact of differences in educational systems across countries.

17. Exceptions include Rostas 1948, an early study of intraindustry productivity differences between firms in the United States and Great Britain, and Caves 1980, an updated look at the same topic.

The work that has been done on cross-industry differences in productivity growth has shown that significant differences do, in fact, exist. These result, in large part, from differences in expenditures on research and development.[18] Productivity differences have also been found among firms within a given industry, and these are affected by a number of factors including differences in the age of the capital stock, in internal organization, in technological knowledge and access, and in local market conditions.[19]

In sum, productivity studies of firms, industries, and entire economies have provided important empirical insights. Comparable work on the industry of education and on specific institutions within it is reviewed below after a discussion of attempts to measure outputs and inputs.

Measuring the Output of Education

The major problems with properly measuring the output of education are that it is multidimensional, heavily affected by outside factors, and usually cannot be contemporaneously observed.

Studies have run the gamut in the scope of their analyses. The most basic output measure is certainly the number of years of schooling, undifferentiated by differences in quality. While relying on a crude abstraction, studies using years of education as an explanatory variable have nonetheless produced a number of important insights into the varied consequences of education. These include effects on job satisfaction, personal health, political socialization, criminal behavior, marriage and divorce, the ability to perform complicated tasks and to adopt to changing conditions, and, as discussed above, economic growth.[20]

It is natural that this simplest of output measures, years of education, would also be used by economists in estimating earnings equations and in examining the occupational distribution. The assumption is that more education—what most economists call investment in human capital—eventually means higher levels of production in the workplace. There is a massive literature on this topic, although, like in any exercise in which the quantity of education is used, we learn nothing about the effects of qualitative differences among educational institutions.[21] In fact, this output measure

---

18. See Nelson and Winter 1977.

19. See Nelson 1981.

20. Michael 1982 and Haveman and Wolfe 1984 review this literature. Specific studies include Grossman 1973 on health; Niemi and Sobieszek 1977 on political socialization; Ehrlich 1975 on criminality; Becker, Landes, and Michael 1977 on marriage and divorce; and the sources cited in note 15 on adaptability and performance. See McPherson and Schapiro 1983 for additional discussion of the link between education and economic growth.

21. For literature reviews, see Mincer 1970 and Rosen 1977. It should be pointed out that there is a massive literature on many of the topics discussed below and that, while sample studies are cited, an exhaustive listing is clearly impossible.

likely suppresses a great deal of information since it is reasonable to expect that the economic, social, and political impact of a year of schooling varies considerably depending on the particular school setting.

Many studies of earnings functions have sought to improve on this aggregate measure by replacing years of education with some measure of individual test scores.[22] The assumption here is that the educational experience leads to greater cognitive skills, which translate into more productive workers, and that test scores are a better measure of these skills than the number of years of schooling.

However, there are problems in interpretation that accompany the analysis of the effects of education on wages, and these are not limited to the usual concerns about adequately controlling for background factors such as native ability. The finding that more years of education (or higher test scores) are associated with higher earnings does not necessarily imply that education makes people more productive workers. Obviously, a link between wages and the value of a worker must be assumed, and even with this assumption, it is not clear whether the effect of education is to actually produce marketable skills.

An alternative hypothesis for why higher levels of educational attainment are often associated with higher wages is that the principal function of education is to screen for individuals with the greatest motivation and innate ability.[23] If this were the case, the private returns to education as indicated by increases in wages would exceed the returns to society since schools would be merely identifying the more able students rather than increasing their skills. If education were shown to have no effect on wages once background factors were controlled for, both the human capital and screening functions of education would be discredited.[24]

The use of years of education as an output measure would be more interesting if some additional information were available. Knowledge of the type of educational institution (community college, four-year liberal arts college, engineering institute, research university, etc.) could be of considerable value in an earnings analysis, as long as there are appropriate adjustments made for noneducational factors. This would enable the researcher to compare the added effect of a year of education from one type of institution to another.

What about using wages themselves (or occupational attainment) as an output measure? From the viewpoint of a particular institution, the effect of

---

22. These include Griliches and Mason 1972; Hause 1972; Hanushek 1973 and 1978; Taubman and Wales 1974; and Hansen, Weisbrod, and Scanlon 1970. Some studies have examined the effects on earnings of characteristics of individual schools. These are discussed in the third part.

23. See, for example, Spence 1973, Wolpin 1977, Riley 1979, and Weiss 1983.

24. Jencks et al. 1972 and Bowles and Gintis 1976 contain discussions of this type.

their education on the future income of their graduates might be of interest if it is assumed that higher wages reflect a greater educational output. However, collection of income data, say through an alumni survey, may nonetheless be of limited value. Without an appropriate control group it is not possible to determine the proper counterfactual, that is, the earnings that members of the student body would have achieved had they not attended the institution. Thus, comparing earnings data across institutions could be misleading if the quality of the incoming students differed substantially. On the other hand, a wage comparison between alumni of institutions with similar entrance requirements would be a better indicator of the relative monetary values of the different educational experiences.

Of course, the qualifications mentioned above—the relationship between wages and worker value, and screens versus human capital accumulation—are also relevant here. In addition, there is the important caveat that some careers which are valued highly by society are nonetheless among the lowest paid. Hence, wage comparisons, even with a proper control group, must be made with a great deal of caution.[25]

While years of education, and perhaps wages, can be interesting measures of educational output if used in the proper manner, there are other simple measures that may be used instead. Examples include the size of the graduating class, the percentage of entering freshmen who eventually graduate, and the percentage of seniors who continue on for graduate education. Each of these numbers is a basic, readily available measure of educational output that could be compared across similar institutions.

A more complicated measure involves test scores. While they are thought to be a less than perfect measure of the multidimensional outcomes of education, they are nonetheless a commonly used assessment tool.

Institutions interested in measuring how much their students have learned can contrast the results of standardized tests of their seniors with those from other institutions, but of course, if the entrance standards differ, this comparison is meaningless. The best way to control for prematriculation quality is to test the students early on and use these results as a basis for comparison with later tests. This is what has been done at Northeast Missouri State University, an institution that has been at the leading edge of the assessment movement in this country.

---

25. An earnings comparison within an occupation—say teaching—may be of some interest as long as adjustments are made for differences in the quality of incoming students. While recognizing that many alumni surveys measure occupational and economic status, Pace 1985 recommends survey questions aimed at measuring what college contributes to a student's learning and development and, in turn, what these students contribute to society. This point is returned to below.

There are a number of choices in terms of standardized tests.[26] A prominent example is the American College Testing (ACT) Program exam, which has four parts—English, math, social science, and natural science. This is one of the exams used at Northeast Missouri State University, where a large number of sophomores are tested and their scores compared with prematriculation results. For those who question the validity of such an exam as a measure of the outcomes of higher education, the ACT also has a broader evaluation tool called the College Outcomes Measures Program's (COMP) Assessment, which has been used by over 250 colleges and universities in the United States.[27] The COMP assessment has three options—the composite exam, the objective test, and the activity inventory. The composite exam covers three "process" areas—oral and written communication, problem solving, and clarifying social values—and three "content" areas—functioning within social institutions, using science and technology, and using the arts. The objective test covers the same areas except that, unlike the composite exam, it contains no oral section and no essays. The activity inventory covers the same general areas but is aimed at both current students and alumni in seeking to determine what use they are making of their education.

The Educational Testing Service (ETS) has standardized tests of their own that can be used for assessment purposes. They have three general education tests which are in the areas of the humanities, social sciences, and natural sciences, as well as a major field exam in business. They also have their College-Level Examination Program (CLEP), which has general exams in English composition, math, humanities, natural sciences, social sciences, and history.

In addition, the ETS offers Graduate Record Exams (GREs) in seventeen different areas, while the ACT Proficiency Examination Program (PEP) Exams along with the CLEP Subject Exams from the ETS cover the subject matter within particular courses. These can serve as external instruments for determining knowledge in the major field or in particular areas within the field although, again, care must be taken in comparing results across institutions with different quality students.[28]

Standardized tests are by no means limited to those of the ACT and ETS. A number of states have developed their own testing devices.[29] The California

---

26. Harris 1986 provides an excellent discussion of the usefulness of various standardized tests as assessment tools.

27. Harris 1986, 18.

28. Harris 1986 points out that the cost of the different exams (in time and money) varies substantially and that this should be considered in choosing the appropriate assessment tool. Hartle 1986 provides information on assessment costs at the state level. Ewell and Jones 1986 give a detailed description of the direct costs of an institutional assessment program.

29. See Hartle 1986.

state system uses a writing assessment exam on each of its nineteen campuses. The university system of Georgia has its own reading and essay tests. The state of Florida has a series of required tests in communication skills and in mathematics. While the aim of these tests is generally to ensure minimum proficiency, there is no reason that they could not be given at different points in a student's college experience and thereby serve as an assessment device.

However, some observers doubt whether any standardized exam can be used to measure accurately the output of education. John Chandler, President of the Association of American Colleges, has recently written that:

> The use of standardized tests holds great promise for elevating minimum standards of student performance. But if standardized tests assume too prominent a role in an institution, they can have a stultifying effect on teaching and learning. Such tests are not well suited for permitting a student to demonstrate his or her capacity for aesthetic judgement, critical thinking, moral sensibility, and other more subtle and elusive qualities of mind and character.[30]

The criticism enunciated above is only one of several that are offered against an overconcentration on standardized exams. Another is the fear that faculty members will sacrifice substance in "teaching to the test." Not only is the authority of the instructor undermined by required standardized examinations, but these exams may encourage him or her to gear the course material to the norms of a general test, potentially sacrificing the risk-taking associated with individual prerogative.[31]

An alternative to the use of standardized tests as a measure of the output of higher education is to use either outside evaluators or a panel of on-campus faculty members. A popular complaint about U.S. higher education is that teaching and the certification of learning is usually "bundled," that is, done by the same individual.[32] The use of a senior comprehensive examination or

---

30. Chandler 1986, 7–8. See Boyer 1987 and Adelman 1986 for a similar argument and Wigdor and Garner 1982 for a comprehensive discussion of issues in testing. Pascarella 1985 provides a general review of research on the cognitive outcomes of higher education. Whitla et al. 1977 contains a detailed analysis of methods aimed at measuring the intellectual and social development of students. These include logic and rhetoric tests to measure communication skills; other tests and analyses to evaluate the ability to solve problems, to master new concepts and materials, to understand society, and to be sensitive to ethical and interpersonal determinations; and surveys to test for the broadening of intellectual and aesthetic interests and experiences.

31. See Rentz 1979 for evidence that this has happened in states where institutional funding is tied to test results. On the other hand, Adelman 1986 argues that there is nothing necessarily wrong with teaching to the test.

32. See for example, O'Neill 1983, Wang 1975, Harris 1972 and 1986, Troutt 1979, and Chandler 1986. Boyer 1987 provides an historical perspective on this issue.

paper where students are evaluated by a panel of examiners would be a step in the direction of separating the teaching from the testing functions.

This is not exactly a novel idea. Swarthmore College, for example, has had an external examination system since 1922 under which faculty from other institutions not only grade a major written exam but also give an oral examination. The novelty results from the variety of new ways in which external examiners are being used.

The Association of American Colleges is presently conducting an experiment (funded by the Department of Education) in which participating colleges and universities are grouped by threes according to size, character, and region and faculty examiners are exchanged among the schools.[33] For each school, a team consisting of faculty members from the other two schools in the group uses oral and written exams to assess how well seniors have been prepared in their major field. The particular assessment tools as well as the areas of coverage are worked out in advance by the entire team. The idea here is to implement an assessment program that recognizes the value of a curriculum within the major that has some degree of uniformity across similar institutions but retains a role for individual autonomy.

Is it possible to collect information on those aspects of educational output—leadership potential, moral integrity, and the ability to respond to new ideas and opportunities, for example—that cannot be measured on tests, from wage surveys, or from outside examiners? There are a number of survey instruments that seek to measure attitudes and behavior. These include eleven such surveys from ACT, eight from ETS, student outcome surveys from the National Center for Higher Education Management Systems, along with "value inventories" that can be used to examine changes in student values during their academic careers.[34] Of course, in order to measure the effect of education, surveys should usually be completed early in the educational experience and again at a later point, although a meaningful comparison could be made between the results from alumni surveys from different institutions as long as their enrollment pools were similar.[35]

---

33. See Chandler 1986.

34. See Harris 1986. Ewell 1983, Pace 1975, 1979, 1983, and 1984, and McKenna 1983 discuss the formulation and analysis of student and alumni surveys. Stevenson, Walleri, and Japely 1985 and Endo and Bittner 1985 examine the organization of the alumni data base.

35. Pace 1985 gives reasons why pretests and posttests are not always appropriate. It is important to note the possibility that value-added results may not adequately control for background factors. A student coming from a certain background may not only have a higher prematriculation test score or a particular set of survey responses but may also be able to learn more quickly or change more readily while in college, regardless of institution-specific characteristics. Whitla 1977, however, failed to find evidence of an interaction effect between background and learning, after proper adjustments were made for background factors. Another point regarding the use of value-added results involves the manner in which the dependent variable is specified.

Thus far a variety of ways of assessing output have been reviewed, ranging from the simplicity of years of education to the standardized test to a series of survey instruments. One of the well-known examples of an institution that has been very serious in assessing educational output, Northeast Missouri State University, mainly relies on standardized tests but also conducts attitudinal surveys of students and alumni.[36] The University of Tennessee, Knoxville, along with all state-supported institutions of higher learning in the state, uses a combination of standardized exams, external reviews, and student, alumni, and employer surveys.[37] An even more famous example— Alverno College in Milwaukee, Wisconsin—has gone quite a bit further in carrying out the technical meaning of the word *assessment.*[38]

Alverno uses an elaborate system of written and verbal schemes (ranging from simple writing exercises to complex group simulations which last for more than a week) to evaluate student progress in eight areas that stretch across all disciplines and programs: communications, analytical capability, problem solving, valuing in a decision-making context, social interaction, individual/environment relationships, responsible involvement, and aesthetic responsiveness. Students must pass through six levels of performance in each of the areas.

Can this experience be widely generalized? Probably not since Alverno College, a small (1,500 students), closely knit, liberal arts college for women, with an unusual amount of faculty-student interaction, is far different from most colleges and universities. The fact that the members of one particular college community can agree on the institutional goals and are willing to pay the high cost of such a time-consuming exercise does not mean that other institutions could—or even should—follow their example. Nevertheless, something can certainly be done in terms of assessment for every institution.

Thus far, the discussion of output measures has been limited to the teaching side of the educational production process. Faculty in many academic institutions also engage in research activities whose output could be evaluated.

Like in the case of student learning, there are a variety of output mea-

---

Hanushek 1986 presents a number of reasons why the initial achievement measure should be included as one of the inputs rather than differencing the dependent variable.

36. See McClain and Krueger 1985 and Northeast Missouri State University 1984.

37. See Banta 1985.

38. Alverno College Faculty 1979 and Mentkowski and Loacker 1985 describe the Alverno assessment system in detail. MacKinnon 1975 defines assessment as being a psychological evaluation of individuals involving testing and observation by a study team, with the aim of predicting behavior in a variety of roles and situations. The list of institutions that are known for their assessment efforts is expanding rapidly. Ewell 1987 discusses a number of "lead institutions" that have been selected by their states in order to experiment with assessment.

sures. These include the number of published books and articles, the number of citations of their work in the literature, the value of research grants received, and finally, a measure with a long tradition in the United States, peer-based departmental rankings—especially at the graduate level.[39] The next step would be to incorporate teaching effectiveness with research output and calculate a composite measure. The difficulty in establishing the relevant output measures and their respective weights probably explains why productivity analyses in the United States have treated the two separately.

In sum, a great deal of work has been going on in the United States in evaluating educational output. Of course, an institution producing a high level of output, however measured, is not necessarily an efficient producer if it turns out that it has used extraordinary amounts of inputs. The next section discusses these inputs, and then productivity, the ratio of outputs to inputs, is considered.

Measuring the Inputs into the Educational Process

The previous sections have described the increasing concern with assessing the output of education. An increase in output—higher test scores, a higher graduation rate, etc.—is certainly desirable, but at what cost? It is clear that the achievement of high levels of output does not necessarily mean efficient production (getting the most out of the least) and that input use must be carefully identified in order to evaluate productivity, the subject of the next part.

One way to begin a discussion of the inputs into the educational production process is to return to the previously mentioned literature on earnings functions. The use of years of education and test scores as explanatory variables was described above, but there have been other earnings analyses in which characteristics of individual schools have been used instead.[40] These include school expenditures and measures of specific school resources and of teacher quantity and quality.

---

39. An important evaluation source is Jones, Lindzey and Coggeshall 1982, the Conference Board of Associated Councils' five-volume study of doctoral programs in 228 universities, using fifteen criteria for evaluation including the number of publications, success of graduates, peer rankings, etc. See the discussions in Tan 1986 and Bourke 1986 and, for samples of the extensive literature on departmental and institutional quality, see Cox and Catt 1977; Lawrence and Green 1980; Adams and Krislov 1978; Cartter 1966; Clark, Hartnett, and Baird 1976; Drew and Karpf 1981; Blau and Margulies 1974; Roose and Anderson 1970; Webster 1983; Astin 1982; and Smith and Fiedler 1971. Solmon and Astin 1981 and Astin and Solmon 1981 review rankings of undergraduate departments that include credit for commitment to teaching.

40. See Hanushek 1986 for a summary of this literature. Sample studies include Wachtel 1976, Johnson and Stafford 1973, Ribich and Murphy 1975, Akin and Garfinkel 1977, Welch 1966, and Behrman and Birdsall 1983.

Expenditure data may take several forms. There are total expenditures which include capital costs and interest on debt, current expenditures which are limited to the operating budget, expenditures on teaching, expenditures on staff, etc.[41]

Measures of school resources tend to be in units other than dollars. Library facilities may be measured in thousands of books, classrooms in square feet, and absolute numbers are often used for computers, administrators, staff, etc. In terms of teacher characteristics, number employed, average salary, degree level, experience, and test scores are some of the measures that have been used.

For all of these inputs, the particular output measure being examined dictates the precise form in which inputs are utilized. For example, a study of test scores would likely put the inputs in per capita terms—faculty per student, staff members per student, computers per student, etc. On the other hand, if the output measure were the number of graduates, then the number of faculty members, staff members, etc., would normally be used as inputs.

The list given above, while certainly not exhaustive, provides an indication of the key inputs identified in the education literature. But there are other inputs that should be considered.

One such input is the curriculum. While it is certainly difficult to quantify, it is of obvious importance in the production process. Another is the students themselves. It should be clear from the sections above that adequate controls for student quality and background are necessary conditions for producing reliable estimates of the educational production function. Further, the opportunity cost of the time of the students reflects the use of a scarce resource and should be considered. Therefore, the total economic cost of education includes direct expenditures by schools, direct expenditures by students, plus the cost of foregone earnings.

There is obviously a major difference between expenditure data and the use of separate inputs. In some analyses of educational productivity, inputs are entered separately and the contribution of each factor to increasing educational output is estimated. On the other hand, it is possible to use a shorthand productivity measure such as the average increase in test scores per additional faculty member or other input. Thus, the increase in test scores per thousand library books, per computer, etc., can be computed. This is obviously not possible if inputs are put into dollar terms and aggregated. An input measure such as total educational expenditures subsumes information on the size of the faculty, staff, library, etc., but does produce a potentially useful summary measure.

The appropriate treatment of inputs in terms of their degree of aggrega-

---

41. Bowen 1980 contains a detailed compilation of expenditure data.

tion depends on the purpose of the analysis. If there is a meaningful quality-adjusted output measure and the goal is to contrast productivity across institutions, then expenditure data may reasonably serve this purpose. If, on the other hand, the goal is to assess the differential impact of various educational inputs, they should be included separately. This point becomes clearer when studies of educational productivity are described in the next section.

Studies of Productivity in Education

The first part presented an overview of the ways in which economists use production functions in analyzing productivity at various levels of aggregation. Applications to the study of education have followed suit in examining the relationship between inputs into the educational production function and a variety of outputs. However, the pursuit of useful, realistic estimates of educational production functions has been adversely affected by one critical factor, the lack of a homogenous output measure.

Studies of this type in the United States have had to overcome the notoriety of an early example, the well-known Coleman Report.[42] After collecting information on a large number of students from a variety of primary and secondary schools, the authors examined the contribution of different school-specific inputs to student performance. Their much publicized finding (later to be questioned in a number of studies) was that a large amount of the variation in performance among students was attributable to differences in family background and characteristics of their fellow students rather than differences in expenditures and other inputs that vary across schools.[43]

How far have we come from the Coleman report? A recent review of the education literature pointed out that, while there have been a substantial number of studies of the production process in elementary and secondary schooling in the United States, "Economic studies of higher education have been largely concerned with distributional questions related to access and costs faced by different groups, with government subsidy policies, and with attendance decisions; virtually no attention has been given to production processes or the analyses of specific programs."[44] Another summary of U.S.

---

42. See Coleman et al. 1966.

43. For criticisms and extensions of this study, see Hanushek and Kain 1972, Bowles and Levin 1968, Cohn 1972, and Cain and Watts 1970.

44. Hanushek 1986, 1143. He notes a few exceptions dealing with graduate school education that are discussed below. Hanushek speculates that the lack of empirical studies results from the fact that the production function approach has not been widely accepted, in part because of the usual finding that schools tend to be very inefficient, but also because of the general reluctance to do any quantitative evaluation of education and the difficulty in formulating meaningful productivity measures. Bok 1986 discusses reasons why the results of serious studies of educational outcomes tend to be ignored within the educational community.

research on higher education agrees that "Remarkably little work has been attempted on relating inputs to outcomes in a systematic way."[45]

Given the paucity of empirical results at the level of higher education, it seems reasonable to look first at studies of primary and secondary school education with the aim of determining whether either the findings or the methodology appear to be relevant at a more advanced educational level.

These studies are divided between examinations of individual student performance and aggregate performance of schools or districts.[46] Output measures are typically scores on a standardized test and input measures include the teacher/pupil ratio, teacher education and experience, and expenditures per pupil.

The empirical results show little support for the importance of either the teacher/pupil ratio or teacher education and only mild support, at best, for teacher experience. While higher expenditures per student do seem on the surface to be positively associated with student performance, even this result tends to disappear when family background characteristics are properly controlled for. What, then, does explain the variation in student performance at the primary and secondary school levels?

Family background variables such as the education and income of parents do make a difference. In addition, there is some evidence that characteristics of teachers other than their education and experience play a role, especially their scores on tests measuring verbal ability. What does all of this mean for U.S. higher education?

In terms of the results, it would obviously be of considerable interest to see whether school characteristics such as teacher/student ratios and expenditures per student matter at the postsecondary level. But the greatest lesson derived from this literature may be methodological. In any analysis, family background variables must be adequately accounted for or the results are likely to be misleading (as was the case with expenditures per pupil in some studies of student performance at the primary and secondary levels). Further, as was pointed out in earlier sections, the output measure must be homogeneous. That is why it is more common to use the results from standardized tests rather than the number of high school graduates, the dropout rate, or other measures in which the quality dimension cannot be controlled for.

Keeping these lessons in mind, it is easy to see why observers have

---

45. Bourke 1986, 16.

46. Hanushek 1986 reports that, since the Coleman Report came out in 1966, 147 separately estimated public school production functions found in thirty-three articles and books have appeared in the literature. Samples include Beiker and Anschek 1973; Boardman, Davis, and Sanday 1977; Bowles 1970; Brown and Saks 1975; Hanushek 1971 and 1972; Levin 1976; Link and Ratledge 1979; Perl 1973; Ribich and Murphy 1975; Sebold and Dato 1981; Summers and Wolfe 1977; and Tuckman 1971. See Hanushek 1986, 1160–67, and Hanushek 1981 for a discussion of the results of these and other studies.

concluded that, for the most part, existing productivity studies of postsecondary education in the United States leave a lot to be desired. One study looked at a large number of colleges and universities in an effort to determine the relationship between various input measures, the number of senior faculty, for example, and output measures such as the number of full-time undergraduates.[47] The results indicate that there is considerable variation in efficiency across institutions of higher learning. Efficient institutions have far fewer senior faculty than the average institution or, looking at it from the other direction, efficient institutions have far more students for a given number of senior faculty.

This finding is not surprising given the discussion of intraindustry productivity differences in the first part. In fact, a similar conclusion was reached in another study, this time of Ph.D.-granting chemistry departments.[48] There, the effect of faculty and research expenditures on the number of graduate and undergraduate degrees as well as on the number of faculty publications was considered. Again, productivity among departments was shown to vary considerably.

These studies used simple productivity measures, such as the number of graduates per faculty member or the average cost per student, that are readily available and have been used in studies of educational productivity in other nations.[49] When these measures are compared across countries, it appears that productivity in higher education varies widely across nations just as it does across institutions within a given nation. However, do we really learn anything from measures of this sort?

The studies of U.S. higher education reviewed above obviously suffer in comparison with those of primary and secondary education in their use of an output measure that is unadjusted for qualitative differences. A reason why so many institutions have gone to so much trouble to measure value added test scores, attitudes, etc., is that simple measures such as the number of graduates cannot usually be used to compare output across institutions at a given time or even at a particular institution over time. This implies that productivity measures should be more detailed than, for example, the number of graduates per dollar.

A recent study uses an output measure which does a better job of controlling for quality: the number of alumni from private, undergraduate colleges

---

47. Carlson 1972.

48. Gray 1977.

49. See Bowen 1981 for a discussion of the historical trend in cost per student in the United States. O'Neill 1976 uses a unit cost measure as a productivity proxy and examines changes over the period 1930–67. Her conclusion is that productivity increases within higher education were less than in other industries, although she cautions that the use of a better, quality-adjusted output measure may alter this finding. Carlson 1976 summarizes several studies that examine expenditures per student.

who went on to receive Ph.D. degrees.[50] Again, input measures reflecting student and faculty quality as well as expenditures per student were tested in a productivity analysis.

A number of these variables proved to be significant including academic and administrative expenditures, faculty salaries, class size and library facilities.[51] Curiously, scores on standardized tests (used here as an input) were shown to be insignificant. While this particular output variable is rather limited, the attempt to control for output quality by concentrating, presumably, on high quality graduates, should be applauded.

Studies of primary and secondary education recognize the quality problem and normally use test scores as an output measure, not the number of graduates. Does the quality of postsecondary education vary less than at lower levels? I think not, and therefore conclude that productivity analyses that do not attempt to adjust their output measure for differences in quality are of limited value.

There are some studies of U.S. higher education that adjust for quality by examining the effects on standardized tests of different characteristics within institutions and academic departments.

A pioneering study examined college-wide test scores in an attempt to identify the important inputs from a list of socioeconomic and institution-specific variables.[52] The results indicate that institutional quality measures had little if any impact on increases in test scores during the college years once background factors were included as explanatory variables.

A number of more recent studies have concentrated on particular departments. In one example, four areas—biology, business, math, and psychology—were considered, but no significant associations between departmental characteristics and student performance on these exams were discovered.[53] Another study looked at learning gains of biology students and found that they were associated with several departmental variables including the number of faculty and the percentage of faculty with a doctorate.[54]

Other analyses replace standardized test scores with results from student surveys.[55] In an excellent example of this type of research, a series of departmental outcome measures within a single university, including student satis-

---

50. Dolan, Jung, and Schmidt 1985.

51. In a similar study, Perl 1970 found that increases in university expenditures per undergraduate student raised the proportion of graduates who eventually enrolled in graduate and professional schools. Perl 1976 also found that increases in the level of instructional expenditures per student raised the probability that an undergraduate would pursue a graduate degree.

52. Astin 1968.

53. Hartnett and Centra 1977.

54. Hartnett 1976.

55. See, for example, Gregg 1972 and Heiss 1967.

faction, graduate school admissions, and employment, were examined.[56] An interesting finding is that increases in student satisfaction are associated with reductions in faculty workload but not with increases in the amount of faculty-student contact.

A more unusual output measure is the grade point average (GPA). One study, using data from one of the campuses of the University of California, adjusted GPA scores for grading differences across departments and found that an aggregate proxy for university resources (average class size, support services, etc.) was an important explanatory variable.[57]

A number of other studies have concentrated on scholarly output. One analysis found that faculty publications were related to several variables including the percentage of nontenured faculty in the department.[58] Another looked at the scholarly output of alumni of graduate programs in economics and tested for the effects of departmental characteristics such as program size and faculty quality.[59] Faculty research activity was shown to have an important positive impact on the eventual publication records of graduate students as does the quality of entering students.

In sum, there are productivity studies in which the output variable is more than just a quantity measure that is unadjusted for quality. However, even here, the output variable is usually far removed from what most people consider to be the more important outcomes of higher education (increased adaptability, greater social awareness, etc.). In addition, many of these analyses suffer from serious statistical problems arising from such factors as collinearity among the independent variables, simultaneous equations bias, heteroskedasticity (unequal variances due to differences in the size of institutions or departments), and the absence of adequate controls for background variables.[60] The lack of technical sophistication probably explains why so many of these studies tend to be ignored in the economic literature on higher education.

Another form of productivity analysis is found in the returns to education literature. As described above, monetary returns can be used as an indicator of educational output and, after computing the rate of return on educational investment, this can be contrasted with the return to other types of investments within a given country or across several countries.

However, as was mentioned previously, there are many problems with measuring educational output in terms of the increase in earnings. The diffi-

56. Bare 1980.
57. McGuckin and Winkler 1979.
58. Dressel, Johnson, and Marcus 1970.
59. Hogan 1981.
60. Chizmar and Zak 1983 discuss alternative ways to estimate educational production functions.

culty in controlling for background factors, the assumptions that wages equal the value of the worker and that education increases human capital rather than provides screens, and the fact that certain jobs with relatively low rates of monetary return are of high value to society (presumably, people who choose to enter these occupations receive compensating differentials in the form of high prestige, security, etc.), can be supplemented with other concerns. Education has a consumption element in addition to being a type of investment. Moreover, it creates positive externalities (by making someone a better citizen, for example). Both of these factors imply that private monetary returns understate the returns to society.[61] In total, there are many good reasons to doubt whether a productivity measure that uses earnings as a proxy for the social returns to education can be used to compare efficiency levels among institutions of higher learning.

Hence, the conclusion cited above that research on U.S. higher education has not yet reached the level where a significant number of productivity analyses have provided meaningful results seems entirely well-founded. Compared with the study of inputs and outputs, the study of the ratio of the two is just beginning. The appropriate direction is to incorporate some of the better measures of output discussed above into productivity studies. To do less is to seriously undermine their relevance.

Conclusions and Suggestions for Future Research

One way to evaluate the U.S. experience with analyzing productivity in higher education is to contrast the state of the literature in the United States with that of other countries. In an international comparison, the United States does very well in certain aspects. In terms of measuring output, for example, the array of standardized tests and attitude/behavior surveys is impressive. However, as explained above, as far as comparing these output measures to input use in a satisfying manner, there is a lot of work that remains to be done.

Exercises with a high probability of a fruitful return include additional work in the following areas:

1. The estimation of earnings functions with years of education as an input, disaggregated by type of institution[62]

---

61. See Cohn 1972 for an interesting discussion of the conceptual and statistical limits to the returns-to-education approach. For a clear description of the methodology involved in these studies, see Eckaus 1973.

62. In all cases, proper controls for background factors must be in place. Klitgaard 1985 summarizes the results of studies in which the differential earnings impact of the degree of selectivity of colleges is considered. He also presents an excellent discussion of the many problems associated with the use of earnings as a measure of the output of higher education.

2. The use of value-added test results as a dependent variable with the usual collection of inputs used as explanatory variables
3. The use of results from student and alumni surveys in which output data are calibrated in a variety of ways as dependent variables and various inputs are used as explanatory variables
4. The study of how technological change alters the contribution of different inputs in the production of educational outputs. For example, an examination of the interaction between the use of computers in teaching and the number of students per faculty member would allow us to see whether the use of computers makes the student/faculty ratio a less important input[63]
5. The study of the degree to which education contributes to increased adaptability, particularly in the context of the diffusion of technology
6. The study of the effect of the curriculum on value-added test scores and on more general measures of educational output
7. The study of the effect of "unbundling" on student learning

The above list highlights some particularly interesting areas of research and is not meant to be exhaustive. There are a wide range of topics that should be explored. However, I agree with those who caution that a productivity analysis in the absence of a legitimate output measure is either pointless or worse.[64] In order for productivity studies to proceed in a constructive manner, the interesting and valuable literature on measuring educational output should be drawn upon. It seems a great waste that the interchange between output studies and productivity analyses has been so limited.

But what about studies of educational productivity in which cost per graduate or the number of graduates per faculty member is used as the productivity measure? These may tell us something about relative efficiencies, but I wonder how much. Like in any productivity analysis, the output measure must be standardized to make any sense. Otherwise it is a question of apples and oranges.

Living in the Commonwealth of Massachusetts, I wouldn't think of calculating a variable that simply adds up the number of graduates from all of the colleges and universities, divide by total expenditures, and contrast that ratio with one from, say, the State of New Jersey. There is no reason to expect that the educational quality is similar enough across the states to give any real meaning to this productivity variable. Yet this sort of productivity measure is used in international studies. Does it make any more sense to compare this

---

63. Various aspects of this issue are discussed in several papers in Harrison and Stolurow 1975. Murnane and Nelson 1984 provide an interesting look at the link between research and development and educational innovation.

64. The empirical problem becomes very real when government funding is tied to the results of a less than meaningful analysis of productivity.

type of ratio for the entire United States with that of England or France? I don't think so.

On the other hand, I know of no suitable standardized measure of educational output and am therefore skeptical about whether international studies of educational productivity are possible at this time. As indicated by my suggested research agenda, it is my view that efforts should be directed to studies within particular countries, not among several.

The work on assessment in this country has paved the way for useful analyses of productivity in higher education. Which inputs are important in increasing output? How do institutions vary with regard to efficiency? It is my belief that we have only just begun to address these questions in a meaningful manner. However, as we continue to develop comprehensive output measures, we are setting the stage for important analyses of productivity, work that will finally enable us to evaluate efficiency in U.S. institutions of higher learning.

REFERENCES

Adams, Arvil V., and Joseph Krislov. "Evaluating the Quality of American Universities: A New Approach." *Research In Higher Education* 8(1978): 97–109.

Adelman, Clifford. *The Standardized Test Scores of College Graduates, 1964–1982.* Washington, DC: National Institute of Education, 1985.

———. "To Imagine an Adverb: Concluding Notes to Adversaries and Enthusiasts." In *Assessment in American Higher Education: Issues and Contexts,* edited by Clifford Adelman, 73–82. Washington, DC: Office of Educational Research and Improvement, U.S. Department of Education, 1986.

Akin, John S., and Irwin Garfinkel. "School Expenditures and the Economic Returns to Schooling." *Journal of Human Resources* 12(4) (Fall 1977): 460–81.

Alverno College Faculty. *Assessment at Alverno College.* Milwaukee: Alverno College, 1979.

Association of American Colleges. *Integrity in the College Curriculum: A Report to the Academic Community.* Washington, DC: Association of American Colleges, 1985.

Astin, Alexander W. "Undergraduate Achievement and Institutional 'Excellence.'" *Science,* August 16, 1968, 661–68.

———. "Why Not Try Some New Ways of Measuring Quality." *Educational Record* 63 (Spring 1982): 10–15.

Astin, Alexander W., and Lewis C. Solmon. "Are Reputational Ratings Needed to Measure Quality?" *Change,* October 1981, 14–19.

Banta, Trudy W. "Use of Outcomes Information at the University of Tennessee, Knoxville." In *Assessing Educational Outcomes: New Directions for Institutional Research,* edited by Peter T. Ewell, 19–32. San Francisco: Jossey-Bass, 1985.

Bare, Alan C. "The Study of Academic Department Performance." *Research in Higher Education* 12(1980): 3–22.

Becker, Gary S., Elisabeth M. Landes, and Robert T. Michael. "An Economic Analysis of Marital Instability." *Journal of Political Economy* 85(6) (December 1977): 1141–47.

Behrman, Jere R., and Nancy Birdsall. "The Quality of Schooling: Quantity Alone is Misleading." *American Economic Review* 73(5) (December 1983): 928–46.

Beiker, Richard F., and Kurt R. Anschek. "Estimating Educational Production Functions for Rural High Schools: Some Findings." *American Journal of Agricultural Economics* 55 (August 1973): 515–19.

Bennett, William J. *To Reclaim a Legacy: A Report on the Humanities in Higher Education.* Washington, DC: National Endowment for the Humanities, 1984.

Binswanger, Hans, and Vernon Ruttan. *Induced Innovation: Technology, Institutions, and Development.* Baltimore: Johns Hopkins University Press, 1978.

Blau, Peter M., and Rebecca Z. Margulies. "The Reputations of American Professional Schools." *Change,* Winter 1974, 42–47.

Boardman, Anthony, Otto Davis, and Peggy Sanday. "A Simultaneous Equations Model of the Educational Process." *Journal of Public Economics* 7(1) (February 1977): 23–49.

Bok, Derek. *President's Report: 1984–85.* Cambridge, MA: Harvard University, March 1986.

Bourke, Paul Francis. *Quality Measures in Universities.* Bedford Park, South Australia: Flinders University of South Australia, Commonwealth Tertiary Education Commission, 1986.

Bowen, Howard R. *The Costs of Higher Education: How Much Do Colleges and Universities Spend per Student and How Much Should They Spend?* San Francisco: Jossey-Bass, 1980.

———. "Observations on the Costs of Higher Education." *Quarterly Review of Economics and Business* 21 (Spring 1981): 47–57.

Bowles, Samuel. "Toward an Educational Production Function." In *Education, Income and Human Capital,* edited by W. Lee Hansen, 11–60. New York: NBER, 1970.

Bowles, Samuel, and Herbert Gintis. *Schooling in Capitalist America.* New York: Basic Books, 1976.

Bowles, Samuel, and Henry M. Levin. "The Determinants of Scholastic Achievement—An Appraisal of Some Recent Evidence." *Journal of Human Resources* 3(1) (Winter 1968): 3–24.

Boyer, Ernest L. *High School: A Report on Secondary Education in America.* The Carnegie Foundation for the Advancement of Teaching. New York: Harper & Row, 1983.

———. *College: The Undergraduate Experience in America.* The Carnegie Foundation for the Advancement of Teaching. New York: Harper & Row, 1987.

Brown, Byron W., and Saks, Daniel H. "The Production and Distribution of Cognitive Skills Within Schools." *Journal of Political Economy* 83(3) (June 1975): 571–93.

Cain, Glen G., and Harold W. Watts. "Problems in Making Policy Inferences from the Coleman Report." *American Sociological Review* 35(2) (April 1970): 328–52.

Carlson, Daryl E. "The Production and Cost Behavior of Higher Education Institutions." Ford Foundation Program for Research in University Administration, Paper P-36. University of California, Berkeley, 1972.

————. *A Review of Production and Cost Function Estimation for Higher Education Institutions.* Davis: University of California, 1976.

Cartter, Allan A. *An Assessment of Quality in Graduate Education.* Washington, DC: American Council on Education, 1966.

Caves, Richard E. "Productivity Differences Among Industries." In *Britain's Economic Performance,* edited by Richard E. Caves and Lawrence B. Krause, 135–98. Washington, DC: The Brookings Institution, 1980.

Chandler, John W. "Assessment: A View From the Campus." Paper presented at the ETS Invitational Conference, "Assessing the Outcomes of Higher Education," New York City, October, 1986.

Chizmar, John F., and Thomas A. Zak. "Modeling Multiple Outputs in Educational Production Functions." *American Economic Review,* May 1983, 18–22.

Clark, Mary J., Rodney T. Hartnett, and Leonard L. Baird. *Assessing Dimensions of Quality in Doctoral Education: A Technical Report of a National Study in Three Fields.* Princeton: Educational Testing Service, 1976.

Cohn, Elchanan. *The Economics of Education.* Lexington, MA: Lexington Books, 1972.

Coleman, James S., Ernest Q. Campbell, Carol J. Hobson, James McPortland, Alexander M. Mood, Frederic D. Weinfeld, and Robert L. York. *Equality of Educational Opportunity.* Washington, DC: U.S. Government Printing Office, 1966.

Coleman, James, Elihu Katz, and Herbert Menzel. "The Diffusion of an Innovation Among Physicians." *Sociometry,* December 1957, pp. 253–70.

Congressional Budget Office. *Trends in Educational Achievement.* Washington, DC: Congressional Budget Office, 1986.

Cox, W. Miles, and Viola Catt. "Productivity Ratings of Graduate Programs in Psychology Based on Publications in the Journals of the American Psychological Association." *American Psychologist* 32 (October 1977): 793–813.

Denison, Edward F. *The Sources of Economic Growth in the United States and the Alternatives Before Us.* New York: Committee for Economic Development, 1962.

————. *Why Growth Rates Differ: Postwar Experience in Nine Western Countries.* Washington, DC: The Brookings Institution, 1967.

————. *Accounting for United States Economic Growth, 1929–1969.* Washington, DC: The Brookings Institution, 1974.

————. *Accounting for Slower Economic Growth: The United States in the 1970s.* Washington, DC: The Brookings Institution, 1979.

Dolan, Robert C., Clarence R. Jung, Jr., and Robert M. Schmidt. "Evaluating Educational Inputs in Undergraduate Education." *The Review of Economics and Statistics* 67 (August 1985): 514–20.

Dressel, Paul L., F. Craig Johnson, and Philip M. Marcus. *The Confidence Crisis.* San Francisco: Jossey-Bass, 1970.

Drew, David E., and Ronald S. Karpf. "Ranking Academic Departments: Empirical Findings and a Theoretical Perspective." *Research in Higher Education* 14(1981): 305–20.

Eckaus, Richard S. *Estimating the Returns to Education: A Disaggregated Approach.* A Technical Report Sponsored by the Carnegie Commission on Higher Education. Berkeley: The Carnegie Foundation for the Advancement of Teaching, 1973.

Education Commission of the States, Task Force on Education for Economic Growth. *Action for Excellence: A Comprehensive Plan to Improve Our Nation's Schools.* Denver: Education Commission of the States, 1983.

Ehrlich, Issac. "On the Relation Between Education and Crime." In *Education, Income and Human Behavior,* edited by F. Thomas Juster, 313–37. New York: McGraw-Hill, 1975.

El-Khawas, Elaine. "Campus Trends, 1986." Higher Education Panel Report Number 73. Washington, DC: American Council on Education, August 1986.

Endo, Jean, and Terry Bittner. "Developing and Using a Longitudinal Student Outcomes Data File: The University of Colorado Experience." In *Assessing Educational Outcomes: New Directions for Institutional Research,* edited by Peter T. Ewell, 65–79. San Francisco: Jossey-Bass, 1985.

Ewell, Peter T. *Student-Outcomes Questionnaires: An Implementation Handbook.* 2d ed. Boulder, CO: National Center for Higher Education Management Systems, 1983.

———. "Editor's Notes." In *Assessing Educational Outcomes: New Directions for Institutional Research,* edited by Peter T. Ewell, 1–5. San Francisco: Jossey-Bass, 1985.

———. "Assessment: Where Are We? The Implications of New State Mandates." *Change,* January/February 1987, 23–28.

Ewell, Peter T., and Dennis P. Jones. "The Costs of Assessment." In *Assessment in American Higher Education: Issues and Contexts,* edited by Clifford Adelman, 33–46. Washington, DC: Office of Educational Research and Improvement, U.S. Department of Education, 1986.

Fiske, Edward B. "Colleges Prodded to Prove Worth." *New York Times,* January 18, 1987, 1, 27.

Gray, Robert G. *Understanding Joint Production Process: A Convex Hull Approach.* Unpublished doctoral dissertation. University of Colorado, Boulder, 1977.

Gregg, Wayne E. "Several Factors Affecting Graduate Student Satisfaction." *Journal of Higher Education* 43 (June 1972): 483–98.

Griliches, Zvi. "Measuring Inputs in Agriculture: A Critical Survey." *Journal of Farm Economics* 42 (December 1960): 1411–27.

Griliches, Zvi, and William Mason. "Education, Income and Ability." *Journal of Political Economy,* May/June 1972, part II, pp. S74–S103.

Grossman, Michael. "The Correlation between Health and Schooling." In *Household Production and Consumption,* edited by Nestor E. Terleckyj, 147–211. New York: NBER, 1973.

Hahn, F. H., and R. C. O. Matthews. "The Theory of Economic Growth." In *Surveys of Economic Theory,* vol. II, *Growth and Development,* edited by American Economic Association and the Royal Economic Society, 1–124. New York: St. Martin's Press, 1967.

Hansen, W. Lee, Burton Weisbrod, and William J. Scanlon. "Schooling and Earnings of Low Achievers." *American Economic Review* 60(3) (June 1970): 409–18.

Hanson, Katharine. *Exploring Assessment: Issues and Concerns for COFHE.* Washington, DC: Consortium on Financing Higher Education, May 1986.

Hanushek, Eric A. "Teacher Characteristics and Gains in Student Achievement: Estimation Using Micro Data." *American Economic Review* 61(2) (May 1971): 280–88.

———. *Education and Race: An Analysis of the Educational Production Process.* Cambridge, MA: Heath-Lexington, 1972.

———. "Regional Differences in the Structure of Earnings." *Review of Economics and Statistics* 55(2) (May 1973): 204–13.

———. "Ethnic Income Variations: Magnitudes and Explanations." In *American Ethnic Groups,* edited by Thomas Sowell, 139–56. Washington, DC: Urban Institute, 1978.

———. "Throwing Money at Schools." *Journal of Policy Analysis Management,* Fall 1981, 19–41.

———. "The Economics of Schooling: Production and Efficiency in Public Schools." *Journal of Economic Literature* 24(3) (September 1986): 1141–77.

Hanushek, Eric A., and John F. Kain. "On the Value of 'Equality of Educational Opportunity' as a Guide to Public Policy." In *On Equality of Educational Opportunity,* edited by Frederick Mosteller and Daniel P. Moynihan, 116–45. New York: Random House, 1972.

Harris, John. "Baccalaureate Requirements: Attainments or Exposures?" *The Educational Record,* Winter 1972, pp. 59–65.

———. "Assessing Outcomes in Higher Education." In *Assessment in American Higher Education: Issues and Contexts,* edited by Clifford Adelman, 13–31. Washington, DC: Office of Educational Research and Improvement, U.S. Department of Education, 1986.

Harrison, Shelley A., and Lawrence M. Stolurow, eds. *Improving Instructional Productivity in Higher Education.* Englewood Cliffs, NJ: Educational Technology Publications, 1975.

Hartle, Terry W. "The Growing Interest in Measuring the Educational Achievement of College Students." In *Assessment in American Higher Education: Issues and Contexts,* edited by Clifford Adelman, 1–11. Washington, DC: Office of Educational Research and Improvement, U.S. Department of Education, 1986.

Hartnett, Rodney T. "Departments within Colleges Differ in Impact," *Findings* 3(1976): 5–8.

Hartnett, Rodney T., and John A. Centra. "The Effects of Academic Departments on Student Learning." *The Journal of Higher Education* 48 (September/October 1977): 491–507.

Hause, John C. "Earnings Profile: Ability and Schooling." *Journal of Political Economy,* May/June 1972, part II, pp. S108–S138.

Haveman, Robert H., and Barbara L. Wolfe. "Schooling and Economic Well-Being: The Role of Nonmarket Effects." *Journal of Human Resources* 19(3) (Summer 1984): 377–407.

Heiss, Ann M. "Berkeley Doctoral Students Appraise Their Academic Programs." *Educational Record* 48 (Winter 1967): 30–44.

Heywood, John. *Assessment in Higher Education.* New York: John Wiley & Sons, 1977.

Hogan, Timothy D. "Faculty Research Activity and the Quality of Graduate Training." *The Journal of Human Resources* 16(3) (Summer 1981): 400–415.

Jencks, Christopher, Marshall Smith, Henry Acland, Mary J. Bane, David Cohen, Herbert Gintis, Barbara Heyns, and Stephan Michelson. *Inequality: A Reassessment of the Effects of Family and Schooling in America.* New York: Basic Books, 1972.

Johnson, George E., and Frank P. Stafford. "Social Returns to Quantity and Quality of Schooling." *Journal of Human Resources* 8(2) (Spring 1973): 139–55.

Jones, Lyle V., Gardner Lindzey, and Porter E. Coggeshall, eds. *An Assessment of Research-Doctorate Programs in the United States.* 5 vols. Washington, DC: National Academy Press, 1982.

Jorgenson, Dale W., and Z. Griliches. "The Explanation of Productivity Growth." *Review of Economic Studies* 34 (July 1967): 249–83.

Kendrick, John W. *Productivity Trends in the United States.* New York: NBER, Columbia University Press, 1961.

———. *Postwar Productivity Trends in the United States, 1948–1969.* New York: NBER, Columbia University Press, 1973.

Kendrick, John W., and E. Grossman. *Productivity in the United States: Trends and Cycles.* Baltimore: Johns Hopkins University Press, 1980.

Kinnick, Mary K. "Increasing the Use of Student Outcomes Information." In *Assessing Educational Outcomes: New Directions for Institutional Research,* edited by Peter T. Ewell, 93–109. San Francisco: Jossey-Bass, 1985.

Klitgaard, Robert. *Choosing Elites.* New York: Basic Books, 1985.

Lawrence, Judith K., and Kenneth C. Green. *A Question of Quality: The Higher Education Ratings Game.* Washington, DC: American Association for Higher Education, 1980.

Levin, Henry M. "Concepts of Economic Efficiency and Educational Production." In *Education as an Industry,* edited by Joseph T. Froomkin, Dean T. Jamison, and Roy Radner, 149–91. Cambridge, MA: Ballinger, 1976.

Link, Charles R., and Edward C. Ratledge, "Student Perceptions, I.Q., and Achievement." *Journal of Human Resources* 14(1) (Winter 1979): 98–111.

MacKinnan, Donald W. *An Overview of Assessment Centers.* Greensboro, NC: Center for Creative Leadership, 1975.

McClain, Charles J., and Darrell W. Krueger, "Using Outcomes Assessment: A Case Study in Institutional Change." In *Assessing Educational Outcomes: New Directions for Institutional Research,* edited by Peter T. Ewell, 33–46. San Francisco: Jossey-Bass, 1985.

McGuckin, Robert H., and Donald R. Winkler. "University Resources in the Production of Education." *The Review of Economics and Statistics* 61 (May 1979): 242–48.

McKenna, Barbara. *Surveying Your Alumni: Guidelines and 22 Sample Questionnaires.* Washington, DC: Council for Advancement and Support of Education, 1983.

McPherson, Michael S., and Morton Owen Schapiro. "Economic Public Policy Implications of an 'Outmoded' Work Force." *Educational Record* 64(4) Fall 1983, 50–54.

Mentkowski, Marcia, and Georgine Loacker. "Assessing and Validating the Outcomes of College." In *Assessing Educational Outcomes: New Directions for Institutional Research*, edited by Peter T. Ewell, 47–64. San Francisco: Jossey-Bass, 1985.

Michael, Robert T. "Measuring Non-Monetary Benefits of Education: A Survey." In *Financing Education: Overcoming Inefficiency and Inequity*, edited by Walter W. McMahon and Terry G. Geske, 119–49. Urbana, IL: University of Illinois Press, 1982.

Mincer, Jacob. "The Distribution of Labor Incomes: A Survey with Special Reference to the Human Capital Approach." *Journal of Economic Literature*, March 1970, 1–26.

Murnane, Richard J., and Richard R. Nelson, "Production and Innovation When Techniques are Tacit: The Case of Education." *Journal of Economic Behavior and Organization* (September–December 1984): 353–73.

Nadiri, M. Ishaq. "Some Approaches to the Theory and Measurement of Total Factor Productivity: A Survey." *Journal of Economic Literature* 8 (December 1970): 1137–77.

National Commission on Excellence in Education. *A Nation at Risk: The Imperative for Educational Reform*. Washington, DC: U.S. Government Printing Office, 1983.

National Governors Association. "The Governors' Report on Education: Text of the Section on College Quality." Reprinted in *The Chronicle of Higher Education*, September 3, 1986, 79–80, 82–84.

Nelson, Richard R. "Research on Productivity Growth and Productivity Differences: Dead Ends and New Departures." *Journal of Economic Literature* 19 (September 1981): 1029–64.

Nelson, Richard R., and Edmund Phelps. "Investment in Humans, Technology Diffusion, and Economic Growth." *American Economic Review*, May 1966, 69–75.

Nelson, Richard R., and Sidney Winter. "In Search of Useful Theory of Innovation." *Research Policy*, Summer 1977, 36–76.

Niemi, Richard, and Barbara I. Sobieszek. "Political Socialization." *Annual Review of Sociology* (1977): 209–33.

Northeast Missouri State University. *In Pursuit of Degrees with Integrity: A Value-Added Approach to Undergraduate Assessment*. Washington, DC: American Association of State Colleges and Universities, 1984.

O'Neill, Joseph P. "The Crisis of Integrity," paper presented at the annual meeting of the American Educational Research Association, Montreal, Canada, April, 1983.

O'Neill, June. "Productivity Trends in Higher Education," in *Education as an Industry*. Eds. Joseph T. Froomkin, Dean T. Jamison, and Roy Radner. Cambridge, MA: Ballinger, 1976, 349–65.

Pace, C. Robert. *Measuring Outcomes of College*. San Francisco: Jossey-Bass, 1979.

———. *College Student Experiences: A Questionnaire*. 2d edition. Los Angeles: U.C.L.A. Higher Education Research Institute, 1983.

————. *Measuring the Quality of College Student Experiences.* Los Angeles: U.C.L.A. Higher Education Research Institute, 1984.

————. "Perspectives and Problems in Student Outcomes Research." In *Assessing Educational Outcomes: New Directions for Institutional Research,* edited by Peter T. Ewell, 7–18. San Francisco: Jossey-Bass, 1985.

Pace, C. Robert. *Higher Education Measurement and Evaluation Kit.* Los Angeles: Laboratory for Research on Higher Education, U.C.L.A., 1975.

Pascarella, E. T. "College Environmental Influences on Learning and Cognitive Development." In *Higher Education: Handbook of Theory and Research,* edited by J. Smart, 1–61. New York: Agathon Press, 1985.

Pavitt, Keith, ed. *Technical Innovation and British Economic Performance.* London: Macmillan, 1980.

Perl, Lewis J. *The Role of Educational Investment and Family Background in the Production and Distribution of Educational Services.* Unpublished doctoral dissertation. University of California, Berkeley, 1970.

————. "Family Background, Secondary School Expenditure, and Student Ability." *Journal of Human Resources* 8(2) (Spring 1973): 156–80.

————. "Graduation, Graduate School Attendance, and Investments in College Training," In *Education as an Industry.* edited by Joseph T. Froomkin, Dean T. Jamison, and Roy Radner, 95–135. Cambridge, MA: Ballinger, 1976.

Rentz, Robert R. "Testing and the College Degree." In *New Directions for Testing and Measurement.* San Francisco: Jossey-Bass, 1979.

Ribich, Thomas I., and James L. Murphy, "The Economic Returns to Increased Educational Spending." *Journal of Human Resources* 10(1) (Winter 1975): 56–77.

Riley, John C. "Testing the Educational Screening Hypothesis." *Journal of Political Economy,* October 1979, part II, pp. S227–S252.

Roose, Kenneth D., and Charles J. Anderson. *A Rating of Graduate Programs.* Washington, DC: American Council on Education, 1970.

Rosen, Sherwin. "Human Capital: A Survey of Empirical Research." In *Research in Labor Economics,* edited by Ronald G. Ehrenberg, vol. 1, 3–39. Greenwich, CT: JAI Press, 1977.

Rostas, Laszlo. *Comparative Productivity in British and American Industry.* Cambridge: Cambridge University Press, 1948.

Ryan, Bryce, and Neil Gross. "The Diffusion of Hybrid Seed Corn in Two Iowa Communities." *Rural Sociology,* March 1943, 15–24.

Sebold, Frederick D., and William Dato. "School Funding and Student Achievement: An Empirical Analysis." *Public Finance Quarterly* 9(1) (January 1981): 91–105.

Smith, Richard, and Fred E. Fiedler. "The Measurement of Scholarly Work: A Critical Review of the Literature." *Educational Record* 52 (Summer 1971): 225–32.

Solmon, Lewis C., and Alexander W. Astin. "A New Study of Excellence in Undergraduate Education—Part One: Departments without Distinguished Graduate Programs." *Change,* September 1981, 22–28.

Solow, Robert M. *Growth Theory: An Exposition.* Oxford: Clarendon Press, 1970.

Southern Regional Education Board, Commission for Educational Quality. *Access to*

Quality Undergraduate Education. Reprinted in *The Chronicle of Higher Education,* July 3, 1985, 9–12.

Spence, A. Michael. "Job Market Signaling," *Quarterly Journal of Economics* 87(3) (August 1973): 355–74.

Stevenson, Mike, R. Dan Walleri, and Saundra M. Japely. "Designing Follow-Up Studies of Graduates and Former Students." In *Assessing Educational Outcomes: New Directions for Institutional Research,* edited by Peter T. Ewell, 81–91. San Francisco: Jossey-Bass, 1985.

Study Group on the Conditions of Excellence in American Higher Education. *Involvement in Learning: Realizing the Potential of American Higher Education.* Washington, DC: National Institute of Education, 1984.

Summers, Anita, and Barbara Wolfe. "Do Schools Make a Difference?" *American Economic Review* 67(4) (September 1977): 639–52.

Tan, David L. "The Assessment of Quality in Higher Education: A Critical Review of the Literature and Research." *Research in Higher Education* 24 no. 3 (1986): 223–65.

Task Force on Teaching as a Profession. *A Nation Prepared: Teachers for the 21st Century.* Washington, DC: Carnegie Forum on Education and the Economy, 1986.

Taubman, Paul, and Terence Wales. *Higher Education and Earnings.* New York: McGraw-Hill, 1974.

Troutt, William E. "Unbundling Instruction: Opportunity for Community Colleges." *Peabody Journal of Education* 56 (July 1979): 253–59.

Tuckman, Howard P. "High School Inputs and Their Contribution to School Performance." *Journal of Human Resources* 6(4) (Fall 1971): 490–509.

Twentieth Century Fund, Task Force on Federal Elementary and Secondary Education Policy. *Making the Grade.* New York: Twentieth Century Fund, 1983.

U.S. Department of Education. *The Nation Responds: Recent Efforts to Improve Education.* Washington, DC: U.S. Department of Education, 1984.

———. *What Works: Research about Teaching and Learning.* Washington, DC: U.S. Department of Education, 1986.

Wachtel, Paul. "The Effect on Earnings of School and College Investment Expenditures." *Review of Economics and Statistics,* 58(3) (August 1976): 326–31.

Wang, William K. S. "The Unbundling of Higher Education." *Duke Law Journal* 1975: 53–90.

Webster, David S. "America's Highest Ranked Graduate Schools 1925–1982." *Change,* May/June 1983, 14–24.

Weiss, Andrew. "A Sorting-Cum-Learning Model of Education." *Journal of Political Economy* 91(3) (June 1983): 420–42.

Welch, Finis. "Measurement of the Quality of Schooling." *American Economic Review* 56(2) (May 1966): 379–92.

———. "Education in Production." *Journal of Political Economy* 78(1) (January/February 1970): 34–59.

Whitla, Dean K. *Value Added: Measuring the Outcomes of Undergraduate Education.* A study conducted by the Office of Instructional Research and Evaluation. Cambridge, MA: Harvard College, 1977.

Wigdor, A. K. and W. R. Garner, eds. *Ability Testing: Uses, Consequences, and Controversies*. 2 vols. Washington, DC: National Academy of Sciences, 1982.

Wolpin, Kenneth I. "Education and Screening." *American Economic Review* 67(5) (December 1977): 949–58.

CHAPTER 4

The Economics of Cost, Price, and Quality in U.S. Higher Education

Michael S. McPherson and Gordon C. Winston

The cost-quality quandary in American higher education is, to simplify some-what, really two problems. On one hand is the problem many states are struggling with of raising the quality of undergraduate instruction at state-run institutions. At these institutions, cost to the buyer is not a major issue because state operating subsidies keep tuition relatively low. And the major issues regarding resource costs in public higher education center more on expensive research facilities than on the cost of undergraduate teaching. On the other hand is the problem that at elite private colleges and (some) univer-sities, where the intensity of commitment to high quality in undergraduate teaching has traditionally been highest, costs to the buyer seem to be going through the roof.

A natural link between these two problems is suggested by the role tuition revenues play in the finances of these two sets of institutions. At public institutions, tuition from students is a relatively unimportant source of reve-nue, and the incentive to respond to the market by teaching well is corre-spondingly attenuated. Unless tuition policy changes radically, the problem for states is to figure out ways to provide other incentives to public univer-sities and colleges[1] to teach well. At private colleges and universities one source of rapid cost increases facing students is the heavy dependence of these institutions on tuition, for two reasons. First, when revenues are needed, higher tuitions are the most obvious source private institutions have to get them. Second, and more surprisingly, the great attention to student demands and preferences at private colleges may cause them to raise tuitions faster because it pays for costly items that either provide or symbolize quality and because high tuition may itself be a signal of quality.

---

1. Hereafter, for the sake of economy of expression, we will use the labels *college* and *university* interchangeably, except where the context otherwise makes clear.

To make it a slogan, quality is a problem in public higher education because student demands matter too little, and cost is a problem in private higher education because student demands matter too much.

This proposition, however much it needs to be qualified and complicated, may provide a useful starting point for exploring some issues about quality and cost in higher education. The following chapter takes up these questions more from the standpoint of private than of public colleges, and especially of elite private colleges, partly because they are what we know more about and partly because the current concern about costs in higher education focuses so heavily on that small but influential group of schools. Issues about quality and cost in public higher education are certainly worthy of more attention than we have managed to give them here.

After a preliminary attempt to sort out the various meanings the terms *cost* and *quality* assume in higher education, we take up some issues about problems of cost and pricing in contexts where reliable information about quality is hard to come by. We then examine some special issues that arise from the practice in higher education of charging different prices to different customers through the vehicle of financial aid. We conclude by raising a number of issues about federal policy that are, we hope, illuminated by this analysis.

Unpacking the Notion of *Quality*

Quality and Heterogeneity

There may be some goods and services that can meaningfully and unambiguously be ranked from *best* to *worst*, but the services of higher education institutions are surely not among them. Products that can be so ranked are generally quite homogeneous and can be ranked along a single, measurable dimension, such as chemical purity or butterfat content.

But colleges and universities are too various in their missions and clienteles for any single dimensional ranking to make much sense. In fact, it is important to notice that this heterogeneity is of more than one kind.

First, most colleges and universities are multiproduct firms, aiming to provide more than one, and often many, kinds of services. The large state university, with its concerns for undergraduate, graduate, and professional teaching; for pure and applied research; for public service; for semiprofessional athletics; and so on, is the clearest example, but even simpler institutions like community colleges or liberal arts colleges have multiple objectives.

Second, even if we focus on a single broadly defined function—say the improvement of students' writing skills—institutions differ dramatically in the clienteles they serve. A team of instructors who are superbly well qualified to improve the writing performance of students who have completed four years of honors-level English in high school may be thoroughly inept at teaching basic grammar and usage to students with poor high school training, and vice versa. A high quality education for a particular group of students is one that is well adapted to their needs and capacities, thus frustrating any notion of a single scale of quality.

The closest we can get to a fully unambiguous quality ranking is to focus separately on groups of schools with similar missions and similar clienteles— or, where schools have multiple missions or clienteles, to try to compare their components separately.

Quality and Value

Another cut on the quality issue requires distinguishing these questions:

1. How well does a college do with the resources it has? versus
2. How great are this college's resources?

Back in the 1970s, we tended to think that the Volkswagen Beetle was a very high quality car in the former sense, while the Mercedes or the BMW was plainly a better car than the Volkswagen from the latter point of view. Various American car companies at the same time devoted themselves to showing that simply putting a lot of resources into a car was not enough to ensure high quality in either of these senses. Question 1 is often thought of as the question whether a product or service provides good value for the money.

It should be possible, at least in principle, to answer this "value for the money" question for schools that expend about the same amount of resources per student, provided that they have similar clienteles and missions. Similarly, if schools are at least roughly equal in cost-effectiveness (and have similar missions and clienteles) but differ substantially in the resources they make available per student, it should be possible to compare those schools in terms of question 2. Thus, one would expect the school that was deploying more resources to have smaller classes, better dormitory furniture, a more industrious or learned faculty, and the like.

It is, of course, no easy matter to compare the cost-effectiveness of schools that deploy different amounts of resources, especially since in reality there are always *some* differences in clientele and mission to deal with as well. Putting those aside, it may be meaningful to say that one school, which costs society more, is, in absolute terms, higher in quality than another less expensive school. But is the extra expenditure worth it? Does the more expensive school provide as good or better value for the money? To answer this question requires some sort of judgment about what the added quality is worth, a judgment on which different people may disagree.

Quality and the Eye of the Beholder

Still another complication in judging quality arises from the fact that, even holding constant mission, clientele, and resources per student, quality may be judged differently by different constituencies that matter to a college or university. Parents may feel differently about heavy homework assignments than students do; alumni may have a distinctive view of what good teaching is; the public at large may have a stake in educating students for citizenship that other constituencies do not feel so acutely; faculty often have a distinctive view of their institution's mission and central concerns. A full list of groups with a stake in a college's or university's conduct would surely include, among others, students, parents, alumni, faculty, staff, trustees or governing board members, legislators, and citizens. What quality is depends on how you perceive and why you care about a college.

Student Quality and Institutional Quality

A final complication in thinking about college quality is the interplay between the quality of the students and the quality of the school. In general, one of the things students care about most in choosing a school is the quality of the students. The evidence, not too surprisingly, is that the typical student wants to attend a school where his or her classmates will be somewhat, but not too much, more accomplished than he or she is (Litten 1991). Doubtless this is partly a matter of reputation—the job market prospects of a student, for example, are to some degree influenced by the average quality of his or her classmates—but there is a real educational point to this preference too. Students learn from their colleagues, and it is quite plausible that a student will typically learn most from peers who are near him or her in capacities and accomplishment, and perhaps preferably a little above.

Students function, then, both as consumers of education and as inputs to one another's education. This function considerably complicates thinking about educational quality. Thus, a school that held constant the quality and amount of all its other resources and improved the quality of its student body somewhat, say by replacing a few of its weakest students with a few high achievers, would thereby become, in a perfectly objective sense, a better institution for most of its students. At the same time, the change would improve the reputation of the school and demand for its services, thus likely making it easier for the school to improve the quality of its other resources as well.

This institutional interest in admitting high quality students is compatible with the substantial meritocratic component in American ideas about distributing higher education, which implies that more able students should receive more expensive educations. Both the strong demand for the services of institutions that serve high ability students and this disposition to provide such students with better educational resources result in the familiar fact that, by and large, more selective institutions provide more costly educations. This fact complicates the task of disentangling the quality of the educational resources an institution provides from the quality of the clients who receive them.[2]

It would be possible to imagine a higher education system that systematically devoted more resources to less well-qualified students, perhaps out of a desire to use the educational system to compensate for social disadvantages or out of a sense that the most able students can learn pretty well on their own and from each other.[3] Contemplating such a system brings out the ambiguity inherent in notions of what constitutes a good college, since presumably in such a system the better paid and more effective teachers, the smaller classes, and the more comfortable dormitories would be found at the schools that were easiest to get into. Conceivably, such a system could produce bizarre incentive effects, as students might underperform to get into a better school.

Whatever the merits of such a system, it would clearly be quite different from the one we have now, in which a hierarchy of institutions ranked by resources per student, subsidy per student, and academic performance of students would all (with significant exceptions) be quite similar. A bit of evidence on this point is presented in Lee 1987, which shows measures of expenditures per student and total subsidy per student in higher education according to the ability ranking of students.

Cost and Quality

We might pull together these different aspects of the notion of quality by considering some alternative interpretations of the complaint that the most expensive colleges and universities cost too much, referring here to the resource costs of the institutions rather than their price. There are at least these possible interpretations:

1. These institutions simply waste resources: they could produce exactly the quantity and quality of educational services they do now while using fewer resources.
2. These schools spend too much money on items that, while desired by

---

2. For a more extended treatment of these complicated issues, see McPherson and Schapiro 1990.

3. It is not clear that society's resources are best spent on remediation at the level of higher education; there is reason to suspect that early intervention, before primary school, is more productive.

some constituencies, are not genuinely educationally valuable; such frills add to the cost of education without providing comparable benefits.

3. Too much money is spent on the education of the most able students relative to what is spent on others. Society should find ways to redirect resources from this elite education to the education of lower achieving students in other higher education institutions.

4. Too much money is spent on higher education altogether. Fewer resources should be devoted to the education of both more able and less able students in higher education, and the freed resources should be devoted to other social uses that have higher priority.

Only the first of these possibilities conforms unambiguously to an economist's understanding of waste. In every other case, the implied changes would reduce the cost of the most expensive colleges and universities only by reducing their quality, at least according to the values of some participants. The last three possible interpretations all raise questions about educational *priorities*, whether among the diverse educational missions and constituencies colleges serve, between institutions serving different categories of students, or between higher education and other social concerns.

Unpacking the Concept of Cost

Despite its prominence in recent debate, the notion of *the cost of a year of college education* is fraught with ambiguity. Indeed, the complications seem no less pervasive than those surrounding the idea of the quality of higher education. Some of the ambiguity about costs is due to the degree to which colleges and universities fail to follow our intuitive and usually accurate ideas about economic transactions between buyers and sellers; some ambiguity comes from our embedding in the pricing of higher education social objectives antithetical to the profit motive; and some comes from curious and arcane traditions of college and university accounting that distort their own sense of their own costs.

Whose Cost, the Buyer's or the Producer's?

The distinction between a product's price—the cost to the buyer—and its production costs—the cost to the producer—is a familiar one. But the twists and turns that distinction takes in higher education are not familiar, and intuition, schooled in ordinary commercial transactions, can be seriously misleading. In commercial transactions, there is typically not much difference between price and production costs—an oft-extolled virtue of a competitive economy. When monopolistic elements intrude, to be sure, price can exceed average production costs, and indeed, that is the rationale of the antitrust policies that are intended to eliminate such distortions.

But in higher education, in sharp contrast, prices often differ from production costs markedly, behaving quite unlike those of commercial markets. Our natural analogy fails. The price of a year of Williams education, to take a handy example, is currently $20,760 while per student production costs measured on a current services basis are on the order of $34,000. Prices in higher education are not only typically lower than production costs—the opposite of monopoly—but it is not uncommon for production cost to be one and a half to two times the price. Though our example refers to a well-endowed and expensive private college, it is not at all atypical of that influential group of colleges and universities. At public colleges and universities, it is rare for tuition revenues to cover as much as 30 percent of operating costs, and they often cover much less.

So in colleges and universities, a substantial part of the costs of production are not passed on to the consumers in the prices they pay. Instead, these institutions use endowment income, current gifts and grants, and public revenues from taxpayers—in quite different proportions depending on institution type—to reduce the price charged the student. There are, of course, quite widely shared social motives for doing this. The point here is simply that the contrast between the market institutions of higher education and the commercial markets we are more familiar with is fundamental: in higher education production costs are higher than price, and often by a very great margin.[4]

A dynamic parallel to the unique cost-price relationship of higher education derives from the fact that changes in prices need not be closely related to changes in costs. For profit-seeking enterprises, the markup between price and cost is generally set by market conditions, so that changes in price and production cost are closely linked. The intervention of gifts, public appropriations, and endowment income introduce more discretion for colleges. Particularly for private institutions that hold endowments in trust, there is a need to plan for a distant future—the obverse of the way their current fortunes depend on a distant past. One of the principal advantages of an endowment, in fact, is the capacity it gives a university to unlink expenditures and prices in the short run, helping to avoid stop-start patterns of financing that sometimes disrupt poorly endowed or public institutions. It is striking to notice that the capitalized value of the stream of revenues major state universities receive from their legislatures would be equivalent to an awesomely large endowment, but the inflexibility and uncertainty of that payment stream make it much less valuable than an equivalent endowment.

---

4. For a more thorough analysis of the wealth-equivalence of such income streams, see Bradburd and Mann 1991.

Generously endowed private universities have in principle the flexibility to gear their tuition pricing decisions to their judgment of current market conditions while tailoring their expenditure decisions to other forces like curricular need and trends in faculty labor costs. In practice, the ability of such institutions to raise substantial revenue from tuition and save the proceeds is more doubtful, given the internal pressures to spend whatever money is available.

Price and Sticker Price: The Effect of Financial Aid

Even the novel relationship between price and production costs found in higher education (and some other nonprofits) is complicated further by the injection of strong social and institutional objectives into pricing policy. For many colleges and universities, the price is only a sticker price, systematically adjusted for individual students according to their individual characteristics—traditionally, academic or athletic performance and family income. Since most institutions have at least some sources of subsidy that hold price below average production cost, the typical situation is that no student pays a price equal to the full cost of his or her education and many students—over 50 percent at some of the most expensive private institutions—do not pay even that subsidized price, paying, instead, a price lowered by scholarship grants and subsidized loans.

The motives and consequences of these discounts will come in for further discussion below. Here it is sufficient to note that colleges justify expenditure on both need and merit based aid partly on social grounds, of equity or of reward for excellence, and partly on grounds of institutional self-interest. Merit awards attract able or fleet-footed students who add to the institution's prestige, while need-based aid contributes to goals of diversity and social justice by lowering the price to those who are less able to pay—the classic strategy of a price-discriminating monopolist. Those institutions that could not fill their classes with students paying the sticker price may, like the airlines, gain more in revenue by selling some seats at a discount than by leaving them empty.

Resource Costs and Money Costs

For neither student nor college is all cost captured by money cost; even the actual money price, adjusted for financial aid, will typically not describe all the costs of going to college, while even the accounted production costs will typically not describe all the costs of producing that education. By going to college, the student sacrifices earnings that are often considerable in comparison to the price; meanwhile, the institution leaves out of its cost accounts significant parts of the resource costs of its education.

Sacrificed Student Earnings

Students give up potential earnings when they go to college full time, and even part-time study at night school may carry a cost in lost leisure or earning opportunity. These are the opportunity costs of economic theory that are not included in the money costs of education but are nonetheless very real and play an often crucial role in student decisions. So even the fully aided student who pays a zero price to go to school may incur significant opportunity costs if the student's absence from the workforce deprives the student or his or her family of essential earnings. Because the magnitude of these opportunity costs depends solely on what else the student would be doing if he or she weren't in school, it is, at one and the same time, important, idiosyncratic, and hard to measure.

Capital Costs and Depreciation

The institution's money costs fail to reflect real resource costs for quite different reasons, though opportunity cost again plays a central role. Capital costs plague the dubious traditions of college accounting. Colleges and universities own massive amounts of physical capital in the form of buildings, equipment, land, and facilities. Though reported values of that capital stock have their problems, a reasonable rule of thumb might be that for every dollar of operating cost, there are six to eight dollars of physical capital; so a school with a $50 million yearly operating budget may work with $300–400 million of physical capital.

But if the institution owns that capital stock, the services it yields never show up as a cost of producing the education. Two comparisons may convey the depth of that anomaly.

Some colleges own most of their capital stocks; some colleges rent theirs. (Rented capital is a fact of life especially at large urban institutions that are squeezed for on-campus space.) Yet that difference in ownership clearly cannot matter to the real resource costs of producing an education; in two otherwise identical schools, students take their classes inside heated buildings, walk on paved sidewalks, live in dry rooms, and so on. Yet the conventions of college accounting would show that the college that owns its own capital incurs much lower costs than the college that rents its capital. Rent payments include normal depreciation—wearing out—of the capital stock, and rents include as well the opportunity cost of putting those buildings to another use, reflecting their real resource value. But little of that would show up on the books of the school that owned its own capital.[5] It would, despite its

---

5. Repair and renovation costs would typically appear, and they would be included, too, in a rental charge.

being identical to the other in all real respects, appear to be more efficient, producing the same education at a lower cost.

The other useful illustration involves a slightly greater leap of imagination to a college that owned not only its buildings and grounds but its faculty and staff. In that slave system, our present college accounting conventions would happily show that the faculty and staff carried no costs except analogous to maintenance and repair, those of feeding, clothing, housing, and medical care. All else—all the productive value of their services that we now include as a central component in the cost of higher education—would be considered to be free.

The assumption of college accounting is that what the institution owns has no value and carries none other than direct costs; the opportunity costs of those resources, physical or human slave resources, are ignored.

Note that there are two distortions here in the way capital costs are accounted. One is that no costs are routinely recognized for the regular wearing out of the capital stock—colleges do not depreciate their capital. The other is that the value of capital resources in alternative uses is routinely ignored. Although there is some movement in college accounting to recognize depreciation costs, the substantially larger opportunity costs of capital are likely to continue to be ignored. Together, these two cost components represent a significant underaccounting of the real resource costs of higher education. For Williams, as one example that is amply endowed with buildings and resources, the recognition of capital costs adds almost 50 percent to total costs read straight from the operating budget; cost per student goes from $34 to roughly $49 thousand per year.

Wealth and Debt

Colleges and universities are increasingly going into debt; their borrowing typically is available for and used to finance capital projects, but given the fungability of resources, college borrowing raises broader questions than that restriction might imply. Induced by government grants of tax exempt status for their bonds, colleges and universities have run up significant debt. Although recent changes in the tax law curtail tax subsidies for such borrowing at private institutions, it is not clear that, having acquired the habit, schools will stop borrowing as a result.

Increased indebtedness is not obviously related to costs—indeed, a major incentive to borrow has been the revenues earned by interest arbitrage when institutions can take out loans at lower rates than they earn in their portfolios—but it is highly relevant to the gap between cost and price. Prudent accounting practice apparently endorses a university's issuing debt in amounts as much as one third the value of the endowment, yet such institutions traditionally issued no debt at all. Two consequences would seem to follow from such massive debt issue. An endowment illusion appears evident even at this stage—the tendency to think of endowments as if they still represented the unencumbered wealth they once were when, in fact, they are increasingly offset by outstanding debts. Institutions will think themselves quite wealthy on the basis of their gross endowments when much of that wealth is cancelled by offsetting debt. The business concept of net worth, rather than gross endowment, has become relevant, yet universities and colleges seem rarely to think in net worth terms, and indeed we have been unable to discover published data on universities' net worth despite frequent reports—lists, tables, rankings—of gross endowment. Debt service at public institutions may in a similar way represent an inadequately recognized encumbrance on future revenue streams. Along with this illusion of wealth come declining returns on gross endowment—though return on net worth may rise owing to interest arbitrage, it will be increasingly diluted by debt service.

A happy consequence of increased indebtedness is that it appears to be inducing at least a sporadic and partial recognition of the costs of capital services. So Stanford, for one, is including in its operating budget a charge for debt service on any building built with borrowed money. Though they do not yet recognize the same real resource costs for buildings built with their own gift or endowment money, what they are doing is clearly the entering wedge; it seems unlikely that they will long live with the anomaly of having two identical operations housed in identical buildings, in one of which operating costs do and in the other do not include the costs of capital. As that uncomfortable anomaly is eliminated, the recognition of capital costs may well become general. In the meantime, tax-exempt debt issue has the power significantly to alter the relationship between price and costs of higher education.

Pricing and Quality with Imperfect Information

Price, Quality, and Imperfect Information: Economists' Insights

Looked at as a product that is for sale in a market, one leading characteristic of a college education is that its quality is hard to judge. Higher education shares this characteristic with a good many other goods and services, among them medical and legal services, electronic equipment, and scholarly papers. In the last two decades, economists have examined with much more care the implications for the functioning of markets of the fact that information about the quality of products is often scarce, unreliable, and costly. Although the economic work has tended to focus on consumer goods marketed by profit-seeking firms, it is instructive to review some of the leading ideas that have emerged from the economics literature.

A good starting point is the distinction between *experience* and *inspection* goods. The quality of inspection goods can be easily observed by the buyer—some foodstuffs and many items of clothing come close to being pure inspection goods. But many consumption items can only be adequately judged by experience—books must be read, restaurant meals must be eaten, cars must be driven for years, and so on. For some such goods, the experience can be gained at low cost—unfortunately for the Coca-Cola company, it was easy enough to find out what the "New Coke" tasted like—but for others, experience takes time, and the opportunity for repeat purchases is rare. Trial and error is a risky way to select either a heart surgeon or a college education.

Both buyers and sellers have incentives to overcome the information gap that exists for experience goods; but, unfortunately, the market also generates incentives that interfere with the free flow of information. Producers of a new high quality car have incentives to advertise its exceptional performance and reliability. Unfortunately, producers of a new low quality car have incentives to make exactly the same claims. Because the enforcement of rules against misleading advertising claims is itself costly and unreliable (after all, no one knows for some years how reliable a new car will prove to be), it is very hard for a firm to make a credible advertisement of its product's special virtues. Intelligent consumers will be skeptical about all advertising claims. There is a symmetrical problem on the consumer side. A seller could say, "you try the product, and pay me what it is worth"; the buyer than has an incentive to understate the value of the product.

Both buyers and sellers look for ways to reduce buyer's uncertainty about product quality. Buyers talk with their friends and pay for the services of agencies and magazines that provide disinterested information about products. Sellers offer legally enforceable warranties. However, although these strategies can often reduce uncertainties, they cannot usually eliminate them. Products can be guaranteed against certain objectively observable defects, but a guarantee that a product will provide a consumer with a higher level of satisfaction will suffer from the problem noted above: consumers will have an incentive to report themselves unsatisfied. The generation of information from independent agencies is impeded by the fact that good information is costly to acquire and is itself hard to sell at its true value: how do you get those who value the information to pay you for it, rather than borrow a friend's copy of *Consumer Reports?* Because such information is a public good, the market will tend to produce too little of it. Government agencies may step in to add to the flow of information, as much consumer protection legislation tries to do, but government action must be limited to objective and verifiable information, while it is often more intangible or subjective aspects of a commodity that matter most to consumers. Current government interest in increased accountability in higher education, however, may well include elements of both.

When the provision of such direct information about product quality is inadequate, buyers are likely to seek, and producers will try to provide, *indirect* or *symbolic* indicators of product quality. One of the most fascinating developments in modern economics has involved the systematic exploration of the implications of such quality indicators for the performance of markets in which information is imperfect. The phenomenon is familiar: firms advertise their longevity, their prestigious customers, their size. None of these provides direct evidence about product quality, but all these items speak indirectly to the quality of the firm's performance: it has had enough satisfied customers to stay in business for eighty years or to grow large or to pass inspection from the (presumably demanding) agents of (say) the Queen of England.

Other symbolic expressions of a firm's reliability may be more subtle. Firms selling high quality products may worry inordinately about insignificant details of a product's finish or packaging. Buyers may care little about these details as such but are likely to respond to the signal such care sends about the firms' approach: if they care that much about the quality of the printing on the package, surely they must care also about the quality of the parts in the motor. More generally, most experience goods have some features that are open to inspection: the looks of a car, the leather on the chairs in a lawyer's waiting room, or the manicure of a lawn on a college campus. Firms attend to those as a signal of their willingness to attend to more substantial matters.

However, such signaling poses an obvious risk to consumers. It is easy enough to put a real turkey of a camera in a fancy box; why should consumers put any more faith in these signals than in the puffery of advertising claims? Several economists have offered an ingenious reply to this query. Suppose the signal or quality indicator is itself costly to produce. By investing in the signal, the firm is, in effect, saying, "We believe in this product. We are willing to spend money to get you to try the product once, or anyway to induce you to give it a very close inspection. If the product is a turkey, we won't get many repeat purchases or survive many close inspections. If we expected that result, it wouldn't pay us to invest in the signal." The signal, precisely because it is expensive to produce, has a kind of self-validating quality.

Philip Nelson has tellingly applied this notion to the familiar phenomenon of content-free advertising. When Pepsi pays Michael Jackson or Michael J. Fox millions of dollars to make a commercial, the only information that commercial conveys is that Pepsi believes its product is worth spending millions of dollars to advertise. If they expected the product to flop, they would not throw away money on the ads. What Veblen called "conspicuous waste" may thus serve an economic function in an information-poor environment: spending lavishly on the package really does testify to the quality of what is inside. Locating your shop in a high-rent district, running a newspaper advertisement that is mostly white space, having the waiters outnumber the customers—all these may be ways of signaling that the product is so good you can afford to invest lavishly in making it available to people.[6]

Another important signal or quality indicator is the price of the product itself. In a well-functioning market, one would expect better quality versions of a product to sell for a higher price. Given the costliness or unavailability of adequate direct information, it may be quite reasonable for buyers to judge quality by the price. The producer of a high-quality product may consciously stress its costliness as a mark of its quality. However, the preceding analysis suggests a serious problem here. Charging a high price is not an expensive signal to send. What is to prevent sellers of low-quality products from sending a misleading signal by charging a high price?

It is easiest to see the answer to this question by turning it around. What prevents a seller who has been marketing a high-quality product at a high price from dropping the quality, thereby reducing costs and adding to profit? The answer lies in the negative impact this action would have on future sales. The high price is in effect a promise of high quality; failure to keep the promise will harm the firm's reputation and hence reduce repeat purchases and produce negative word-of-mouth advertising. (A firm that knew it was going out of business would have an incentive to shortchange its customers in its closing months; the resulting customer suspicion is one reason firms tend to keep news of plans to close down quiet.)

Returning now to the original question, we can see that a low-quality producer can gain in the short run by charging a misleadingly high price only at long-run cost to its reputation. Even reverting to the former low price may not restore customer loyalty, since customers may anticipate a further quality reduction. The fly-by-night strategy of overpricing and underperforming may work if it is possible to pull up stakes easily and reestablish the business in a new location. It will not work well if there are large setup and shutdown costs in the business or if buyers are sufficiently alert to look to other reputational indicators, such as length of time in the business, in selecting the producers they deal with.

---

6. Plainly, this signaling function is likely to be only part of the explanation for some of these phenomena. The high-rent district is a convenient place to shop, and diners enjoy close attention from waiters.

An important subtlety in Nelson's analysis is that neither the firms nor the customers need to be aware of the signaling function for it to work. Customers will find that buying heavily advertised products works, and firms that produce high-quality products will find that it pays to advertise, while producers of low-quality products will find it does not pay to advertise. The practices can sustain themselves even if both the firms and the consumers have quite other ideas about what is going on.

Thus a firm in a stable market that raises its price to signal an improvement in quality is going to have to make good on the signal, by investing the added revenues in providing a better product. In markets that function this way, it is rational for consumers to judge quality by price and rational for producers to set price according to quality.

These signaling mechanisms all represent imperfect responses to the problem of costly and inadequate information about product quality. Image advertising and other conspicuous waste use up resources without providing any direct benefits. Firms will devote more attention to aspects of product quality that are easily observed than they would if information on all aspects of the product were easy to get. When buyers judge quality by price, high-quality products tend to sell at a premium compared to the price that would be charged with perfect information.[7] All these strategies may be vulnerable to exploitation by opportunistic sellers who succeed in faking the relevant signals.

Yet while these market-oriented solutions are imperfect, it is not clear that any perfect solution to costly information exists. To outlaw image advertising or other conspicuous waste would, for example, deprive consumers of one more-or-less reliable source of information on product quality. To combat the phenomenon of judging quality by price through a scheme of price control that prevented charging a premium for high-quality products would eliminate the incentive for high-price producers to maintain high quality. (See note 7.) If information were perfect, of course, these problems would not arise, but wishing for perfect information is not an effective policy.

Pricing and Quality in the Higher Education Marketplace

It is our sense that these developments in the economic theory of markets with imperfect information offer useful insights about recent developments in the higher education marketplace. At the same time, they help us to recognize some important features of higher education that depart from the assumptions that lie behind the economists' models.

Applying the Pricing-Reputation Framework
It requires no argument to show that college education is a service whose quality is hard for the inexperienced consumer to judge. It is also apparent that

---

7. A firm producing a high-quality product is in effect making an investment in reputation: it maintains high quality now so that it will have strong sales in the future. If the firm did not expect a positive return—a premium—on this investment in reputation, it would not undertake it. It can be shown that the more information poor the environment in which the firm operates is, the larger the premium that must be paid to encourage firms to keep quality high (Shapiro 1983).

both colleges and students have invested in a number of the strategies for coping with this uncertainty that we have just surveyed. The publication of guides to colleges has become a significant industry, as families turn to independent sources for information about college quality. Colleges have engaged in increasingly explicit and extensive marketing activities, intended to provide consumers with information that will influence their choices. Also increasing, we would suggest, are activities by colleges and universities intended to offer signals of high quality to prospective customers.

The signaling we have in mind involves both various forms of image advertising and an increase in various categories of expenditure that serve to signal quality indirectly to buyers who have limited access to reliable direct information about quality. Colleges have devoted increasingly substantial resources to improving the presentation of the materials they mail to prospective customers. More extensive (and quite expensive) use of full-color reproductions in catalogs and viewbooks, the development of differentiated information packets to students with different backgrounds and interests, investments in yield parties and the cultivation of alumni networks—to be sure, each of these conveys some information about the institution, but each also carries an important indirect message. That message is, we believe that if you look hard at this place, you will be impressed, and we are willing to put substantial money behind that belief.

A similar kind of signaling may be involved in the choice of on-campus investments. As noted above, some aspects of the educational enterprise are very hard to learn about except through experience, while others are more-or-less available to inspection. Investment in the latter provides some direct information about the quality of the school but also serves the purpose of signaling that the school has the confidence to put substantial resources behind those aspects of the enterprise that most attract students. These investments would not be worthwhile if other aspects of the institution proved disappointing once students were on scene.

Colleges seem to be paying substantial attention to presenting their campuses well in these respects. One would expect considerable attention to the quality and appearance of grounds and physical plant, as well as investments in architecturally striking buildings, devoted to activities whose benefits students can readily grasp. Theaters, athletic facilities, computer centers, museums, and the like would rank high on a list of such facilities, and prestigious colleges and universities have been energetic in developing such facilities in recent years.

Investment in marketing efforts and more generally in the presentation of the institution has, we believe, grown markedly in recent years, especially among the more prestigious private institutions. The economic analysis suggests some reasons why that should be so. One key point is that the mechanisms for signaling quality are all aimed principally at attracting new or poorly informed customers. For a variety of reasons, elite colleges and universities have been making strenuous efforts in the last decade to broaden their clientele. One important reason for this broadening has been a concern for diversity, to make the institution known and attractive to students of ethnic and social backgrounds that have not been well represented at these schools. Elite institutions, like others, have also been quite concerned about the decline and significant geographical shifts in the college-age population. Strenuous marketing efforts have aimed to increase the fraction of the college-age population applying to these institutions, as a way of countering the shrinkage of the pool. Anxiety about competing effectively with high-quality public institutions has also played a role.

A second relevant factor is that colleges and universities have become more dependent on students as a source of revenue. Federal support for research and graduate education has lagged since the early 1970s, while the federal money that is available has increasingly been channeled through students as student aid. In the states, the picture is more mixed, but many states have suffered financial reverses that have reduced the relative contribution of state appropriations to public university and college revenues. At the same time, a relatively strong economy through much of the 1980s, particularly for upper-middle- and upper-income families, increased the attractions of a high-price, high-quality marketing strategy. The economic reversals of the early 1990s have certainly caused colleges to rethink that strategy.

With heightened marketing efforts across a wider range of student groups, high-cost colleges and universities have become much less cozy places than they were before World War II. In the old days, there was a much clearer understanding about what sort of people (i.e, mainly upper-class white men—or upper-class white women at the "Seven Sisters") went to the elite colleges, and in those circles, information about these institutions was relatively easily gotten, from parents and friends who had gone to these schools. In attempting to communicate with a larger and more diverse clientele, these institutions must necessarily adopt techniques that are more impersonal. Among groups where they are not well known, these institutions must also anticipate that their claims will be treated more skeptically. Simply saying the institution is good may no longer be enough; it has to demonstrate it in visible, albeit symbolic, ways to a clientele that is literally as well as figuratively from Missouri.

It is difficult to judge how much such demonstration efforts have actually contributed to cost increases. It does seem clear, though, that these efforts have contributed to an atmosphere in which quality is more closely identified with visible, and often expensive, symbols of quality.

This brings us, finally, to the notion of judging quality by price. Such an indirect quality signal is likely to be more important in a marketplace that contains more potential customers who lack other sources of reliable information on institutional quality. One good way for a college to send a strong signal that it is a high-quality place is to make sure its price is not below the price of schools that are lower in quality.

A university may in fact succeed in the short run in improving its reputation for quality simply by raising its price, but unless the university validates that signal by supplying a quality level that matches the price, it is likely to suffer in the longer run. Both word-of-mouth and repeat business (from particular families or particular high schools) will suffer if the quality claim implied by the price is not credible. A marketplace in which schools are struggling to attract an increasingly diverse student body from a declining pool of students—and in which information about quality is scarce—seems likely to exhibit both rising prices and rising quality.

The success of that strategy may rest on an environment of considerable affluence. In more stringent times, a reputation for quality can abruptly become a reputation for extravagance.

Problems with Viewing Education as a Reputational Good
This economic framework helps us to understand and, in some measure, to sympathize with the efforts of schools to polish their images and pay more attention to some relatively superficial aspects of their operation which are, nonetheless, important in communicating in an information-poor environment. Yet there are also ways in which a recognition of the reputation game can make for uneasiness. Two points stand out.

First, the economic analysis here pays no attention to the variety of quality concepts that are relevant in higher education. Quality, in economic models of consumer goods markets, is simply understood as whatever dimensions of the product consumers value; it may be associated with durability or reliability or convenience, but it is ultimately understood in a purely subjective way as whatever consumers care about.

But quality in higher education includes perspectives beyond those of the student and his or her family. As noted earlier, quality may be differently defined by faculty, alumni, public officials, and other interested parties. Indeed, one of the reasons that higher education institutions are accorded not-for-profit status is precisely to recognize that there is more to the business of higher education than pleasing the paying customers. Increased attention to the marketing of the institution to potential students (and, in another context, to potential donors) means increasing the weight of that constituency in university decision making.

It is easy to see that choices faculty might wish to make, particularly regarding curriculum and program, could conflict with the institution's marketing aims. Indeed, this could be true even of choices that would in fact be in the long-run interest of students. This need not imply that students are short-sighted or Philistine: it is important to remember that they are selecting a college in the midst of a bewildering variety of choices about which, inevitably, they know relatively little. Strong, simple signals are very important.

It is worth underlining what we are *not* saying here. Schools that are responding to market pressures to supply a high-price, high-quality, high-prestige product are very likely doing exactly that. As we have argued, economic pressures will tend to make schools that charge high prices deliver the goods by providing quality commensurate with the price. In dynamic terms, if a college adds a couple of percentage points to its rate of tuition increase, that college is likely to use the added resources to develop a new program or facility or to improve an existing one. If the college simply wastes those resources, spending them on items that do not matter to students or parents, the cumulative effect of such price increases will be to make the college less competitive. The difficulty is that this is quality as judged by the consumer—and indeed it will be especially those aspects of quality that are easiest for the consumer to observe and judge. The trouble is that these aspects of quality may not be those that other persons interested in higher education would regard as the most important.

A second point is that the quality of a higher education should be understood relative to the needs and capacities of the particular student. As noted earlier, the best school for a given student may not be the best school, simply. This principle is true only to a much more limited extent of most of the consumer goods economists have in mind with price-quality models. Although there clearly are variations with individual need and circumstance, there is a fairly clear sense in which (ability to pay aside) a BMW simply is a better car than a Chevy Nova, and almost anybody would be better off with the former car. However, there are plainly students for whom a Harvard or a Williams education is simply ill suited.

Unfortunately, this signal is quite difficult to send in a noisy and confusing marketplace. The symbols of high quality that are easy for students to grasp do not lend themselves to neat differentiation along dimensions of student need and capacity: high prices, attractive campuses, splashy athletic facilities, and the like are features that would attract almost any student. The fact that the best institutions in terms of rich physical resources also tend to attract the best students and therefore to provide the best career prospects provides further encouragement to a one-dimensional ranking of schools that makes much less sense than a similar ranking for cars or television sets.

Costs and Subsidies in Higher Education

Unlike commercial products, as we noted above, most college educations are priced below cost. This practice reflects a social judgment—or, better, the cumulative effect of a variety of judgments by social groups—that the purposes of college education are not best served by making its supply maximally dependent on the market. The effect of the subsidies provided to higher education institutions is to give those who run them more discretion about whom to admit, what to teach, and what prices to charge than they otherwise would have.[8] Much of the subsidy takes the form of contributions to operating costs, either through public appropriations or through the income generated by private gifts and grants. In addition to such generalized aid, further awards are made to individual students on the basis of their characteristics or those of their families, reducing the price for them below even the sticker price. These two kinds of aid carry several implications for costs, pricing, and quality in higher education.

Subsidies and Generalized Aid

It is possible for colleges and universities to charge a sticker price that does not cover costs because of institutional subsidies. These subsidies make the production and sale of higher education so different from conventional transactions. Public institutions are directly subsidized by current taxpayers while private subsidies are based on voluntary gifts (encouraged or discouraged by tax laws), present and past. Though subsidies to public institutions may reflect a consensus among the voters, it remains that the tax subsidies are inherently coercive transfers from the public to students. In private colleges and universities, past gifts to endowment or physical plant yield current returns in the form of income and capital services. All together, these subsidies to the institutions allow current students to pay less than the costs of their education.

The issue of coercive tax support of public higher education has been much studied with considerable emphasis on the redistributive effects of general tax support of a present and potential elite (Hansen and Weisbrod 1969). But the role of private endowments has, until quite recently, attracted much less analytical attention despite the central role endowment and gift-based subsidies have played in the production of the highest quality—at least, most costly—colleges and universities in the United States. In the past two years, however, both Henry Hansmann (1990) at Yale and William Massy (1990) at Stanford have addressed the question, why endowments? And while the issue is now firmly on the agenda, neither of their analyses has captured what seems to be the essential aspect of endowments: that they are a device by which the

---

8. Colleges and universities might encounter legal difficulties with their expenditures on student aid if they were profit-seeking institutions, for their selective discounting policies might be judged to be price discrimination. Imagine if a used car dealer required you to fill out a form detailing your income and assets before the dealer would tell you what the car would cost you.

elite of one generation subsidize the education of the elite of the next. And while the role of endowments is worth understanding in its own right, that understanding is given urgency by current federal threats to tax endowment income.

Our premises are two, and probably quite unexceptionable: that costly, resource-intensive education better serves to develop the talents of superior students and that those students are typically more successful than most students, with that success reflected, on the average, in higher lifetime incomes.

What appears, then, to be happening is that a very expensive high-quality education is provided at a lowered price to the superior students of one generation through an implicit loan from the preceeding generation that is to be repaid by subsequent (consequent?) increases in earnings. So a large endowment permits the sale of very high-quality education at low current prices to a highly selected (quantity-rationed) young elite whose subsequently superior performance carries with it higher average incomes, which are then voluntarily shared in repayment of that implicit loan with the next generation of elite through maintaining and expanding the endowments of these institutions. It is an intergenerational aid program among an elite leadership.[9]

This means of finance has two critical consequences for the operation of high-cost, highly selective institutions. First, were any generation to pay the full costs of its own expensive education, ability to pay would play a larger role in determining who attends, and selectivity on academic and other indices of promise would be less. Second, if the high-cost institutions had to cover their full costs from tuition, their education offerings would likely be lowered in cost and quality. Any particular student and his or her family has to view the investment in high-quality education as risky: there is considerable uncertainty about any one individual's own future success. From society's standpoint, however, that risk is effectively pooled in the admission of a highly selected student body to highly selective schools. The general subsidy to these highly selected youth, then, provides an incentive to keep the quality of education provided to the most able high school graduates high and to make

---

9. At a somewhat more parochial level, and with more baggage, it is often asserted that an institution will maximize long-term income if it keeps current tuition charges lower than its students are willing to pay, thereby increasing the implicit loan to them, increasing, in turn, their sense of future obligation and hence their future contributions. While that hypothesis has not, to our knowledge, been tested (though it seems it easily could be), it has been offered as an explanation for less-than-market levels of tuition and, especially, as a warning to those who would charge a sticker price that was all its market would bear.

A different implication of this hypothesis is that as the proportion of current costs covered by explicit loans is increased, subsequently successful students will view the repayment of those loans as fully satisfying their obligation to the institution and hence to future generations. Those effects could clearly be estimated with difficulty but with considerable value.

ability to pay count for less and merit (as judged by the various qualities that secure admission to a selective institution) to count for more in admission to high cost schools. Among the reasons for emphasis on promoting racial and ethnic diversity in the highly selective colleges and universities is a desire to ensure that the social and professional leadership positions to which these schools provide entry are open to a wider range of the nation's populace.

An analogous argument can be (and indeed has been[10]) advanced regarding education at flagship public universities. These institutions were created with the idea in mind of broadening access to higher education, more for a technical than for a professional and social elite. Selectivity was traditionally provided more by a rigorous flunk-out policy than by selective admissions, although a number of states now follow a California model of selective admissions to the top tier of state institutions. Prices have been kept low by state operating subsidies, financed through taxes. This subsidy can be interpreted in intergenerational terms if one views the higher taxes paid by graduates of the state's institutions as providing the revenues that finance the operating subsidies. This, of course, stretches the point compared to private university subsidies, where alumni of a particular institution generally provide the bulk of the donations to that institution.

Merit, Equity, and Aid to Individual Students

Generalized aid, whether from tax revenues to public institutions or from gifts and endowment income in private institutions, is augmented by further reductions in price based on the characteristics of individual students or their families—traditionally on academic, athletic, or artistic performance or on family income. The criteria on the basis of which this individual aid is granted have become a source of contention in higher education, one that is of special importance among the high-cost and highly selective colleges and universities we have been discussing. It involves a conflict between student performance (merit) and family income (need). It is a conflict that, we will argue, is more apparent than real, though it is more dangerous for that reason.

The dominant criterion used in the past thirty years for the granting of individual aid in selective colleges has been, with few exceptions, need or ability to pay, as judged primarily by family income and wealth. This criterion is used in both public and private higher education, although the higher tuition levels in private colleges make need-based aid a much larger budget item at those schools. Combined with strict admissions standards and the fact that the more selective institutions tend to have more resources to devote to their students, the policy of need-based aid has tended to produce a meritocracy—

---

10. Freeman 1973.

the best education in the nation has been made available to the best students in the nation without regard to their parents' ability to pay for that education.[11]

The best of U.S. education, of course, is pricey. As noted above, it costs in the neighborhood of $50,000 to produce one year of a Williams or Harvard or Swarthmore education, and undergraduate education at the most prestigious public institutions, such as the University of California at Berkeley, is quite costly as well. But even though the student who pays the highest published sticker price pays only a fraction of that cost at many institutions, that still leaves a very large bill for the student or her family. The current disagreement centers on which characteristics should be considered in giving further discounts to individual students.

Both need and merit criteria have immediate appeal. Need-based aid satisfies our deeply ingrained desire for economic justice—that deserving young people are offered similar opportunities, regardless of their parents' financial success or lack of it. It is the essence of American equal opportunity. On the other hand, merit-based aid appeals to our deeply ingrained desire to build on the best, rewarding talent and effort and perseverance and reaping the social benefits of preparing talented people for important economic and social responsibilities.

Merit-based aid has the additional appeal, always included in pragmatic discussions of aid policy but rarely in discussions of principle, that the quality of an institution's students plays a very large role in determining the quality of the education it offers, both in the minds of the consuming public and in fact. So any institution that wants to improve (or protect) the quality of its educational product is sorely tempted to use merit-based aid to make the price of its education selectively lower for the most desirable students, to "buy" good students, if you will, in recognition of their central role in determining how good the school is and is perceived to be.

And there's the rub. The outcome of that parochial temptation is, in the language of game theory, a nearly classic Prisoners' Dilemma.[12] It is in the

11. Two important qualifications to this statement need to be registered. First, the best students here are those with the strongest academic credentials *when they graduate from high school*. The educational opportunities and home environments of students from different social and economic backgrounds differ enormously. Hence, the process that determines who will turn out to have strong qualifications for attendance at a highly selective college is not itself meritocratic. Second, even among selective institutions, only a handful follow a policy that combines need-blind admission with a policy of full-need financing. The rest either deny admission to some students because they would require too much aid or admit some students without offering them enough aid to make the institution affordable.

12. The district attorney has two prisoners on a misdemeanor but can convict either on a major felony if the other confesses. If one confesses and the other does not, the squealer goes free and the unfortunate partner gets ten years. If both confess, they get five years each. The misdemeanor gives them just six months each. A little thought will show that, no matter what Prisoner

best interests of any individual school to use its limited financial aid resources to lure the best students away from a competing school. If it can improve its student quality, it will improve its reputation and its educational quality. To put the same thing the other way around, if its competitors are trying to bid away a school's best students, the quality of its own education will fall unless it retaliates. Those are not idle possibilities but concrete results of competitive merit-aid bidding for good students.

A strong institutional self-interest is served by merit-based aid. Against this interest is usually set the rather fragile defense of need-based aid, that it is more just. It appears that the choice is hard—merit-based aid rewards individual accomplishment and educates a deserving elite while need-based aid serves compelling interests of justice and equity.

But this appearance is wrong. Consider all the elite, high-quality colleges and universities together. They have stuck, with some wavering, to need-based aid. What has that policy produced? It has produced both equity of access to the best and most costly education and the reward, recognition, and efficiency of meritocratic selection. The best, most able students are admitted to the best institutions without regard to their financial abilities. For this set of institutions, taken as a whole, two quite different policies determine who goes and who does not: admissions policies and aid policies. Only the best students are *admitted* to these schools—that is the merit component, embedded in admissions policy—and among those good students, only the most needy are *given financial aid*—that is the equitable component, embedded in financial aid policy. Collectively, the limited aid resources have maximum impact on both quality and equity.

What is going on, of course, is that when all these schools are considered together, there are two different policies to accomplish the two different goals of equity and excellence. When one school is considered alone, aid policy has to carry the burden of both objectives. And it cannot.

To see this situation clearly, it is helpful to take the perspective of someone at one of these institutions. If we try to jockey for position using our limited financial aid resources to bid the best students away from competitors and they use their limited aid resources to counter our seductive offers, we will wind up using our aid resources, collectively limited, in a bidding war for the best students without regard to their financial need. The end result, it is easy to see, would be a set of elite schools peopled by students who either are

---

A does, Prisoner B is better off confessing (if Prisoner A confesses, Prisoner B cuts his term from ten years to five by also confessing; if Prisoner A stays mum, Prisoner B can walk by ratting him out). The same incentives apply to A. Selfish individualists then both confess (the district attorney is too smart to let them talk to each other and cut a deal) and go up the river for five years, whereas if they thought of the larger (i.e., their partner's) interest, they could each get out after six months.

very very good, absorbing a lot of aid dollars whether they need them or not, or can pay the sticker price in full. Those who lose out are the students who are very good but cannot afford the sticker price of these schools—students who are now heavily represented in the elite colleges but who would not be there if we had spent our aid funds on those who can well afford to pay the price.

Alternatively, it can be recognized that our very strong urge to equity is being served now along with recognition of merit. Thus a pure need-based aid program is pure need-based only from the perspective of a single institution. Among all such institutions, it is both a need- and a merit-based program.

Take a simple example. There are five rich and five poor students who want to go to Stanford and Williams. All are highly qualified, but three—two rich and one poor—are clearly the best. There are some other rich students out there, but they are not nearly as good as any of these ten. The five poor students need $5,000 each to be able to go to either school; the five rich students can pay the full $20,000 sticker price. Together, Stanford and Williams have $25,000 available for financial aid.

Under the need-based aid system, all ten wind up at Stanford or Williams—the $25,000 financial aid budget is given to the five poor students at $5,000 each, so they can go; the five rich students pay the full $20,000 sticker price, even though two of them are real hot shots. But with the bidding war inherent in a merit-based system, all $25,000 of available aid funds are spent on the three hot shots, two rich and one poor. Nothing is left for the four highly qualified poor students. So they settle for an institution that is less suited to their aptitudes while Stanford and Williams fill up their classes with the marginally qualified rich students who can afford to pay the price.

Under a need-based system, all ten of the best students can go to the best colleges; five are rich, five are poor. Under a merit-based system, nine out of ten at Stanford and Williams are rich, including four who are marginally qualified rich students, while four much better qualified poor students are denied access.

The moral of the story, of course, is that among the elite colleges, bidding against each other for merit students will not increase their number but will increase the amount of aid that goes to students who do not need it, leaving—since aid funds are inevitably limited—less for well-qualified students who do. Some individual schools may improve the quality of their students, at least for a time, but at the social cost of denying high-quality education to high-quality students who cannot afford it.

The temptations of this myopia, of institutional chauvinism, are strong, and unfortunately, they are supported by some appealingly principled-sounding arguments. The Stanford faculty, looking at its own admissions policies, is said to have taken umbrage at the fact that Stanford rewards one kind of merit handsomely, through liberal aid to quarterbacks and breast-strokers and point guards, while it still rejects academic or intellectual merit as a basis for aid. What is the sense of that in an institution dedicated to academic and intellectual values? Another apparently high road to the low road of the Prisoners' Dilemma is the argument that schools that agree on aid awards for individual students were "colluding in restraint of free, competitive trade," breaking the nation's antitrust laws.

What the first of these arguments does, of course, is simply to argue that a university should look out for its own parochial interests in increasing its own student quality without regard to what that myopia does to the broader community or society. The other antitrust argument has the same tinge of rationalizing an antisocial self-interest. It is, indeed, against U.S. law for firms to collude to fix prices. But that law exists because it is widely believed—for reasons routinely rehearsed in Economics 101—that such behavior harms society in significant ways when profit-making firms engage in it. What is markedly different here is that colleges are not profit-making firms and that their collusive behavior protects the use of limited resources for unexceptionably valuable social purposes. Unlike profit-making firms, non-profit institutions typically charge prices that are less than production costs; unlike profit-making firms, collusion assures that we further lower our prices, in concert, to reach only the socially most deserving students. A government dedicated to society's best interests certainly should not apply the private firm concept of collusion to the universities' effort to make superior education available to students who cannot afford it.

The issues become more tangled when one considers the problem of no-need merit scholarships at institutions that are not at the top of the pecking order. Recent years have seen more intensive efforts by less selective private institutions to lure some students from the elite colleges through merit awards and increasing attempts by state systems and institutions to encourage more high-achieving students to attend home-state institutions. In each of these cases, there is obviously a Prisoners' Dilemma aspect to the situation, when one considers each such institution or system against its close competitors. Thus, regarding state systems, there is a clear irrationality if, say, New Jersey's merit awards lure students home from the University of Virginia, while Virginia's merit awards pull Virginia students home from Rutgers. And regional private institutions may similarly find themselves drawing down scarce aid funds simply to move students around among essentially similar institutions.

Things are more complicated, though, if the merit awards serve in part the purpose of moving some students from more elite to less elite institutions. The institutions offering the awards (whether public or private) presumably believe that adding some more high-achieving students to their mix will improve both the educational quality and the image of the institution, and it is difficult to know how to judge whether the gain to students at the less elite institution will exceed the negative educational impact at the more elite institution resulting from the loss of one of its powerful students. The less elite institution could add an equity argument: because the generalized aid subsidy per student is typically larger at a more selective institution, if both students limit their aid awards to measured need, the student will get a larger subsidy at the more selective institution.[13] No-need awards could then be said to even the competition. One could even describe the no-need award as a payment to the student for the educational benefits that student will provide for his or her classmates.

It seems plausible that, in moderate doses, the use of no-need awards at institutions of moderate selectivity could do more good than harm from society's perspective. However, competitive forces make moderate doses of non-need-based aid hard to sustain. Institutions higher up the pecking order will find it hard to resist responding to raids from other institutions, while institutions at any particular level in the pecking order are likely to find it necessary to respond to their peers. Since more selective institutions tend to have deeper pockets, wholesale no-need competition would likely result in very little net movement of students among classes of institutions but in a sharp drop in the prices paid by high-ability students with low or no need. If the drain of resources into no-need aid comes at the expense of need-based aid, needy students of widely varying ability would find their college opportunities curtailed.

There is certainly room for debate about whether society spends too much or too little on the higher education of the highest achieving students compared to lower achievers as well as about whether the degree of stratification of college students by academic achievement is too large or too small. However, no-need awards are at best a limited and risky instrument for modifying those distributions in desirable ways.

Student Aid and Price Restraint

Has the increasing reliance of many colleges on student aid discounts contributed to the rapid price increases of the 1980s? A good deal of ink has been

---

13. A numerical example may help. Suppose the more selective school, institution A, charges $15,000 and has a resource cost per student of $30,000. Institution B, less selective and less well endowed, charges $12,000 and costs $25,000. The student and his family can pay $10,000. Then at institution A a need-based system would provide the student with $5,000 in individual aid plus a $15,000 generalized subsidy. At institution B the need-based award would be $2,000 and the generalized subsidy $13,000. Hence at A the student gets a total subsidy under a needs-based system of $20,000, and at institution B just $15,000. B could argue that a $5,000 no-need award, on top of the $2,000 need-based grant, would just even things up.

spilled on the notion that federal student aid has stimulated colleges and universities to raise their prices rapidly. This is a dubious argument at best, but a different kind of argument, having to do with institutions' own use of resources for student subsidy, may have more bite.

The federal aid argument is simple to state: if the federal government is willing to pay a certain fraction of college costs, colleges can capture more federal revenue by raising their prices. Because a (presumably substantial) part of the increase will be borne by federal payments rather than by families, the market provides little discouragement to this kind of activity.

There are two obvious difficulties with this argument. First, it is simply not the case that a typical college—certainly not the high-cost colleges that have borne the brunt of this attack—can get much extra federal aid by raising price. Unlike the arrangements that hold for much medical insurance (including, until recent reforms, the federal Medicare program), federal student aid programs do not commit the government to picking up a certain fraction of costs. In most cases, a student's Pell grant is determined by his or her family income and will not rise if the student attends a costlier school. The campus-based programs that pass money to schools to be spent on student aid were, in principle, designed to give more money to schools that have bigger aid budgets, and those aid budgets do tend to rise with tuition, but in fact, funding for those programs has fallen consistently below the thresholds where raising tuition could generate extra dollars. It is true that some middle-income students can qualify for bigger guaranteed student loans at more costly schools, but the amounts of subsidy involved make it very unlikely that these extra dollars are an important factor.

The second, quite simple point is that in the 1980s when costs went up fast, federal student aid did not, while in the 1970s when student aid went up fast, costs did not. In fact, it is much more plausible that the many institutions that have experienced declines in the share of their expenses covered by student aid revenue in the 1980s have raised tuition in part to finance some of those student aid expenses themselves.

There is, however, a quite different route through which the practice of discounting tuition through student aid probably does contribute to lessened price restraint in higher education. Typically, when an institution has extensive need-based student aid, aid awards to needy students automatically go up to offset tuition increases. If an institution can afford to practice full need financing, those students who lack the ability to pay are in effect held harmless from tuition increases. That makes it easier for schools to raise tuition in part because it seems—and indeed is—morally less troubling to raise tuition if you insulate those who cannot afford the increase from its effects. But it is also a straightforward matter of economics that those who are more likely to resist price increases are those who have less ability to pay, and this fact exerts a restraining influence on pricing. Thus, in many markets, the middle-class customers perform the service for more affluent customers of keeping prices lower than they would otherwise be, since, if everyone pays the same price, the price has to be geared to capture enough of the less affluent customers. If more sellers had the capacity to charge different prices to different customers, we would expect the more affluent customers to pay more than they do now and the less affluent ones to pay less.[14]

Some Policy-Oriented Questions

How do the analytical perspectives developed above bear on thinking about national policies toward higher education cost and quality, especially at the federal level? We attack this issue through posing for discussion a number of policy-oriented questions. After asking what the problems are, we consider first possible strategies for direct federal intervention to control higher education prices and costs and then indirect means the federal government might employ to influence cost, quality, and prices.

Is the Best of American Higher Education Too Good?

Few critics of American higher education would put the point this bluntly, but the question is surely worth asking. It emerges most forcefully with public reactions to high-cost, high-selectivity colleges. Can *any* college education really be worth $200,000—a fair estimate of the cost of the resources supplied by a college like Williams to an average undergraduate? It is worth noting that the analogous question is now being asked about medical care, an area that has also long been exempt from such queries.

It is not clear by what standard such a question can be posed for higher education. Certainly a market test, combining the willingness of families to pay with the willingness of donors to give, suggests that the purchasers and supporters of such educations see them as worth the price. They obtain a wide range of benefits from their investment in college, from improved job skills to valuable social contacts, from cultural enrichment to opportunities to participate in athletic programs. Donors presumably gain satisfaction from contributing to these activities and from being made to feel part of the college or university enterprise.

---

14. This does not happen more frequently partly because price discrimination is illegal. Probably at least as important as the legal prohibition is the technical difficulty of discriminating in the sale of products that can be resold. If camera stores charged affluent customers more, low-income people would be hired to buy cameras for wealthy people. Services like medicine, education, and transportation are easier to police against such resale practices, and price discrimination is more common in those industries.

It is natural to want to duck the hard question about whether these institutions are too good by transforming it. Perhaps these colleges and universities could supply precisely the same range of services at lower costs through becoming more efficient. Or perhaps their costs should be covered differently, say by spending more out of the endowment to lower the cost to families of present education at the expense of higher prices or reduced quality for future generations. However one answers these questions, the more basic question is also worth keeping in focus: perhaps these very expensive colleges and universities really are over the top in the quality and variety of services they attempt to provide.

But if this really were the case, wouldn't the market let us know? Our earlier discussion suggests two reasons why the market here may not be a fully adequate means of settling on quality levels in elite higher education. First, the student cost of this kind of education is heavily subsidized, partly by governments but mainly by donors. If students and their families had to bear the full costs of this education, they would be likely to search harder for bargains and thereby induce cost- and quality-cutting pressures. These pressures would be further increased if need-based student aid were reduced, since that would increase the price sensitivity of an important segment of the market.

This partial insulation of higher education from the market is a product of conscious social policy; public funds and encouragement to private donations are provided because it is thought that families would underspend on higher education without such support and because it is thought that educational priorities within colleges and universities should not be too much dictated by the market. But it then becomes essentially a political and social judgment how intense or lavish this education should become; there is no magic to the levels of resource use at which we have arrived. Perhaps the only thing to be said is that those who genuinely think these colleges are too good should make some effort to say precisely what they should do less well as a way of saving money and be prepared to defend that judgment against constituencies for whom those disfavored items are a high priority.

The second weakness of the market solution stems from the signaling phenomenon discussed earlier. The poverty of information about college quality encourages institutions to invest in visible, and costly, symbols of quality, one of which is a high price. This process, it is important to stress, is not unchecked; if the symbols do not correspond to what students discover when they arrive on campus, that word will eventually spread. Still, the importance of signaling in an environment where schools are trying to broaden their client base has a dynamic that bears a certain analogy to the arms race. Each institution may wind up spending more than it wants—indeed charging more than it wants—to offset the signaling efforts of other schools.

To see the problem, imagine a university that believed it could deliver a better product, from the students' point of view, at a lower cost, through reorganizing in some ways and dispensing with some conspicuous expenditures that had little more than cosmetic value. How does this university get the message out? Surely an announcement that the institution is cutting its price, getting rid of three club sports and two interdisciplinary programs, and replacing its IBM computer facility with two minis is likely to send the wrong signal. Saying that the university is taking these steps not because it is desperate for students but because it sees ways to improve the institution's quality by refining its focus will not cut much ice, because that is precisely what an institution that *is* desperate for students would say. The competitive dynamic in an information-poor environment clearly has aspects that bias institutions toward higher costs and prices.

Has the Cost-Price Spiral Spun Itself Out?

The forces generating a cost-price spiral are not unlimited, and signs of their slowdown have become amply evident in the 1990s.

First, and quite importantly, the intense marketing efforts of elite colleges and universities are closely connected with two current developments: an urgent desire to recruit a more diverse student body and a concern to offset the demographic implications of the baby bust. The baby bust will end in a few more years, and familiarity with elite higher education among minority and disadvantaged groups is growing rapidly. Efforts to signal quality are most intense when trying to reach new clienteles (just as new brands get substantially more advertising than established brands); it is reasonable to suppose that as leading institutions become more completely known in the national market and as the echo of the baby boom approaches, these pressures for higher cost will ease.

Second, quality consciousness appears to be turning to cost consciousness among important segments of the public that higher education wants to reach. Something like this happened, albeit temporarily, in the automobile market after the oil price hike changed public views about transportation. The two kinds of conditions that have generated such a reaction in higher education appear to be, first, developments in the national economy that have made families more reluctant to pay top dollar for education and, second, a growing suspicion among students and families that the most expensive features of elite higher education are badly overrated. The political rhetoric that has nurtured this worry has not encouraged families to distinguish between extravagance and those features that are the essence of high-quality education.

Should the Federal Government Attempt to Dictate
Higher Education Prices?

One policy option the federal government could consider in its worries about college costs is simply imposing price ceilings or cost ceilings on colleges and universities. Few observers have advocated anything so drastic, but it may clarify issues to pose the matter directly. Such action might also raise constitutional questions, which we are incompetent to judge, but those worries aside, is this approach at all feasible or attractive?

The idea of the federal government literally stipulating prices or expenditure levels for the more than 3,500 nonprofit and public colleges and universities is prima facie absurd. Besides posing enormous bureaucratic difficulties, such a step would fly in the face of the traditions of decentralization and pluralism in American higher education.

Two alternatives to this blunderbuss approach are not so categorically unworkable. One would be to legislate maximum rates of increase in costs or prices for all institutions. Any such action always raises complications regarding measurement: which expenditures count? are prices per credit hour or per semester? and so on. Any price control system sets up incentives for sellers to do the accounting in ways that evade the intent of the controls; although not serious in the short run, such distortions become cumulatively more distorting as time goes on.

A more serious problem is that controls that were tight enough to be binding on either price or cost would involve the federal government quite deeply in the setting of educational priorities for the nation's institutions. Either expenditure or price controls would make it very hard for individual institutions to change their missions and programs substantially, unless there were a system in place for providing approved exceptions to the limitations. But any board empowered to rule on such exceptions would in effect have the authority to determine the directions of change in program and mission for all the colleges and universities in the United States. If price controls were to extend to public higher education, the federal government would play a key role in determining the sharing of costs between state governments and students, a role few would find desirable.

A second strategy, and one that would likely be more politically popular, would simply be to regulate the costs or prices of the most expensive colleges and universities. A simple version of this regulation would be to say, for example, that no college or university whose total charges (tuition, room, and board) exceeded, say, $15,000 could raise its charges by more than, say, 1 percent per year above inflation. Imposing such regulations would compel these institutions to cut back on quality improvements, find ways to become more efficient, or draw down their endowments more rapidly or, most likely, to produce some combination of the three.

This approach is vulnerable to several strong objections. First, this approach would make the federal government the ultimate arbiter of the question whether the best of American higher education is too good. In a pluralist society, it is not at all clear that we want a univocal federal answer to that question. Second, for many high-cost institutions, undergraduate education is only one of many activities they undertake, and one that has to struggle for resources and attention with the rest. If the revenues from that activity are curtailed, while others such as graduate education, research, and consulting are not, a disproportionate withdrawal of energy and resources from the constrained activity is likely. This withdrawal might produce a sharper decline in the effectiveness of these institutions' undergraduate efforts than anyone would prefer. Finally, the approach would be a kind of sumptuary legislation with strong paternalistic overtones. If families and private donors want to sustain an educational enterprise at a rather luxurious level, why should they be prevented from doing so? It is hard to imagine federal efforts to regulate the prices of luxury cars or boats, yet even the most costly higher education seems less extravagant than those.

Should We Restrict Federal Aid to High-Cost Colleges?

This last point suggests a more limited direct federal response to high-cost education: to deny or limit federal student aid to those who elect to attend the highest cost institutions. The argument here would be, "It's fine if some family wants to spend their own money for Maserati-class education, but I'm darned if my tax dollars should support it."

This outlook plainly has a certain intuitive appeal. The appeal is partly grounded in the belief that low-income students qualify for much more federal aid by attending high-cost institutions. As we noted above, this belief is largely spurious. The fact is that it costs the federal government very little, if any, more to support a student at a high-cost, highly selective institution than at most other schools. The bulk of the aid received by needy students at high-cost institutions is in the form of institutional discounts and grants rather than federal support.

Indeed, the denial of federal support for education at high-cost institutions would likely result in more rather than less governmental expenditure on the education of the affected students. For many of these students would likely enroll instead in state-run institutions, where state appropriations cover a substantial fraction of costs.

Such a strategy of denying federal aid to high-cost places also conflicts with the unique role graduates of these institutions play (for better or worse) in our society. As we noted earlier, the need-based aid strategy has served to keep these highly selective institutions open to all students regardless of their ability to pay, and this has helped to improve access to influential social and economic positions for students from a variety of social and economic backgrounds. This process could be substantially set back by a refusal to provide federal support to students at high-cost institutions.

The hope in such a proposal might be not that these schools would become inaccessible to low-income students but rather that the schools would respond to these rules by containing their own costs. However, federal student aid support is a relatively small income item at the most expensive institutions, and its threatened loss would not be an overwhelming consideration in the policies of these institutions.

Can We Improve the Flow of Information to Students and Parents about College Quality?

If direct federal intervention to control college and university costs and prices seems unpromising, are there steps the federal government could take to create an environment in which better decisions about cost and quality would be made?

If potential consumers of higher education were perfectly informed about the characteristics and the long-run benefits of attendance at particular higher education institutions, many of the difficulties that concern us would evaporate. Judging quality by price would cease to be an issue, as would the whole range of marketing and signaling efforts colleges and universities engage in. Perfect information is, of course, a daydream, but even improved information could be an important aid.

Better direct information about what colleges had to offer would reduce the emphasis on indirect information and allow colleges to concentrate more on conveying subtler messages concerning the particular characteristics of their programs.

Both because it is difficult for schools to convey accurate information about themselves and their competitors in a credible way and because the production of information is a public good, there is plainly, in principle, a role for the federal government in certifying educational quality and disseminating information about educational alternatives. Perhaps the kind of information that would be most useful is that which would help students gauge the fit between their needs and capacities and what different schools have to offer. Such information would encourage families to make educational choices less on the grounds of overall institutional prestige and more on the basis of how well a school serves a given student.

Unfortunately, it is far from clear what practical steps can be taken to advance this goal. Markets for commercial products suffer from the same difficulty. Certain minimal characteristics of a product can be established through regulatory and certification processes: the medicine is very likely not to kill you, the car's wheels hardly ever fall off. But the kind of information that really matters in the choice between products—or between educational institutions—is extremely subtle and, in the case of higher education, varies from one individual to another. The problem is especially difficult in the current context because the concern about costs centers on the most expensive institutions. These are not schools for which the usual accrediting processes, or even suitably tuned-up versions of those, will reveal anything of interest. Neither are objective quantitative measurements, of the kind the assessment movement is attempting to popularize, likely to prove illuminating for the relatively subtle differences on which the choice among such schools depends.

Nor is it unreasonable to worry that government efforts at the dissemination of information might do more harm than good if their measures are inaccurate or if they provide information on so small a part of the overall picture—like the current call for crime statistics on campuses—that they are misleading.

It might be more useful to attempt to improve the channels of information colleges and students rely on now. Thus, efforts, such as those that the College Board has undertaken, to improve the preparation and knowledge base of high school guidance counselors, could be helpful. Perhaps ironically, another measure that might help is to search for ways to accelerate and extend the marketing efforts of the colleges themselves. To some degree, the present situation is a disequilibrium in which colleges are trying to become better known among clienteles that have traditionally been poorly informed about them. After these schools achieve more success in these efforts, it is reasonable to suppose that these intense marketing efforts will ease off, with some consequent easing in efforts to demonstrate high quality in costly ways. It is not clear what the federal role may be in stimulating such efforts. However, local, regional, and consortial efforts to sponsor college fairs and encourage other forms of information exchange may be of use in this regard.

Should We Reduce Colleges' and Universities' Dependence on the Market?

In the last decade, college and university finance has become more dependent on student payments as a revenue source. Declines in research expenditures as a share of revenues, weak economies in some states, and most recently changes in tax law that in several ways reduce the degree of tax subsidy for higher education have contributed to this trend. These trends tend to increase the weight attached to student preferences in decisions about college and university resource allocation and increase the pressure on colleges to undertake expenditures that signal high quality to students.

The argument here can be generalized. Burton Weisbrod has recently examined models in which nonprofit institutions engage in some activities they find intrinsically satisfying and others they undertake to generate revenues. The larger the contributions to institutional revenues made by autonomous sources not linked to these revenue-raising activities, the more the institution concentrates its resources on the activities it most cares about. Weisbrod has argued that the relative reduction in autonomous revenue sources has increased colleges' commitment of resources to revenue producers like creative financing schemes, souvenir stores, and the like (much to the displeasure of the small business community). In the same vein, one could regard the educational services provided by colleges as including some that they ("they" might be regarded as the faculty and the administration) intrinsically value and some that they undertake essentially as revenue raisers that serve to attract paying student customers. Teaching American history might fall in the first category while conducting yield parties or recruiting high-powered student athletes might fall in the latter. A greater dependence on student tuition will tend to increase institutions' emphasis on the latter kinds of activities.

A policy response would be to provide more general purpose subsidies to institutions that are not closely linked to their performance in recruiting students. Such subsidies might be provided either directly or through increased encouragement to private donations. This would tend to increase the influence of faculty and administrators (and possibly trustees) relative to other constituencies in determining internal resource allocation.

There is an important weakness in this strategy, beyond the point that it costs money. In effect, the assumption is that the institution will care more about and have a clearer view of educational quality than students and parents do. That may be true of some institutions, but the faculty and administrators at other institutions may have objectives they rank much higher than effective undergraduate instruction. Given autonomous control over resources, they may not be at all inclined to allocate them toward undergraduates but instead use them to support, for example, research and graduate instruction.[15]

In effect, this is a fair picture of the dilemma that faces legislatures in many states, where the objectives of public institutions are very much ori-

---

15. Compare James 1978.

ented toward professional prestige and any discretionary resources go toward prestige-enhancing activities like research. It has proved very difficult to design effective incentives to encourage attention to undergraduate teaching. The fact that most private institutions strongly depend on tuition revenues provides an important incentive for effective teaching.

Should We Encourage Colleges and Universities to Collude on Price?

We noted earlier that some of the pressure for higher prices and for conspicuous expenditure at high-cost private institutions is the result of competitive pressures: a desire to provide the assurance of high quality in a market where reliable information is scarce. Such quality competition has, like the closely related competition for high-quality students through merit scholarships discussed above, an important Prisoners' Dilemma aspect. This phenomenon has been widely noted in commercial markets, where, for example, high advertising expenditures for a particular brand of cosmetics may serve mainly to offset the impact of advertising for other brands. Both producers and buyers might be better off if the producers could agree to de-escalate the conflict. But explicit agreement on pricing, product, and advertising strategies runs afoul of the antitrust laws. Most economists would probably agree that in commercial contexts the general policy of encouraging competition is justified, despite that on occasions competitive action leads to some waste of resources.

David Breneman has suggested that college pricing and the provision of new programs suffers from an excess of competition. As president of Kalamazoo College, he felt he could not afford to moderate his institution's rate of price increase unless other high-quality Midwestern institutions did the same. To cut the rate of price increase unilaterally would have risked sending a signal that Kalamazoo was in trouble; at the same time the resultant slowed growth of revenues would have impeded Kalamazoo's ability to add interesting new features to its programs while its competitors continued to do so. On the other hand, if all the Midwestern private liberal arts colleges moved in concert to keep prices in check, none of them would suffer a relative disadvantage.

There is a delicious irony here: the suggestion is that "a conspiracy in restraint of trade" could be used as a vehicle for keeping prices down—not what our economics textbooks or our experience with the OPEC cartel would lead us to expect. A couple considerations make this more plausible than it might seem at first glance. First, quality competition is an expensive and demanding proposition for colleges and universities. For colleges to collude in keeping prices down while keeping expenditures up would indeed fly in the face of economic logic, but the proposition is that colleges would forego some expensive building and programmatic changes at the same time they exercised more price restraint. This prospect is more reasonable for the institutions to contemplate. Second, these are not profit-seeking institutions. More collusion on price and program quality would mean, in effect, a reduction of the influence of the student market compared to that of other constituencies in determining institutional priorities. In this respect, encouraging greater collusion on price would have similar effects to providing colleges with more autonomous revenue.

The approach would have the same drawbacks as well. In the first place, the quality improvements that would be foregone through a policy of price restraint would be at least in part a genuine loss from the standpoint of buyers of higher education. Whether consumers would value their dollar savings more than the loss in the development of new wrinkles at the institutions they or their children attend is a difficult judgment to make. More seriously, the appeal of this proposal depends on the assumption that the other constituencies at the institutions in question—principally faculty and administration—in some sense have the best interests of the students at heart. But easing the pressure of the student market is likely to have quite different effects at different types of institutions. While it may be plausible that liberal arts colleges would take advantage of collusion on price and quality in ways students and parents would approve of, other sorts of institutions might substantially devalue student interests without competitive pressures.

Despite these drawbacks, it may well be that the encouragement of more agreement among groups of comparable institutions on policies toward pricing, marketing, and the development of new programs would be worthwhile. Explicit agreements on price and marketing strategies would certainly provoke nervousness in light of the current Justice Department investigation. While it might not seem reasonable to have higher education join baseball as an institution with a blanket exemption from the antitrust laws, some more limited protection to encourage agreements on price restraint and certain other kinds of coordinated action might well become an attractive public policy.

Conclusion

This paper has been offered in a spirit of exploration. Its purpose has been both to clarify and to complicate, to make distinctions involving cost and quality in higher education, but also to warn against too much precision in debate where there is in fact less. *Quality* is a word, and a goal, with many meanings; even *cost*, a term that has the ring of hard facts and bottom lines, turns out to be a much more ambiguous and multifaceted notion in higher education than may at first appear.

The tools we have used—and, more important, the perspective and framing of the issues—are those of an economist, with an economist's emphasis on imperfect information and efficiency, on pricing and equity, and also an economist's concern with public policy. Nationally, these are issues central to higher education that are yet deeply unsettled at the beginning of the 1990s; sorting them out will require a good grasp of the economist's perspective and a great deal besides. We hope our contribution to that enterprise will prove to be of some value.

REFERENCES

Bradburd, Ralph, and Duncan Mann. "Wealth in Higher Education Institutions." Unpublished, 1991.

Freeman, Richard B. "On Mythical Effects of Public Subsidization of Higher Education: Social Benefits and Regressive Income Redistribution." In *Does College Matter? Some Evidence on the Impacts of Higher Education,* edited by Lewis C. Solmon and Paul Taubman. New York: Academic Press, 1973.

Hansen, W. Lee, and Burton Weisbrod. *Benefits, Costs and Finance of Public Higher Education.* Chicago: Markham, 1969.

Hansmann, Henry. "Why Do Universities Have Endowments?" *Journal of Legal Studies* 19 (January 1990): 3–42.

James, Estelle. "Product Mix and Cost Disaggregation: A Reinterpretation of the Economics of Higher Education." *Journal of Human Resources* 13 (Spring 1978): 157–86.

Lee, John B. "The Equity of Higher Education Subsidies." Unpublished paper, 1987.

Litten, Larry. *Ivy Bound: High-Ability Students and College Choice.* New York: College Board Press, 1991.

Massy, William F. *Endowment: Perspectives, Policies and Management.* Washington, DC: Association of Governing Boards, 1990.

McPherson, Michael, and Morton Schapiro. *Selective Admission and the Public Interest.* New York: College Board Press, 1990.

Shapiro, Carl. "Optimal Pricing of Experience Goods." *Bell Journal of Economics* 14 (Autumn 1983): 497–507.

Weisbrod, Burton. *The Nonprofit Economy.* Cambridge, MA: Harvard University Press, 1988.

CHAPTER 5

The Economics of Academic Tenure:
A Relational Perspective

Michael S. McPherson and Gordon C. Winston

The main argument advanced in favor of the institution of tenure is the
protection it provides for academic freedom.[1] Defenders of tenure seem ready
to concede its economic inefficiency but see it as a necessary price to pay to
protect scholarly independence. Those who question the value of academic
freedom, or see other ways to protect it, then see little to recommend the
institution of tenure. Indeed, in one of the few economic articles on tenure,
Armen Alchian explained its existence cynically as an expensive and wasteful
luxury indulged in by a professoriate freed through the nonprofit status of
colleges and universities from the rigors of the competitive economy.

Such a negative view of the economic role and consequences of tenure
seems to us one-sided and importantly misleading. The implicit assumption
that the world outside the academy provides most workers with little effective
job security is false, and the idea that colleges and universities could function
efficiently by operating on the basis of personnel policies analogous to the
longshoreman's shape-up is mistaken. Indeed, some of the most interesting
empirical work in labor economics of late has emphasized what Robert Hall
(1982) calls, in the title of one of his papers, "The Importance of Lifetime
Jobs in the U.S. Economy." And much of the most exciting recent work in
analytical labor economics, and in macroeconomics as well, has aimed at
understanding the mutual interest workers and firms have in sustaining stable

We are grateful to the Faculty Development Program at Williams College for support of this
research. The views presented in this paper are those of the authors. We have been helped by
comments from Richard Chait, Lee Alston, Joseph Kershaw, and members of the Williams
College Economics Department. Throughout the paper we follow the convention of using the
masculine pronoun to refer to both men and women.
1. A representative sample of writings is Smith 1973. Valuable material on the legal and
historical aspects of academic tenure is in Keast and Macy 1973.

long-term employment relations and in protecting each other from the vagaries of the market.[2]

Academic tenure, of course, differs importantly from the kind of job protection seniority affords to production workers or (more to the point for comparison with academics) the kind that corporate employment policies provide to middle-level managers. But, we suggest, the difference lies less in the degree of job security afforded[3] than in the nature of the job guarantee and, surprisingly, in the explicit and risky probation that precedes obtaining the guarantee. To put the latter point somewhat polemically: the striking thing about the university, compared to a typical corporation, is not the number of college graduates employed there with secure jobs but the number of high-level employees who don't expect to be allowed to stay. This point is closely related to our first point, the nature of the job guarantee. For academic employees are assured not only continued employment with the "firm" but continued employment in a highly specific and well-defined position: teaching, for instance, eighteenth-century French literature. The system of rigorous probation followed by tenure is a reasonable way of solving the peculiar personnel problems that arise in employing expensively trained and narrowly specialized people to spend their lifetimes at well-defined and narrowly specialized tasks. The character of this problem, and of this solution, moreover, helps to explain a good deal about academic employment.

It is these themes that we shall develop. They will show that the tenure institution has some desirable efficiency properties that are often overlooked. This, of course, does not prove that tenure should not be reformed or abolished, especially in light of an emerging situation which may raise some of the costs of tenure. Neither does it suggest that we dismiss arguments for tenure based on academic freedom; we merely put them to one side. But we do suggest that any serious proposal for the reform of tenure has to show how alternative arrangements would solve the personnel problems tenure solves; both theory and experience suggest that the implicit alternative of providing faculty with no job guarantee does not solve these problems. Our major aim, in any event, is not to evaluate alternative policies but to contribute to understanding how tenure actually works in the context of the university.

In developing this analysis, we draw heavily on the emerging literature in

---

2. Two recent papers concerned with the academic labor market that build on this literature are Freeman 1977 and James 1980. Neither is centrally concerned with the topics of interest in this paper.

3. Legally, of course, tenure is not a job guarantee. In institutions following American Association of University Professors (AAUP) guidelines, tenured faculty are (a) appointed "without regard to term"—that is, without a specific end date—and (b) are assured of a certain formal procedure prior to dismissal. Dismissal must be for cause, but the cause quite explicitly can be incompetence or economic exigency. That few people get fired is a practical more than legal consequence of the working of these rules in an academic setting.

a field which we call—generalizing a term of Victor Goldberg's—"relational economics." The predominant theme of this literature is that the fact of uncertainty in economic life undermines the usual assumption of anonymity in economic transactions and instead makes it valuable for the parties to economic transactions to develop sustained relationships with one another. This perspective has been applied to good purpose in studying the economics of organizations (Arrow 1974, Williamson 1975 and 1979), the economics of law and contract (Goldberg 1980, MacNeil 1974), labor economics (Leibenstein 1976), macroeconomics (Okun 1980), and elsewhere. The analysis of tenure is only one of its many potential applications to the operation of academic institutions.

Our analysis will proceed by contrasting "stylized" or "ideal-typical" pictures of the corporation and the academic institution. Corporate employees, we will assume, are hired with an effective lifetime job guarantee, perhaps following a brief and largely perfunctory probationary period and barring gross malfeasance or severe economic hardship for the corporation (these latter qualifications corresponding to comparable limitations on the academic tenure commitment). Corporate employees are not, however, guaranteed a particular assignment, with well-defined tasks and perquisites, but rather face an array of possible career paths along which the corporation has discretion to move them at varying rates. University employees in contrast do not receive an immediate employment guarantee but face instead an extended and serious probation. But when they *are* guaranteed employment, it is a guarantee of employment in a specific set of tasks with well-defined perquisites.

These pictures are exaggerations but, we think, recognizable ones. The notoriety of corporation jobs that lack an implicit employment guarantee—those of CEOs or advertising executives—only stresses the contrast with the more usual case. And the narrowly defined and well-ensured tasks of the academic fit the picture of the research universities and the more prestigious colleges better than they fit other places. But we think accounting for the differences in our extreme cases will shed light on the wider range of corporate and university personnel policies encountered in the real world.

Our analysis proceeds in several steps. First is a brief explanation for why employers and employees (outside and inside academics) value secure employment relationships and a brief statement of the difference it makes when the commitment is to a narrowly defined job. In the third section is an analysis of the reasons why academic institutions commit themselves to providing faculty with security in a specific job. There follows an analysis in the fourth section of the central implications of this specific job commitment for the character of the academic employment relationship and of academic life more generally. The fifth section discusses alternatives to tenure, and conclusions appear in the sixth section.

Job Security, Job Specificity, and
Organizational Effectiveness

One of the central insights of analytical labor economics over the last decade has been the recognition that the productivity of an organization depends heavily on the character of the work environment it is able to provide. The classical picture is of the profit-maximizing firm, sensitively adjusting the wage rates of workers and hiring and firing ruthlessly to get the most out of its work force at minimum cost—such a firm turns out on a careful view of its internal requirements not to be maximizing profits at all. Most obviously, the implicit assumption of "no transactions costs" embodied in this picture of the rapidly adjusting firm is wrong. Turnover is costly to firms because of training costs and the value of accumulated information about present employees, information that cannot be cheaply or reliably purchased in the market. At the same time, mobility is expensive to workers—they value job security—because of search and relocation costs and because of information they accumulate about the firm they work for. So firms can hire a labor force of given quality more cheaply by pursuing a policy that reduces involuntary turnover of employees.[4]

Within the firm, moreover, workers need to train other workers, which they will be reluctant to do if the trainee is a viable candidate for the trainer's job (Thurow 1975; Solow 1980). It is also often cheaper for employers to evaluate the performance of a team or group of workers than to judge the performance of individuals within the group, so that neither wage nor dismissal incentives may be easily targeted at individuals (Alchian and Demsetz 1972; Williamson 1975). More subtly, firms need to create an "atmosphere" (to borrow Williamson's word) within the work group that conduces to a cooperative attitude; elements of wage and employment competition within the group may poison the atmosphere and discourage workers from revealing information to higher management that might be useful in reassigning tasks, making judgments about promotions, and the like.

Williamson, Wachter and Harris (1975) have analyzed the resulting structure of "internal" labor markets at length. Firms will maintain an active position in the "external" labor market only for a relatively few positions in the job structure: the bulk of positions in the job hierarchy will be filled by promotion from within. The wage attaching to a particular job in the hierarchy will be largely independent of who occupies it; differential success in performance will be rewarded by more rapid promotion through the hierarchy rather than by more pay for better workers within a rank. The perennial prospect of promotion provides workers with an individual incentive to stay with the firm

---

4. This literature is usefully condensed and cited in Okun 1980 (chap. 3).

and produce, without exacerbating the tendency toward destructive competition between workers at the same grade.

The wage and promotion structure also helps to cement the relation between the worker and the firm. The firm invests in the worker, both by training and—importantly—by accumulating information about his particular strengths and weaknesses. The worker signals his willingness to stay through and past the initial investment period by accepting a relatively low initial wage: a strategy which makes sense only if he plans to stay. He is willing to do so in part because he believes the firm will find a "slot" for him that fits his capacities and interests. Within limits, the resulting wage/promotion arrangement will be self-enforcing: the worker and the firm will have a mutual interest in getting the worker into a job where his productivity is high and where his pay is high enough both to ensure continued employment with the firm and to make other workers in the firm aspire to such high productivity jobs. The need for the firm to present itself to employment candidates as a good place to work provides it with an additional incentive for "honest" promotion and job assignment practices.

Essential to this picture, however, is the presumption that there exists in the firm a variety of jobs of varying wage and productivity which workers might be willing to accept. One might see the firm as having internalized some of the functions of a placement agency: because information about worker capabilities is a by-product of the production process, it makes sense for firms to offer to workers the service of finding the job that fits them best. Other things equal, the firm will be more attractive to workers the wider the array of potential jobs it offers.[5]

But in academic employment there is very little of this internal job mobility: it is a crucial fact that people who are hired to the faculty either stay on the faculty or are dismissed: they do not move to alternative employment within the institution, except for the relatively few who move into academic administration. And, of course, nonacademic employees are hardly ever promoted to the faculty. Reasons for this crucial fact will be discussed shortly, but first it is important to note that it radically reshapes the structure of the employment problem that colleges and universities face, compared to that of large corporations.

To the degree that firms can freely assign workers to jobs and career paths with differing wages and productivities, they can avoid the risk of radical mismatches between wage and productivity for individual workers while still avoiding the costs of high turnover. Moreover, the return on invest-

---

5. It might seem that all that matters is the number of "good" jobs available. But this is not so, since for workers who are uncertain about their productivity, the absence of low-productivity jobs means not assurance of a good job but a higher probability of dismissal.

ment in information about worker performance will be increased by its dual role in the organization: the same information which is useful in monitoring the worker's performance in his present job also has value in determining when and whether to reassign him.

The university, lacking this flexibility in assigning responsibilities to workers, is thus in a difficult spot. When a worker is inflexibly attached to a particular job, mismatches between wage and productivity can only be avoided by (a) adjusting wages to match individual productivities, (b) accepting the costs of higher turnover by dismissing low productivity employees, or (c) introducing more intensive and costly initial screening. Alternative (a) is of course used within limits, but unrestrained use of wage differentials is unattractive because it requires costly monitoring of the performance of every individual faculty member throughout his career and because of the disruptive and demoralizing effects of introducing large wage differentials for faculty with comparable rank and responsibilities. Freeman (1976) notes the constraints academic institutions feel in establishing wage differentials between and within academic departments. (Notice that, without extensive initial screening for faculty quality, wage differentials might need to be very large indeed to reflect productivity differences. With such screening in place, the expected productivity of the monitoring needed to sustain wage differentials is lower.) Alternative (b), if seriously pursued throughout every employee's career, also requires expensive monitoring throughout the career (which itself has negative "atmospheric" effects) and introduces employment insecurity which is costly to both workers and the firm.

Academic employers have thus settled on a version of alternative (c)— more intensive initial screening—as a central element of their personnel policies. This takes the form both of more intensive preemployment screening than corporations undertake for entry-level positions and of intensive on-the-job screening concentrated in the first few years of employment. These considerations help account for several of the key features of academic employment policy.

First, and most centrally, we can understand why such "a big deal" is made out of promotion and tenure decisions. The decision to employ a person permanently in a well-defined position is momentous both for the worker and the firm: the worker gets not merely employment security but something close to a guarantee of status and lifetime income prospects; the firm is locked into not only a stream of future wage payments but a stream of future productivity from the worker over which it will have very little control. It follows therefore that firms will invest quite heavily in the scrutiny of their nontenured employees and that workers will attach great importance to perceived fairness of the institutions for making tenure and promotion decisions. The result is a concentration of everyone's energy and attention on that single point in the career, which is quite the opposite of the more diffuse but more sustained attention to worker performance in the corporation.

The obverse of close attention to the academic worker's performance prior to tenure is the marked inattention to performance after tenure. This too can be seen as a rational response to the academic employment situation. In the corporation, with its flexible job assignment policies, a principal role for the continual monitoring of employee performance is the making of continual marginal adjustments in workers' job assignments: increasing the productivity of the existing labor force by reallocating tasks among workers. But in the university, where the tasks are final once the employment guarantee is made, monitoring performance has little value, for there is little to do with the information. To be sure, information about tenured faculty can influence the rate of wage advance to some degree and can serve as a basis for moral suasion, but the central use to which such information is put in the corporation, to shape the path of the worker's career advance, is markedly less available within an academic institution.

These considerations also help account for the existence in academia of a sharply defined "nodal point" by which time a decision of "up-or-out" on tenure must be made. Personnel decisions in the corporation are almost always taken at the margin: to hasten or delay promotion; to expand or contract the range of responsibility. In academics, the possible decisions at any time are two: the marginal one of continuing employment for another year or the dramatically non-marginal one of terminating employment. If the former decision is always available, there will be an almost inevitable tendency to evade the latter one, which is bound to be difficult and unpleasant. To force a decision by a fixed moment serves both to legitimize the harsh decision to let someone go—the option of another chance just isn't available—and provide an incentive to gather the large amounts of costly information needed to make such a weighty decision responsibly. (See Brewster 1972.)

These remarks show the fundamental differences between the personnel problems of the academic institution and the corporation that follow from the narrowness and specificity of the academic job commitment. Much more remains to be said in elaboration of the implications of these points for the operation of colleges and universities. But it is time now to examine with care the reasons for this crucial structural difference between the university and the corporation: why do universities not offer—and why do faculty not seek—the wide range of career paths offered within a typical corporation?

Sources of Job Specificity in the University

The fact that individuals are hired to do quite narrowly defined and rigidly specified jobs is central to the economics of tenure and describes the major structural contrast between university and corporate employment. The sources of this difference lie on both the production and demand sides of the market. The "organizational technology" of the university is such that it attaches relatively little value to preserving its freedom to change the job assignments of particular workers. At the same time, worker preferences are such that a faculty member would typically prefer to continue his occupation (say, teaching physics) at another institution than to stay with the "firm" in a different job. Behind these differences in organizational technology and preferences lies an important difference between the corporation and the university in the kinds of "knowledge capital" workers acquire to do their jobs. In the university, this knowledge is predominantly tied to the worker's academic subject: it is specific to the *occupation* and not to the firm. In the corporation, there is likely to be a greater premium on *firm-specific* human capital: knowledge of the particular codes, practices, and procedures of *that* corporation as opposed to others. (For the importance of firm-specific human capital in the corporation, see Arrow 1974 and Becker 1964. The distinction between occupation- and firm-specific human capital is drawn in Rosen 1977.)

This contrast is reflected in the differences in training patterns for corporate and university work. In academic employment, training is for a specific academic discipline and not for a specific employment or firm. Academic training is an extreme case of the classic "nonappropriability" of worker training—the fact that firms are reluctant to invest their resources in the training of their employees and more so the less specific is that training to that firm—the more generally valuable it is in other firms. Training for university employment is so extreme a case of nonappropriability that the firm—the hiring university—refuses to provide any training and, instead, hires its employees with virtually their full complement of training (the Ph.D.) secured elsewhere and at someone else's expense. This is underscored by the curious, if familiar, fact that the new academic employee does the same thing— teaches the same sorts of classes in the same way and writes the same sorts of articles and books—as the thirty-year veteran. Quality, it is hoped, improves with maturity, but the duties of faculty members remain remarkably the same.[6]

---

6. This shifting of the training function entirely out of the employing institution is especially interesting in light of the fact that the same institutions are involved in both roles, even while keeping separate. Not only does the firm have the competence to train its own workers but it is often engaged in just that activity in its own graduate schools. So the Massachusetts Institute of Technology (MIT) hires a new Stanford Ph.D. to train its Ph.D. candidates at the same time that Stanford hires a new MIT Ph.D. to train its Ph.D. candidates. Even when the formal identity of competence is not so glaring, much of the anomaly remains: when Kermit Gordon and Emile Despres were on the Williams faculty, Charles Kindleberger referred to Williams as "the best graduate school in economics in the country, only you've got to be an Assistant Professor to get in."

Again, the corporation presents the antithesis in its widespread employment of individuals trained as generalists who are subsequently put through a highly firm-specific training followed by a career of additional training in different, again firm-specific, activities. The multiplicity of suitable corporate jobs with their often differentiated internal training requirements and the individual worker's multiple job assignments, seriatim, over his career are aspects of the high degree of substitutability among those jobs. An important reason for the substitutability appears to be the absence of high levels of requisite prior training; conversely, the absence of much prior training before workers enter the firm tends to make all jobs similar for the generally talented but not specifically trained individual.

This difference in training and human capital accumulation patterns naturally shapes worker interests in the character of the job guarantee they will seek. Individual academics will typically prefer to substitute one employer for another while retaining their occupations rather than to scrap their costly training in favor of taking a different job at the same institution. Moreover, it is reasonable to expect that only workers with a relatively strong prior commitment to the occupation will undertake training in the first place, so that the commitment to the profession is a result of preferences as well as the opportunity cost of the specialized investment in training. The academic worker will thus put little value on a guarantee of employment which is not specific about the kind of employment guaranteed.[7] The new corporate employee, on the other hand, with less investment in occupation-specific training, and less knowledge about where his skills and interests lie, will care more about job security as such and may put positive value on the corporation's implicit offer to match his job assignment to his aptitudes, as information about those aptitudes emerges.

The tendency to job rigidity in the university is compounded by its objectives of doing its job of education and research (producing its product) at reasonable cost. An important aspect of the technology of university production, the result of the specialized human capital possessed by academics, is that it is rarely as easy to substitute employees among jobs as it is to hire new employees from outside for those particular jobs. If the university has an opening for a worker to teach and do research in particle physics, the productivity in that job of a professor of French Literature currently employed by the university is unlikely to be nearly as high as that of a new employee trained specifically in particle physics—someone currently in graduate school or employed in the physics department of another university. The occasional Renaissance Man, of course, is the exception that proves the rule. It will

---

7. Presumably, he'd like to have his cake and eat it too. Both sorts of security—especially since they are rights and not obligations—are nice to have. The point here is simply that if one has to choose, the choice will typically be in favor of keeping the occupation and not the employer.

similarly be unlikely that the best person for a nonacademic job opening will be a faculty member—in many cases it seems true that intense academic training does as much to *dis*qualify as to prepare people for other kinds of work. So on pure productivity grounds, too, the university will accommodate these sharp technological differences in productivity among individuals and will hire French scholars to teach French and physicists to teach physics.

The corporation, of course, shows that this employment pattern is far from inevitable. It hires the liberal arts graduate—often a history or English major—for a broadly defined "management" training program from which he or she may be assigned to a specific job in production management or financial management or sales or . . . . And even a cursory examination of corporate management careers makes it clear that once assigned to sales or production or finance, the corporate employee will often be reassigned to quite different sorts of managerial employment throughout his career with the firm. Indeed, even employees (like engineers) who may be hired for their specific skills will often, if successful, "graduate" into jobs that do not depend on those skills.

So both sides of the market lead to narrowness and rigidity of academic employment: the technology of production sharply reduces flexibility in inter-job substitution at the same time that the preferences of workers sharply reduce their willingness to change fields rather than changing firms. Neither appears dominant.[8]

It is understandable, then, in light of the important differences in the interests of work in the academic and corporate employment settings that the form of the agreements ensuring job security will differ. As Simon (1957) has stressed, the contract governing any employment relation will be importantly "incomplete," with the worker ceding an important amount of discretionary authority to the firm about exactly what activities he must undertake. In the corporate setting, the firm's authority generally extends to granting the firm considerable freedom to determine what position in the firm the worker will fill, not only to begin with but through the career. The quid pro quo is an implicit commitment by the firm to retain the employee in some capacity, barring markedly unusual circumstances. But in the university, the faculty member cedes much less authority to the "firm" to determine the content of his job. Indeed, it can be argued that this is one of the most attractive features of academic employment—the fact that workers are, to a remarkable extent,

---

8. It is futile to ask whether it is workers' rigid preferences or universities' rigid productivity requirements that explains the job specificity and rigidity of academic employment. The more flexible, adaptable job environment into which the corporate employee is hired, too, is the result both of greater flexibility in production and greater indifference on the part of the worker whether he is assigned to one job or another within the firm.

asked to do very little they don't choose to do. They get paid for reading, thinking, talking and writing about those things that they find interesting and rewarding. The result, of course, is that the university has little authority to reassign workers to different work; it may make offers and suggestions, but the presumption is that an academic worker always has the right to stick to his job. An offer of tenure ensures this security in a specific job permanently. The quid pro quo is, however, a little different than in the corporate world: job security comes only following a lengthy and rigorous period of probation.

Personnel Decisions in the University

The university and the corporation, then, face sharply different sorts of personnel problems.[9] The corporation can feel relatively relaxed about the "quality" and characteristics of the persons it hires into entry-level positions and can follow an implicit policy of "instant (or almost instant) tenure" simply because it has available a wide range of job slots requiring differing capacities and offering different wages and because it retains freedom to allocate employees among those jobs, and to reallocate employees as time goes on. The essence of the corporate personnel management problem is to ensure a steady and reliable flow of information about employee performance and to maintain a responsive institutional structure to reallocate employee responsibilities on the basis of that flow of information. Economists, notably Arrow (1974) and Williamson (1975), are beginning to appreciate what a subtle and important problem this is.

The university, however, essentially *knows* what its people are going to do and, if it is to attract good employees, it cannot allow itself very much discretion about how much it will pay people to do it.[10] Its problem then is to ensure that it gets good quality workers into the "firm" and to ensure that they stay motivated in the absence of sensitive marginal incentives. The probation-

---

9. Many of the points in this section emerge, from a somewhat different perspective, in section 4 of James and Neuberger 1979.

10. This latter point deserves elaboration. The corporation, we assume, will fix a wage for a given job. But people's expected incomes will vary with the jobs (and career paths) they are assigned to. Why could the university not achieve a similar result by varying pay according to teacher performance? Besides the general arguments about morale implications and difficulties of productivity measurement noted earlier, there is a further problem. With a flexible array of jobs, the corporation has an interest in putting high-productivity people in high paying jobs. This tends to keep the corporation "honest," since to put a potentially high-productivity person in a low-paying job costs the firm product, as well as costing the worker income. But with the job assignment fixed, the university could save itself money by asserting falsely that a particular professor had low productivity. So there would be more ground for suspicion that the university might use its power to set wages in "unfair" ways that don't match productivity differences.

tenure system is a reasonable response to this distinctive employment problem. We shall discuss in turn some aspects of the probation period, the tenure decision, and the problem of motivating senior faculty.

The Probation Period

It is possible to identify four distinct ways in which a lengthy and explicit probationary period is valuable.

(1) Performance monitoring.   In any economic transaction, people need to know what they are buying. The productive organization—including the university—must have ways of knowing about the performance of its employees in doing the things that produce the firm's output. But among workers and jobs, there is very great variety in the ease with which that performance can be measured by the firm: the ditch digger quite unambiguously has or has not moved a specific amount of dirt by noon; the theoretical biologist may or may not have spent the morning in pursuit of his research objectives—he may have been daydreaming about making a killing in the stock market. Differences in the inherent measurability of different occupations are essentially technological, attaching irreducibly to the specific activity (Leibenstein 1976). Given these inherent technological measurement problems, incentives to misrepresent performance may compound the difficulties of measurement. Workers and firms may both try to give a misleading picture of what the worker is actually doing, but absent the underlying technological measurement problems in the first place, incentive distortions cannot persist: if performance can easily be monitored, there is no room for attempted misrepresentation.

The performance of the activities of academic workers—teaching and scholarship—is certainly hard to measure.[11] These activities do not produce concrete, measurable products of easily discernible quality; neither their output nor their inputs are easily observable or measurable.

It is not necessary to this analysis to assert that corporate productive activities are any easier to measure than those of academia. What counts for

___

11. But not equally. There seems little doubt that teaching performance is even harder to measure than scholarship, if only because the inherent qualitative judgments made about both are made by more knowledgeable people and more publicly in the case of scholarship. Furthermore, those judgments are made by much the same people over time—there is continuity in the population of judges in the case of scholarship but a constantly changing group in the case of teaching. This difference between teaching and scholarship, while not directly relevant to the present analysis, would certainly be central in any analysis that differentiated between university and college faculties.

the present analysis in differentiating the two organizations and their labor markets is, simply, that the university combines measurement difficulties *and* job-specific employment while the corporation combines its measurement difficulties with job-flexible employment: the corporation can second-guess and the university cannot.

But "hard to measure" is a bit too imprecise for our purposes. What it means is that a worker's actual job performance can be known by the firm only with the expenditure of resources—on things like record keeping but most importantly in the form of attention, time, and effort. Performance that is inherently harder to measure simply takes more of those resources. Of course, it may be both undesirable and exorbitantly expensive to try to know with certainty the quality of a performance. So what's relevant is often the achievement of a given level of confidence in that knowledge. Again, the "harder to measure," the more resources are needed to get to that level of confidence.

This applies to measurement of the performance of an individual worker at a particular point in time. There are two important additional dimensions. Spence and Williamson note the frequently greater ease—the lower cost—of measuring the performance of a *group* of workers than that of an individual worker alone. Alchian and Demsetz (1972) relied on such "nonseparability" of performance measurement for their influential analysis of internal organizations—their illustration was the difficulty of the separate measurement of the work performance of two men lifting a box onto a truck. As a group, their performance is easily measured; individually it is not.

The even more relevant—and neglected—dimension of measurement is simply the duration of the period over which the performance is measured. A repetitive activity—like either teaching or scholarship—may be very costly to monitor quickly but be quite easy to judge over a longer period. So in addition to the differences among jobs in their inherent static costs of performance measurement, there will also be differences in the way performance information accumulates with the duration of observation.

The relevance of this time dimension for academic employment is obvious. Academic job performance is unusually difficult to measure quickly. The ease with which accurate judgments can be made clearly increases with a longer period of observation. While it would be very difficult to judge scholarly potential, for instance, in a week of even very intensive observation, it is easy to achieve a reasonable judgment over a five-year period. In general, a longer period of observation of any repetitive activity yields a given degree of measurement accuracy at lower total resource cost. For these reasons, the lengthy probationary period for faculty can be a useful method of quality control.

(2) Self-selection.[12]   One hazard facing the university is analogous to the problems of moral hazard and adverse selection in the insurance industry. Given the assured status and security of the tenured academic position, there is danger of persons misrepresenting themselves—their basic attitudes, work habit, goals, etc.—in order to obtain tenure and showing their "true colors" afterwards. This problem, of course, exists for the corporation too, but it is mitigated by the fact of job flexibility. The worker who has led his superiors to overestimate his potential can be either downgraded or "kicked upstairs" in response.

The interposition of a probationary period, with relatively low pay and a relatively high dismissal probability, reduces the incentive for misrepresentation of this kind. The longer the period over which one has to "fake" desirable attitudes, the greater the cost of doing so, and since levels of performance after tenure are not so intensively monitored or enforced, there is a strong premium on granting tenure to those who genuinely enjoy their work. The longer the probationary period, the greater the tendency to screen out those who don't.

(One might add to this a point originally due to Pascal, who noted that merely acting out religious ritual may eventually produce real belief. There may be a tendency for one who tries to act the part of a well-motivated academic to actually become such eventually. Those among us who feel surprised at how hard they continue to work after receiving tenure may be cases in point.)

(3) Time to tenure as an economic variable.   With relatively rigid wages and job descriptions, the university faces a problem in adjusting the attractiveness of its employment offering to changes in market conditions. The corporation, of course, faces a comparable problem which it solves in part by varying promotion prospects and rates of promotion in response to market conditions. The university can, in a similar way, use variations in the likelihood of promotion and in the length of the probationary period to vary the value of its employment offer as market conditions change. There is extensive empirical evidence that such variation is in fact an important feature of the academic labor market (Kuh 1977; Weiss 1981).

(4) The focusing of monitoring resources.   As noted earlier, fixing a terminal point to the probationary period enforces a concentration of attention and monitoring effort that encourages careful evaluation of candidates for promotion. In the absence of such a focal point, the tendency will be to postpone the

---

12. The phenomenon of self-selection in labor markets has received much attention recently. See Spence 1974, Salop and Salop 1976, and the articles referred to in Okun 1980 (chap. 3).

difficult decision to fire anyone and to dissipate the energies needed to stage a serious evaluation.

The Tenure Decision

While it is useful in some contexts to speak of the "university" as making decisions on tenure and job security, in fact specific individuals within the institution are charged with making them. The arrangements in the university are quite different from typical corporate arrangements, and these differences can be at least partly understood in terms of the analysis developed here.

In the corporation, decisions about promotions are typically made in a hierarchical manner, with those at higher levels in the hierarchy deciding on those lower down, and with a well articulated structure of levels shaping the whole. In the university, however, while deans and presidents may be involved in decisions, most of the weight of the tenure decision is typically borne by those members of the discipline who have already been given tenure: peer review is the order of the day.

Several aspects of these arrangements can be addressed in our framework. Why is it disciplinary peers, rather than "higher ups" within the institution who bear the weight of the decision? Why is it peers within the institution rather than peers outside the institution who are central? And why is it tenured faculty, rather than all those in the discipline at the institution, who decide?

The rationale for peer, rather than hierarchical, authority is clearly linked to the specialized nature of academic job assignments: judgment of an employee's performance during the probationary period must be made by those who are competent in his field since his main productive activities are specific to that field.[13] Just as the university cannot usually hire a French professor to teach particle physics, so it cannot rely on a French professor (or a dean or president trained for that role) to judge the performance of a particle physicist. Of course, formally the role of peers may only be advisory to those with hierarchical authority, but higher-ups will rarely have grounds to overrule strong recommendations from departments, and, if such recommendations are often overruled, the higher-ups will undermine the incentive for departments to put much effort into evaluations.

Peer judgments could, in principle, be made by committees of outsiders. Their advice is, of course, sometimes obtained but rarely given weight comparable to that of the candidate's colleagues. This is so despite the fact that it is sometimes alleged that outsiders could be more fair and objective. One

---

13. This is more clearly the case in scholarship than in teaching. This would lead us to hypothesize that the role of disciplinary peers in tenure decisions is stronger at schools that put more emphasis on research.

reason for the importance of "locals" is that they can more cheaply be informed about aspects of a colleague's performance other than published work. Such information could only be made available to outsiders through extensive visits and observation. This fact is especially important since (as we discuss further below) an important part of the judgment is a forecast about the candidate's likely behavior *after* receiving tenure, and this requires a subtle view of the candidate's motivations, which is harder for outsiders to obtain.

Another, perhaps more important, reason for giving weight to local views concerns the motivation of the evaluators. The fact that local evaluators must live with the results of their decision and they presumably care about the reputation and quality of the department they are affiliated with gives them a stronger reason to judge with care than outsiders would have. We should add, of course, that insider evaluation is subject to abuse, for which the obtaining of outside views may be a partial corrective. The attribution of motivation may become an intrusive and arbitrary exercise, and the concern with needing to "live with" a colleague may lead to undue emphasis on traits of congeniality or even obsequiousness. But it is not clear that there is any feasible system for evaluating academic personnel which can avoid these hazards.

Last is the question why nontenured people are typically excluded from the group of peers who decide on tenure. One obvious reason is the potential conflict of interest in evaluating a potential competitor—or conversely the potential conspiracy on the part of candidates to support one another's interests. Indeed, the need for objective evaluations has been cited by some observers (we think wrongly) as the key rationale for the institution of tenure itself: without job security, faculty would be motivated to resist retaining workers superior to themselves (Freeman 1980). A separate reason for excluding nontenured personnel from tenure decisions is the relatively brief time over which they can expect to be associated with the institution, which may lead them to give undue weight to the short-term interests of the institution in making decisions.

Motivating Senior Faculty

Like universities, corporations generally avoid instituting wide merit-based pay differentials for different workers doing similar jobs: wages within grade, in fact, are closely linked to seniority (Medoff and Abraham 1981). But corporations can use promotion ladders and job reassignment as devices to continue to motivate effort among workers who are not threatened with dismissal. As we have argued, these options are much less available to universities. So the question arises, how *does* one motivate senior faculty? This is a large question, worthy of a paper (at least) in its own right, but a few observations related to the themes developed here are warranted.

First, a negative point: given the logic of the academic employment structure, it is far from obvious that intensive hierarchical efforts to evaluate and motivate senior faculty in fact make much sense. Monitoring worker performance is an expensive activity, and it may in itself have a negative impact on morale. It may be perfectly sensible, if there is little to be done with the information that is gathered anyway, to limit monitoring to what is needed to detect gross malfeasance and to the spontaneous monitoring of each colleague by his peers and to accept that a certain amount of "deadwood" is an unavoidable by-product of the system.

An interesting extension of this point has been suggested by Oliver Williamson (1975, 55–56). If, in fact, it is difficult to monitor or regulate the performance of faculty in their central activities of teaching and scholarship, it may prove *counterproductive* to monitor those ancillary activities (like use of the telephone or of paperclips) where regulation is possible. If there is no alternative but to trust faculty on important matters, it may be prudent to trust them on small matters as well, in order to make that attitude of trust as visible and pervasive as possible. More broadly, the general attitude of autonomy and mutual respect which universities try to foster among faculty can be seen as a reasonable response to their inability to monitor and regulate their central activities.

The fact that marginal incentives are hard to supply for senior faculty affects importantly the character of the screening process for nontenured faculty. It is necessary to determine not only what faculty are capable of doing but also to form a judgment about what they will be *inclined* to do, in the absence of marginal incentives. It is crucial to select for promotion faculty who have a strong "internal" motivation to perform, or, alternatively, faculty who are readily subject to "moral suasion" or "peer pressure" in regulating their performance levels. This is plainly a difficult judgment to reach, since it involves inferring by observing someone who is subject to sanctions how he will behave when he is not subject to those sanctions. The point made earlier about the self-selection function of the probationary period is relevant here, since the longer the probation, the higher the cost to the candidate of acting against his inclination. A further implication is that the need to form judgments about a candidate's inclinations and motivations argues against reducing the tenure decision to a set of purely "objective" indicators, like number of publications. As noted, reaching judgments about motivation and about likely performance under changed conditions creates opportunities for abuse, but they seem to be unavoidable.

The discussion to this point has focused on incentives internal to the institution. It is necessary to note as well the incentive for tenured faculty to perform well in the hope of achieving a better position at another university— "better" in terms of pay, prestige, or other factors that matter to the person in question. Active markets for senior faculty only exist, however, at a relatively small number of institutions. Predictably, they are the ones where research figures most prominently in the work of the faculty, since research performance is much easier for "outsiders" to evaluate and so to provide a basis for competing offers. At this group of universities, the external market functions as a partial substitute for the other motivating factors discussed here.

Term Contracts as an Alternative to Tenure

The logic of the present analysis may be usefully underscored by a brief comparison of tenure arrangements to the most familiar kind of employment arrangement commonly thought of as an alternative to the tenure/probation system.[14] This is the alternative of term contracts: appointing faculty to renewable contracts of relatively short (three- to five-year) duration. Under a term-contract system, faculty are offered a series of fixed-period renewable contracts. The notion is that under such a system each faculty member's performance is constantly reviewed during his career, with each contract renewal contingent on performance in the preceding contract period. The "naturalness" of this alternative no doubt stems from the rather odd idea— derived from taking textbook economic theory too literally—that this is how "real world" employment markets work. And indeed, judged by textbook criteria of the working of timeless markets, term contracts have a strong appeal in economic efficiency terms: "deadwood" workers are constantly being got rid of on the basis of their recent performance, and everyone is continually spurred to strong efforts by the threat of dismissal.

Our theoretical perspective, however, makes us strongly doubtful that things will work out this way in practice. Moreover, a valuable recent book on tenure by Richard Chait and Andrew Ford (1982) provides strong case-study evidence supporting our theoretical view. If the decision about contract renewal were more than nominal, it would prove very costly to universities committed to it. The resources required to evaluate everybody seriously every few years would be simply enormous. If such evaluations did not result in many dismissals, they would be largely wasted. If they did, the university would bear the costs of greater turnover. Moreover, the threat of job insecurity might make it more difficult to hire good faculty at wages comparable to those

---

14. A different and in some ways rather intriguing alternative to a tenure/probation system would be the adoption of an "instant tenure" system like that of the corporation. This could only work efficiently if universities retained more discretion over the job assignments of faculty than they now do and if there were a wider range of jobs available in universities than are now. This could conceivably come about if universities were branches of multiproduct corporations. To pursue the "thought-experiment" of organizing universities in that way would take us away from the main point of this paper, but it may be worth attempting on another occasion.

at places offering more security. And against the potential incentive advantages of more intense monitoring would have to be weighed the potential negative morale implications of that practice.

But in fact the more likely outcome is that contract renewals will become routine, and the system will approximate instant tenure. Two strong incentives contribute to such a shift from nominal job insecurity to actual job security. First, in perpetual reevaluation there is no moment of truth, no special time when the resources of the institution need be brought to bear on evaluating an employee's performance. Since that evaluation is both time and resource consuming and it risks a quite unpleasant outcome—and since another opportunity for evaluation will come along soon—the incentives are there to prevent a real and meaningful evaluation with each (or any) termination of a fixed-period contract. In a tenure decision, where the issue is a lifetime commitment, it is much more difficult to be slack and to procrastinate.

The second incentive is the simple fact of mutuality—the judges are also the judged. Since everyone on the faculty is in the same contract renewal boat, there is obvious pressure for the judges to be gentle and compassionate and not to evaluate their fellows too harshly—when one's own turn is on the horizon, only the slightest imagination is needed to see the value of such a precedent.

The schools employing term contracts that Chait and Ford examined (Hampshire College, Evergreen State College, and the University of Texas at Permian Basin) support this view of the consequences. Reappointments become routine and turnover is quite low. Chait and Ford (1982, 12) quote a Task Force established at Hampshire to review the term contract policy as asserting that "The current system also has an adverse impact on the faculty's quality by diverting inordinate faculty time away from teaching [and other work]. The involvement of so many faculty in the review of over twenty of their colleagues a year seriously drains important resources from the main educational functions of the college." The authors (p. 13) further note that the faculty, "referees today and candidates for reappointment tomorrow, fear retribution as well as strained relationships." Hampshire has since moved to create a "tenure-like" decision for a ten-year reappointment after the first two three-year appointments to create a "crunch decision" that will focus attention and resources. Evergreen has not made such a shift, but the absence of pressure for making difficult decisions seems to have been felt there too. The authors report an interview with the president of Evergreen in which he said, "Sometimes I say to myself, 'My God, we have instant tenure!'"

Instant tenure, of course, is precisely what, in our analysis, corporations have. But, to repeat our earlier point, they do not provide instant tenure to a specific job with specific responsibilities and perquisites. Universities with instant tenure are likely either to be forced toward extremely intensive prescreening of candidates for appointment, which is intrinsically quite difficult, since close observation of the candidate, over a long period of time, doing work like that he will be asked to, is required or else to accept a decline in quality of personnel.

One perhaps surprising point here is the potential advantage of a probation/tenure system over term contracts from the standpoint of minority employment. To the degree that term contracts amount to instant tenure, the cost to the university of making "mistakes" will rise, and there will be pressure in hiring to rely on established channels of historic reliability in locating candidates. (An illustration is the practice at Oxford, which has instant tenure through term contracts, to hire its own graduates.) To the degree that those historic channels embody past policies of discrimination, instant de facto tenure will militate against change and experiment. A similar problem arises to the degree that disadvantaged groups are victims of "statistical discrimination," having their individual qualities discounted because of (correct or incorrect) beliefs about average characteristics of their group (characteristics which may themselves be the result of discrimination). (See Akerlof 1970; Thurow 1975.) The opportunity to observe an individual during probation will reduce the reluctance to judge the individual on his own merits rather than on group averages and may also over time lead to the undermining of the beliefs that sustain the statistical discrimination. This line of reasoning may apply not just to racially and sexually disadvantaged groups but to graduates of less prestigious universities as well.

Conclusion

The central message of this paper can be summed up as follows: the institution of tenure is not simply a constraint imposed on universities, whether to protect faculty jobs or to ensure academic freedom, but an integral part of the way universities function. The tenure/probation system is a reasonable response to the highly specialized nature of academic work and to the long training such work requires. An intelligent understanding of the operation of universities and a constructive approach to the reform of their personnel policies needs to take these realities into account.

This conclusion need not be so complacent as it may sound. One could, for example, question whether academic training needs necessarily to be so specialized as it has become. It is also true that our analysis presents a somewhat idealized picture of how tenure and promotion decisions are made, and there is room for argument about how close to these ideals various colleges and universities come in practice. Our point, however, is that criticism of the tenure system and proposals for reform must come to grips with the quite real and special academic personnel problems the tenure system responds to. Much existing criticism, by failing to understand the economic functions of tenure, fails to do that.

A further step away from complacency may be taken by recalling some of the special pressures that may arise for the tenure system in the near future. Our analysis incorporates two key assumptions about the workings of the academic labor market: one, that the typical individual will enter the academic career with a stronger commitment to the occupation than to a particular institution; the other, that the granting of tenure amounts to a lifetime employment guarantee in practice. Both these have for the most part been true over the fifty years or so that the institution of tenure has been in full force in America, but of course tenure is always granted subject to financial exigency for the institution, and people can only pursue a lifetime commitment to academic employment if jobs are available.

Many observers expect the impending decline in college age population to produce substantial strains on the academic labor market (Cartter 1976; Dresch 1975; Freeman 1976; Bowen 1981; Oi 1979).[15] As the likelihood of financial crises at academic institutions rises, the value of obtaining a tenured position falls. At the same time, the familiar academic career pattern of starting out at a prestigious institution and then moving on to tenure at a less prestigious institution if necessary has ceased to be viable in many fields. For the next fifteen years, fewer people will enter academics with the expectation that it will be a lifetime career. Thus, some of the basic assumptions of our analysis will be at least partly undermined in the future. The operation of the tenure system has in the past been closely tied to the background of an expanding university and college system. A period of contraction is likely to stimulate a search for alternatives on the part of both employers and workers. Whether the pressures will be sufficient to cause such an alternative to emerge is difficult to say. But constructive thought about the form such an alternative to tenure might take, and especially analysis of its likely consequences for the performance of universities and colleges, will need to draw on the kind of functional analysis of tenure we have begun to develop here.

We would like, finally, to point toward two kinds of further work that need to be done both to extend and to strengthen the foundations of this study. First, our analysis contains a number of implications about the behavior of academic institutions which it would be desirable to test. We would expect, for example, that institutions where faculty play more specialized roles would be more likely to conform to the "ideal typical" tenure model. We would also expect that academic hiring practices in fields where there is closer substitution between academic and nonacademic employment of skills (business and medicine may be examples) will be less likely to adhere to the classic proba-

---

15. For a sceptical view of these projections, see Ahlburg et al. 1981.

tion/tenure pattern. These and other implications should be developed and tested. Second, it is possible to think of some segments of industry with labor market institutions similar to tenure (e.g., the Army's up or out policy) and also to think of occupations with similar characteristics (rigid job description and high costs of measuring performance) to academics (accounting and medicine may be examples). It would be valuable to see if there is indeed a match, as our view would suggest, between tenure-like labor market institutions and academic-like occupation characteristics.

REFERENCES

Ahlburg, Dennis, Eileen M. Crimmins, and Richard A. Easterlin. 1981. The outlook for higher education: A cohort size model of enrollment of the college age population, 1948–2000. *Review of Public Data Use* 9: 211–27.

Akerlof, George. 1970. The market for "lemons": Quality uncertainty and the market mechanism. *Quarterly Journal of Economics* 84 (Aug.): 488–500.

Alchian, Armen. N.d. Private property and the relative cost of tenure.

Alchian, Armen A., and Harold Demsetz. 1972. Production, information cost, and economic organization. *The American Economic Review* 62, no. 5 (Dec.): 777–95.

Arrow, Kenneth J. 1974. *The limits of organization.* New York: W.W. Norton.

Becker, Gary S. 1964. *Human capital: A theoretical and empirical analysis, with special reference to education.* New York: National Bureau of Economic Research.

Bowen, William. 1981. Report of the President: Graduate education in the arts and sciences: Prospects for the future. Princeton University: Princeton, NJ, April.

Brewster, Kingman, Jr. 1972. On tenure. *AAUP Bulletin* 58 (Dec.): 381–83.

Cartter, A. 1976. *Ph.D.'s and the academic labor market.* New York: McGraw Hill.

Chait, Richard, and Andrew Ford. 1982. *Beyond traditional tenure.* San Francisco: Jossey-Bass.

Dresch, Stephen. 1975. Demography, technology, and higher education: Toward a formal model of educational adaptation. *Journal of Political Economy* 83 (June): 535–69.

Freeman, R. B. 1976. *The overeducated American.* New York: Academic Press.

———. 1980. The job market for college faculty. In *The demand for new faculty in science and engineering,* edited by M. McPherson, 85–134. Washington, DC: National Academy of Science.

Freeman, S. 1977. Wage trends as performance displays productive potential: A model and application to academic early retirement. *Bell Journal of Economics and Management Science* 8: 419–43.

Goldberg, Victor. 1980. Relational exchange: Economics and complex contracts. *American Behavioral Scientist* 23 (Jan./Feb.): 337–52.

Hall, Robert. 1982. The importance of lifetime jobs in the U.S. economy. *American Economic Review* 72 (March): 716–24.

James, Estelle. 1980. Job-based lending and insurance: Wage structure in tenured labor markets. Working paper no. 228. Economic Research Bureau, State University of New York at Stony Brook, Dec.

James, Estelle, and E. Neuberger. 1979. The university department as a non-profit labor cooperative. Revised version of paper presented at the U.S.-U.K. Conference on Collective Choice in Education, Boston, MA, Dec. Mimeo.

Keast, W. R., and J. W. Macy, Jr., eds. 1973. *Faculty tenure.* San Francisco: Jossey-Bass.

Kuh, Charlotte. 1977. Market conditions and tenure for Ph.D.'s in U.S. higher education. A report for the Carnegie Council on Policy Studies in Higher Education. Mimeo.

Leibenstein, Harvey. 1976. *Beyond economic man: A new foundation for microeconomics.* Cambridge, MA: Harvard University Press.

MacNeil, I. R. 1974. The many futures of contract. *Southern California Law Review* 47 (May): 691–816.

Medoff, James, and Katherine Abraham. 1981. The role of seniority at U.S. work places: A report on some new evidence. Working paper no. 618. National Bureau of Economic Research.

Oi, Walter. 1979. Academic tenure and mandatory retirement under the new law. *Science* 206 (Dec. 21): 1373–78.

Okun, Arthur. 1980. *Prices and quantities: A macroeconomic analysis.* Washington, DC: The Brookings Institution.

Rosen, Sherwin. 1977. Human capital: A survey of empirical research. In *Research in labor economics: An annual compilation of research,* edited by R. Ehrenberg, vol. 1, 3–40. Greenwich, CT: JAI Press.

Salop, J., and S. Salop. 1976. Self-selection and turnover in the labor market. *Quarterly Journal of Economics* 90 (Nov.): 619–29.

Simon, Herbert. 1957. A formal theory of the employment relationship. In *Models of man,* 183–95. New York: Wiley.

Smith, B., ed. 1973. *The tenure debate.* San Francisco: Jossey Bass.

Solow, Robert. 1980. On theories of unemployment. *American Economic Review* 70 (March): 1–11.

Spence, A. Michael. 1974. *Market signaling: Information transfer in hiring and related screening processes.* Cambridge, MA: Harvard University Press.

Thurow, L. C. 1975. *Generating inequality: Mechanisms of distribution in the U.S. economy.* New York: Basic Books.

Weiss, Yoram. 1981. Output variability, academic labor contracts and waiting times for promotion. Working paper no. 26-81. Foerder Institute for Economic Research, Faculty of Social Sciences, Tel Aviv University, Ramat Aviv.

Williamson, Oliver. 1975. *Market and hierarchies: Analysis and anti-trust implications.* New York: Free Press.

Williamson, Oliver E. 1979. Transaction-cost economics: The governance of contractual relations. *Journal of Law and Economics* 22: 233–61.

Williamson, Oliver E., Michael Z. Wachter, and Jeffrey E. Harris. 1975. Understanding the employment relation: The analysis of idiosyncratic exchange. *The Bell Journal of Economics* 6, no. 1 (Spring): 250–78.

Part 3
Student Finance

CHAPTER 6

How Can We Tell if Federal Student Aid Is Working?

Michael S. McPherson

That question has come, in various forms, to be a major preoccupation of legislators, administrators, and analysts concerned with higher education finance. Twenty years of large-scale federal support for student aid have resulted in a complex and interconnected set of programs. Some observers of the aid system see it as an essential underpinning of our existing college and university financing system that provides essential services to disadvantaged students and contributes to the financial health and stability of higher education as a whole. Others see it as a wasteful and ill-structured mess that spends money ineffectively and distorts the incentives of students and institutions.

How can we make progress in assessing the effectiveness of the aid system? No doubt we will always have both demagogic assaults on and apologetic defenses of federal aid programs, but most participants in the debate over the federal role in student finance want something more and better than that. They would like more agreement on standards of assessment of aid effectiveness, a more systematic grasp on the data and, perhaps most important, a deeper understanding of the role aid actually plays in the overall working of the higher education system—an understanding of how it influences the choices made by students *and* the behavior of institutions.

Assessing the effectiveness of student aid requires a framework broad enough to capture the major issues at stake but limited enough to provide a focus to investigation and judgment. We need to figure out what questions we have some hope of answering and we need to understand why some questions that *look* like they should have easy answers—how many students will drop out if we cut Pell grants?—are actually very hard. This paper does not propose to answer the question, "How well is federal student aid working?" but rather to help us ask it more constructively.

135

That basic question can be interpreted quite broadly or very narrowly. The narrowest formulation is, "Does federal aid money go where the statutes and regulations say it should go?" This question has been pursued in a number of "quality control" studies undertaken by the Department of Education. The aim is not to learn whether aid accomplishes its purposes but simply whether the administrative machinery works. At the other extreme, a highly ambitious formulation would be, "Does federal student aid make the United States a happier and more productive society?" This must in some sense be the ultimate purpose of student aid; it is a dauntingly difficult question to answer, or even approach, however, for several reasons. Not only are the terms "happier" and "more productive" uncomfortably vague, but the question also calls for a comprehensive understanding of the role of higher education in American society as one part of its answer.

Both the narrower and broader questions are worth asking in certain contexts. For our purposes though, we want something broader than the "quality control" issue and narrower than the "quality of life" issue. We should look beyond the former because the quality control studies seem to show that the shortcomings in the student aid delivery system are not so dramatic that they defeat the main intents of the system and, moreover, they are not beyond improvement. At the same time, before we can reach a judgment about the "cosmic" questions, we need answers to some intermediate ones. We cannot judge how aid policies affect the quality of American life until we know what impact they have on schools and students. This then is a good place to start.

The discussion will be built around several questions of the "middle range"[1] that ask whether student aid has achieved (is achieving) its broad social purposes. Consider three issues, framed as historical questions about the impact of the aid policies of the last twenty years:

1. Has federal student aid expanded educational opportunity? Has it, that is, encouraged the enrollment and broadened the educational choices of disadvantaged students?
2. Has federal student aid made the distribution of higher education's benefits, and the sharing of its costs, fairer?
3. Has federal student aid made higher educational institutions work better, by making them financially more secure and educationally more effective?

This agenda of questions is broader than the one that has become most common in discussions of aid effectiveness. We have fallen into the habit of

---

1. See the partly related use of this notion in Merton 1968.

equating the issue of aid effectiveness with measures of the effect of student aid on the enrollments of low-income students. This is natural, because, as our first question suggests, helping deprived students is obviously a central purpose of the aid effort and because it at least looks somewhat measurable. But limiting inquiry to that first question produces an unreasonably narrow framework for assessing the role and impact of student aid. It is worth taking a moment to elaborate that point.

Take first the question of fairness, a term most social scientists would be happy to avoid, if they could. Is it correct to say that our concern with the fairness of the aid system is captured in finding out if aid allows poor students to get to college who otherwise could not? This would allow us to limit discussion to our first, and most comfortable, question. But I think it is clear that a lot of the energy in the student aid debate comes from questions about who *should,* and not simply who *can,* carry the burden. Once a system that helps some families is put in place, one needs systematic rules about where to draw lines determining whom to help and in what amounts. Those concerns have, for example, been at the heart of the continuing wrangle over how far up the income scale subsidies should extend.

Even when we consider only poor families, our concerns about aid are not exhausted by the aim to get more of their members into higher education. Some low-income families, no doubt, have made extraordinary sacrifices to send their children to college without aid. Most people, I believe, would feel strongly that it is unfair to ask that kind of sacrifice of some parents while others have a much easier time of it. Surely this kind of judgment should figure in our assessment of the aid system. This is so even though for such families—ones who would actually make the extraordinary sacrifice if not helped—student aid just improves the family living standard and does not increase enrollment.

The impact of aid on institutions and on the financial stability of higher education similarly must be in the picture. Although we pin the label "student aid" on some of the dollars the federal government disburses, the fact is that those dollars inevitably become part of the stream of financial resources on which colleges and universities rely. In the immortal words of David Stockman, those aid dollars help colleges and universities "finance their budgets."[2] It is quite likely that federal aid policies affect college pricing and aid policies, admissions policies, curricular and staffing decisions, and so on. Aid, that is, affects the *supply* as well as the *demand* for education. Moreover, the history of the federal student aid programs makes it fairly clear that

---

2. "Now you are going to get a lot of pressure from the colleges on it. They're not worried about the student, they're not worried about equity in America; they're worried about financing their budgets." David A. Stockman, quoted in *The New York Times,* February 8, 1985, page 1.

Congress anticipated and implicitly endorsed the notion that federal aid would contribute to the financial health of colleges.[3] These impacts must be part of our story.

Student Aid and Educational Opportunity

Although, as we have just observed, there is more to the story, a central purpose of federal student aid has undoubtedly been to provide needy students with more resources in order to encourage them to attend college as well as to broaden their choice among colleges. How well has that strategy worked?

Attempts to answer this question come up against one preeminent obstacle: need-based federal student aid is only one strand in a highly complex and varying web of factors that determine students' educational decisions. It would be most convenient if we could "rewind the tape" of the last twenty years and see what higher education would look like if we had never had, say, Pell grants but everything else had been unchanged. Or—a subtler question— if we could see what would have happened had Pell grants been fully funded and the Pell formula for determining grant awards been left untouched over the period.

But that is impossible, and we are left with basically two kinds of substitutes for replaying history. One, what I will call "before and after" study, involves looking at the actual historical record to try to see how the world with federal student aid is different from the world without it. The trouble, of course, is that we can never be sure if the results that show up in the actual record were produced by factors other than or additional to student aid—precisely the sort of possibility we could rule out if we had the power to replay history with just the changes we wanted to examine.

The alternative is to build a statistical model of the processes that generate the historical outcomes, estimate the parameters of that model, and try to "simulate" the replaying of history through the model, by running the model with and without some variety of federal aid. The danger here— besides all the pitfalls of statistical estimation—is that of omitting from our model some of the key relationships that shape "real-world" change. Suppose, for example, that federal student aid has indirect effects on the behavior of institutions—maybe more generous aid makes them raise their admissions standards. The actual historical record will be shaped by these indirect effects, but the simulated history will not.

Since neither approach is adequate in itself, the obvious thing to do is to try both approaches and see if the two sets of findings can be reconciled. It is

---

3. See the illuminating treatment in Gladieux and Wolanin 1976.

not my aim to *do* that job here.[4] What I will try to do is sketch out what the "raw material" for that job would look like—that is, what in broad terms the historical record and existing statistical studies seem to tell us—and what the task of reconciling them is like. It will be convenient to focus discussion on the Pell grant program, introduced through the Higher Education Amendments of 1972 (and called Basic Educational Opportunity Grants, BEOGs, until 1980) and generally regarded as the flagship of the national effort to expand educational opportunity.

Statistical studies. Almost all statistical studies of the effect of student aid on enrollment try to get at the problem from the demand side: aid, in the form of grants or subsidized loans,[5] "buys down" the student's or family's cost of college and thereby encourages enrollment demand or the choice of more costly schools. The majority of demand studies in fact estimate the influence of price changes on enrollment behavior; to decide what these studies imply about aid effects requires a judgment about whether a dollar of grant aid or a dollar's worth of loan subsidy is more, less, or equally as effective as a one dollar price cut in stimulating enrollment.

Available studies differ widely in data sources, statistical methods, and findings.[6] They do, however, tend to agree on two main points: student decisions to enroll in college respond positively, and nontrivially, to price cuts; and decisions about where to attend school also respond nontrivially, and in the expected way, to changes in relative prices of alternative schools. Those studies that have been able to look separately at the effect of aid awards on enrollment decisions find similar things: both grants and loans stimulate enrollments, with (as we would expect) a dollar of grants having more effect than a dollar of subsidized loans (which is less than a dollar of loan subsidy).

Rather than attempting yet another survey of this large and somewhat technical literature, let me make these findings more concrete by focusing on one exemplary study, that done by Charles Manski and David Wise several years ago (Manski and Wise 1983).

Manski and Wise examined data for a sample of 1972 high school graduates. They estimated a statistical model that best explained the choices

---

4. Leslie and Brinkman 1988 survey both historical and statistical studies of enrollment effects of student aid in chapter 8.

5. "Work-study" or subsidized work raises other complications. If the student is paid more than she could get without the subsidy, the difference might be viewed as being like a grant. If not, the subsidy really goes to the employer. Things get even more complicated if the issue turns on job availability rather than pay rates. The federal college work-study program has, in fact, been a rather small component of the overall federal aid effort, and for simplicity I will leave it aside here and concentrate on loans and grants.

6. A number of able reviews of the literature on demand for higher education exist. A recent one, which provides references to many of its predecessors, is Leslie and Brinkman 1987.

these young people made among schooling and nonschooling alternatives, on the basis of the characteristics of the students (family income, parental education and the like) and of their post–high school alternatives (prices and aid offers from colleges they were eligible for, employment opportunities, and so on). A number of their main results confirmed findings of other studies—for example, that the enrollment choices of low-income families are more sensitive to price than those of higher income families and that enrollments are more sensitive to price at two-year than at four-year colleges.

Manski and Wise then used their model explicitly to attempt the kind of exercise described above: they tried to simulate with their model the effect of the Pell grant program on 1979 enrollments. They did this by estimating their model with and without the Pell program, holding all other variables constant. The results, summarized in table 1, suggest that Pell grants "should" have had (if their model is correct) a significant positive impact on enrollments, especially of low-income students. The enrollment effects, given the parameters of their model, are much larger at two-year than at four-year colleges, and much larger among low-income than among higher income grant recipients.

These latter results are worth underlining, because they imply that the enrollment impact of federal grants is very sensitive to how the grants are distributed. In 1979, the year Manski and Wise simulated, the Pell program was much more generous toward middle- and upper-income students than it was earlier, or than it is now. Manski and Wise estimated that just under half of all Pell awards in 1979 would go to low-income students (by their definition) compared to 86 percent targeted on that group in 1977. If lower income students are more responsive to aid awards, this change in targeting tends greatly to dilute the enrollment impact of the program. Thus, Manski and Wise estimate that in 1977, 39 percent of Pell awards went to "induced enrollees"—students who would not attend without the award. This figure dropped to 25 percent in 1979.

The Manski and Wise results are not out of line with most other econometric estimates of price responsiveness of enrollment demand. They estimate that the 1979 Pell program raised enrollments by 21 percent compared to a world without Pell. A "consensus" estimate of demand elasticity arrived at by Leslie and Brinkman (1987) on the basis of their extensive literature survey would put that figure modestly lower, at something more like 10 to 15 percent.[7] There is also some reason to believe that the Manski-Wise estimate of enrollment responsiveness at two-year colleges is too high, and at four-year colleges too low.[8] The finding that lower income families are more price

---

7. A fuller treatment of the Manski and Wise work and details of the estimation procedure used in obtaining the "consensus" estimate reported in the text are in McPherson 1988.

8. For discussion of these points, see McPherson 1988.

TABLE 1. Predicted Distributions of Enrollments in 1979 With and Without the BEOG Program (in thousands)

Income Group	Predicted enrollments							
	All Schools (1)		Four-Year Schools (2)		Two-Year Schools (3)		Voc-Tech Schools (4)	
	With BEOGs	Without BEOGs	With BEOGs	Without BEOGs	With BEOGs	Without BEOGs	With BEOGs	Without BEOGs
Lower (less than $16,900)	590	370	128	137	349	210	113	23
Middle	398	354	162	164	202	168	34	22
Upper (more than $21,700)	615	600	377	378	210	198	28	24
Total	1,603	1,324	667	679	761	576	175	69

Source: Manski and Wise 1983.

sensitive than others has been confirmed in a number of other studies.[9] In all, the Manski and Wise effort fairly represents the state of the art in the econometric study of higher education demand.

The historical record. Simulation results are inevitably a kind of fiction, an attempt to answer the question, "What if?" We would naturally like to know if historical experience confirms the simplified picture of reality captured in the statistical models. Has the presence of the Pell program actually produced the results the simulations suggest?

A first look at the overall pattern of enrollments during the period Pell was expanding consistently—roughly 1974 through 1980—suggests a mixed answer to this question. Some features of the period confirm the econometric expectations rather nicely. Two-year college and vocational-technical school enrollments grew more rapidly than four-year college enrollments over the period, as we would expect if grants to low-income students were a primary stimulus to enrollment. (Manski and Wise estimate that 60 percent of 1979 vocational-technical school enrollments were generated by Pell grants.) College participation rates of black high school graduates and of low-income high school graduates grew modestly over that period, as we should also expect.

On the other hand, because Pell grants reduce the price to low-income students compared to that facing high-income students, we should expect Pell grants to increase the relative participation of students from lower income families in college—that is, participation rates of lower income students should grow faster than others. And this, as Hansen (1984) has argued, we do not find.[10] In fact, enrollments of families with above average and below average incomes grew at about the same pace from the early to the late 1970s—and this is true of men, of women, of blacks, and of whites. Hansen has suggested that this implies that the enrollment trends were dominated by factors common to both richer and poorer families (the women's movement as an encouragement to female enrollment is an example) and that grants to lower income students did not have much effect.

Unfortunately, neither the supportive nor the skeptical observations just reported can carry very much weight in deciding how effective aid is. The rapid expansion in community college enrollments in the 1970s was at least in part the product of a tremendous effort by states to increase the supply of such places. We do not know to what extent potential students in an earlier time

---

9. See McPherson 1978 for a review of evidence on this point.

10. Hansen's piece has stimulated much controversy. It has been argued that his results may be sensitive to choices of definition of income bands, to choice of starting and ending years, to details of enrollment definitions, and the like. See Lee 1982 and 1986 and Frances 1982. Although there are important limitations to Hansen's study, I do not believe these further studies have succeeded in overthrowing Hansen's main findings for the period in question. The proper implications to be drawn from those findings are, as I argue in the text, another matter.

would have attended community colleges, located close to home and with open admissions policies, even without federal grant support, because in many areas those schools didn't exist.[11] And, of course, that supply effect can help account for increasing participation of disadvantaged students without necessarily looking to aid for the explanation.[12] (But would states have built and sustained those schools without the promise of federal aid? That subtler question about the supply side effects of federal aid arises in the third section below.)

What about the failure of low-income enrollment gains to outpace those of other groups? This evidence is weak because it ignores the possibility that other factors at work in the 1970s were differentially boosting the enrollment of upper income groups, or retarding lower income enrollments. To the degree that is so, the conclusion should be not that Pell grants had no effect but that in the absence of Pell grants, lower income enrollments would have fallen compared to others.

The 1970s were a complicated decade. The Vietnam War strongly influenced the choices of young people in the early years of the decade; inflation and poor real performance of the economy may have affected judgments about the affordability of and the returns to higher education later in the decade; throughout the decade, the baby boom college classes of the 1960s and early 1970s flooded markets for educated labor and reduced the job prospects of college graduates (Freeman 1976). The relative impact of these factors on students from richer and poorer families is not well understood.

One obvious, and ironic, factor tending to promote expansion in upper income enrollments was the growth of federally supported financial aid to upper income students. In 1978, Congress passed and the president signed the Middle Income Student Assistance Act (MISAA), which (as already noted) greatly increased the proportion of Pell dollars going to families with incomes above the median and also made subsidized, federally guaranteed student loans available to all students, without regard to financial need. This legislation resulted in a dramatic redistribution of federal financial aid in the space of a year or two.

---

11. Much of the increase in supply of community colleges predates the introduction of basic grants in the early 1970s, with almost 400 such institutions constructed during the years 1963–1973 (Center for Statistics 1986, 121). There is, in fact, evidence that the income distribution of college enrollments shifted in favor of lower income families during the late 1960s (Davis and Johns 1982). Some of the enrollment effects of this supply increase would likely carry over into the 1970s. It is also true that community college construction continued to be relatively rapid in the late 1970s, with 109 such institutions opening between 1973 and 1981.

12. It is harder to see a comparable supply-side push on proprietary education, and in my view the rapid growth of the proprietary sector in the 1970s is the clearest evidence of the enrollment impact of aid. But the proprietary sector, although growing rapidly, was still relatively small at the end of the 1970s.

144   Paying the Piper

Some sense of the magnitude of the shift can be gleaned from table 2, which reports on federal aid dollars per full-time freshman resident student for several years during the period 1975–1984. (The dollars are averaged over recipients and nonrecipients of aid and are expressed in real terms.) The table reports Pell grant dollars per student, federal loan dollars per student, and an estimate of the "value" of aid per student, with federal loan dollars being valued at half the loan amount, for students grouped by family income.[13] Income is measured in dollars of constant (1978) value.[14]

Comparing 1976 to 1980, we see that MISAA significantly increased federal subsidies to students from more affluent families.[15] While the value of per-student subsidies to the poorest students stayed about constant in real terms, those to families with incomes between $10,000 and $20,000 increased by more than a third. Percentage increases were still higher for families with higher incomes than that, although in absolute dollars the amounts remained fairly small. This redistribution resulted partly from an easing of the income restrictions on Pell, which benefited moderate-income students especially, and partly from the "uncapping" of Guaranteed Student Loans (GSL), which made significant amounts of federal subsidy dollars available to very high income students. The implied redistribution of federal subsidy dollars is quite substantial. Between 1976 and 1980, federal student aid subsidies to freshman resident students with real family incomes below $10,000 fell by about $100 per student in real terms; for students in every higher income

13. The major subsidy elements in federally guaranteed loans are the payment by the federal government of all interest while the student is in school and the payment of a fee by the federal government to the lending institution that reflects the difference between the student's interest rate and a market rate of return while the loan is being repaid. Subsidies in the National Direct Student Loan Program take a different form but are similar in magnitude. Estimates that put the subsidy value in the vicinity of 50 percent can be found in Hauptman 1982 and in Bosworth, Carron, and Rhyne. 1987.

14. The data set relied on here has well-known limitations. All values are self-reported estimates by college freshmen, who may not be well informed either about their parents' income or even about the amount and, more especially, the form of the aid they receive. The bulk of the sample of schools from which the data are drawn are schools that have elected to participate—it is not a statistically controlled sample. (Within a school, however, the data are not used unless most freshmen take the survey.) Finally, the questionnaires are not issued under controlled conditions. For all these reasons, these data must be interpreted cautiously.

There are, however, three good reasons for relying on these data. First, in examining trends over time, some sources of error are likely to be consistent over years—it is plausible, in particular, that in any year freshmen are likely to misestimate their parents' income in a similar way. Second, gross movements in the data—for example, the runup in federal loans to affluent students after MISAA—show up in a reassuring way. Finally, these data have the cardinal virtue of existing, in a consistent format, over a period of years. They are the only national data on student aid that have that property.

15. These changes are relevant to the comparisons Hansen makes, since he focused on comparing 1972 to the years 1979 and 1980, the two years when MISAA had its largest influence.

TABLE 2. Federal Aid per Student, All Institutions, Freshmen

Income	1974	1976	1978	1980	1982	1984
$10K or less						
Real Pell	$565.07	$731.75	$736.82	$590.90	$443.76	$426.80
Real federal loans	346.11	300.62	328.06	396.74	528.31	597.05
Real value of federal aid	869.00	1,021.37	1,025.00	922.17	792.63	807.46
$10K to $20K						
Real Pell	166.70	246.77	230.64	267.37	172.35	149.14
Real federal loans	358.69	332.80	417.48	572.19	564.16	633.69
Real value of federal aid	384.57	478.88	502.37	620.76	497.51	510.59
$20K to $30K						
Real Pell	58.45	76.47	60.56	95.16	54.23	32.66
Real federal loans	241.09	245.58	358.31	581.73	393.21	446.67
Real value of federal aid	187.93	218.80	261.09	411.31	266.86	272.28
$30K to $50K						
Real Pell	43.24	33.74	28.46	42.72	27.35	12.51
Real federal loans	179.19	113.91	174.16	513.45	224.97	246.75
Real value of federal aid	139.64	95.23	123.06	308.47	146.68	141.25
$50K or more						
Real Pell	15.29	15.27	12.76	17.27	17.50	8.10
Real federal loans	74.79	39.06	54.77	407.59	119.44	142.21
Real value of federal aid	55.89	37.54	42.99	224.73	80.55	82.30
ALL						
Real Pell	162.02	202.28	186.03	217.37	144.21	132.66
Real federal loans	282.88	234.55	306.05	520.70	410.62	465.25
Real value of federal aid	339.89	364.96	381.42	529.90	381.94	398.78

Source: Calculated from Cooperative Institutional Research Program (CIRP), American Freshman Survey. Amounts and incomes in 1978 dollars. Real value of federal aid is sum of Pell, SEOG, and one-half of federal loans. Data are for full-time freshmen resident students. Both recipients and nonrecipients of aid are in the population base.

group (including those from families earning more than $50,000 per year) such subsidies increased by about $200 per student.

If the 1970s provide only ambiguous evidence on the effects of expanding the federal student aid commitment, the 1980s may shed more light on the impact of aid cutbacks. Although Congress has strongly resisted the sharp reductions in federal student aid repeatedly proposed by the Reagan administration, Congress has, especially in the early 1980s, permitted erosion in the real value of appropriations in some aid programs.[16] At the same time, in an environment of limited total aid funding, the increasing flow of aid funds to students at proprietary institutions and to adult students has implied reductions in the real value of aid available to the "traditional" college population— young people attending state-run and nonprofit postsecondary schools full time. Data from the American Freshman Survey indicate that Pell grants for the lowest income students (family incomes of $10,000 and below in 1978 dollars) have fallen by 30 to 50 percent (depending on type and control of institution) on an inflation-adjusted, per-student basis for full-time resident students between 1979 and 1984. Some of this drop has been made up by expanded use of student loans, but the total amount of federal subsidy going to these students has clearly fallen substantially.

We have had, then, something approaching a "natural experiment" in the impact of cutting student subsidies since 1980. Of course, like the aid expansion of the 1970s, the "experiment" has hardly been conducted with scientific purity. Aid to upper income students was cut back almost as sharply after 1980 as it was increased in the two preceding years. Real college tuitions starting rising rapidly at about the same time aid started to decline. The turmoil surrounding proposed aid cutbacks also complicates the picture: at various points in the 1980s headlines may have made potential students believe that aid prospects were much more dismal than they really were. These beliefs may have had real impacts on enrollment decisions.

We have not yet had systematic studies of trends in enrollment patterns in the 1980s comparable to those done for the 1970s. Fragmentary evidence, however, suggests that the aid reductions may have had a significant impact on enrollments of lower income students. This may be part of the explanation for the decline in black enrollments that has been receiving considerable attention. Black students come disproportionately from families that are eligible for need-based student aid, and evidence from the freshman data sug-

---

16. The most dramatic step was the decision in 1981 to eliminate the provision of benefits to social security recipients' children while they were in college. (Before this change, benefits ended at age eighteen for nonattendees but continued to age twenty-one for those who enrolled in college.) The higher education community expected that the savings from eliminating this arrangement would be plowed back into need-based student aid programs; this never happened.

gests that this group has shared in the general decline in federal aid subsidies. Arbeiter (1986) has shown that the enrollment rate of young blacks in traditional higher education has dropped substantially in the 1980s. He argues that part but probably not most of the drop may be accounted for by increased black enrollment in proprietary vocational-technical schools (on which we do not have good enrollment information).[17]

Other fragments of evidence of the impact of aid include widespread suggestions—and some statistical corroboration—that public university students are more affluent than earlier, an indication of shifts from full-time to part-time enrollment, and the weak enrollment performance of public community colleges, which tend to enroll a lower income clientele.

The missing part of the picture for the 1980s is systematic study of enrollment trends by income class of students—work for the 1980s comparable to that done by Hansen and by others for the 1970s. Even with such studies, of course, the usual cautions about drawing causal inferences from historical trends will need to be invoked. But clearly we need to know more about these trends. If the evidence of the 1970s suggests that expanding educational opportunity through student aid is a tough uphill climb, the fragmentary evidence of the 1980s seems to indicate that rolling down the hill is much easier.

Fairness

Judgments about the fairness of the U.S. higher education system turn mainly on some of its key structural features that are largely independent of the federal role. The United States sends significantly more of its young people on to postsecondary education than most other countries do and asks them (or their parents) to pay more of the costs than most other countries do—two features that are almost certainly related. The United States is also highly unusual in maintaining a mixed system of state-run and private institutions, with the former basing relatively low tuitions on substantial state operating subsidies and the latter depending for financing more on tuition and private philanthropy.[18]

The federal student aid effort has not challenged these structural features directly and has set up only rather mild incentives for changing them indirectly.[19] It has instead worked essentially within the existing structures and

17. This too may be partly the result of changing federal student aid patterns—with reduced federal subsidies covering more of the costs of a short-term vocational program than of traditional higher education.
18. Johnstone 1986 provides a highly illuminating study of college financing practices in several European countries.
19. The State Student Aid Incentive Grant Program was designed deliberately to encourage

helped mainly but by no means exclusively with financing the education of lower income students. In fact, as will be explained further below, even within the more limited context of student financial aid, the federal government has tended to work within a larger structure of "need-based student assistance" that in its main principles predates the federal effort.

Inevitably in these circumstances, judgments about the fairness of the federal student aid effort get tied up with larger questions about the fairness of the overall system of higher education financing in the United States. In deliberating about fairness, then, there is room both for large-scale discussion about the fairness of the overall institutional structure, as well as for more limited inquiry into the fairness of the federal effort given that larger institutional context.[20] Here we will stress mainly that second, more modest level: within the mixed system of public and private colleges in the United States, does federal student aid make the distribution of benefits and burdens in U.S. higher education fairer than it otherwise would be?

Even after limiting the discussion in this way, it is helpful to divide it into two parts. We will look first at "macro-fairness"—at the implications of federal student aid for the distribution of the burden of higher education finance among income groups in the population and between public and private sectors in higher education. The issue of "micro-fairness"—the details of how awards to individuals are determined—will be looked at in turn.

Macro-fairness. The key institutional feature of U.S. higher education that shapes deliberation about macro-fairness is the provision of higher education on a large scale by both state-run and independent, nonprofit institutions. Regarding public higher education, does the low-tuition strategy do enough to relieve the financing burdens of those less affluent families who attend there? And, on the private side, do considerations of fairness argue in favor of federal efforts to help bridge the gap between tuitions in the public and private sectors (a gap that is the product more of state subsidies than of cost differences between the sectors)? These questions correspond more or less to the trite labels of "access" and "choice."

It is important in getting a handle on these questions to get a sense of what the federal aid system, as it has evolved over the last twenty years, actually does in these respects. The basic logic of the federal role has been heavily shaped by the principles of "need-based" student aid, originally

---

states to put resources into student aid; a possible by-product might have been fewer resources for direct subsidies of public institutions and so higher tuitions. This is about as close as the federal government has come to trying explicitly to shape state higher education financing policies.

20. The best recent discussion of the fairness of the overall U.S. system for distributing higher education resources appears in Gutmann 1987. John Lee 1987 provides an eye-opening account of the total amount of subsidy received by students of differing incomes at various types of institutions.

worked out by a group of colleges in the 1950s to guide the allocation of their own student aid resources. These principles, in fact, when fully fleshed out, amount to a rather comprehensive view—indeed, an ideology (a term I mean not at all negatively)—of student finance.[21]

The key principles of the need-based aid ideology are these:

1. The first responsibility for paying for postsecondary education lies with the student and his or her parents.
2. The ability of a family to meet those responsibilities should be measured through a thorough, explicit, and objective assessment of its financial capacity.
3. Financial aid should be awarded only to students who can demonstrate need for it as measured by family ability to pay.
4. A student's ability to pay should influence his or her choice of college less as increased aid resources are available. Ideally, if resources permit, cost of college should be eliminated as a factor in college choice for students with demonstrated need. That is, aid should be sufficient that a family's expected contribution to college cost is independent of what school the student attends.

It is worth pausing a moment to note how widely accepted these principles are in higher education—both by the colleges and by the American public—and how thoroughly unique they are, within American society, to higher education. Nobody suggests that one's choice of cars or houses or food should be independent of one's capacity to pay. Medical care is perhaps the only other example in America of a marketed commodity in which we try to sever the link between capacity to pay and quality of service received.[22] And not even for medical care are families of average or above average means asked to bare their financial souls as they do, rather readily, for colleges. Plainly, the willingness of schools to ask for and parents to comply with this degree of financial probing is based squarely on a perception that access to college is so important in our society that this way of doing business is fundamentally fair.

---

21. By calling the principles of need-based aid an "ideology," I mean only to stress their comprehensiveness and principled basis, as well as to suggest some of the fervor with which members of the aid community are attached to them. I do not in any way mean to imply that the doctrine is stupid, shallow, insincerely held, or politically partisan—none of which is true.

22. The link between health and education here is no accident. Indeed, public provision of elementary and secondary education reflects in part a similar desire to reduce the effects of family ability to pay on quality of services received. These two "commodities," health and education, are widely seen as basic determinants of social opportunity—"basic goods" in Rawls' sense of goods that we need in a society like ours to pursue almost any reasonable plan of life. See Rawls 1971 and Daniels 1985.

This is not to say, I hasten to add, that colleges ever have lived up to this ideology fully, or indeed that the ideology is itself unproblematic. At the level of practice, almost all colleges and universities give at least some aid based on merit (athletic, academic, or other) unrelated to need, and very few have provided enough aid to all qualified needy applicants to eliminate costs as a factor in college choice. At the level of principle, the notion of family or parental responsibility applies awkwardly to adult students and to young people whose parents just refuse to act "responsibly" (as that term is understood in the needs ideology). The challenge of measuring ability to pay raises all sorts of problems, some rather technical (dealings, for example, with tax shelters), some more principled (taking account of families' longer run capacity to save and borrow in assessing their ability to pay).

Indeed, some observers would reject the need-based aid ideology altogether, arguing that parental resources should be ignored. Leaving parental resources out of the picture might imply large amounts of subsidy to all students, on the grounds that they are all, on their own hook, "needy." A different way of taking parental resources out of the picture is to argue that students, as prime beneficiaries, should pay for their educations themselves through long-term unsubsidized loans. Accepting either of these positions would imply a radical revision in our thinking about how to pay for college. These are, for the moment, distinctly minority views. The predominant position in America has been that substantial amounts of need-based aid are needed to compensate for differences in family background that would otherwise distribute the burdens and benefits of higher education quite unfairly.

A look at the historical record shows that federal aid policy has been powerfully shaped by the "needs" ideology. Indeed, among the "generally available" student aid programs, only the GSL Program has fallen outside the "needs-based aid" framework—and even that, as we shall see below, is changing.

The first general purpose federal student aid grant program, inaugurated in 1965, worked explicitly through the needs analysis systems the colleges had developed on their own. Money was provided through Educational Opportunity Grants (as well as through college work-study) for colleges to distribute through their financial aid offices to students whom they judged "exceptionally needy." Later National Defense (renamed Direct) Student Loan funds were folded under the same framework.

When the federal effort expanded with the introduction of BEOGs (later Pell grants) following the 1972 Education Amendments, a federal formula dictated the grant distribution. (Campus-based grants were preserved and renamed SEOGs). The formula was similar in structure to the needs analysis methodologies then in place, making award amounts depend on families' financial condition and cost of college. Thus, although college financial aid offices had no discretion over these funds, their distribution was shaped by needs analysis principles.

Two critical features of the BEOG method of award determination shaped the distribution of awards. First, a ceiling was set on the award any one student could get, a ceiling determined by the family's ability to pay (and more fundamentally by the limits on what Congress was willing to spend on the program). Going to a higher cost college would not permit a student to get more than this ceiling amount, although going to a low enough cost college could reduce a student's need, and so her award, below that ceiling. In principle, a big enough maximum grant would make awards under the program highly sensitive to tuition levels—students at low-tuition schools would cease to have need at award levels lower than those available to students with the same family income at more expensive schools. In practice, the "ability to pay" ceiling has been the binding constraint for most students most of the time (that is to say, very few students have had their full need met by Pell aid, given the funding limits), so that award amounts in the Pell or BEOG programs have not been very sensitive to tuition levels.

The other feature was a rule that no student could receive a BEOG award amounting to more than half of his total educational cost (more recently changed to 60 percent). Private colleges have supported this provision as a way of limiting the flow of aid dollars to public institutions with low tuitions. This constraint, which does not at all follow from the logic of the "needs" ideology, has been binding mainly for the lowest income students at low-tuition community colleges.

These programs—the basic grant or Pell program and the "campus-based" programs, such as SEOG, college work-study, and National Direct Student Loan—fit quite comfortably within the larger framework of need-based student aid created by the nation's colleges and universities. In fact, it is helpful to see these programs essentially as a federal effort to fund part of the colleges' need-based aid strategy. (Many state student aid programs can be viewed in the same light.) Federal regulations prohibit students from receiving more support from these programs combined than the amount he or she would be determined to "need" by the needs analysis methodologies schools use, and indeed for the most part (especially at private institutions) federal resources provide only part of the aid funds needy students receive.[23]

What part of need has the federal government been willing to fund? It is in addressing this question that we begin to gain some insight into the treat-

---

23. During the late 1970s, following the passage of the MISAA, the Pell methodology was made less stringent in some respects than private methodologies, so some students who would not have qualified for aid from their schools may have received Pell grants. This pattern was quickly reversed in the 1980s.

ment of "access" and "choice" or of public and private schools by the federal need-based aid programs. Most state-run schools have low tuition and offer relatively little aid from their own resources (state support goes predominantly for operating subsidies that support the low tuition). Low tuition implies that federal need-based aid has to go to students from families of low or modest incomes (others will not have need), and the paucity of institution-based funds means that for most such students the bulk of their aid comes from the federal government. Thus, in public higher education, federal need-based aid acts in effect as a *supplement* to the low-tuition strategy in keeping down the costs facing low-income families. The fairness of that supplementary aid has to be viewed in the context of state policies that already provide very substantial subsidies (through low tuition) to all attendees regardless of income. The federal aid introduces an element of income sensitivity into what is otherwise a fairly regressive pattern of subsidy in public higher education.[24]

The situation in private higher education is quite different. Private institutions spend a fair amount of their own resources on need-based grants and price discounts—partly owing to the need to compete with low-cost public institutions. Even without federal intervention, therefore, subsidy policies in private higher education are already rather income sensitive. Federal aid directed to private colleges thus does two things. First, it federalizes some of the costs of aid policies that the colleges would, within the limits of their resources, undertake anyway. (This is clearest with the campus-based programs that pay money directly into schools' financial aid budgets, but it applies more indirectly to Pell as well.) Second, it probably increases the total resources going into need-based aid at private colleges and focuses more of them on higher need, lower income students than the colleges would themselves.[25] Some sense of the latter point can be gathered from table 3, which shows the distribution of federal and other grant aid per student (averaged over aided and nonaided students) by income class of students' families in private higher education for several years. It is clear that the schools themselves tend to devote more resources to relatively low-need students, while federal aid tends to go to higher need types.[26]

---

24. "Regressive" here is used in the sense of tax policy. A regressive tax policy increases taxes less than proportionately with income; a regressive subsidy policy reduces benefits less than proportionately with income.

25. "Probably" because the actual effect depends on how colleges' own policies would be different if federal aid did not exist.

26. It should be noted that these figures include non-need-based as well as need-based aid, and that "other" aid includes aid through state scholarship programs and other third parties as well as institution-based aid. Perhaps the schools would redistribute their own aid money down the income scale if the federal contribution were reduced? It is impossible to be sure, but there is no evidence that this has happened in recent years as the relative importance of federal grant aid has declined.

TABLE 3. Grant Aid per Student,[a] Private Institutions

Income	1974	1976	1978	1980	1982	1984
$10K or less						
Real federal grants	$892.23	$995.05	$1,052.08	$909.06	$650.89	$611.23
Other grants	507.64	776.62	929.53	763.30	729.29	778.67
$10K to $20K						
Real federal grants	324.82	417.73	436.23	488.71	320.80	265.92
Other grants	438.00	790.97	955.77	786.56	748.97	818.77
$20K to $30K						
Real federal grants	114.12	148.39	148.75	202.99	122.14	83.78
Other grants	214.00	605.93	763.69	627.51	598.50	642.84
$30K to $50K						
Real federal grants	78.53	58.41	58.05	80.84	54.39	27.76
Other grants	146.60	276.28	399.15	351.55	327.78	391.83
$50K or more						
Real federal grants	18.38	19.89	15.96	26.82	25.75	13.77
Other grants	48.24	97.77	124.55	157.18	154.21	227.32
ALL						
Real federal grants	270.47	299.82	299.34	352.99	227.79	200.59
Other grants	304.30	545.41	667.65	582.07	537.93	603.90

Source: Calculated from CIRP, American Freshman Survey. Amounts and incomes in 1978 dollars. Real federal grants is sum of BEOG and SEOG. Other grants include state and external as well as institution-based grants. Data are for full-time resident students.
[a]Both aided and nonaided students.

Whether federal aid going to public institutions promotes distributive fairness depends on judgments about whether it is desirable to introduce some income sensitivity into the pattern of subsidies in that sector.[27] Whether federal contributions promote fairness in private higher education depends on judgments about whether the federal government should bear part of the costs of "choice"—of sharing with families and private colleges part of the burden of making these institutions available to needy students. It is important to stress that the federal government does not come anywhere near picking up all of these costs. In recent years, about 57 percent of Pell revenues have gone to

27. This is put in a way that takes the existence of substantial operating subsidies in public higher education as given. Some observers would prefer to recast the financing of public higher education in order to make state subsidies income-sensitive, by changing the form of state support from operating subsidies to portable student aid. But this question is part of the larger agenda of how we finance higher education that I am trying to avoid.

public institutions, about 21 percent to proprietary vocational schools, and only about 23 percent to nonprofit private institutions. Campus-based funds are targeted more heavily at private institutions, which gather about 43 percent of them (College Board, 1986). This level of support, however, implies that these sources pay only about a third of the costs low-income students face at private institutions and around a quarter of the costs facing middle-income students at these institutions.[28] The issue, then, given actual and likely funding levels, is not whether the federal government should stand ready to underwrite the full costs of an expensive private higher education for needy students but whether fairness is promoted if it picks up part of the burden of bridging the gap between public and private charges.

The major exception to the generalization that federal aid fits under the broad umbrella of "need-based aid" is the GSL program, which has at various times excepted all or some of its recipients from needs analysis and/or subjected them to a less stringent needs test than either the Pell methodology or the "uniform methodology" used to distribute most non-Pell grant aid.[29] In fact, the recent reauthorization of the Higher Education Act for the first time limits all provision of GSLs to students with demonstrated need. Part of the rationale for keeping GSL out of the needs analysis framework over the years has been that even students who are not "needy" may still need to borrow money to finance college expenses, and they will have trouble gaining access to credit markets for higher education loans if they lack suitable collateral. This group includes both middle-income students at relatively low-tuition public institutions and more affluent students at higher cost private colleges. The recent tightening of GSL eligibility rules has produced cries of "foul" from both groups but especially from public college students, who until now have not had to meet a needs test at all if their family incomes were under $30,000.

Yet GSL not only provides access to credit markets, it provides that access on fairly heavily *subsidized* terms. The actual subsidy a student receives depends on how long he or she goes to school and how long it takes to repay, as well as on fluctuations in market interest rates. But most estimates suggest that 30 to 50 percent of the real cost of a federal guaranteed loan is ultimately carried by the federal government. Although affluent students may need access to credit markets, it is hard to explain why they "need" such subsidies, at least if need is understood in anything like the way it is in the rest of the need-based aid system. The impulse to make credit for college widely

---

28. See Miller and Hexter 1985a and 1985b.

29. Only in the years 1978–81 were subsidized GSLs freely available to all students, with no means test at all. Earlier, families had to have incomes below a specified ceiling to qualify for GSL subsidies. This tended to target the funds to lower and middle class students, but without the more systematic targeting provided by a full-fledged needs analysis.

available—an impulse motivated importantly by considerations of fairness—here runs smack into the fairness-inspired belief that subsidies should be targeted on students with demonstrated financial need. This conflict cannot be avoided as long as the two different goals of providing subsidies and providing access to credit are locked together in one program.

Microfairness. Mies van der Rohe, in a context far removed from higher education finance, said "God is in the details." The point may apply nonetheless. Details about exactly who qualifies for federal student aid, and how much, may be just as challenging to work out fairly as broader distributive questions—and, if handled poorly, they may be at least as threatening to the viability of the aid system.

Perhaps a useful way to think about the problem is this. There is a clear "core case" of a student from a needy family—an image we have in mind of the person need-based aid fundamentally aims to help. For most of us, the image is that of a struggling young person, born in or near poverty, whose parents would like to help her get through college, but really can't, at least not without tremendous sacrifice.

No doubt some people would deny that a person in this plight deserves federal subsidy, but not very many. Disagreements about federal aid arise mainly because any federal aid system needs to have a response to a variety of kinds of cases that deviate in one or another dimension from that "canonical" picture. How should we view the family that is not bad off in the long run but is temporarily short of funds? Or the family with substantial net worth but whose assets are tied up in a farm or a house? The family that could have saved but did not? What is the responsibility of a noncustodial divorced parent? What about the increasing numbers of adult and part-time students? How should we treat the scion of the family, who at twenty-five is "independent" of his parents but still expects to inherit?

It is important to see that, even for those who agree that the federal government has a basic responsibility to subsidize the education of needy students, these are intrinsically hard questions. It is impossible for any actually operating aid system to be silent about them, and our basic principles are not precise enough to guide us to unambiguously best answers about all of them. And even when we know what we would like to do—as perhaps with the "scion"—it may be impossible to write a set of rules which is manageable and still gives the outcome we want in every case.

All this is sure to become more difficult as the financial affairs of American families become more complex and as rising college costs make more affluent families eligible for need-based aid (even though relatively little of the aid they get may come from federal sources). As in the tax system, there is a real tension between simplicity and fairness—one needs the details to handle hard cases, yet getting the details may prove intrusive and oppressive.

It is also true that, even more than the tax system, needs analysis systems depend on voluntary compliance; although some procedures exist for verifying aid applications, nothing at all comparable to the Internal Revenue Service's auditing and enforcement capacities exists or is imaginable for student aid.

There is a further complication. As the federal government has come to fund a larger fraction of all student aid, it has taken an increasingly aggressive stance toward dictating the needs analysis methodologies colleges and universities use in awarding some of that aid. Most recently, Congress has written into the law a methodology that schools must use in distributing *all* the aid going to a student who gets *any* federal aid. Such a congressionally legislated methodology is subject not only to all the technical problems mentioned above but to enormous and fluctuating political pressures.

It is clear that the "microfairness" of the aid system is coming under increasing pressure. The system of need-based aid may well not survive unless procedures are found for developing and modifying the "rules of the game" in acceptable ways. Two things seem to be missing right now. One is a scheme for distinguishing families with relatively simple financial circumstances and claims from those more complex cases that need a full-blown needs analysis. The other is a visibly impartial body that can oversee the details of needs analysis methodologies—a body that will be publicly accountable but insulated from the immediate political pressures and the enormous demands on timing facing members of Congress.

Institutions and Student Aid: The Supply Side

I mentioned at the outset that we cannot really assess the effectiveness of student aid without attention to its impact on how, and how well, institutions operate. This issue has been pushed into the headlines of late by the secretary of education's strong insistence that increasing student aid does not help needy students cope with college costs, because the main effect of aid is simply to cause schools to raise their prices. It would be remarkable if this story were true in its extreme form—that *all* federal aid is simply absorbed in aid-induced tuition increases—and we have seen no credible evidence to support it. But it would be just as remarkable if schools' decisions about pricing and the allocation of their own aid funds were entirely independent of federal student aid policy.

In fact, it is not impossible that aid and tuition are linked, but in just the opposite way from the secretary's hypothesis. It is possible, that is, that *decreases* in federal student aid may *raise* the prices some schools charge. If schools feel obliged, either for competitive or humanitarian reasons, to replace lost federal aid for needy students, that revenue has to be made up from somewhere. And the revenue source most institutions (especially private institutions) have some control over is tuition. This would provide a link between tuition and aid exactly inverse to the one the secretary has emphasized.

Indeed, the crude data we have offer more support for this hypothesis than the other. Schools have raised their institutional expenditures on student aid quite rapidly as federal support has fallen relative to costs. And tuitions have tended to go up more rapidly when federal aid is scarce or falling than in the 1970s, when it rose rapidly. Needless to say, this evidence is far from ironclad.[30]

It would, however, be a serious mistake to limit assessment of the institutional impact of aid to the narrow question of aid and pricing. Let me suggest the broader agenda by offering a few illustrative examples of important "supply-side issues."

1. Tom Mortensen, when he was with the Illinois State Scholarship Commission, offered the following assessment of developments in that state. When lower income Illinois students started receiving less federal grant assistance in the 1980s, the Scholarship Commission reacted by targeting more state student aid on lower income students. As a result, higher income students attending private institutions started receiving less (or no) state aid and began applying in greater numbers to public four-year institutions. This excess demand from relatively well-qualified applicants helped induce the public institutions to raise their admission standards, a step that implied denying admission to larger numbers of low-income blacks, whose credentials tended to be relatively weak. If this analysis is correct, it suggests that cutbacks in federal student aid can affect the opportunities available to disadvantaged students through channels that have nothing to do with the standard "demand-side" story about changes in aid affecting those families' capacities to pay. Whether or not this can actually be shown to have occurred in Illinois, it is plain that indirect effects of this kind could develop at various points in the supply system.

2. The expansion of federal student aid has been accompanied by a remarkable increase in numbers of proprietary vocational institutions and in enrollments in that sector. Reliable data on this sector are hard to come by, but one piece of evidence is the growth in the share of Pell revenues going to students at proprietary institutions over time —from 9 percent in 1974–75 to over 20 percent in 1984–85 (Gillespie and Carlson 1983; College Board 1986). The cause and effect seem clear. Pell grants and student loans allow low-income students, many of

---

30. For further discussion see Hauptman and Hartle 1987 and McPherson 1988.

whom are not qualified for or not interested in traditional higher education, to pay for vocational training. Small, entrepreneurial proprietary institutions, often operated as chains, have responded to this market with enormous energy, notably through aggressive advertising and through strong job placement efforts for their graduates. The lobbying presence of this sector in Washington has also become powerful.

The supply of this kind of education was in very substantial measure called into being by federal policy choices—although the development seems to have been thoroughly unanticipated. Indeed, serious efforts to measure enrollments and describe performance in this sector are only now getting under way. Congress is groping toward ways of regulating this sector it helped bring into being. It seems clear that the emergence of this sector is of first-rate importance for the educational future of American youth. It is a phenomenon that must be understood from the supply side.

3. A final illustration is the history of affirmative action toward minorities in U.S. higher education. It is clear that in the 1970s many colleges and universities in both public and private sectors became much more aggressive in pursuing affirmative action policies in student recruiting and admissions and in modifying their curricula to accommodate students with different needs and interests. To an important degree, these developments were products of the social consciousness of the time. But it is significant that need-based federal student aid reduced the cost to states and institutions of enrolling disadvantaged minority students, since part of the aid cost would be borne by the federal government. It was, in particular, less burdensome for states and localities to operate open admission community colleges after the federal government began picking up part of the tab. It seems very likely that federal student aid policy increased the supply of places for disadvantaged minorities in higher education and encouraged their recruitment, although we do not know how to measure the extent of this effect. It is also plausible that the reduced emphasis on aggressive recruiting of disadvantaged minority students at many institutions in the 1980s is related to changes in federal policy, although again the climate of the times also has much to do with it.

These examples illustrate the importance of improving our understanding of how federal aid policies influence institutional policies and behaviors. Comparatively speaking, we have lavished attention on the "demand-side" implications of student aid, through studies like those discussed in the first section above, while hardly touching the supply side. It is as though studies of agricultural price supports never looked at the behavior of farmers, or studies of housing subsidies never looked at builders. To begin to fill this gap, we need to work on models of institutional behavior, encompassing state-run,

independent nonprofit, and profit-seeking suppliers.[31] We also need to identify and work with sources of data in which there is significant variation in the
variables affecting supply, so that impacts of changing supply conditions can
be studied. We might, for example, investigate the comparative institutional
behavior of schools in states with very different state student aid policies. The
problems are not easy, but if we want a rounded picture of the effects of
student aid they are extremely important.

What are the policy implications of introducing a supply-side perspective
on student aid? Some of them obviously depend on empirically supported
answers to questions such as those raised above. But some comments can be
made at a more general level. It is, after all, plain that federal student aid has
become a major source of institutional finance in the United States—schools
do rely on aid as a means of "financing their budgets." Not all student aid, by
any means, serves this purpose. It would be foolish to suppose that if the $20
billion dollars of federal aid disbursements suddenly dried up schools would
be $20 billion dollars poorer. A substantial part of the loss—certainly the
majority—would land on families who would be forced to come up with the
money themselves or who would withdraw their children from higher education (suffering then an educational rather than a financial loss). But still the
loss of that revenue flow would be a substantial blow to colleges and
universities.

Federal student aid is then in part a way of giving federal aid to institutions.[32] We need to ask whether, from a policy point of view, this is a good
thing. That is really a two-part question: (1) Should the federal government
provide some institutional support to colleges and universities? (2) If so, is
student aid a good vehicle for providing such support, compared to alternatives that are realistically available?

A full-dress treatment of these questions is not my purpose here. Instead,
I want to urge that these questions—which received serious national attention
in the late 1960s when the issue of federal support for higher education was
being seriously debated—be put back on the agenda. We cannot say how well
federal student aid is working without thinking these questions through.

One kind of answer to the first question is that the federal government
should *not* be in the business of providing institutional support. Let states do
that through state-run institutions (if at all); the federal government should
simply purchase from universities those services it requires—notably research
and the education of disadvantaged students. Any institutional support univer-

---

31. Such studies would connect with the literature on public choice and on the behavior of
the not-for-profit sector more generally. See Hoenack and Pierro 1986 and the essays in Rose-
Ackerman 1986.

32. For a more complete discussion, see McPherson 1987.

sities derive from these purchases is just an unavoidable byproduct of buying the services and should be minimized.

Taken to its extreme, this proposes a competitive market model of higher education, where schools derive their revenues from the sale of services to customers. If we accept that logic, it becomes doubtful that higher education institutions should be tax exempt or nonprofit, or indeed that states should run them. This market model has, of course, considerable appeal on grounds of economic efficiency. Perhaps the most cogent argument against it derives from the observation that for many hundreds of years, societies have chosen not to run academic institutions in that way. It has been seen as desirable to place some kind of buffer between the various demanders of services from universities and colleges and their internal operations, a buffer that has been supplied at times by a framework of religious insulation, at times by state support and protection. General institutional support provides universities with a base of resources that allows them at times to refuse to do what their clients want, and also to do things their clients will not pay for. Whether the combination of state institutional support for public colleges and charitable support (encouraged by favorable tax treatment) for private institutions does enough to provide this buffer, or whether additional direct federal support is called for, is hard to judge, but there is considerable reason to resist the presumption that a pure "purchase of services" approach is ideal.

If one reaches the conclusion that federal institutional support is justified, there remains the question whether federal student aid is a good way to provide it. The most obvious alternative is direct formula-based institutional aid, which would go to schools in proportion to their enrollments, or the number of degrees they grant, or some more complicated scheme. Congress looked hard at such schemes in 1971 and 1972 and finally drew back. The short-run political problem was to find a formula that would not be seen as biased against some particular sort of school; any given formula would be seen as over-weighting or under-weighting graduate students, as allowing too much or too little for differences in educational costs, and so on. In the longer run, the danger in any formula is its rigidity. The political problem of revising any formula once in place (except in ways that gave everybody more—and even then how much more is a problem) would be overwhelming. Moreover, any politically viable formula would be inclined to reinforce the status quo—tending to finance exactly the pattern of institutions that then existed and tending to disadvantage institutions that differed from existing norms.[33] States that operate institutions have more control in this respect; they can, at least in

---

33. There is an excellent discussion in U.S. Department of Health, Education, and Welfare 1969.

principle, gather the detailed knowledge needed to reallocate subsidies in response to changing conditions—although they plainly do not find it all that easy to do so. For the federal government to do the same for thousands of institutions is unimaginable.

Student aid as institutional aid has some advantages. It gives institutions an incentive to attract and to respond to the requirements of disadvantaged students. It has some built-in flexibility, because funds will flow toward institutions and sectors that expand and away from those that contract. It avoids the need for an explicit federal judgment about how much institutional support any particular institution or type of institution should get.

There are disadvantages, too. For much the same reasons that formulas for direct institutional aid would be hard to revise, the complex of institutional interests that impinge on aid distributions—encompassing not only schools of various descriptions, but banks, loan guarantee agencies, forms processors, needs-analysis services, and so on—make those formulas hard to revise as well. This is one reason that the existing set of aid programs has become so bewilderingly complex: when somebody has a stake in every existing provision, the number of provisions is almost certain to rise over time. The student aid "vehicle" may deliver large amounts of resources to types of institutions where Congress is not eager to see them go, yet there is no convenient way to regulate the mechanism. Finally, reliance on the student aid vehicle for delivering institutional aid causes arguments about student needs and institutional needs to become thoroughly blended together, promoting incoherent discussion of public policy.

Ultimately, if federal institutional support for higher education is judged worthwhile, the question about student aid as a vehicle for delivering it must be put in comparative terms. What feasible alternative would work better? If the nation were to cut back sharply on federal aid without putting such an alternative in place, the overall level of federal support for higher education institutions would drop substantially. Perhaps that would be judged a desirable outcome; it is not something we should do by accident.

Conclusion

I have identified three broad points of view from which to evaluate the effectiveness of federal student aid: those of promoting wider opportunity for postsecondary education, of distributing the burden of college costs fairly, and of contributing to the general institutional health of colleges and universities. It is natural to conclude by asking about the relationships among those goals—are they compatible or conflicting?

It is clear that any one of these goals, pursued single-mindedly, could conflict with the others.[34] For example, exclusive concern with promoting opportunity would imply denying aid to any family that would somehow scrape the resources together without aid. But this would deny aid to just those poor families who were willing to make heroic sacrifices to pay for higher education, and that seems plainly unfair. Similarly, if all one cared about were promoting the financial well-being of institutions, one would want to detach aid expenditures thoroughly from any encouragement to institutions to enroll more needy students. The way to maximize the contribution of federal subsidies to the institutions' financial health is to give them money for doing exactly what they would do anyway, so that all the federal revenue is "gravy." The effort to enroll more needy students will absorb some of those revenues the schools would get to keep if aid were provided to schools with "no strings attached."

Yet despite these areas of conflict, the three goals may well be compatible to a striking degree. Consider the relationship between fairness and opportunity. Most people would agree that a fair structure of student aid would give more aid to needier families, a feature that tends to promote greater enrollment of disadvantaged students and hence more equal opportunity. It is, of course, the case that some arguments made in the name of fairness cut the other way, as when middle-class or part-time or adult students argue for "equal" treatment with low-income young people, and interpret "equal treatment" as meaning they should receive generous aid. But the appeal to fairness here may be superficial: it is not really fair to treat people the same if their circumstances are different. The standard of fairness calls for working these kinds of cases through carefully, paying attention to differences in need and capacity to pay. Given scarce aid resources, fairness arguments will probably often support opportunity arguments for targeting resources on the needier students.

It is perhaps more surprising to note that "institutional support" arguments often reinforce "opportunity" and "fairness" arguments. Student aid helps an institution when it enables more qualified students to go or when it relieves the institution-based aid budget for students who would receive aid from the school if federal aid were not available. Aid does not help a school when it simply picks up expenses the family would otherwise have paid themselves—in that case it is the family budget rather than the institution's budget that benefits from the aid. But, in general, money that goes to needier students is more likely to affect their enrollment decisions and/or to affect institution-based aid allocations. It is when money goes to families who can

---

34. It is not so clear that "fairness" pursued single-mindedly would conflict with other goals, but then it is not so clear what single-minded pursuit of fairness would mean: fairness is perhaps better viewed as a constraint on the pursuit of other goals.

afford to pay the full bill at the colleges of their choice that it helps the institution least.[35] Thus, in a broad way, if student financial aid is to help institutions, it is better that it be targeted on needier students, as both fairness and opportunity arguments urge.

These broad points about compatibility and conflict among goals plainly leave a lot of room for further investigation and discussion. They do not settle questions, for example, about proper targeting on public versus private institutions, about the right treatment of independent students from these several points of view, or about how rapidly aid should fall with rising income.

But it was never my intention to settle such questions here; rather I hope that I have raised them in a more illuminating way.

---

35. For further discussion, see McPherson 1987.

REFERENCES

Arbeiter, Solomon. 1986. "Minority Enrollment in Higher Education Institutions: a Chronological View." *Research and Development Update of the College Board* (May): 1–9.

Bosworth, Barry P., Andrew S. Carron, and Elisabeth H. Rhyne. 1987. *The Economics of Federal Credit Programs.* Washington, DC: The Brookings Institution.

Center for Statistics, Office of Educational Research and Improvement, U.S. Department of Education. 1986. *Digest of Education Statistics.* Washington, DC: U.S. Government Printing Office.

College Board. 1986. *Trends in Student Aid: 1980–1986.* New York: The College Board.

Daniels, Norman. 1985. *Just Health Care.* New York: Cambridge University Press.

Davis, Jerry S., and Kingston Johns, Jr. 1982. "Low Family Income: A Continuing Barrier to College Enrollment?" *Journal of Student Financial Aid 12* (February): 5–10.

Frances, Carol. 1982. "Basic Facts on College-Going Rates by Income, Race, Sex, and Age, 1970 to 1980." Prepared for the National Commission on Student Financial Assistance.

Freeman, Richard. 1976. *The Over-Educated American.* New York: Academic Press.

Gillespie, Donald A., and Nancy Carlson. 1983. *Trends in Student Aid: 1963–1983.* Washington, DC: Washington Office of the College Board.

Gladieux, Lawrence E., and Thomas R. Wolanin. 1976. *Congress and the Colleges; The National Politics of Higher Education.* Lexington, MA: D. C. Heath and Company.

Gutmann, Amy. 1987. *Democratic Education.* Princeton, NJ: Princeton University Press.

Hansen, W. Lee. 1984. "Economic Growth and Equal Opportunity: Conflicting or Complementary Goals in Higher Education?" In *Education and Economic Pro-*

ductivity, edited by Edwin Dean. Cambridge, MA: Ballinger Publishing Company.

Hauptman, Arthur M. 1982. *Financing Student Loans: The Search for Alternatives in the Face of Federal Contraction.* Washington, DC: The College Board.

Hauptman, Arthur, and Terry Hartle. 1987. "Tuition Increases Since 1970: A Perspective." *Higher Education and National Affairs,* February 23, pp. 1ff.

Hoenack, Stephen A., and Daniel J. Pierro. 1986. "An Econometric Model of a Public University's Income and Enrollments." Unpublished.

Johnstone, Bruce. 1986. *Sharing the Cost of Higher Education.* New York: The College Board.

Lee, John. 1982. "Changes in College Participation Rates and Student Financial Assistance, 1969, 1974, 1981." Prepared for the National Commission on Student Financial Assistance.

———. 1986. "Changes in Student Participation Rates." Proceedings of the NASSGP/NCHELP Research Conference, Chicago, Illinois, June 1986.

———. 1987. "The Equity of Higher Education Subsidies." Unpublished.

Leslie, Larry, and Paul Brinkman. 1987. "Student Price Response in Higher Education: The Student Demand Studies." *Journal of Higher Education* 58 (March/April: 181–204.

———. 1988. "The Effects of Student Financial Aid." *The Economic Value of Higher Education.* New York: Macmillan.

Manski, Charles F., and David A. Wise. 1983. *College Choice in America.* Cambridge, MA: Harvard University Press.

McPherson, Michael S. 1978. "The Demand for Higher Education." In *Public Policy and Private Higher Education,* edited by David Breneman and Chester Finn, 143–96. Washington, DC: The Brookings Institution.

———. 1987. "Student Aid as Institutional Aid." Unpublished. April.

———. 1988. "On Assessing the Impact of Federal Student Aid." *Economics of Education Review* 7, no. 1: 77–84.

Merton, Robert K. 1968. "Sociological Theories of the Middle Range." In *Social Theory and Social Structure.* New York: Free Press.

Miller, Scott E., and Holly Hexter. 1985a. *How Low-Income Families Pay for College.* Washington, DC: American Council on Education.

———. 1985b. *How Middle-Income Families Pay for College.* Washington, DC: American Council on Education.

Rawls, John. 1971. *A Theory of Justice.* Cambridge, MA: Belknap Press of Harvard University Press.

Rose-Ackerman, Susan, ed. 1986. *The Economics of Not-for-Profit Institutions.* New York: Oxford University Press.

U.S. Department of Health, Education, and Welfare. 1969. *Toward a Long-Range Plan for Federal Financial Support for Higher Education.* Washington, DC: Government Printing Office.

CHAPTER 7

Federal Student Aid Policy: Can We Learn from Experience?

Michael S. McPherson

Experience, we are often told, is the best teacher. But if that is so, we must at least admit that her lesson plans are not very clear. Federal student aid, along with other social programs introduced in the activist days of the Johnson and Nixon Administrations, has now been around long enough to provide a substantial record of experience. Increasingly we are being asked to decide what lessons can be drawn from that experience. Has student aid (or low income housing, or Food Stamps, or Medicaid) "worked"? Can we use our experience to make it work better—and preferably, given budgetary stringencies—work better for less money?

It's not so easy. It is surprising, and perhaps instructive, that more high-quality analytical work was done on student aid in the years prior to the blossoming of the federal programs in 1972 than has been done since.[1] Apparently a relatively clean slate has its advantages. One can analyze the workings of programs in the pristine form of their imagined state. And, lacking real data, one can get by on plausible-sounding made-up numbers. Once the programs exist, however, the analyst is faced with actual programs that never fully embody the simplicity of the theoretical model and real data that are hopelessly contaminated by reality. At the same time, the analyst's attention is readily drawn to the little glitches and curlicues of the programs' actual

The author acknowledges support of the Andrew Mellon Foundation for the research underlying this chapter. Mary Skinner assisted in research, and Meropi R. McCoy did the text processing. The views expressed are those of the author and should not be attributed to other staff members, officers, or trustees of the Brookings Institution.

    1. An entire issue of the *Journal of Political Economy,* a leading economic journal, was devoted to higher education finance in 1972. Proposals for income-contingent loans generated substantial analytical work (Shell et al. 1968; Dresch and Goldberg 1972; Hartman 1971). The Joint Economic Committee of the U.S. Congress also published a volume of studies on higher education finance in 1969.

operations, and away from the larger questions of purpose and design that motivated the efforts in the first place.

The problems of learning from experiences are in fact at least two-fold. One is the sheer opacity of experience. How can we hope to disentangle the effects of a particular government program from those of all the other variables that are changing at the same time—especially when the program itself is likely to be continually modified in response to interest group pressures and to the perceived effects it is having? Even large scale social experiments, useful as they are, can never fully reproduce the conditions of a permanent national program. What we require is Douglas Hofstadter's imaginary device, the "subjunctivision." This looks much like a regular TV with a video recorder attached. The important difference is that on the subjunctivision we can replay events with critical assumptions changed. We could, for example, see how the recent Redskins-Oilers game would have come out if the officials had correctly awarded the Oilers a touchdown on that controversial pass play. (Washingtonians would oppose this.) Or, by pushing some other buttons, we could see how that game would have gone if the teams were allowed five downs per series.

With this device in hand, we could go back and see how history would be different if Congress had supported institutional aid instead of student aid in 1972, or if it had decided simply to abolish the federal aid programs in that year. Lacking this device, we are instead thrown back on the resources of statistical analysis and of our imaginations in trying to see what difference the federal programs have made.

The second difficulty in learning from experience confronts us even when our understanding of that experience is adequate. That is the problem of modifying programs once they are in place. Bureaucracies quickly form around programs, and interested parties develop a firm grasp of the advantages of the status quo. Since any significant change will produce losers as well as winners, consensus politicians will tend to converge on leaving things where they stand. There is no need to belabor this point before an audience familiar with student aid policy.

These two difficulties in learning from experience—what might be called the *cognitive* problem of deciphering that experience and the *strategic* problem of implementing the lessons—are not as separate as I have implied. For programs can be set up in ways that either encourage or discourage bureaucratic entrenchment, and that makes it easier or harder to get information about their workings. When we think about program design prospectively, we need to look at programs not only from the standpoint of their capacity directly to achieve goals but also from the standpoint of the capacity of the organizations they create to learn and to adapt over time. Richard Nelson among others has argued that increasing attention to this *procedural* or *evolutionary* dimension of policy analysis has been a most important development in recent years.[2]

In what follows, I want to explore some implications of this "evolutionary" or "institutional" approach to policy analysis for our thinking about federal student aid. I have two main topics. The first concerns the problem of determining how effective student aid programs have been in promoting the college enrollment of lower income and disadvantaged students. I will argue that that problem looks very different once the key role of state and institutional *responses* to federal policies are taken into account.

The second part of the essay looks more directly at the institutional means through which federal aid policies have been implemented. Over the years, Congress has made several key decisions about *how* students and their families would be aided. I'll examine some implications of those choices for the evolution of aid policy. Then follows a brief look at policy implications and some concluding remarks.

Enrollment Effects of Student Aid

Nearly everyone agrees that raising the college enrollment of lower income and disadvantaged students has been among the central purposes of federal student aid. It would certainly be a mistake to construe this as Congress' *sole* purpose in providing aid, since it's quite clear that at various times national defense, the needs of "middle income" students, and the financial health of colleges have also motivated Congressional actions on student aid. Still, the concern with aiding the disadvantaged is sufficiently clear and central that it is naturally the first place to look in trying to see if the programs have "worked."

When they have looked, analysts have been less than pleased with what they have found. The enrollment rates of lower income students have not shown any clear upward trend since the major low-income-oriented aid program, BEOGs (now Pell), was introduced in 1972. The picture, in fact, is quite mixed, as John Lee (1983) has shown in comparing data for 1974 and 1981. Among dependent students, lower income whites had substantial increases in college participation, but lower income blacks experienced an even sharper decline. Lower income female dependents shared in the general increases in female enrollment during the 1970s, while lower income male participation declined. For dependent students as a whole, participation fell substantially for those with family incomes below $7,500 (in 1980 dollars), and rose for those earning from $7,500–$12,500. Meanwhile, the participa-

---

2. See Nelson 1977 and Nelson and Winter 1982. Another volume in a similar spirit is Lindblom and Cohen 1979.

tion rate of lower income independent students dropped substantially. It's hard to discern anything like a consistent movement toward more participation of disadvantaged students during the years when the federal student aid effort was most prominent.

The same sorts of results emerged from Lee Hansen's 1984 study, in which he examined changes in the participation rates of lower income and higher income students from the early to the late 1970s, using several data sources. As it is well known, he found little or no systematic change in the ratio of lower and upper income enrollments over that period. Hansen had been willing to go further than Lee in drawing policy implications from these findings. He concludes that the old programs have had little effect on advancing the important goal of equalizing educational opportunity.

Obviously, we need Hofstadter's subjunctivision to decide if this conclusion is warranted. We know that a good deal besides federal aid policy changed during the 1970s: the war in Vietnam ended (and with it the military draft), inflation rose and economic growth languished (at least in part as a result of the oil crisis), and markets for educated labor were flooded with unprecedented numbers of college graduates. It's not unlikely that some of these factors would have affected the relative participation of lower and upper income students.

The fact that federal aid served purposes other than aiding the disadvantaged creates further complications. After 1978, with the passage of MISAA, large portions of the Office of Education's student aid budget went to provide subsidized loans and (to a lesser extent) grants to students from families with above median incomes, tending to reduce the real levels of support for the less advantaged. Early in the 1970s important amounts of federal student aid were also distributed outside the Office of Education, through GI Bill payments to veterans and through payments to surviving children of social security recipients. The total amount of grant aid, taking into account all these federal sources, actually reached its real dollar peak in 1975–76, so that the picture of "little aid in 1972, lots in 1980" is misleading.

These complications make the simple "before and after" comparisons of Hansen and Lee suspect. Statistical manipulations can go part of the way to overcoming the difficulties, by introducing further variables to the analysis that "control" for the effect of factors other than changing levels of federal aid to lower income students. That is what's accomplished by the econometric literature on enrollment demand. This literature produces estimates of the effects of price changes at colleges on the propensity to enroll, while controlling for other factors that may vary with the price. By assuming that the effect of a grant is the same as the effect of a price cut of the same size (or, in a few cases, by relying on direct estimates of the impacts of grants), we can estimate what effect the federal BEOG program would have had on lower income enrollments, in the absence of complicating factors like wars ending and other aid programs expanding and contracting. I have estimated elsewhere, using this approach, that the availability of Basic Grants should have boosted enrollments in the lower income population by 20 to 25 percent, compared to what they would have been otherwise.[3]

This sort of statistically corrected estimate is certainly helpful but misses an important further dimension or complexity in trying to replay the past. It tries to determine what effects the Pell program would have had if various disturbing factors had not intervened. However, in order to do so, it makes the ruthless assumption that the *only* effect the grant program had was to reduce the net price facing students. The implicit assumption is that other aspects of state and institutional behavior, such as pricing, levels of state budgetary support, offers of institution-based aid, and so on, are unaffected by federal policy change. We would presumably want our subjunctivision to be more imaginative than that!

A lively illustration of this further dimension of complexity can in fact be drawn from New York State. An alert reader of the *Chronicle of Higher Education* noticed a recent story in which the Chancellor of the City University of New York objected to the Reagan Administration's plans to shift the burden of higher education finance toward the states. The reader reminded us that one of the recommendations of the Keppel Task Force report of 1972 was to introduce tuition at the City University in order to capture more federal student aid funds. He quoted the report as emphasizing that "New York State students and institutions will fail to some degree to qualify for federal funds under the new statutes unless the public institutions charge higher tuition than they do at present . . . [We] consider it extremely important that the State take maximum advantage of federal funding in order to reduce the burden on state taxpayers."[4]

There is nothing at all nefarious about proposing to take advantage of changing federal rules in this way; indeed, it would be extremely odd, and probably irresponsible, if state governments and both public and private institutions of higher education failed to consider changing their own operations in response to changing federal student aid policies.

But to understand the effects of federal aid policies, it is clearly necessary that these indirect responses be taken into account.[5] The examples of

3. See McPherson 1985. The estimate is for 1979, relying on a "consensus" estimate of price sensitivity of enrollment reported in Leslie and Brinkman 1985.
4. Thackrey 1985. The quotes are from pages 5 and 15 of the report (Task Force on Financing Higher Education 1972).
5. To draw an analogy to the football game viewed on subjunctivision, neglecting these indirect effects would be like seeing what happened if one team changed its offensive strategy and the other stuck to its old defense.

such indirect effects that come most readily to mind (at least to one trained as an economist) are ones, like this, that tend to *offset* the effects of the aid. Others of the same sort might include hikes in private tuition or reductions in institutions' own expenditures on aid. But plainly not all the effects work in that direction.

It's clear, for example, that the availability of federal aid makes it easier for both state and private institutions to pursue policies that encourage the admission of lower income students. Recruiting such students becomes less costly if the federal government pays part of their maintenance and tuition costs. It's even possible that the availability of federal aid could induce some institutions to devote *more* of their own aid resources to needier students, because the federal aid may lower to a more feasible level the gap that the institutions' own resources have to fill.

Sorting these potential effects out, and weighing their magnitude, is a major empirical/analytical project, one that I am currently trying to make some progress on. I can offer here some preliminary hypotheses and conclusions.[6]

1. Despite the Keppel Task Force's hopes, and Secretary of Education Bennett's frequently voiced fears, there is not much evidence that the availability of federal student aid has lent a substantial upward push to higher education prices. Superficially, federal student aid arrangements look at lot like third-party medical care payment schemes, where the provider can get more money from the government or the insurer simply by raising the price. But, in fact, most student aid doesn't work that way. For the most part, the size of a student's Pell grant or of a campus's allotment under the campus-based programs is determined by a formula that is insensitive to price.[7] In fact, as table 1 shows, college costs rose considerably faster (relative to inflation) in the 1960s, when federal aid was small, and in the 1980s, when it had been falling, than in the 1970s, when it grew. This evidence is hardly conclusive, but it should give pause to those who see federal aid as a major source of higher education cost inflation.

---

6. A fuller discussion of some of these findings is in McPherson 1985, on which the following pages draw in part.

7. The exception, which the Keppel Task Force had its eye on, is the provision in the Pell program that limits a student's maximum award to half the cost of attendance. A low-cost college with many students up against that ceiling could garner added federal resources simply by raising its price. In fact, however, the other limits on Pell awards have lagged so far behind inflation in college costs and other prices that for some time there have been few schools in a position to take much advantage of the provision by raising their prices. The formulas for dispensing "campus-based" aid to institutions are in principle cost-sensitive, but in reality they are so heavily "grandfathered" that at current funding levels the cost sensitivity is lost.

TABLE 1.   Annual Real Rates of Increase in Costs of Attendance at Selected Categories of Colleges and Universities, 1963–83

Years	Private University	Public Four-Year College	Community College
1963–70	2.2%	1.5%	3.2%
1970–80	−0.5	−0.8	−0.9
1980–83	6.3	4.6	2.6

Source: Gillespie and Carlson 1983; Gillespie and Quincy 1984.

One exception to the general price insensitivity of most federal aid is worth noting. Under rules that have been in effect since 1982, the amount of subsidized loans that some higher income students are eligible for rises with the cost of the college they attend. It is possible that this link is connected to the recent rapid run-up in charges at private colleges.

2. It's very clear that efforts to recruit minority and disadvantaged students increased substantially in the 1970s, continuing a trend begun in the 1960s. In the public sector, this took the form largely of the creation of new "open-access" institutions, mostly community colleges; while at private institutions and many public four-year colleges, revised admissions criteria, affirmative action programs, and curricular revisions were more important.

   It's hard to show a cause-and-effect link between expanded federal aid and expanded recruitment, but it is clear, as noted above, that federal aid reduced the costs to schools of pursuing these policies. In the case of public community colleges, for example, the federal government went from supplying 7 percent of their educational revenues in 1968 to supplying 15 percent in 1979, with most of the increase being due to Pell.[8] This shift in financing may well have encouraged states to increase the supply of places at these institutions.

3. The most provocative statistical relationship I have discovered concerns the relationship between federal student aid and institutions' use of their own resources for aid, whether through price discounting or direct expenditures. As table 2 shows, inflation-adjusted aid per student grew by more than 5 percent per year in both public and private institutions from 1966 to 1973, the period just preceding the introduction of BEOGs. From 1973 to 1980, it fell by 7 percent per year in public institutions and by 3 percent per year in private institutions. Total real spending on institution-based aid was lower in both sectors

---

8. Calculated from data in Gillespie and Carlson 1983 and U.S. Department of Education, National Center for Education Statistics various years.

TABLE 2.   Institution-Based Scholarship Aid Selected Years, 1966–1982[a]

Year	Current Dollars			1967 Dollars			Per Student,[b] 1967 Dollars		
	All	Public	Private	All	Public	Private	All	Public	Private
1966–67	429	156	273	441	160	281	69	37	138
1969–70	701			638			80		
1972–73	1,067			851			92		
1973–74	1,133	537	596	851	403	448	89	54	205
1974–75	1,204	581	623	815	393	422	79	49	189
1977–78	1,543	718	825	851	396	455	75	45	187
1978–79	1,626	717	909	832	367	465	73	42	188
1980–81	1,858	779	1,079	753	316	437	61	33	166
1981–82	2,138			785			63		
1982–83	2,333			806			65		

Source: National Center for Education Statistics, *Financial Statistics of Colleges and Universities,* various years; *Digest of Educational Statistics, 1983–84;* and Office of Student Aid, *OSFA Data Bank,* various years.
[a]Total institutional scholarship expenditures less supplemental educational opportunity grant revenues, as reported by institutions in the Higher Education General Information Survey and by the Department of Education's Office of Student Financial Aid.
[b]Total scholarship aid divided by total enrollment (including graduate and part-time).

in 1980 than in 1973. Although detailed data are not available for the most recent years, it appears that real spending on institution-based aid has begun to grow again in the 1980s as federal aid has been cut back. Anecdotal information suggests that the growth in institution-based aid is currently quite rapid at many private institutions.

These changes, especially at private institutions, are large. Had real per student spending on institution-based aid at private colleges continued to grow from 1973 to 1980 as it had earlier, spending per student would have been higher by $344 (1980 dollars) in 1980 than it in fact was. This compares to Pell grants per student in private higher education of $544 in 1980.[9]

Again, many factors other than student aid policy were at work over this period, but the pattern present in these numbers is highly suggestive. The most straightforward interpretation is that institutions cut back on their own aid efforts as the federal government expands its aid. That interpretation, however, raises as many questions as it answers, for example:

9. All per student figures are per total enrollment, including graduate and part time. Undergraduate full-time equivalent enrollment data are not available for some years covered in the data.

- Could institutions have found the resources to fund expanded levels of aid in the 1970s, had the federal government not intervened as it did? The response by institutions might instead have been to cut back on their commitment to need-based aid, with the resources instead used for other purposes—perhaps merit aid or perhaps activities unrelated to student finance.
- If institutions had continued to expand their aid budgets during the 1970s at the rate they did in the 1960s, who would have borne the costs of greater aid? The most obvious possibility is that other students and their families would have, in the form of more rapid increases in tuition. There may in this sense be a link between the historical pattern of aid expenditures and of tuition. When federal aid resources are rising, tuition increases may slow, because the cost of expanded aid is picked up by the national government. But when they are low or falling—as in the late 1960s and in the 1980s—tuitions may have to rise to finance increased aid from institutional revenues.
- Would institutions have directed aid to the same set of students the federal government did? Even if institutions continued to aim their dollars at needy students, they might have distributed them differently than federal programs did.

  One possibility is that institutions competing for students might have diverted their aid budgets toward "low need" middle class students, for whom relatively small awards might make a real difference in choice of school. This would have restricted opportunities for needier students, relative to the outcome with federal intervention.

Plainly much more work is needed in investigating the character of the linkages mentioned here and other possible ones. But it does appear that awareness of these institutional relationships may lead us to think about the role of federal aid policy in a somewhat different light. The U.S. Congress does not, after all, have the power within our federal system to directly *put* low-income students into college. All it can do is try to direct the flow of federal funds in ways that permit and encourage the other actors in the system—states, colleges, and families—to move in that direction. From that perspective, a more accurate description of the aim of federal student aid policy embodied in BEOGs (and the campus-based programs) would be this: to bolster the market stability and financial health of postsecondary institutions that encourage the enrollment of lower income and disadvantaged students.

This interpretation is consistent with the legislative history of the 1972 amendments, where Congress seemed to display almost as much concern with the financial plight of colleges as with the plight of disadvantaged students.[10] This interpretation of Congressional intent also suggests an interpretation of the developments in the 1970s and 1980s which plays rather well, at least on my "subjunctivision." It goes like this:

During the latter part of the 1960s, both public and private institutions undertook major efforts to provide expanded educational opportunity for needy and disadvantaged students. In the private sector, these efforts took the form of the expansion in need-based aid already noted and in programs for recruitment of minority and disadvantaged students. There was also an expansion of need-based aid in public higher education, but the development of community colleges and other open-access institutions, often in urban areas, was probably more important to the public effort.

Although data on student income distributions for those years are weak, there is some evidence that these efforts had a real effect. Davis and John's (1982) analysis of data from the American Council on Education (ACE) survey of freshmen suggests that the percentages of freshmen from families below the U.S. median income jumped between 1966 and 1971—by 35 percent at various categories of private four-year colleges and by somewhat lesser amounts at public and private universities. Since then, these percentages have been roughly constant.[11]

Perhaps colleges and universities overreached themselves in making these efforts in the late 1960s. In response to a climate of opinion in the 1960s that greatly valued efforts toward more equality, they may have undertaken efforts they couldn't—or anyway wouldn't—sustain at growing cost in the longer run. As noted earlier, there was considerable concern at the end of the 1960s about the financial viability of many private colleges as well as about the fiscal capacity of state governments. Without federal support, private colleges might have backed off their commitments to recruit and help finance the education of disadvantaged students, and state governments might have backed off their commitments to support open-access institutions. If so, federal intervention may have had the effect of sustaining the gains made in the late 1960s, in the face of financial pressures that would otherwise have eroded them. The fact that low-income and minority enrollments have declined in the 1980s, as federal support has been cut back, provides circumstantial evidence in favor of this interpretation.

This story is consistent with Lee Hansen's and John Lee's "before and after" data for the 1970s, but it would lend those data a very different norma-

---

10. See Gladieux and Wolanin 1976. Readers will recall that concern about the financial stability of colleges, especially private colleges, was quite widespread around 1970. The most influential of the reports that appeared at that time was Cheit 1971.

11. The Carnegie Council (1979) reports a similar trend based on census data.

tive significance than Hansen provides. For it would suggest that the federal programs, rather than *failing* because they failed to raise enrollments, instead *succeeded* by preventing lower income enrollments from falling.

This story is conjectural, but it does, I think, provide a suggestive interpretation of the recent past. Of course, even if the story is completely right, it by no means provides a blanket justification for existing federal student aid policies. Perhaps other feasible policies would have been more effective in moving institutions in the directions Congress desired, or in accomplishing results more cheaply. Such policies would, however, need to be analyzed in light of the kinds of institutional interdependencies noted here.

Strategic Choices: Replaying the Past

One way to get a handle on the consequences of alternative policies is to think back over major policy alternatives Congress has actually entertained and to try to imagine (the subjunctivision again) what differences the choice of these other alternatives might have made. It's especially important, as was noted at the outset, to compare alternative policies in terms of the capacities of the organizations they create to learn, to adapt, and to yield up information about their performance.

In schematic terms, Congress can be said to have made three fundamental choices over the last twenty years that have shaped the existing structure of federal student aid. First, chronologically, in 1965, Congress decided to embark on providing federal support for subsidized educational loans by working through private financial markets rather than through a government supported "Student Loan Bank." Second, in 1972, Congress chose to expand its commitment to support of higher education through creating a program of grants to lower income students (the BEOG program) rather than through providing direct operating subsidies to colleges and universities—subsidies that were at that time being actively sought through the major higher education associations. Finally, in 1978, Congress elected to respond to strong pressure to subsidize the college costs of "middle income" students by extending the availability of need-based grant and loan aid to more affluent students, rather than by providing tax credits for college tuition. I will argue that the latter two choices were fundamentally correct ones but that the 1965 decision to work through private loan markets has turned out to be an important mistake.

Student Aid Versus Institutional Aid

The decision to channel most aid to students rather than to provide direct federal subsidies to institutions implied allowing the educational marketplace to determine where federal subsidy money would go.[12] One of the influential early discussions of the institutional aid alternative identified a fundamental organization defect in the notion:

> It will probably be concluded that a formula is a good device if it does not lead to a relative decline in the importance of any class of institutions. Consequently, one of the disadvantages of institutional aid by formula is that it encourages the status quo. Clearly, a system which tries to maintain the relative shares of different types of institutions will not be particularly adaptable to the changing needs of students and society in general. (U.S. Department of Health, Education and Welfare 1969, 26)

In principle, either a discretionary commission (like the University Grants Committee in Britain) or a sufficiently ingenious and complex formula for distributing aid could avoid endorsing the status quo, instead directing institutional behavior in desired directions. However, besides the political difficulties of establishing any such apparatus in so decentralized a system of institutions as the United States, the informational requirements would likely prove unmanageable. It's hard to imagine a system of institutional aid at the federal level which would generate reliable information about what activities the aid was supporting and how effective the results were.

By contrast, direct aid to students gives institutions a straightforward incentive to respond to those students' demands. Students voting with their feet can over time reshape the mix of institutions substantially. At the same time, such aid can be targeted at lower income students and thereby help to promote more equal opportunity.

Perhaps the most striking consequence of strengthening the influence of lower income students through providing them with direct aid has been the rapid growth of the proprietary (for profit) sector in postsecondary education. Proprietary schools, which received less than 7 percent of Pell grant funds in 1974, received 18.9 percent of those funds in 1984, more, in fact, than public two-year colleges received (Lee 1985, table 3). We may well feel ambivalent about this result. Presumably it reveals that these students obtain something valuable from the proprietaries which they wouldn't have gotten (and which we wouldn't have known about) without the existence of portable aid. On the

---

12. Congress has continued to provide small amounts of institutional aid for library expenditures, for "developing institutions," and in some other ways. The relatively small "campus-based" aid programs, which give money to institutions to provide to needy students, are somewhere between institutional and student aid. But in the discussion leading up to the 1972 education amendments there was serious consideration of large-scale, formula-driven operating subsidies to be provided to all colleges and universities. It was this alternative to expanded student aid that Congress turned away from.

other hand, we know relatively little about many of these institutions and have suspicions about the educational value of some, and, as they grow in importance, we may with justice want to see them brought within a more adequate regulatory structure. Despite this ambivalence, the emergence of the proprietaries is a good illustration of the way portable aid to students encourages innovation in education and makes the system responsive to student preference.

It's worth stressing that these criticisms of institutional aid at the federal level do not necessarily carry through for the states. States for the most part operate the institutions they finance and thereby gain greater control over the uses to which subsidies are put. Also, because most states provide operating subsidies to only a limited number of institutions, the informational and incentive problems noted above may be less acute.

Tax Credits Versus Aid Expenditures

In 1978, the Carter Administration concluded that the only way to head off a bill providing tax credits for college tuition was to support the extension of student aid to middle and upper middle income students. The resulting MISAA removed all needs tests from the GSL Program and made the needs test in the BEOG program substantially more generous. The result was a rapid and substantial shift of student aid funds toward students from families with incomes above the median.

In retrospect, it seems clear to most observers that this was a bad piece of legislation.[13] It disrupted the traditional commitment of aiming student aid subsidies predominantly toward lower income families. Moreover, the unrestricted availability of heavily subsidized loans encouraged even families with no shortage of funds to borrow, if only to take advantage of the interest rate spread by reinvesting the proceeds. Besides the concerns about equity these issues raised, it rapidly became apparent that the budgetary commitments implicit in that legislation would lead to large and continuing increases in the student aid budget, increases that were probably unsupportable.

Despite these important drawbacks of the 1978 legislation, it seems clear that from an evolutionary point of view that legislation was superior to introducing tax credits. For one thing, the embarrassing consequences of the legislation that passed were highly visible—in rapidly increasing budgetary costs and in aid awards to affluent students. Indeed, in the years since 1980, the extensions of aid to higher income students have been largely reversed through further legislative action. Had tax credits been introduced instead, both their budgetary costs (in terms of foregone tax revenue) and their distributional implications would have been much less visible. Because tax measures generate less infor-

---

13. A valuable volume in the Carnegie Council series (Carnegie Council 1979) was devoted to proposals aimed at undoing the negative effects of that legislation.

mation about their functioning, they are less prone to correction over time. In fact, it seems likely that once tax credits for college expenses were introduced, the pressures to increase their amounts and to broaden whatever income restrictions they began with would prove irresistible.

In these two basic respects, then, focusing on supporting students rather than institutions and relying on the expenditure rather than the tax side of the budget, existing federal higher education programs seem well structured.

Guaranteed Loans Versus a Loan Bank

However, in deciding to operate the principal federal loan program for higher education through private financial institutions, Congress may well have made a strategic mistake. This financing mechanism has in fact plagued the GSL Program since its inception.[14] The basic strategy of the program has been to encourage banks to lend money to students by insuring those loans against default and to encourage students to borrow by having the government pay their interest costs while they are in school (and in certain other special statuses).

Ironically, for the first decade of the program's existence, its major problem lay in getting banks to make enough loans. Students were wary of borrowing; banks, unfamiliar with the loans and put off by what they saw as high administrative costs and doubtful profitability, were reluctant to lend; and states, who were supposed to help oversee the program, saw little advantage in becoming involved. Loan volume, especially to minority and disadvantaged students whom lenders might see as less desirable, was much less than desired.[15]

We have, it would appear, fixed that problem. This has been accomplished, essentially, by *paying* everybody to participate: banks receive a "special allowance" from the government that guarantees them a return above their cost of funds, the interest rate students pay is set below market rates, and state agencies that administer the loans have received administrative cost allowances and interest-free loans from the government to encourage their cooperation.

From the point of view of establishing an institutional structure with the potential to evolve in a constructive way, these arrangements have very serious drawbacks. First, it is extremely hard to tell, with this setup, where all the federal money is going and whether the payments are justified. There is no market test of whether the current level of payments to banks is needed to

---

14. The National Defense (later Direct) Student Loan Program (which predates GSL) provides federal capital directly to colleges to use in making loans. It is much smaller than the GSL program.

15. These problems are examined in Rice 1977.

make the student loan business profitable for them, nor of whether the payments to state agencies are required.

Second, the system sets up perverse incentives for all the actors. Because banks and state agencies are essentially fully insured against defaults, they have no financial incentive to try to collect loans. Although the program gives the appearance of being market based, since it operates through profit-making financial institutions, efforts at collection of loans by banks and agencies are in fact induced not by the market but by regulatory "due diligence" requirements, which have become increasingly elaborate over time. Meanwhile, the subsidy offered to students tends to encourage them to borrow more than they need to finance their education; the response to this is still another set of regulations that limits loan amounts and restricts loan eligibility to the needy.

A third drawback is that the system discourages innovation in such matters as repayment periods and the introduction of variable repayment schemes. The key elements of the loan agreement are in effect written into the law, by the rules according to which the government distributes subsidy payments. Not only is it cumbersome to modify these legislated rules, the complex set of interests created by the subsidy structure makes it very hard to arrive at an agreement for any change.

Finally, and importantly, the current setup introduces a bias in congressional deliberations about aid. Congressional budget practice implies that only current outlays on loans appear in the budget Congress deals with; the contractual commitments the government undertakes when new loans are granted do not register on the books until they come due. As a result, any curtailment of new guaranteed loans has only a minor short-term effect on the budget. Most of the budgeted costs of the loan program for the next few years are to pay the costs of special allowances, interest subsidies and defaults on past loans. By contrast, reductions in grant awards show up as immediate budgetary savings. As a result, the real value of aid awarded to students from programs other than GSL has been dropping rapidly under the recent pressure to cut federal expenditures—it is now less than half what it was in 1978. During the same period, the inflation adjusted value of GSL aid has grown by 285 percent.[16]

It seems likely that other institutional arrangements for college lending would have fared better than GSL has done. Not that all the problems would have disappeared. GSL interest rates were originally set at more or less unsubsidized levels; the rise in interest rates that accompanied inflation at the beginning of the 1970s began the pattern of subsidy to both banks and students who were repaying loans.[17] That unanticipated run up of interest rates

---

16. Computed from data in Gillepsie and Carlson 1983 and Gillespie and Quincy 1984.
17. The in-school interest subsidy was always part of the program for needy borrowers.

would probably have pulled any federal lending program at least temporarily into giving subsidies.

However, some version of a national Student Loan Bank would seem to have advantages both in providing more information about how the program was performing and in giving it the potential to learn from and adapt to experience. Such a bank would be empowered to borrow at government rates and lend (presumably through colleges and universities) to qualified students. The bank could be expected to set rates to cover its costs, including the insurance of defaults. If instead a subsidized loan rate were desired, the cost of that subsidy would show up as an operating loss of the bank, which would have to be covered from federal appropriations. It would be relatively easy to gauge the extent and identify the beneficiaries of the subsidy. Such a bank could also be given considerable latitude to experiment with alternative financing instruments and terms for college lending.[18]

The decision to rely on private financial institutions rather than a national bank to finance educational loans may by now be irretrievable. The existing system has a formidable list of constituencies on its side. Banks and state agencies have a direct interest in the present system, while schools and students may prefer "the devil they know." Still, unless some basic restructuring is done, it seems likely that these important structural problems will persist and will increasingly dominate federal decision making about student aid. Perhaps the best hope is to develop some incremental strategy for "weaning" the system of its dependence on GSL, perhaps, as Arthur Hauptman has proposed, through expanded reliance on a modified form of the direct lending mechanism embodied in the existing small National Direct Student Loan Program (Hauptman 1985).

Summary

Is there any general lesson to be drawn from this schematic review of history? One, perhaps, is to beware of general lessons. It's often said, for example, that we should rely on the market as much as possible and prefer decentralized to centralized solutions to problems. But, while the decentralized, market-based approach of portable need-based grants has worked out rather well, the decentralized, market-based approach of running the loan program through banks has not worked well at all—worse, in all probability, than a more centralized National Bank, using schools as lending agents, would have done. In general, as Nelson and Winter have observed, "serious policy analysis [in areas where many actors are involved] requires detailed understanding of the

---

18. Helpful recent discussions of the Loan Bank notion are in Carnegie Council 1979, chapter 13, and Hauptman 1986 (draft).

institutions, mechanisms, interests, and values at stake" (Nelson and Winter 1982, 385). Close analysis has to substitute for easy generalization.

A second lesson may be of more comfort. Both the decision to rely on student rather than institutional aid and the decision to favor expenditures over tax credits were the product of deliberate and extended debate in Congress and among the informed public. By contrast, the decision to adopt a guarantee mechanism over other possible forms of lending was apparently taken much more casually. GSL started as a small and not heavily subsidized program, and full blown proposals for a National Student Loan Bank were not developed until the late 1960s, when GSL already existed. We might conclude, then, from this admittedly small sample of congressional actions, that Congress performs better when it deliberates more fully—a result that might strike some as counterintuitive.

Some Policy Implications

My main purpose in presenting this analysis has been to suggest some constructive ways of looking at student aid policy, rather than to defend detailed policy proposals. Still, it may advance the discussion if I spell out some policy implications that seem to me to follow naturally from the prospectives developed here.

1. Need-based portable grant assistance to students continues to look like the most attractive vehicle for carrying the main burden of federal subsidies to undergraduate education. The case that such assistance "doesn't work" in promoting the enrollment of the disadvantaged has to be judged "not proven." Given the institutional complexities and the limited state of our knowledge it's hard to "prove" this case one way or the other.

   However, if Congress wants to help finance the colleges, and wants to do it in a way that encourages the system to respond to the needs of disadvantaged students, need-based grants are a more effective and institutionally manageable way to do it than any alternative that has been suggested. This broad conclusion of course leaves plenty of room for detailed debate about the desirable level and terms of grant subsidies. The pressing concern here is that the real level of Pell grant awards has lagged very badly behind rising college costs (the current $210 maximum is worth only about three-quarters as much as the $140 maximum in effect in 1975). It seems quite likely that this is part of the explanation for the sharp recent drop in minority enrollments in college. Getting grant awards back to the real levels of the mid-1970s—perhaps at the expense of loan funding—is an important priority.

2. The GSL Program is in need of basic reconstruction. For the reasons set out above, the financing mechanisms established in that program do not work well. Converting the system to a more straightforward and manageable arrangement like a National Loan Bank makes basic sense. I should stress that I do not base this conclusion mainly on the currently popular concerns about defaults or about excessive loan burdens. Both of these are in important measure by-products of the more basic failings of present arrangements and would be helped by an institutional setup that gave lending institutions an incentive to collect loans and to devise more flexible and longer term repayment arrangements.

   The short-term defect in the GSL program that I would be most inclined to stress is the large federal subsidy cost of the existing program—the product more of interest subsidy than of default costs. It's quite unclear who benefits from this subsidy or what social goals it promotes, and the growing federal cost starves other, probably more important, aid programs like Pell. In the longer run, perhaps the most serious defect with the guarantee program is precisely that it discourages "learning from experience"—despite its apparent decentralization, it's not a setup that invites, or even permits, much experimentation, innovation, or response to changing conditions.

3. The idea of formula-based institutional aid as a substitute for federal student aid is perhaps permanently dead (and little mourned), but the notion of subsidizing student costs through the tax rather than the expenditure side of the budget lives on. The currently most popular notions are not tax credits for college tuition but various schemes to provide tax breaks for college savings. Each such scheme must be looked at on its own merits, and some of them may have features that make them superior to the simple tax credit notions of years past. Moreover, increasingly widespread tax support for other uses of savings—including retirement, home ownership, and life insurance—may create a "second-best" argument for extending such support to educational saving as well.

   Still, all tax subsidy schemes suffer from the important institutional drawbacks identified earlier. With both their costs and their consequences less visible than expenditure programs, they are less likely than expenditure programs to receive careful oversight or to evolve in constructive ways.

4. An issue has surfaced in the current debate over reauthorizing the Higher Education Act which raises in a sharp way the concerns expressed in this paper about fostering constructive change and adapta-

tion. In the past, Congress has elected to leave considerable scope for nongovernmental groups to develop systems for computing the financial need of applicants for aid other than Pell grants (Pell awards have already been determined by federal formula). There appears now to be a strong possibility that Congress will write into the law a detailed needs analysis system to apply to *all* aid (including state and institution-based aid) going to any student who receives any federal aid at all.[19] The current rules instead allow organizations like the ACT Service and the College Scholarship Service to develop their own needs analysis systems, which they then provide to colleges, as long as the systems conform to broad federal guidelines.

A legally mandated needs analysis system would be a regrettable step toward rigidity. Needs analysis, especially for the relatively affluent students who may be eligible for aid at higher cost schools, is a complex affair. Systems must be revised over time to account for inflation, for changes in tax laws, and for other developments. Preserving equitable treatment requires difficult judgments about matters that are both technical and emotionally charged—like taxing home equity, farm assets, and tax-sheltered income—matters that are politically hard for Congress to deliberate about and mechanically difficult to write into law in a timely way. Meanwhile, over the last five years, the existing needs analysis systems have been evolving toward a more comprehensive and coherent assessment of family finance.[20]

Although in the short run this is a fairly small and rather technical element of the student aid debate, it could eventually prove consequential. For if, as I think likely, a legally mandated needs analysis formula becomes in time both obsolete and heavily politicized, it could tend toward undermining the credibility of the student aid system as a whole.

Conclusion

When my son was six, he would often embark on projects of rather striking ambition—usually drawings of mural size. After some minutes of intense effort, a difficulty would arise, and he would dissolve in frustrated tears, abandoning not just that drawing, but the very *idea* of making drawings—or

---

19. The wide reach of this system would apply because of the so-called "overaward" rule—no student who receives federal aid can receive a total aid package that exceeds his or her demonstrated need.

20. This judgment is based largely on my service for several years on the College Scholarship Service's Committee on Standards of Ability to Pay—which service may, however, have biased my perception of this issue.

indeed of trying things in general. Our politics at the moment have a little of that flavor. Exaggerated hopes in the 1960s have led to exaggerated disappointments, and too sweeping reactions, in the 1980s. We're prone, I think, to ask overly simple questions (Did the Great Society succeed or fail? Does Student Aid work?) and to demand overly conclusive answers.

Constructive social policy requires instead greater awareness of the complexity of social institutions and consequently of the limitations as well as the strengths of the analytical tools we can use in assessing policies. We need the patience both to ask less sweeping questions and to expect complacency; we also need to remain honestly critical of the shortcomings of our policies and institutions. I have tried in these remarks on student aid to embody something of this approach, one that I think is essential if we are to "learn from experience."

I'm happy to report that my son, who's just turned nine, seems to be learning to moderate his cycles of overambition and excessive despair. With luck, our society will do the same.

REFERENCES

Carnegie Council on Policy Studies in Higher Education. *Next Steps for the 1980's in Student Financial Aid: A Fourth Alternative*. Washington, DC: Jossey-Bass Publishers, 1979.

Cheit, Earl. *The New Depression in Higher Education: A Study of Financial Conditions at 41 Colleges and Universities*. New York: McGraw-Hill Book Company, 1971.

Davis, Jerry S., and Kingston Johns, Jr. "Low Family Income: A Continuing Barrier to College Enrollment?" *The Journal of Student Financial Aid* 12, no. 1 (February 1982): 5–10.

Dresch, Stephen P., and Robert D. Goldberg. "Variable Term Loans for Higher Education—Analysis and Empirics." *Annals of Economic and Social Measurements*, January 1972: 59–92.

Gillepsie, Donald A., and Nancy Carlson. *Trends in Student Aid: 1963 to 1983*. Washington, DC: College Entrance Examination Board, 1983.

Gillespie, Donald A., and Lynn Quincy. *Trends in Student Aid: 1980 to 1984*. Washington, DC: Washington Office of the College Board, 1984.

Gladieux, Lawrence E., and Thomas R. Wolanin. *Congress and the Colleges: The National Politics of Higher Education*. Lexington, MA: D.C. Heath and Company, 1976.

Hansen, W. Lee. "Economic Growth and Equal Opportunity: Conflicting or Complementary Goals in Higher Education?" In *Education and Economic Productivity*, edited by Edwin Dean. Cambridge, MA: Ballinger Publishing Company, 1984.

Hartman, Robert. *Credit for College: Public Policy for Student Loans*. New York: McGraw-Hill, 1971.

Hauptman, Arthur. *Federal Costs for Student Loans: Is There a Role for Institution-Based Lending?* Washington, DC: American Council on Education, June 1985.
————. *The National Student Loan Bank: The Road Less Traveled.* Draft prepared for NAICU annual meeting, 1986.

Hofstadter, Douglas. *Goedel, Escher, Bach: An Eternal Golden Braid.* New York: Basic Books, Inc., 1979.

Lee, John B. *Changes in College Participation Rates and Student Financial Assistance: 1969, 1974, 1981.* Washington, DC: Applied Systems Institute, Inc., January 1983.
————. *The Distribution of Student Financial Aid: Trends Among the Postsecondary Sectors.* Washington, DC: American Council on Education, June 1985.

Leslie, Larry L., and Paul T. Brinkman. *Student Price Response in Higher Education.* Tucson: University of Arizona, Center for the Study of Higher Education, March 1985.

Lindblom, Charles E., and David K. Cohen. *Usable Knowledge: Social Science and Social Science Problem Solving.* New Haven, CT: Yale University Press, 1979.

McPherson, Michael S. "On Accepting the Impact of Federal Student Aid," Second Annual NASSGP/NCHELP Research Conference, May 31–June 1, 1985, Washington, DC. *Report and Papers.* Springfield: Illinois State Scholarship Commission, July 1985.

Nelson, Richard P., and Sidney G. Winter. *An Evolutionary Theory of Economic Change.* Cambridge, MA. The Belknap Press of Harvard University Press, 1982.

Nelson, Richard R. *The Moon and the Ghetto.* New York: W.W. Norton & Company, Inc., 1977.

Rice, Lois D., ed. *Student Loans: Problems and Policy Alternatives.* New York: College Entrance Examination Board, 1977.

Shell, Karl, F. M. Fisher, D. K. Foley, A. F. Friedlander, J. Behr, S. Fischer, and R. Mosenson. "The Educational Opportunity Bank: An Economic Analysis of a Contingent Repayment Loan Program for Higher Education." *National Tax Journal,* 21, no. 1 (March 1968): 2–45.

Task Force on Financing Higher Education. "Higher Education in New York State. A Report to Governor Nelson A. Rockefeller from the Task Force on Financing Higher Education." 1972.

Thackery, Russell I. "Letter to the Editor: State of New York and U.S. Student Aid." *Chronicle of Higher Education,* June 26, 1985: 30.

U.S. Department of Education, National Center for Education Statistics. "Financial Statistics on Institutions of Higher Education," (fiscal years 1968–69, 1973–74, 1977–78, 1979–80, and 1981–82). Washington DC: Government Printing Office, various years.

U.S. Department of Health, Education, and Welfare. *Toward a Long-Range Plan for Federal Financial Support for Higher Education: A Report to the President.* Washington, DC: Government Printing Office, 1969.

CHAPTER 8

Measuring the Effects of Federal Student Aid: An Assessment of Some Methodological and Empirical Problems

Michael S. McPherson and Morton Owen Schapiro

Certainly no aspect of the evaluation of federal student aid has attracted more attention than the question of its impact on enrollment levels and patterns. Although it is important to note that affecting enrollment is not the whole justification for student aid, the aim of promoting the enrollment of targeted groups has been central to the case for federal student aid throughout its history.[1] Despite quite substantial empirical efforts, the issue of the size—and even the existence—of these enrollment effects remains unsettled.

This chapter provides a crucial review of the major studies of enrollment effects of aid. We give special attention to the seeming conflict between empirical findings based on cross-sectional econometric results that tend to find large effects of aid and the actual historical experience in which these effects are not readily discernible in the aggregate data.

The issue of enrollment effects has several aspects. The main focus has traditionally been on access, interpreted as the effect of student aid on postsecondary enrollment of disadvantaged groups, without reference to the kind of postsecondary education they obtain. A second focus is choice, the effect of aid availability on the range of postsecondary alternatives available to and chosen by disadvantaged students. Expanded choice is usually equated with improved enrollment prospects for disadvantaged students at more costly private colleges and universities. A distinction is also sometimes drawn between the effect of aid on students' initial decision to enroll in a postsecondary institution and their tendency to persist through the completion of a program or degree.

A version of this chapter appears in Chapters 2 and 3 of our book, *Keeping College Affordable: Government and Educational Opportunity* Washington, D.C.: Brookings Institution, 1991.

This work is summarized in our article, "Does Student Aid Affect College Enrollment? New Evidence on a Persistent Controversy," *American Economic Review* 81 (March 1991): 309–18.

The authors wish to thank Michael P. O'Malley, Diedre Goodwin, and Mary Skinner for excellent research assistance.

1. A broader framework of goals for federal student aid is suggested in McPherson 1988.

Commentators have noted that evidence on these various dimensions of aid's influence on student behavior could have important implications for policy. Jensen (1983) and St. John and Byce (1982) emphasize the sharp reversal in trend in federal student aid appropriations in the early Reagan years. After more than a decade of expanded funding, real spending on most student aid programs was either capped or significantly reduced in 1981 and 1982, intensifying interest in the possible behavioral impacts of such sharp changes in spending.

Schwartz (1986) points to the considerable fluctuations in the income targeting of federal student aid from 1965 to 1984. The Higher Education Act of 1965 initiated relatively small-scale programs that were at first targeted fairly closely on lower income groups.[2] Starting in the 1970s, funding increases substantially expanded the amounts of support available to lower income students from these programs, but changes in the programs during the 1970s also significantly increased the share of federal student aid funds for which middle-income students were eligible. As St. John and Byce (1982) show, the distribution of student aid funds had moved substantially toward the middle class in the period following the passage of the MISAA in 1978. This trend toward broadened aid eligibility reversed with the budget-cutting initiatives of the early 1980s, which had the effect of targeting available funds more heavily on lower income students. Schwartz (1986) argues that knowledge of the behavioral effects of aid on students from various income groups is needed to assess the impact of changes in the distribution of aid across income classes.

An additional persistent policy concern has been the effectiveness of aid in increasing the participation of minority students in higher education. St. John and Noell (1988) report evidence that the enrollment rate of eighteen-to-twenty-four-year-old African-Americans increased from the early to the late 1970s as student aid funding expanded but had reached a plateau by 1978 at a level well below white enrollment rates. An analysis of the responses of students from different racial and ethnic backgrounds to student aid offers is important in assessing the effectiveness of federal student aid spending as a device for expanding minority participation in higher education.

Finally, in reviewing reasons for interest in studying the effects of aid on student behavior, we should note a concern with persistence through, and graduation from, college. Although it is quite possible that even abbreviated stays in college that do not result in degrees are productive for students and society, it would plainly be worrisome if an important effect of student aid were to encourage students to enroll in college and then drop out. St. John, Kirshstein and Noell (1988) are among several authors who have attempted to

---

2. From the outset, the GSL program had broader income eligibility criteria than grant and work-study programs.

isolate the influence of aid of varying types on student decisions to persist in college.

Attempts to measure the impact of aid on these varied aspects of student behavior fall into two basic classes, econometric studies and trend or "before and after" studies.[3] "Before and after" studies compare enrollment levels or patterns over a period during which federal student aid policies changed significantly, attributing changes in observed outcomes to the changed policies. Such studies are vulnerable to the criticism that factors other than aid policies that may have changed over the same period may be responsible for the observed outcome. Despite this serious flaw, studies of this kind are sometimes quite influential, because they are relatively easy to understand and because they do link up visibly with the most obvious purpose of the federal programs: to have a noticeable effect on real-world behavior of students.[4]

The econometric alternative to "before and after" studies is to build a statistical model of the processes that generate the historical outcomes, estimate the parameters of the model, and use those parameter estimates to stimulate the effect of changes in federal policy. These models attempt to control for factors that simple before and after studies leave out, although no model can escape the risk that important variables are left out or poorly measured or that the model specifies the relationships among the variables incorrectly.

In principle, one should be able to reconcile the findings of these two kinds of studies: given adequate historical data, it should be possible to use the parameters of a correctly specified econometric model to trace out the historical data used in "before and after" studies. In practice, the two approaches have not seemed easy to reconcile: the econometric studies lead us to expect substantial effects of changes in aid policy on observed student behavior, but such effects have not been seen to emerge clearly in many studies of aggregate historical data.

The principal aim of this paper is to pursue the task of reconciling historical and econometric data more thoroughly than has been done before. We first review, in the next section, the various approaches to measuring aid effects that have been employed in the literature and discuss some of their strengths and limitations. The section after that reviews some of the principal

---

3. A third source of information is the study of student survey responses to questions about how their educational decisions are made, in particular about the effect of aid. These studies cannot be viewed as providing hard evidence, partly because students, as aid recipients, are likely to be inclined to exaggerate its impact, but more importantly because students probably in many cases cannot reliably tell how they would have behaved had aid not been available to them.

4. The most widely cited of the "before and after" studies of federal student aid is Hansen 1983. A comprehensive survey is included in Leslie and Brinkman 1988.

empirical findings from the econometric literature on aid. The next section describes existing studies of historical trends in enrollment and aid patterns and thus poses the problem of the apparent inconsistency between econometric predictions and historical reality. In the following section, we turn to some newly developed data to pursue this historical versus econometric contrast in more depth and to offer our assessment of how it should be reconciled. In the final section, we discuss improvements in econometric testing.

Types of Studies and Their Problems

Although differing in many ways, most econometric studies of enrollment share a background of common theoretical assumptions. They assume, most fundamentally, that the data under examination reveal information about students' *demand* for education rather than decisions about institutions' enrollment *supply*. They generally assume, that is, that if more students with given characteristics (income, academic record, and so on) seek higher education of a particular kind, that added demand will be met without any change in institutions' prices, admission standards, student aid policies, or quality. They usually assume, further, that any increase (or decrease) in the aid funds available to an institution from external sources (such as the federal government) will be completely passed through into reductions (or increases) in the net cost facing prospective students, rather than being absorbed by the institution through higher (or lower) fees or less (or more) aid provided from the institutions' own funds.

These are problematic assumptions, more so in some econometric studies than others.[5] Even if econometric estimates manage to escape contamination from the confounding of supply with demand effects, it remains critical, as developed further below, to allow for supply effects in applying the findings to historical trends, where supply effects clearly do play a role.

Student aid is assumed in these demand models to affect student behavior through affecting the net price (to the student and his or her family) of educational alternatives. Microeconomic theory carries implications for how students should respond to various factors that may change their net cost of education. Other things equal, a fully informed student should have the same reaction to a $100 grant as to a $100 reduction in tuition—both reduce the net cost equally. If, as evidence suggests (Hearn 1980), students are better informed about tuition levels than about aid availability, the tuition decrease should have a relatively larger effect.

---

5. These assumptions of perfectly elastic supply are most troubling in econometric studies that rely on aggregate data, such as state cross-sections or national time-series. They are least worrying in studies of the behavior of individual students.

The analysis of student loans is somewhat more complicated. Typical student loans offer their recipients two things: (1) access to a credit market that would otherwise not be available owing to difficulties in establishing creditworthiness and (2) subsidies in the form of below-market interest charges and direct government payment of interest. For fully informed student borrowers, the impact of the second factor on behavior should be just the same as a grant or a tuition reduction of equal value (that value being determined as the present discounted value of the stream of subsidy payments evaluated at an appropriate market interest rate). The first factor should increase the behavioral effect of the loan beyond that amount.[6] A subsidized loan, that is, should in theory have a smaller effect on behavior than a grant with the same face value, but a larger effect than a grant that equals the value of the loan subsidy—all this assuming that students and their parents are able to figure out what is going on.

In fact, as we shall see, empirical studies have in any event had relatively little success in distinguishing the impact of different sources of reduction in net cost.

A final set of theoretical issues concerns distinguishing the question of *whether* to enroll in college (the access question) from the question of *where* to enroll (choice). It is conceptually helpful (although not necessarily psychologically accurate) to sort the college choice decision into two parts. The student first ranks all the schooling alternatives available to him or her—taking into account price, aid availability, quality, and so on—and then compares the best of those educational alternatives with the alternative of not continuing in school at all. A change in aid policies would affect the net cost to the student of (at least) some of the educational alternatives and therefore may affect which school is ranked highest among educational alternatives. If the top ranked choice changes or if it stays the same but the net cost of that choice is changed by the change in aid policy, then the decision about whether or not to go on to school may also change.

It follows that the change in student behavior produced by changes in aid

---

6. A third form of aid, besides grants and loans, is college work-study, the provision to students of jobs (typically on campus) at governmentally subsidized wages. If the students receiving these jobs would otherwise get similar jobs at similar wages, the subsidy payment is really being made to the school, and should have no enrollment effect. To the extent that students avoid unemployment or receive higher wages because of the subsidy, there should be demand effects. Because college work-study has been a relatively unimportant federal program in dollar terms, it is in any event ignored here. It should be noted that a number of studies indicate that being employed for a limited number of hours in an on-campus job while in school tends to encourage persistence in college, apparently by increasing the students' commitment to and integration with the institution. This phenomenon is apparently independent of the net cost considerations this chapter focuses on. See Newman 1985.

policy is likely to be sensitive to how the policy change affects the net cost of different alternatives. Thus a policy change whose main effect is to increase the aid at alternatives previously ranked low by potential students may affect choice while having little effect on access (principally changing the destinations of students who were college bound anyway), while a change that reduces net costs at all institutions without affecting relative prices may promote access without affecting choice. The actual targeting of aid among institution types is likely to have an important influence on its effects, and these are not easy to sort out.

Findings: A Summary of the Literature

A great many studies over the years have attempted to estimate the impact of the price or net cost of education on students' postsecondary education decisions.[7] A minority of those studies have tried to measure specifically the effect of student aid on enrollment decisions, with the rest focusing on the impact of tuition price.[8] Although the studies differ widely in data sources and estimation techniques, they tend to agree on two main points. First, student decisions to enroll in college respond positively, and nontrivially, to price cuts or aid increases. Second, decisions about where to attend school also respond nontrivially to changes in the relative prices of schooling alternatives.

Rather than providing still another review of this large and complex literature, it may be more enlightening to review one exemplary study in some depth, elaborating the discussion with evidence from other studies and literature reviews. The study to be focused on is that by Charles Manski and David Wise.[9] This study is similar in basic approach to several other studies of individual student behavior, which rely on evidence concerning student characteristics and choices from large-scale surveys of young high school graduates.

Access

The Manski-Wise analysis proceeds in several steps. Starting from data for a sample of 1972 high school graduates, the authors first construct for each student a choice set of institutions to which the student could be admitted, that set depending on the student's academic performance and geographic location. The authors then perform an analysis estimating the amount of aid any given student would have been offered at each institution in his or her choice

---

7. A number of able surveys of this literature exist. A recent one, which provides references to many of its predecessors, is Leslie and Brinkman 1987.

8. Again, Leslie and Brinkman 1988 provide a helpful review of the literature.

9. Manski and Wise 1983.

set.[10] The final step, given knowledge of the characteristics of these young people and of the academic institutions and the nonschooling alternatives available to them, is to estimate a statistical model that best explains the choices these young people actually made among schooling and nonschooling alternatives.

More specifically, the authors develop in this last step an equation that indicates the probability that a person with given characteristics (income, race, academic background, and so on) will select a school with particular characteristics (price, aid offer, quality, and so on). The maximum-likelihood parameter estimates of this multinomial logit model are chosen to yield a predicted enrollment pattern that matches the actual outcomes as closely as possible. This equation can then be used to estimate how actual enrollment patterns would differ if some of these student or institutional characteristics were to change—if, for example, incomes or Scholastic Aptitude Test scores rose or if institutional costs rose.

In particular, the authors were able to simulate the effects of changes in student aid policy on enrollment patterns. They used their model to estimate how 1979 enrollment patterns would differ depending on whether the Pell grant program was or was not available to students. Specifically, the estimated model was used to forecast a student's response to changes in the cost of enrolling at different schools. The sample of students was weighted to match the national population of 1979 high school seniors and predictions were made for Pell awards during the 1979–80 academic year. Enrollment impacts of the program were then computed and compared with the hypothetical situation in which 1979 conditions are preserved but there is no Pell program. Their main finding was that the Pell grant program should have had a substantial effect on access. By their estimate, the Pell grant program left enrollments 21 percent higher than they would have been without Pell, with the increases heavily concentrated at two-year colleges and among students from lower income families. The predicted response by income group varies greatly: there is a 59 percent enrollment increase for low-income students, a 12 percent increase for middle-income students, and only a 3 percent increase for upper-income students.

As with most econometric studies, a detailed look at the Manski-Wise results exposes some puzzles. The large enrollment effect they find at two-year colleges stems from the fact that they find that two-year enrollments

---

10. The National Longitudinal Survey of the High School Class of 1972 does not contain good information on the aid offers students actually did or might have received from institutions in their choice set that they did not attend. The imputations Manski and Wise developed were derived from an equation relating the aid offers students actually received at institutions they attended to such characteristics of the students as their academic achievements and parents' incomes and of the institutions as their tuition and type (four-year or two-year).

respond much more strongly to aid increases than to price cuts. They do not find anything comparable to this result for other types of schools, nor is the finding replicated in other studies. Moreover, as noted above, theory suggests that grant increases should have a smaller effect than price cuts, because they are harder to learn about. If the aid effect at two-year colleges is set equal to the effect of price changes of the same magnitude, the effect of the Pell program on total enrollment drops to 6 percent.

On the other hand, the effect of the Pell program on four-year enrollments in the Manski-Wise study is puzzlingly small (virtually zero percent). Other studies, notably those by J. B. Schwartz, find substantial effects of public grants on four-year college enrollment.[11] It may be that a technical feature of the Manski-Wise estimation procedure produces an underestimate of the enrollment effect at four-year colleges.[12]

Several key features of the Manski-Wise findings on the access effects of Pell grants are corroborated by other studies. Leslie and Brinkman (1988) identify six studies in addition to Manski and Wise that contained useful estimates of the effects of grant aid on enrollment levels.[13] While differing widely in data sources and estimation techniques, the studies all find substantial effects of grant aid on enrollment levels, and find those effects to be stronger among lower income students. Jensen (1983), in a survey of the literature outside the discipline of economics, similarly concludes that there is strong evidence of positive effects of financial aid on access to college, especially among students from relatively disadvantaged backgrounds. Hauptman and McLaughlin (1988), in summarizing the econometric literature, agree that enrollments rise in response to additional aid availability and that lower income students are more influenced by aid than are students from more affluent families.

Estimates developed by Leslie and Brinkman from their analysis of the seven econometric studies suggest that the Pell program as it existed at the end of the 1970s should have raised lower income enrollment by between 20 and 40 percent, implying an increase in total enrollment of roughly 10 to 20 percent. They point out that these results indicate that roughly 500,000 to 1 million low-income students and approximately 400,000 middle-income stu-

---

11. Schwartz 1985 and 1986.

12. Their simulation technique requires the assumption that the availability of Pell grants will not induce any increase in applications to four-year colleges; the only effect allowed for is increased enrollment among students who (without Pells) apply to and are admitted to at least one four-year school but do not enroll. Since, in their sample, about 65 percent of the eligible population never are accepted for admission at a four-year college, this assumption sharply limits the possible effect they could have found.

13. The six studies are Berne 1980, Blakemore and Low 1985, Carlson 1975, Crawford 1966, Carroll et al. 1977, and Jackson 1978.

dents are enrolled in college because of grant aid. The midpoint of the total of these figures is slightly over 1 million students, approximately 16 percent of all full-time students.

Further econometric support for this finding is provided by the many studies that estimate the effect of tuition variations on enrollment behavior. Although changes in grant awards may have somewhat different effects on enrollments from tuition changes that have equivalent effects on net price, the size of those effects and their variation across income classes should be similar. It is therefore reassuring to note that most studies of enrollment demand find significant positive effects of tuition reductions on enrollment levels and find that the enrollment effects (in percentage terms) are larger for lower income students.[14] Leslie and Brinkman (1987) find that a consensus of the studies they survey puts the effects of a price cut of $100 (1982–83 academic year dollars) on national enrollment of eighteen-to-twenty-four-year-olds at about 1.8 percent. On the assumption that a price cut has equal effect with a grant increase of the same magnitude, the Pell program as it existed in 1979 should have boosted total enrollment by roughly 10 to 15 percent, compared to what enrollments would have been in that year without the program.[15] This estimate is roughly comparable to estimates like those of Manski and Wise that try to measure the effect of grant aid directly.

Perhaps the most important limitation of the Manski-Wise effort and most of the other studies discussed so far lies in their reliance on data that predate the major expansion in federal student aid beginning in the early 1970s.[16] Thus, the Manski-Wise effort to stimulate the effects of Pell relies on estimates of student responsiveness to student aid grants available in 1972, under award programs that differed significantly in structure and sources from the Pell program. In the late 1980s, a data set (High School and Beyond) based on a survey of 1980 high school graduates became available from the federal government. Although relatively few econometric studies of enrollment behavior based on these data are yet complete, findings that are available suggest that results from these data will be broadly similar to earlier results. Schwartz (1986), for example, has reported on a study examining the effects

---

14. See Leslie and Brinkman 1987 for a comprehensive survey. For an analytically oriented survey that examines the relation between income levels and price responsiveness of enrollment, see McPherson 1978.

15. This assumes an average Pell award of about $1,000 (1979 dollars) per recipient and that about half of freshmen should have been eligible for Pell under 1979 rules. Manski and Wise (1983, 21) estimate an eligibility rate of around two-thirds and an average award of slightly below $1,000.

16. All but one of the econometric studies of access discussed by Leslie and Brinkman (see note 13 above) rely on data from 1972 or earlier. The first year in which students received awards from the Pell (BEOG) program was 1974.

of grants and loans on enrollment at four-year colleges. He found that about 21 percent of low-income enrollment at four-year colleges was accounted for by Pell, and smaller percentages of higher-income enrollments; results that are broadly consistent with other findings reported here. St. John and Noell (1988), using High School and Beyond along with the National Longitudinal Survey of the High School Class of 1972, also found that financial aid had a positive impact on enrollment decisions, with scholarships and grants having the largest effect among aid packages for minority applicants.

Choice

Empirical findings about the effects of grants on choice—the decision about where to enroll in college—are much more unsettled than the access findings. Part of the reason is that there has been less agreement in the literature about precisely what questions should be studied. Several studies have adopted the perspective of the individual institution, asking to what degree students with particular characteristics may be influenced in choosing that institution by varying the amount or kinds of aid they are offered. These studies, in effect, attempt to help institutions measure the effectiveness of student aid as a marketing or recruiting tool.

Other studies have instead been concerned with the responsiveness of national enrollment patterns to changes in the relative prices of different schooling alternatives, with student aid viewed as one source of relative price variation. Still other studies have been concerned to ask how big an impact the actual patterns of student aid we observe nationally have had on the enrollment destinations of students.

It is important to recognize that each of these types of study is very different from the others. It is conceivable, for example, that differences in aid offers might have a big influence on which school was chosen from within a particular broad class of schools but very little influence on what broad class of school was chosen. To take a Chicago example, perhaps aid offers make a big difference on students' choice between Loyola and Depaul, or between Chicago and Northwestern, but almost no influence on the choice between a Catholic comprehensive university and a secular research university. It is apparent that the outcome of any choice study may be extremely sensitive to just how the alternatives facing students are specified and that attempts to generalize from disparate studies are quite hazardous.

There is also a major difference between asking how responsive students are to relative price changes and asking how large an impact the national aid distribution has on choice. The latter question combines the issue of student responsiveness with the issue of how large an effect the aid pattern has on relative prices (the latter being essentially a supply rather than a demand side question).

Despite these complications, some generalizations do emerge. Institutionally oriented studies tend to show that substantial differences in aid offers can be effective in attracting students. These studies rely on data reporting the relative amounts of aid offered by a particular institution along with other institutions to which a sample of students were admitted. The usual finding is that the attractiveness of the aid package significantly affects student destinations.[17]

Tierney (1980) examined the choices made by Pennsylvania students who were admitted to schools that differed substantially in cost. Tierney had available data files with exceptionally good information on the costs (including aid) facing students at these institutions and on the students' personal and academic characteristics. His studies too show significant responsiveness of choice to relative prices: as differences in tuition between public and private institutions increased, the probability of matriculating at a public institution rose. However, as private institutions offer more grants and scholarships relative to public institutions, the probability of matriculating at a private institution rises.

In summarizing the literature, Jensen (1983) states that financial aid has a substantial influence on institutional choice for students who are accepted by two or more colleges. Leslie and Brinkman (1988) conclude that student aid is an effective way of changing net price differentials among competing institutions—all else equal, an institution can increase its enrollment share by offering more aid. Manski and Wise (1983) also find that college financial aid offers could play an important role in affecting choice among schools. However, in terms of the specific effect of the Pell program on institutional choice, Leslie and Brinkman report that there is less agreement in the literature. Of critical importance is the effect of federal student aid on institutional behavior. Specifically, do institutions raise tuitions in response to increases in federal student aid? We return to this question below.

History: Does Reality Look Like What the Studies Suggest?

These econometric findings create an expectation that it should be possible to detect effects of changing student aid policy in the national time-series data. In this section, we examine evidence on historical trends in pricing, student aid, and enrollment in U.S. higher education, to compare these historical data with the econometric evidence.

---

17. See, for example, Ehrenberg and Sherman 1984 for a study of Cornell.

The econometric evidence suggests that student decisions about whether to enroll and where to enroll are influenced in the expected directions and by significant amounts by changes in the net costs of schooling and of different schooling options. At the same time, federal student aid policies have sufficiently changed over the past two decades in both their magnitude and targeting that they should have had some discernible impact on the relative prices facing undergraduate students.

However, actually tracing these influences is complicated for several reasons. First, changes in federal student aid policy are blended in the time-series data with other forces affecting net costs facing students. Changes in tuition rates and in schools' own expenditures on student aid grants have also been important influences on net costs in recent decades, and both theory and econometric evidence tell us that it is these net costs of attendance that influence student behavior. Second, the distribution of federal student aid among income classes has itself fluctuated considerably in recent years. It is sometimes suggested that federal student aid has been a force consistently lowering the net costs of attendance for lower income students compared to others; but in some years, especially at the end of the 1970s, substantial federal aid went to middle- and upper-middle-income students, complicating the picture substantially. Finally, and related, the mix of federal student aid between grants and loans has changed substantially over time. According to data presented in Gillespie and Carlson 1983 and Lewis 1988, the share of federal loans was only about 60 percent of the total grant and loan volume in 1975 and 62 percent in 1979 and had risen to 71 percent in 1985.[18] Judgments about the relative impact of grants and loans on student behavior should therefore importantly color one's expectations about the influence of federal student aid on enrollment patterns.

A final and quite significant complication is that fully adequate data on aid distributions over time simply do not exist in any consistent series. Data are particularly weak for the period before 1974, when the advent of the Basic Grant program made the need for the collection of student aid data more obvious. Before that time, we have only partial and episodic information. After 1974, the managers of the American Freshman survey began to include a series of detailed questions on the sources and amounts of financial assistance received by surveyed freshmen. These responses provide a fairly complete picture for freshmen of their own perceptions of how their education is being financed. It is necessary to be cautious about interpreting these numbers, since students may be unclear not only about the amount but especially

---

18. The shift toward loans is more dramatic when social security and the GI Bill are included. In 1975, new guaranteed loans were about 21 percent of total federal grants and loans, in 1979 they were 42 percent, and by 1985 they had risen to 63 percent.

about the form (grant versus loan) and source (federal government versus state government versus institution) of the aid they receive.[19] Despite these limitations, however, the American Freshman data, which are used extensively below, provide a helpful baseline for years after 1974 that does not exist for earlier years.

Federal Aid Over Time

Table 1 presents data from the College Board showing the overall magnitudes of federal student aid, expressed in constant dollars, for selected years since 1963. Trends for the 1970s and 1980s are dominated by so-called specially directed aid, funds provided to veterans and to children of social security recipients attending college. Although it makes sense to label each of these programs student aid, since awards are contingent on college attendance, neither was designed principally with higher education in mind, and neither fits the model of need-based student aid. Both programs were very large in the mid-1970s and have dwindled to almost nothing in the 1980s.[20]

When these programs are put aside, the generally available student aid programs administered by the Office (later Department) of Education predominate. The so-called campus-based programs (National Defense [later Direct] Student Loans, College Work Study, and SEOGs) have not grown much since their inception in the mid-1960s, with the result that the GSL Program (now called Stafford loans) and the BEOG (later Pell Grant) program have gradually become the main sources of federal student aid.

The period from 1965 to 1985 can in fact be usefully divided into three subperiods. From 1965 to 1973, a fairly modest total of federal generally available aid was divided between GSL and the campus based programs. From 1973 to 1980, the federal aid budget grew rapidly, with expenditures on Pell roughly keeping pace with growing numbers of dollars lent through GSL. After 1981, GSL growth has continued to be substantial, while real growth has essentially stopped in the Pell grant and the campus-based programs.

This changing mix and level of federal aid must be seen against a background of changing tuition prices in higher education. Figure 1 shows the

---

19. The survey is also forced to rely on self-reported family incomes. This survey is administered by institutions that elect to participate, and the setting in which it is administered may vary among institutions. The sample of institutions is therefore self-selected rather than random (institutions are only included in the sample if they survey a large fraction of their freshmen) and substantially underrepresents two-year colleges. Proprietary institutions, mostly vocational-technical institutions, are not included.

20. The social security benefit to college students was phased out as part of the budget reconciliation process in 1981. The reduction in GI Bill spending results both from changes in the program and from reductions in numbers of young veterans following the end of the Vietnam War.

TABLE 1. Federal Aid Awarded to Students by Source, Selected Academic Years (constant 1982 dollars in millions)

	1963–64	1970–71	1975–76	1979–80	1981–82	1983–84	1985–86
Generally available aid							
Pell grants			$ 1,629	$ 3,113	$ 2,358	$ 2,648	$ 3,163
SEOG		$ 325	350	414	371	342	364
State Student Incentive Grant			34	95	79	57	67
College work-study		552	513	740	640	648	582
National Direct Student Loan	$356	584	800	803	595	647	623
GSL, Parent Loan for Undergraduate Students, and Supplementary Loan for Students		2,466	2,204	4,880	7,407	7,183	7,838
Subtotal	$356	$3,927	$ 5,530	$10,045	$11,450	$11,525	$12,637
Subsidy value of generally available aid[a]	$178	$1,850	$ 3,515	$ 6,464	$ 6,809	$ 6,962	$ 7,825
Specially directed aid							
Social security		$1,212	$ 1,901	$ 1,972	$ 2,047	$ 209	
Veterans	$211	2,724	7,271	2,218	1,385	1,088	$ 753
Other grants	27	39	110	142	112	62	60
Other loans		102	78	52	111	250	330
Subtotal	$238	$4,077	$ 9,360	$ 4,384	$ 3,655	$ 1,609	$ 1,143
Total federal aid	$594	$8,004	$14,890	$14,429	$15,105	$13,134	$13,780

Source: Gillespie and Carlson 1983; Lewis 1988.

[a]Subsidy value calculation values loans at one-half their face value and values work-study aid at $0.

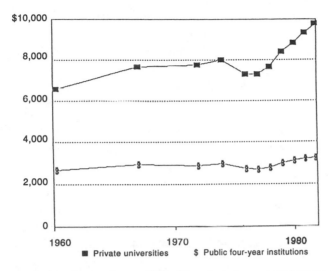

Fig. 1. Costs of attendance, 1963–85, selected years and institution types (in 1982 dollars)

course of real tuition at public four-year colleges and private universities for selected years from 1963–64 through 1985–86. Here again, three rough periods suggest themselves: from 1965 to the early 1970s tuition rose relative to price; from the early 1970s until around 1980, tuition fell behind the rapid inflation of those years; and from 1980 to the mid-1980s, it has been rising rapidly compared to inflation, especially in private higher education. Thus, the overall tendency has been for tuition to rise more rapidly in periods when federal student aid has grown slowly or declined, while slow growth in tuition has coincided with periods of rapid increase in federal student aid.

A more focused picture of trends in the level and distribution of generally available aid can be derived from the American Freshman Survey. The tables and figures that follow focus on a limited subgroup of American undergraduates: young (ages eighteen to twenty-four), full-time freshmen in residence at traditional two- and four-year colleges. This subgroup has always been an important target of the federal student aid programs and has the advantage of providing a fairly well-defined universe for comparisons over time.[21]

21. The specially directed aid programs (principally GI Bill and social security) do not appear importantly in these data, apparently for two reasons. First, much of this money probably went to students outside the subsample reported here, which is limited to first-time, full-time freshman resident dependent students ages twenty-four and below. Second, many students who were recipients of either social security survivor benefits or of GI Bill assistance may not have reported it as student aid.

The distribution of federal aid among income classes of students has by no means been constant over time. MISAA increased the grant and loan money available to higher income students—effects that were gradually reversed in the 1980s. There also was a real contraction in federal grant money for the lowest income students in the 1980s.

Student opportunities throughout this period were affected not just by changes in federal student aid policies but by changes in schools' tuition charges and in aid available from nonfederal sources as well. At private four-year colleges, this nonfederal aid is especially important, amounting in some years to more than a third of the subsidy value of student aid available to low-income freshmen.[22] Moreover, it is not only low-income students who benefit from nonfederal grant aid. At many private institutions, students with incomes between $10,000 and $20,000 receive almost as much nonfederal grant aid per student as the lowest income group. It is also clear that the amount of nonfederal aid going to more affluent students (partly in the form of merit grants) has been rising in recent years.

Although no summary measure can be fully adequate, it is helpful to boil down the changes in tuition and in various forms of aid to a manageable index. One way of doing that is to estimate the subsidy value of the aid received by a particular subclass of students, recognizing that the subsidy value of a loan is less than that of a grant. Per student subsidies are computed here by combining all sources of aid and putting the subsidy value of a federal loan at half the amount lent. These numbers can be combined with estimates of the cost of attendance (including books and room and board as well as tuition) to come up with an estimate of the net cost of attending college. Figures 2 and 3 report these net cost figures for students of different income levels (in 1978 dollars) at public and private institutions.

It is very important to stress that these net cost figures are influenced by factors other than federal aid. At public institutions, the principal contribution to changes in the net cost of education is change in the cost of attendance. That is especially true of the period since 1979, when that factor accounts for more than 80 percent of the change in net cost, except in the lowest income group. At private institutions, changes in nonfederal aid were more important than federal aid in bringing costs down in the 1970s, while increases in the cost of attendance have been the predominant cost-raising factor for most income groups in the 1980s. In general, changes in federal student aid policy play a nontrivial but far from dominant role in producing variations over time in the net costs to students of attending college.

Figures 2 and 3 show that for students at both public and private institutions, and at all income levels, net costs for the 1970s and 1980s have

---

22. The subsidy value calculation is discussed below.

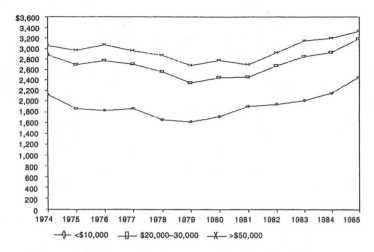

Fig. 2. Net cost of attendance for three income groups, public institutions (in 1978 dollars). (*Source:* American Freshman Survey.)

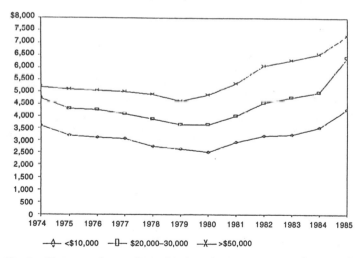

Fig. 3. Net cost of attendance for three income groups, private institutions (in 1978 dollars). (*Source:* American Freshman Survey.)

followed a similar U-shaped pattern. Costs in general fell for all groups of students in the late 1970s and rose in the early 1980s, and in general the dollar amounts of cost change for different groups were roughly similar. For lower- and middle-income students, the cost increase in the 1980s is caused partly by the shift from grants to loans in federal student aid. The overall result is that the student aid system has not succeeded in insulating needier students from changes in the costs of college that affect more affluent students.

To the degree that net costs influence student enrollment decisions, what do these trends lead us to expect to find in the enrollment data that we turn to next? Several points deserve emphasis.

1. It is important to stress that the basic pattern of net cost trends is very similar for different income groups and at different types of institution. All groups tended to benefit from cost reductions in the 1970s and to suffer from cost increases in the 1980s. There is no reason to think federal student aid would have produced strong differentials among enrollment patterns of different groups of schools and students over this period.
2. Still, we should expect to find some detectable influence on the enrollment patterns of the lowest income group of students through this period, both absolutely and compared to other groups, for two reasons.

   a. Lower-income students on the whole experienced a larger percentage reduction in costs in the late 1970s, and a larger percentage increase in costs in the 1980s, than other groups.
   b. The econometric evidence implies that lower income students are more sensitive to price changes of given magnitude than are more affluent students.

We thus should expect to see a relative increase in low-income students' participation rates in the late 1970s and a relative decline in the 1980s.

Enrollment Patterns over Time

It is useful to divide the historical data on enrollment effects of student aid into three periods: that before 1974, preceding the introduction of the Basic Grants program; that from 1974 to 1980, when federal funding for student aid grew sharply in real terms; and that following 1980, when federal student aid funding failed to keep pace with inflation.[23]

Ideally, one would want to control for differences in ability in an enrollment analysis. Obviously, an important aim of federal aid policy is to move toward the equalization of enrollment rates among individuals with similar abilities but different income backgrounds. As indicated in table 2, enrollment rates for students with the highest skills but from the poorest families have not risen from 1961 to 1980 and are still about one-third less than the rates for students with equal ability but from the richest families. Regrettably, our capacity to pursue this important issue in more depth is impaired by the absence of an annual time-series on enrollments by ability and social background.

A further point can be derived from the evidence in table 2. For students in each socioeconomic status group, those with higher levels of academic skills are substantially more likely to attend college. This suggests that policies addressed to raising the academic skill levels of precollege students have the potential to improve access to higher education.

We turn now to evidence on enrollment patterns by income class. The pre-1974 evidence is scattered. Data on the distribution of student aid by income class are very hard to obtain. Evidence on enrollment distributions are also shaky, partly owing to data availability problems but also owing to the fact that large swings in military personnel levels and recruitment policies complicate the interpretation of available data.

Nonetheless, fragmentary evidence suggests that the late 1960s and early 1970s were a period of rapid change in the socioeconomic composition of the U.S. college population. Davis and Johns (1982) examined data on the distribution of college freshmen by income class, as reported in the American Freshman survey. They found a marked increase in the fraction of students from families below the median and below the bottom quartile of U.S. incomes in those years. Similar findings, relying partly on other data, are reported in Carnegie Council (1980).[24]

It seems implausible to attribute very much of this important change to the direct effects of federal student aid policy. The federal commitment of dollars to the main Office of Education programs (Educational Opportunity Grants, college work-study, National Defense Student Loans, and GSL) remained modest through this period, with award levels in 1970 amounting to

---

23. For another discussion of time-series changes in enrollment see Hauptman and McLaughlin 1988.

24. Leslie and Brinkman (1988) discuss additional studies of enrollment changes over time for various economic and demographic groups.

just 9 percent of total tuition revenues in higher education. And of that total, a large fraction (78 percent) was in the form of guaranteed loans, which were not at that time strongly targeted on the neediest students. More likely, the proximate causes of the change in enrollment patterns are to be found in changed policies at the state and institutional levels, and in changed social attitudes. The most prominent state-level effort was the dramatic expansion in community colleges and urban state-run four-year colleges in the 1960s. These institutions were geographically closer to disadvantaged populations than traditional state universities and often adopted open admissions policies that encouraged the enrollment of educationally disadvantaged students, who are disproportionately from poor economic backgrounds. Meanwhile, Gillespie and Carlson (1983) point out that private colleges and universities expanded their own student aid efforts by 149 percent from 1963 to 1970. Further, it may be that they targeted their funds more heavily on lower income students. Finally, the strong societywide concern in the late 1960s for combating poverty and promoting racial equality should not be neglected. These forces led to stronger recruiting efforts directed toward disadvantaged youth, and probably had effects as well on the college-going aspirations of minority and low-income students.

While these effects probably outweighed any direct effects of federal student aid spending in increasing lower income enrollments from 1965 to

TABLE 2. Percent of High School Graduates Entering Postsecondary Education in the Year Following Graduation, by Academic Skills and Socioeconomic Status, Selected Years

Skill Quartile	Year of Graduation	Socioeconomic Status		
		Low	Middle	High
1 (low)	1961–63	13.5	23.8	41.5
	1972	17.8	20.8	34.6
	1980	20.8	25.8	39.7
2	1961–63	23.5	35.8	55.0
	1972	25.3	34.7	52.6
	1980	31.1	39.3	68.1
3	1961–63	37.5	51.0	76.5
	1972	37.7	50.5	71.5
	1980	46.7	59.4	77.4
4 (high)	1961–63	59.5	77.3	91.0
	1972	58.2	67.6	84.4
	1980	58.0	76.3	86.4

Source: Project Talent, National Longitudinal Study, and High School and Beyond, as compiled in The Eureka Project, "The Critical Difference." Reproduced from Hauptman and McLaughlin 1988, table 6.

1974, the indirect effects of federal aid policy on this climate of opinion should not be overlooked. States and private institutions may well have been encouraged in their willingness to expand commitments to education for disadvantaged students by the knowledge that the federal government was putting some support behind those efforts and seemed likely to increase that support. Student expectations may have been similarly affected. The anticipation of an expanded federal role in student finance in the 1970s may have produced some effect on enrollments even before it came into being; it is not possible, however, to measure the magnitude of such a conjectured effect.

The period 1974–85 saw an expanded federal aid commitment that then dwindled, as well as a shift in emphasis from grants to loans. As noted earlier, the period of expanding student aid was also a period of declining tuition (in real terms), while in the 1980s tuition has rapidly risen as the growth in federal aid has slowed. As a result, all groups of students faced lower costs in the 1970s and higher ones in the 1980s.

Can we detect the effect of these swings in net costs on enrollment patterns and levels? Figures 4–6 show enrollment rates, expressed as a percentage of the eligible population, for African-American and white students of different income levels from 1974 to 1985.[25] The enrollment rates are for full-time dependent students, the group on whom federal student aid programs have been most consistently targeted. In these aggregate enrollment graphs, there is no evident effect of net costs of attendance on enrollment for families with incomes above $30,000 (1978 dollars). For families with incomes between $10,000 and $30,000, there appears to be an effect for African-American but not for white students, with the enrollment rate of African-Americans higher in the 1970s when net costs were lower and lower in the 1980s when net costs rose. From 1977 through 1981 the African-American enrollment rate among this middle-income group averaged 38 percent; from 1981 through 1985 it averaged 33 percent.

An even more distinct swing, involving both white and African-American students, is evident for the lowest income group, those with incomes below $10,000 in 1978 terms. The white enrollment rate fell distinctly but modestly from the latter half of the 1970s to the 1980s; the 1975–79 average rate was 33 percent, while from 1981 to 1985 the average rate was 29

---

25. These data are derived from the U.S. Bureau of the Census Current Population Survey data tapes. Enrollments are full time only. The eligible population is defined as persons aged eighteen to twenty-four, financially dependent on their parents, who have completed high school but have not completed four years or more of college. The enrollment figures are for students from this population who are enrolled in college. Figures are reported only for white and African-American students because the "other" race category provides too small a sample for statistical reliability.

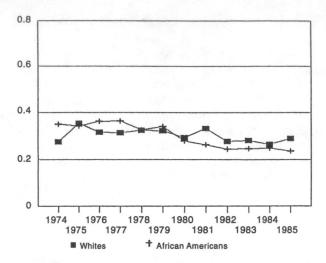

Fig. 4.   Enrollment rates, 1974–85, African-Americans and whites, income below $10,000. Income is in 1978 dollars. (*Source:* Current Population Survey.)

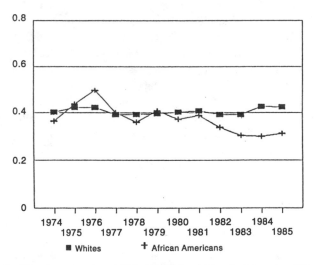

Fig. 5.   Enrollment rates, 1974–85, African-Americans and whites, income $10,000–$30,000. Income is in 1978 dollars. (*Source:* Current Population Survey.)

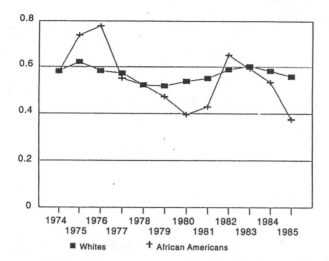

Fig. 6. Enrollment rates, 1974–85, African-Americans and whites, income above $30,000. Income is in 1978 dollars. (*Source:* Current Population Survey.)

percent. For African-Americans, the drop-off is dramatic: average enrollment rates fell from 35 percent to 25 percent between 1975–79 and 1981–85.

Is this general pattern consistent with student aid changes having played a significant role? As noted above, net cost changes in percentage terms were somewhat larger for lower income students, and econometric evidence leads us to expect that that group will respond more sensitively to relative price changes of given magnitude. It thus seems plausible that the change in federal student aid policy, which contributed significantly to the changes in net cost facing lower income students, played a substantial role in reducing lower income enrollment rates in the 1980s.

However, it would be reckless to attribute the whole shift in enrollments to that cause. The 1980s have seen a greater emphasis on imposing demanding admissions criteria on postsecondary institutions, and these standards tend to weigh heaviest on low-income and especially minority students. Many observers also argue that the strong affirmative action commitment to enrolling and retaining African-American and other minority students lost some of its force in the 1980s.

A slightly different way of looking at these data may also prove illuminating. W. Lee Hansen (1983) has suggested that it is useful to look at relative enrollment rates of more and less affluent students in gauging the impact of federal student aid, on the grounds that federal student aid is the most obvious factor that should affect the enrollment behavior of these two groups differentially. He used Current Population Survey (CPS) data in examining enrollment rates for students from families with dependents aged eighteen through twenty-four for two time periods: 1971–72 and 1978–79. He then calculated the ratio of the enrollment rates of below- to above-median-income families in the two periods and found that the ratios declined for whites, African-Americans, men, and women. When a weighted average was taken for whites and African-Americans and for men and women, the ratios again fell between the two periods.

The conclusion from this study is well-known among researchers and policymakers:

> These data force one to conclude that the greater availability of student financial aid, targeted largely toward students from below-median-income families, did little, if anything, to increase access. The results certainly do not accord with expectations that access would increase for lower-income dependents relative to higher-income dependents. (Hansen 1983, 93)

There are some obvious limitations in interpreting this kind of snap-shot comparison at two points in time. First, year-to-year fluctuations may obscure underlying trends, so that increasing the number of years in the comparisons is helpful. Second, controlling for variation in other factors that affect the demand for enrollment is not possible with this methodology. Such factors as overall economic conditions, changes in rates of return to higher education, and changes in opportunity costs of college enrollment (as produced, for example, by changes in the draft law) may influence the comparison if they affect different income groups differently. Finally, this kind of comparison is not responsive to changes over time in the targeting of student aid. As we have noted above, during the 1970s the total amount of federal student aid not only substantially increased but also significantly changed in its distribution. A larger fraction of available aid was targeted at middle- and upper-income students in the late 1970s, tending to obscure any effect on differential enrollment rates that might have occurred.

Some of these limitations can be dealt with by extending the analysis to more years, and by relating the enrollment fluctuations to what we know about year to year fluctuations in amounts and targeting of aid. An extension to more years is offered in figure 7, which displays a three-year moving average of the ratio of the enrollment rates for the lowest (below $10,000) and highest (above $30,000) income groups (in 1978 dollars) over time, looking separately at white and African-American students. Although the trends are similar for both racial groups, the changes are much sharper for African-Americans than whites. The late 1970s saw a relative increase in the ratio of

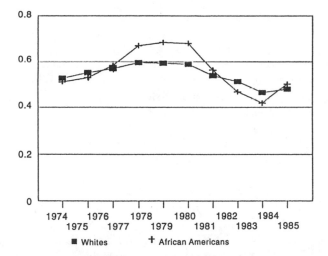

Fig. 7. Ratio of low- to high-income enrollment rates, three-year moving averages, 1975–84 (low-income = $0–10,000 in 1978 dollars, high-income > $30,000 in 1978 dollars)

low-income to high-income enrollment, and the early 1980s have seen a decrease, with some recovery in the mid 1980s. For African-Americans the swing is marked: low-income African-Americans enrolled at more than 70 percent of the high-income African-American rate in 1979; by 1982 the ratio was just over 40 percent. For whites the change in the ratio was from about 60 percent to under 50 percent.

This narrowing of differences between upper-income and lower-income participation rates in the late 1970s was importantly influenced by a decline in upper-income enrollment rates in the late 1970s, a decline for which there is no obvious explanation. (It certainly was not caused by federal student aid policy, which was becoming more generous to affluent students in those years.) It is, however, possible that the reason that lower income students did not share in that decline was that substantial federal student aid was available to them. The underlying reasoning here is that the forces (whatever they were) pressing down on higher income enrollments should have applied across the board; therefore, the failure of lower income enrollments to decline in the late 1970s is backhanded evidence of the effectiveness of aid in bolstering enrollments in that group. This argument is plausible, but not very strong. That the real decline in federal aid in the 1980s was accompanied by a distinct drop in the lower income enrollment rate, while the upper-income rate stayed more or less constant, seems considerably more convincing.

These data suggest that extending the Hansen time-series analysis to more years, and taking closer account of changes in federal aid targeting, raises questions about the strong conclusion that federal aid was without effect. These extensions do not, however, adequately deal with one of the most important concerns about such an examination of trend data: the need for an estimation method in which the strength of the relationship between cost variation and enrollment variation is systematically measured. We attempt to respond to that concern with the regression analysis in the following section.

Further Analysis: Is There Really an Inconsistency between Econometric Results and History?

Summarizing the above discussion, researchers have found significant econometric evidence of a rather large enrollment response to changes in student aid. However, despite substantial variation in aid over time, enrollment responses are not readily detected in national time-series data. This earlier work has failed to subject these data to econometric analysis.

Table 3 summarizes data on net cost of attendance for different income groups from 1974 to 1984. Table 4 summarizes enrollment data by income group over the same period. These data were the basis for much of the discussion in the previous section, and a disaggregated version is now the data source for an econometric examination. Specifically, individual data points are averages of enrollment rates and net cost for particular demographic and income groups.

Since this is a relatively unusual data set, it may be worth a paragraph to spell out more clearly how these regressions should be interpreted. The indi-

TABLE 3. Cost of Attendance, Net of Student Aid, by Income Group (1978 dollars)

	$0–10,000	$10,000–30,000	$30,000+
1974	$3,861	$3,772	$4,055
1975	3,726	3,677	3,955
1976	3,826	3,824	4,039
1977	3,728	3,710	3,945
1978	3,606	3,604	3,860
1979	3,437	3,467	3,742
1980	3,356	3,499	3,992
1981	3,382	3,524	4,108
1982	3,551	3,694	4,396
1983	3,740	3,980	4,734
1984	3,881	4,114	4,881

Source: American Freshman Survey.

TABLE 4.   Enrollment Rates by Income Group, 1974–84

	$0–10,000	$10,000–30,000	$30,000+
1974	0.31	0.40	0.58
1975	0.35	0.43	0.62
1976	0.33	0.43	0.59
1977	0.34	0.40	0.57
1978	0.33	0.39	0.52
1979	0.33	0.40	0.52
1980	0.29	0.40	0.53
1981	0.31	0.41	0.55
1982	0.28	0.39	0.59
1983	0.27	0.38	0.60
1984	0.26	0.41	0.58

Source: CPS.

vidual data points in our regressions are an enrollment rate and an average net cost for a particular population subgroup (e.g., white women, incomes below $10,000) in a particular year. We employ three such data sets: one for public institutions, one for private institutions, and one that averages over public and private institutions. Investigations with the data suggest that small samples in the CPS data for African-Americans and other races make these data points inappropriate for time-series analysis at the level of disaggregation we employ. Therefore, the results we report here are limited to whites only. In the regressions that report on enrollments at public and private institutions separately, we are forced to exclude data for 1980 because mistakes made by the Bureau of the Census in coding the 1980 CPS make it impossible to distinguish public from private enrollments. Thus, regressions using the combined data set are based on sixty-six observations (three income groups, two genders, and eleven years). Regressions for public and for private institutions have sixty observations (three income groups, two genders, and ten years). Dummy variables and interaction terms are used to control for differences among income groups in the strength of the relationship between net cost and enrollment and in the average propensity to enroll. Differences between men and women in the average propensity to enroll are controlled for through the use of a gender dummy. Finally, the regressions contain a time trend testing for secular changes in enrollment propensities that are not captured by our other independent variables.

As noted earlier, students self-reported the data on student aid and family income in the American Freshman Survey. No doubt this self-reporting introduces measurement error in these variables. Nevertheless, we use these data for several reasons. First, they are the only consistently reported annual data on net costs and income. After the National Postsecondary Student Assistance Survey (NPSAS) has been replicated several times, this data file will provide a useful, and probably statistically superior, source for time-series analysis. Since at this point that survey has only been conducted once, it cannot be used in time-series analysis. Second, there is no reason to expect the biases in student reporting of income and costs to vary systematically over time. While it is quite likely that student reported data on family income and ways of paying for college are inaccurate in any particular year, their variation over time should be more reliable. Finally, we know of no reason why any systematic biases in these variables should be correlated with time-series variations in the dependent variable (the enrollment rate). Note that the dependent variable is obtained from a data set that is collected separately from these independent variables.

Nonetheless, we do have significant reservations about the adequacy of the CIRP data, even for time-series comparisons. It would be very useful to undertake some studies aimed at testing the accuracy of these data. One way of doing this would be to compare CIRP data with alternative data sources for particular years when good survey data are available—for example, the year when the High School and Beyond survey was conducted and the year when NPSAS was conducted. This could provide evidence of biases in the CIRP data and of any trends in those biases over time.

Table 5 presents regression results in which enrollment rates averaged across public and private institutions are explained by time-series changes in net cost and other variables. Given the nature of the data set, heteroskedasticity is a natural worry. Therefore, for all of the regression results that follow, estimated asymptotic covariance matrices were computed under the assumption of heteroskedasticity to calculate the standard errors.[26] These adjusted standard errors were used in all tests of significance. The regression equation includes a time trend along with a dummy variable for gender (1 for females and 0 for males) and dummy variables for the medium-income group (income between $10,000 and $30,000 in 1978 dollars) and for the high-income group (income over $30,000).[27] The aforementioned dummies allow the constant term in the regression to vary for different income groups and genders. In addition, the equation includes terms that interact income with the net cost variable, the gender dummy, and the time trend. These interaction terms permit the enrollment impact of net cost to vary across income groups, and also allow us to test for differences across income groups in the time trend

---

26. For the derivation of this technique, see White 1980.

27. The omitted categories for the dummies are incomes below $10,000 and males. The coefficients on the dummy variables in the regression predict differences relative to the omitted categories.

and in the impact of gender differences on enrollment. NETCSTHI interacts NETCOST with the dummy variable representing high income. NETCTMED interacts NETCOST with the medium-income dummy variable. TIMEHI and TIMEMED interact TIME with the income dummies, while FEMHI and FEMMED interact FEMALE with the income dummies.

An example may clarify the interpretation of these interaction effects. The coefficient on NETCOST (call it c) measures the effect of changes in net cost on enrollment among low-income students. The coefficient on NETCSTHI (call it h) measures the *difference* between the effect of net cost on high-income and on low-income students, while the standard error on NETCSTHI indicates the precision with which this difference is measured. The net effect of changes in net cost on enrollment for high-income students is

TABLE 5. Regression Results—Combined Sample

	Dependent Variable: Enrollment Rate		
Root mean square error	0.02282611	R^2	0.9682
Dependent mean	0.4271738	Adjusted R^2	0.9617
Coefficient of variation	5.343517	N	66

Parameter Estimates

Variable	Parameter Estimate	Standard Error	T for H0: Parameter=0
INTERCEPT	0.461157	0.049629	9.292[a]
NETCOST	−0.000068	0.000023	−2.952[a]
TIME	0.003645	0.001755	−2.077[b]
FEMALE	0.048680	0.008753	5.561[a]
MED	−0.142580	0.063266	−2.254[b]
HIGH	−0.209977	0.073307	−2.864[a]
NETCSTHI	0.000155	0.000028	5.526[a]
NETCTMED	0.000091	0.000027	3.357[a]
TIMEHI	−0.003005	0.002773	−1.084
TIMEMED	0.002917	0.002096	1.392
FEMHI	−0.001193	0.013238	−0.090
FEMMED	−0.000261	0.010992	−0.024

Test:	NETCOST+NETCSTHI=0	χ^2:	32.57[a]
Test:	NETCOST+NETCTMED=0	χ^2:	2.85[c]
Test:	TIME+TIMEHI=0	χ^2:	9.59[a]
Test:	TIME+TIMEMED=0	χ^2:	0.40
Test:	FEMALE+FEMHI=0	χ^2:	22.86[a]
Test:	FEMALE+FEMMED=0	χ^2:	53.02[a]

[a]Significant at 0.01 level.
[b]Significant at 0.05 level.
[c]Significant at 0.10 level.

the algebraic sum of c and h. The statistical significance of this net effect cannot be read directly from the t-tests on the individual variables; instead, it is determined by testing the hypothesis that the sum of c and h is equal to zero. As seen in table 5, the Chi-square value equals 32.57, which is large enough to reject the hypothesis that the sum of c and h equals 0. Hence, there is a statistically significant effect of net cost on enrollment for high-income students.

We have the following expectations about the signs of the coefficients. The NETCOST coefficient, which measures the responsiveness of enrollment to net cost for the low-income group, should be negative (higher net cost discourages enrollment). The coefficient on NETCTMED measures the difference between the responsiveness of low- and middle-income students' enrollment to changes in net cost. Cross-sectional studies generally indicate that higher income students are less responsive to price than lower income students. We therefore expect the coefficient on NETCTMED to be positive, muting the negative effect of net cost on enrollment relative to that of lower income students. For the same reason we expect the coefficient on NETSCTHI to be positive (and larger than that on NETCTMED).

As table 5 shows, all the estimated coefficients on these net cost variables are significant with the expected sign. Increases in net cost lead to lower enrollment for the low-income group, and the interaction effects are positive and significant, showing that this effect is smaller for middle- and upper-income students. In fact, the coefficients on the net cost–income interaction terms are larger in absolute value than the coefficient on net cost, implying that the predicted effect of net cost on enrollment in this equation is positive for middle- and upper-income students.[28] For both groups, the net cost coefficient is statistically significant as well as positive. It is possible that this unexpected result for more affluent students is explained by a supply rather than a demand effect: a positive relationship between enrollment and net cost may come about because (particularly in the 1980s) a strong demand among middle- and upper-income students for higher education has caused colleges and universities to raise their prices.[29]

---

28. The values of the intercept and the MED and HIGH dummies imply that for all three income groups the intercept terms are positive but are a declining function of income. This may seem surprising, since we expect enrollment rates to vary positively with income. However, the presence of a negative net cost effect for the low-income group coupled with positive effects for the other income groups means that predicted levels of enrollment evaluated at means in fact increase with income.

29. Because enrollment rates are substantially higher for middle- and high-income students than for low-income students and because these students generally pay higher net costs than low-income students, it is more plausible to expect a supply response to the behavior of middle- and high-income students than to that of the low-income group. Ideally, we could test this

The negative coefficient on net cost implies that for lower-income students a $100 net cost increase results in an enrollment decline of about .68 percentage points, which is about a 2.2 percent decline in enrollment for that income group. We noted above that Leslie and Brinkman find a consensus in the literature that a $100 increase in net cost reduces enrollment rates by 1.8 percent. Converting our estimates in 1978–79 dollars to the 1982–83 equivalent relied on by Leslie and Brinkman, we find that a $100 cost increase results in a 1.6 percent enrollment decline for low-income students. The Leslie-Brinkman figure is in effect averaged over all income groups. As noted earlier, most studies find higher price responsiveness among lower income students. Manski and Wise's results, for example, suggest that a $100 net cost increase for low-income students (in 1979 dollars) leads to a 4.9 percent decline in enrollment.[30] The result here, while lower than the Manski-Wise estimate, seems broadly consistent with typical cross-sectional findings. The important point is that our econometrically controlled time-series analysis supports the view that changes in costs lead to changes in enrollment for low-income students.

We turn next to the coefficients relating to gender and to the time trend. The coefficient on the FEMALE variable indicates that over the 1974–84 period the enrollment rate for women tended to be about 5 percentage points higher than that for men. That the variables interacting FEMALE with income are close to zero and statistically insignificant indicates that this gender effect is constant across income groups. (Chi-square values show that the net effect of the female variable on enrollment is positive and significant for all three income groups.) The time trend is negative and significant for the low-income group, suggesting a tendency for the enrollment propensity for that group to fall over time, but it is important to note that the coefficient is quite small, with the estimated rate of decline being just .36 percentage points per year. The interaction effects imply that there is no significant time trend for middle-income students, but that there is a significant negative time trend of .66 percentage points per year for high-income students.

Tables 6 and 7 examine private enrollment and public enrollment separately. This breakdown is potentially important because the earlier analysis, in averaging over enrollments and over costs in the two sectors, may distort the picture of behavior in each of the sectors considered separately. The structure of the equations is similar to that in table 5, which combines public and private enrollment, except that the net cost variable (NETCSTPU and NETCSTPR, respectively) and the net cost-income interaction terms

---

conjecture about supply-side effects by including demand-shift variables in a multiequation analysis; that, however, is beyond the scope of the present study.

30. This coefficient is computed from information in Manski and Wise's tables 7.2 and 7.4.

TABLE 6. Regression Results—Private Institutions

Dependent Variable: Enrollment Rate			
Root mean square error	0.01379395	R^2	0.9404
Dependent mean	0.1108635	Adjusted R^2	0.9267
Coefficient of variation	12.44228	N	60

Parameter Estimates

Variable	Parameter Estimate	Standard Error	T for H0: Parameter=0
INTERCEPT	0.164585	0.019427	8.472[a]
NETCSTPR	−0.000036	0.000006	−6.272[a]
TIME	0.000487	0.000551	0.884
FEMALE	0.015657	0.004125	3.796[a]
MED	−0.027524	0.027085	−1.016
HIGH	−0.069076	0.053513	−1.291
NTCSTHPR	0.000052	0.000012	4.234[a]
NTCSTMPR	0.000023	0.000008	2.947[a]
TIMEHI	−0.003880	0.002022	−1.918[b]
TIMEMED	0.000156	0.000802	0.195
FEMHI	0.011529	0.009027	1.277
FEMMED	0.005081	0.005152	0.986

Test:	NETCSTPR+NTCSTHPR=0	χ^2:	2.22
Test:	NETCSTPR+NTCSTMPR=0	χ^2:	6.65[a]
Test:	TIME+TIMEHI=0	χ^2:	3.04[b]
Test:	TIME+TIMEMED=0	χ^2:	1.22
Test:	FEMALE+FEMHI=0	χ^2:	11.46[a]
Test:	FEMALE+FEMMED=0	χ^2:	45.11[a]

[a]Significant at 0.01 level.
[b]Significant at 0.10 level.

(NTCSTMPU and NTCSTHPU for public middle- and high-incomes and NTCSTMPR and NTCSTHPR for private middle- and high-incomes) are specific to the sector whose enrollment is being explained. It would be natural to test for the significance of variables measuring cross-price effects (for example, the effect of public sector prices on private enrollment). Unfortunately, a high correlation between the time-series for public and private net costs (on the order of 90 percent) makes it impossible to include both variables in the same equation.

Like in the combined equation, all the coefficients in the private and public equations that are significant have the expected sign. For private enrollment, we estimate that a $100 increase in net cost lowers enrollment by about 3.6 percent for low-income students. In the private equation, the net cost–middle-income interaction is significant, implying that the price responsiveness of students from middle-income families differs significantly from that of students from low-income families. The overall net effect of cost on private enrollment for middle-income families is negative and significant, indicating that, like for low-income students, rises in net cost reduce enrollment for middle-income students as well. The net cost–income interaction variable for students from high-income families is positive and significant, indicating that they are less responsive to price. However, the overall net effect of cost increases on high-income private enrollment is not significantly different from zero.

Continuing with the results for private enrollment in table 6, we find that low-income women have a significantly higher enrollment propensity than low-income men—that is, the coefficient on FEMALE is significantly differ-

TABLE 7.   Regression Results—Public Institutions

Dependent Variable: Enrollment Rate			
Root mean square error	0.02084145	R^2	0.9281
Dependent mean	0.3177716	Adjusted R^2	0.9117
Coefficient of variation	6.558626	N	60

Parameter Estimates

Variable	Parameter Estimate	Standard Error	T for H0: Parameter=0
INTERCEPT	0.327110	0.059491	5.498[a]
NETCSTPU	-0.000038	0.000034	-1.121
TIME	-0.003646	0.001960	-1.860[c]
FEMALE	0.028666	0.008981	3.192[a]
MED	-0.178774	0.072434	-2.468[b]
HIGH	-0.256200	0.076028	-3.370[a]
NTCSTHPU	0.000149	0.000038	3.905[a]
NTCSTMPU	0.000098	0.000038	2.588[b]
TIMEHI	0.003209	0.002350	1.365
TIMEMED	0.002631	0.002246	1.171
FEMHI	-0.007328	0.012655	-0.579
FEMMED	0.001272	0.011050	0.115

Test:	NETCSTPU+NTCSTHPU=0	χ^2:	43.17[a]
Test:	NETCSTPU+NTCSTMPU=0	χ^2:	13.84[a]
Test:	TIME+TIMEHI=0	χ^2:	0.11
Test:	TIME+TIMEMED=0	χ^2:	0.86
Test:	FEMALE+FEMHI=0	χ^2:	5.73[b]
Test:	FEMALE+FEMMED=0	χ^2:	21.63[a]

[a]Significant at 0.01 level.
[b]Significant at 0.05 level.
[c]Significant at 0.10 level.

ent from zero. Moreover, Chi-square values indicate that enrollment propensities in private colleges are also significantly higher for middle-income and high-income women than for men of the same income class. We find a .34 percentage point negative and significant time-trend for high-income students. The time trends for the low-income and middle-income groups are not significant.

Turning to the results for public enrollment in table 7, we find that the coefficient on net cost for low-income students has the expected negative sign but is not significant. As expected, the coefficients on the net cost-income interactions are both positive and significant. For both middle- and high-income groups, Chi-square values indicate that the net effect of cost on enrollment is positive and statistically significant. The FEMALE variable was significant for all income groups. The only significant time trend is a small negative one ($-.36$ percentage points per year) for low-income students at public institutions.

In a further refinement of the analysis, we break down net cost into its two components: the published tuition (the sticker price, called STIK in the table) and the subsidy value of aid (AID). This step serves the purposes, first, of shedding light on the relative magnitudes of the aid and sticker price effects and, second, of pushing the data to see if anomalies or inconsistencies surface. Table 8 reports these results for equations that average over public and private institutions. The coefficient on STIK and AID, which indicate effects for low-income students, have the expected sign—a higher sticker price lowers enrollment, and more aid raises enrollment. The sticker price coefficient is significant, but the AID coefficient fails to be significant at the 10 percent level. It is interesting to note that the parameter estimates are virtually identical (and the same as the net cost coefficient reported above), suggesting that aid and sticker price variations have similar effects.[31] The interaction coefficients all have the expected signs, indicating that both the negative effect of price and the positive effect of aid are muted as income rises. The interactions of STIK with income are statistically significant, while the interactions of AID with income are not. Considering the overall effects of the AID and STIK variables on the enrollment of middle- and high-income students, we find no significant effect of AID for either group, while STIK has a perverse positive effect for middle- and high-income students.

Tables 9 and 10 report the effect of distinguishing sticker price and aid in the equations that examine public and private enrollment separately. These variables are called STIKPU and STIKPR and AIDPU and AIDPR. Table 9 reports results for private institutions. We find that for low-income students,

---

31. The last test statement on table 8 verifies that the difference in absolute value between the STIK and the AID coefficients is not statistically significant.

AID has the expected positive sign and is significant; sticker price has the expected negative sign and is also significant. Again, the aid effect and the price effect are almost identical. The aid-income interaction terms are not significant; the overall effect of aid on enrollment is not significant for middle-income or high-income students. As expected, the interaction term for sticker

TABLE 8. Regression Results—Combined Sample, Separate Price and Aid Variables

Dependent Variable: Enrollment Rate			
Root mean square error	0.02329594	R^2	0.9687
Dependent mean	0.4271738	Adjusted R^2	0.9602
Coefficient of variation	5.453503	N	66

Parameter Estimates

Variable	Parameter Estimate	Standard Error	T for H0: Parameter=0
INTERCEPT	0.459218	0.114308	4.017[a]
STIK	−0.000068	0.000024	−2.818[a]
AID	0.000069	0.000051	1.344
TIME	−0.003635	0.001989	−1.828[c]
FEMALE	0.048684	0.008704	5.593[a]
MED	−0.278997	0.142833	−1.953[c]
HIGH	−0.189528	0.176219	−1.076
AIDHI	−0.000172	0.000106	−1.624
AIDMD	0.000014	0.000064	0.225
STIKHI	0.000150	0.000039	3.855[a]
STIKMED	0.000114	0.000031	3.683[a]
TIMEHI	−0.002410	0.004400	−0.548
TIMEMED	0.001500	0.002349	0.639
FEMHI	−0.001494	0.013533	−0.110
FEMMED	0.000664	0.010839	0.061

Test:	STIK+STIKHI=0	χ^2:	6.93[a]
Test:	STIK+STIKMED=0	χ^2:	5.75[b]
Test:	AID+AIDHI=0	χ^2:	1.23
Test:	AID+AIDMD=0	χ^2:	2.02
Test:	TIME+TIMEHI=0	χ^2:	2.37
Test:	TIME+TIMEMED=0	χ^2:	2.92[c]
Test:	FEMALE+FEMHI=0	χ^2:	20.74[a]
Test:	FEMALE+FEMMED=0	χ^2:	58.36[a]
Test:	STIK+AID=0	χ^2:	0.0003

[a]Significant at 0.01 level.
[b]Significant at 0.05 level.
[c]Significant at 0.10 level.

TABLE 9.   Regression Results—Private Institutions, Separate Price and Aid Variables

	Dependent Variable: Enrollment Rate		
Root mean square error	0.01405429	R^2	0.9420
Dependent mean	0.1108635	Adjusted R^2	0.9239
Coefficient of variable	12.6771	N	60

Parameter Estimates

Variable	Parameter Estimate	Standard Error	T for H0: Parameter=0
INTERCEPT	0.151874	0.049227	3.085[a]
STIKPR	−0.000034	0.000008	−4.449[a]
AIDPR	0.000038	0.000011	3.337[a]
TIME	0.000468	0.000536	0.872
FEMALE	0.015830	0.004210	3.760[a]
MED	−0.039105	0.082808	−0.472
HIGH	−0.134988	0.121489	−1.111
AIDHI	0.000015	0.000108	0.140
AIDMD	−0.000017	0.000024	−0.727
STIKHI	0.000063	0.000020	3.209[a]
STIKMD	0.000024	0.000012	1.957[b]
TIMEHI	−0.007402	0.004866	−1.521
TIMEMED	−0.000183	0.001097	−0.167
FEMHI	0.013390	0.010638	1.259
FEMMED	0.005357	0.005301	1.011

Test:	STIKPR+STIKHI=0	χ^2:	2.55
Test:	STIKPR+STIKMED=0	χ^2:	1.10
Test:	AIDPR+AIDHI=0	χ^2:	0.25
Test:	AIDPR+AIDMD=0	χ^2:	1.02
Test:	TIME+TIMEHI=0	χ^2:	2.06
Test:	TIME+TIMEMED=0	χ^2:	0.09
Test:	FEMALE+FEMHI=0	χ^2:	8.95[a]
Test:	FEMALE+FEMMED=0	χ^2:	43.29[a]
Test:	STIKPR+AIDPR=0	χ^2:	0.06

[a]Significant at 0.01 level.
[b]Significant at 0.10 level.

price and high-income is positive and significant, while the overall effect of price for middle- and high-income students is insignificant.

Table 10 reports results for public institutions. For low-income students, the signs on STIKPU and AIDPU are as expected but are not statistically significant. The interaction term with AID for the high-income group is negative and significant, as we expect. The overall effect of aid for the middle-income group is positive and significant, while for the high-income group, the overall effect is (perversely) negative and significant. The interaction effects for sticker price and income are both significant with the expected positive signs; the overall effects of sticker price are significant and (perversely) positive for both income groups.

These various regression results present a somewhat complicated picture. It may be useful to pull together the most illuminating results in a brief

TABLE 10. Regression Results—Public Institutions, Separate Price and Aid Variables

Dependent Variable: Enrollment Rate			
Root mean square error	0.02053711	R^2	0.9346
Dependent mean	0.3177716	Adjusted R^2	0.9142
Coefficient of variable	6.462853	N	60

Parameter Estimates			
Variable	Parameter Estimate	Standard Error	T for H0: Parameter=0
INTERCEPT	0.380366	0.125456	3.032[a]
STIKPU	−0.000049	0.000037	−1.352
AIDPU	0.000020	0.000066	0.310
TIME	−0.003868	0.002240	−1.727[c]
FEMALE	0.028309	0.008917	3.175[a]
MED	0.438030	0.157962	−2.773[a]
HIGH	−0.092041	0.149601	−0.615
AIDHI	−0.000343	0.000106	−3.230[a]
AIDMD	0.000080	0.000086	0.926
STIKHI	0.000098	0.000043	2.275[b]
STIKMD	0.000152	0.000044	3.442[a]
TIMEHI	0.006152	0.002430	2.532[b]
TIMEMED	0.001606	0.002439	0.658
FEMHI	−0.012045	0.011502	−1.047
FEMMED	0.003761	0.010841	0.347

Test:	STIKPU+STIKHI=0		χ^2:	4.49[b]
Test:	STIKPU+STIKMD=0		χ^2:	17.03[a]
Test:	AIDPU+AIDHI=0		χ^2:	14.95[a]
Test:	AIDPU+AIDMD=0		χ^2:	3.24[c]
Test:	TIME+TIMEHI=0		χ^2:	5.90[b]
Test:	TIME+TIMEMED=0		χ^2:	5.52[b]
Test:	FEMALE+FEMHI=0		χ^2:	5.01[b]
Test:	FEMALE+FEMMED=0		χ^2:	27.05[a]
Test:	STIKPU+AIDPU=0		χ^2:	0.17

[a]Significant at 0.01 level.
[b]Significant at 0.05 level.
[c]Significant at 0.10 level.

summary. Our most important and reliable finding is that increases in the net cost of attendance have a negative and statistically significant effect on enrollment for white students from low-income families. Moreover, the magnitude of this net cost effect is similar to that found in cross-sectional studies of enrollment demand. It is not possible to use our data set to test for net cost effects for African-Americans or other racial-ethic groups because of excessive sampling variation in the estimated enrollment rates for these students.

Our finding that the time-series and cross-sectional results for low-income white students are consistent is an important first step in resolving a long-standing controversy in the literature. These results derive from the fact that we have systematically related changes in net cost to changes in enrollment, rather than simply looking at enrollment levels at two points in time. It is important to appreciate that these findings for low-income students would be obscured in an analysis that aggregated over income groups, since our evidence suggests (in line with the findings of cross-sectional studies) that the behavior of these income groups is quite different.

The next step in our analysis was to break down our enrollment and cost measures into separate variables for public institutions and for private institutions. Once again we found evidence of a negative net cost effect for low-income students attending private institutions; for public institutions the net cost variable had a negative coefficient but was statistically insignificant.

We went on to break down net cost into its two components of sticker price and the subsidy value of student aid. For the combined public-private sample, we found an expected negative and significant coefficient on sticker price among low-income white students; the aid effect was positive, as expected, but insignificant. The point estimates of these two effects were virtually identical, suggesting that students responded equally to price cuts or aid increases. When public and private enrollment were considered separately, all the variables had the expected signs, with the aid and price variables in the private enrollment equation being significant. Point estimates of the aid and price effects in the private equation once again indicate highly similar magnitudes.

Stepping back, we see that the results tell a consistent story about the behavior of low-income white students. In our simpler specifications, the coefficients on variables measuring costs of attendance were significant with expected signs and reasonable coefficients. As we refined the analysis further, for the most part, we continued to find significant coefficients of reasonable magnitude without finding a single significant coefficient with an unexpected sign.

We found a very different picture when we looked at the behavior of more affluent students. We found no evidence in these data that increases in net cost inhibited enrollment in these income groups. In fact, for the upper-income group, there was a fairly consistent positive effect of net cost on enrollment, which may be interpreted as indicating a tendency for high enrollment demand among affluent students to lead to higher net costs for those students. For middle-income students, we found that net cost did not have a consistent effect on enrollment in our equations.

A by-product of our efforts to estimate the effects of net cost on enrollment was a set of estimates of the impact of a time trend and of gender differences on enrollment behavior. To the extent that there has been a trend in enrollment from 1974 to 1984 (after controlling for gender and net cost), it appears to be negative. It is worth pointing out, however, that the magnitude of the estimated trend is small. Finally, we found that, all things equal, women had a greater propensity than men to enroll in institutions of higher education. This is particularly true for the nonpoor.

The above analysis indicates that changes in the net price facing lower-income students have significant effects on their enrollment behavior. An important policy issue, however, is whether changes in federal aid in fact wind up changing net cost. If, for example, increases in federal aid led to decreases in the amount of aid awarded by institutions or to increases in tuition, the effect of aid on net cost would be muted. This issue deserves more systematic treatment than we can give it here. However, preliminary findings from a study of the effects of student aid on institutions that the present authors have underway (McPherson, Schapiro, and Winston 1988) suggest that these potential offsetting effects may not be empirically important. The time-series evidence on net cost further suggests that periods when federal aid is generous coincide with periods when the net cost facing low-income students is lower. This supports the view that these potential offsets are not an important factor.

Pushing the Analysis Forward: Where Do We Go from Here?

While the preceding discussion helps reconcile important points of disagreement in the literature, it also points to further areas of investigation. For one, time-series data on enrollment and net cost by ability would help us get a better handle on the nation's success in achieving a critical goal of aid policy—to enable high-ability students to pursue advanced education regardless of their income background. Although it would be very expensive to maintain such data annually, useful work could be done by pooling data across those years in which large surveys such as High School and Beyond and National Educational Longitudinal Survey of 1988 (NELS88) are undertaken.

A second point is that future attempts to monitor the effectiveness of aid in changing enrollment rates by inspecting enrollment trends over time should attempt to control for actual variations in net cost and other relevant variables. It would be desirable, for example, to include proxies for opportunity costs and rates of return to higher education investments in regressions such as those we have run. Reasonable proxies might be age-, sex-, and income-specific unemployment rates and education-related earning differentials. Whenever the data allow, disaggregating aid by type (grant, loan, and work study) and source (federal, state, local, and institutional) may reveal interesting differences among aid packages. Of course, developing data sets that would permit the analysis of enrollment effects by race over time would be highly desirable. In addition, while our other work thus far has failed to find important effects of federal aid on institutional aid and tuition, further study of the supply side effects of aid is needed to evaluate properly the various links among federal aid, institutional behavior, and enrollment patterns.

Finally, it would be useful to extend the time-series to deal with the question of choice as well as access. Although we were able to estimate separate equations for enrollment at public and at private institutions, collinearity between the public and private price variables impeded our efforts to include cross-price effects in these equations. Such cross-effects, for example, of public tuitions on private enrollment, have considerable importance for institutional and governmental policies. Conceivably, extending the data set over more years or experimenting further with functional forms that might reduce the collinearity would permit meaningful estimates to be developed.

In sum, a more careful analysis of the time-series data has raised serious doubts about the hypothesis that federal student aid has failed to significantly affect enrollment patterns in U.S. higher education over the past two decades. Our assessment indicates that time-series evidence on the enrollment behavior of low-income white students is quite consistent with the many econometric estimates of aid effects in the literature. While further analysis seems warranted, it is nonetheless clear that policy makers must carefully consider potential enrollment effects when determining student aid policy.

REFERENCES

Berne, R. 1980. "Net Price Effects on Two-Year College Attendance Decisions." *Journal of Education Finance* 5 (4): 391–414.
Blakemore, A. E., and S. A. Low. 1985. "Public Expenditures on Higher Education and Their Impact on Enrollment Patterns." *Applied Economics* 17: 331–40.
Carlson, D. E. 1975. *A Flow of Funds Model for Assessing the Impact of Alternative Student Aid Programs.* Menlo Park, CA: Stanford Research Institute.
Carnegie Council. 1980. *Three Thousand Futures: The Next Twenty Years for Higher Education.* San Francisco: Jossey-Bass.

Carroll, S. J., B. M. Mori, D. A. Relles, and D.J. Weinschrott. 1977. *The Enrollment Effects of Federal Student Aid Policies.* Santa Monica, CA: Rand Corporation.

Crawford, N. C. 1966. *Effects of Offers of Financial Assistance on the College-Going Decisions of Talented Students with Limited Financial Means.* Evanston, IL: National Merit Scholarship Corporation.

Davis, J. S., and K. Johns, Jr. 1982. "Low Family Income: A Continuing Barrier to College Enrollment?" *Journal of Student Financial Aid* 12:5–10.

Ehrenberg, R. G., and D. R. Sherman. 1984. "Optimal Financial Aid Policies for a Selective University." *Journal of Human Resources* 19 (Spring): 202–30.

Gillespie, D. A., and N. Carlson. 1983. *Trends in Student Aid: 1963–1983.* Washington, DC: Washington Office of the College Board.

Hansen, W. L. 1983. "Impact of Student Financial Aid on Access." In *The Crisis in Higher Education,* edited by J. Froomkin. New York: Academy of Political Science.

Hauptman, A., and M. McLaughlin. 1988. "Is the Goal of Access to Postsecondary Education Being Met?" Unpublished.

Hearn, J. C. 1980. "Effects on Enrollment of Changes in Student Aid Policies and Programs." In *The Impact of Student Financial Aid on Institutions,* edited by J. B. Henry. San Francisco, Jossey-Bass.

Jackson, G. A. 1978. "Financial Aid and Student Enrollment." *Journal of Higher Education* 49 (6): 548–74.

Jensen, E. L. 1983. "Financial Aid and Educational Outcomes: A Review." *College and University* 58 (Spring): 287–302.

Leslie, L. L., and P. T. Brinkman. 1987. "Student Price Response in Higher Education: The Student Demand Studies." *Journal of Higher Education* 58 (2): 181–204.

———. 1988. *The Economic Value of Higher Education.* New York: Macmillan Publishing Co., Inc.

Lewis, G. L. 1988. *Trends in Student Aid: 1980–1988.* Washington, DC: Washington Office of the College Board.

Manski, C. F., and D. A. Wise. 1983. *College Choice in America.* Cambridge, MA: Harvard University Press.

McPherson, M. S. 1978. "The Demand for Higher Education." In *Public Policy and Private Higher Education,* edited by David Breneman and Chester Finn. Washington, DC: The Brookings Institution.

———. 1988. *How Can We Tell If Federal Student Aid is Working?* Washington, DC: Washington Office of the College Board.

McPherson, M. S., M. O. Schapiro, and G. C. Winston. 1988. "The Impact of Government Expenditures on the Operation of Colleges and Universities: An Empirical Study." Unpublished.

Newman, F. 1985. *Higher Education and the American Resurgence.* New York: Carnegie Foundation for the Advancement of Teaching.

St. John, E. P., and C. Byce. 1982. *"The Changing Federal Role in Student Financial Aid."* In *Meeting Student Aid Needs in a Period of Retrenchment,* edited by M. Kramer. San Francisco: Jossey-Bass.

St. John, E. P., R. J. Kirshstein, and J. Noell. 1988. "The Effects of Student Financial Aid on Persistence: A Sequential Analysis." Unpublished.

St. John, E. P., and J. Noell. 1988. "The Effects of Student Financial Aid on Access to Higher Education: An Analysis of Progress with Special Consideration to Minority Enrollment." Unpublished.

Schwartz, J. B. 1985. "Student Financial Aid and the College Enrollment Decision: The Effects of Public and Private Grants and Interest Subsidies." *Economics of Education Review* 4(7): 129–44.

———. 1986. "Wealth Neutrality in Higher Education: The Effects of Student Grants." *Economics of Education Review* 5 (2): 107–17.

Tierney, M. L. 1980. "Student Matriculation Decisions and Financial Aid." *Review of Higher Education* 3: 14–25.

White, H. 1980. "A Heteroskedasticity-Consistent Covariance Matrix Estimator and a Direct Test for Heteroskedasticity." *Econometrica* 48: 817–38.

CHAPTER 9

Robin Hood in the Forests of Academe

Gordon C. Winston

Tuition season is on us again. Parents, sensitized by Secretary Bennett (William J., '65) if not their own recent experience, are reeling under a new set of numbers describing what they'll have to pay to send their children to America's finest colleges and universities. A sampling: Princeton, $16,918; Williams, $15,666; MIT, $16,970; Yale, $17,020; Stanford, $16,835. It's been front-page news nationwide.

But not all families will actually pay those sticker prices. At most expensive private colleges, a third or more of the students will be charged less than the announced prices because they're "on financial aid," and at some, like Swarthmore, more than half of the student body is given that break.

That sounds generous and even compassionate. But what of those who *do* pay those impressively large tuition bills? A tuition policy that makes wealthier families pay more and less wealthy families pay less, for the same Yale or Amherst education, is what's fashionably being called Robin Hooding in Washington—using tuitions to steal from the rich and give to the poor.

That's a powerful image, suggesting that something basically unfair is being put over on people, especially on wealthier people, by an arrogant educational establishment. And that's not a trivial charge. It deserves an answer; the Robin Hood comparison needs examination.

The underlying issue is price discrimination. A profit-maximizing monopoly does it when it charges two different customers two different prices for exactly the same thing only because they differ in willingness and ability to pay. The price of an airline ticket to New Orleans is less for the casual traveler who's willing to stay over the weekend than it is for a business traveler who isn't. The price is different not because it costs less to transport a family on vacation, but because businesses are willing and able to pay more.

So aren't high tuitions and generous financial aid, together, simply price discrimination?

They are. These schools clearly *do* charge different prices to different

Reprinted from *Williams Alumni Review*, Summer 1987, 29–30. Reprinted with permission.

families on the basis of their different willingness and ability to pay—that is the essence of their financial aid and "need-blind" admissions policies. Aid students get exactly the same high-quality Smith or Harvard education, from freshman orientation through four years to the career counseling office, as those students who pay the full price. These colleges do price discriminate and quite openly.

One thing that distinguishes this price discrimination from that of the airlines or the phone company or the local movie theater is the reason behind the practice. Businesses charge different prices in order to increase their profits. Colleges charge different prices to ensure that able students can have access to an excellent education, regardless of their families' incomes. Firms price discriminate for the private objective of getting higher incomes for themselves. Colleges price discriminate for the social objective of making the best education available to the best students. To put it the other way around, their objective is that of *not* letting the market and wealth alone determine who does and who doesn't get an excellent education.

Though the objectives of colleges may be more laudable than those of monopolies when they price discriminate, aren't they still Robin Hooding?

The most obvious problem with the analogy between the groves of academe and Sherwood Forest, of course, is that the fabled Robin Hood *stole* from the rich to give to the poor. There was not choice: people who didn't want to give were forced to give at bow-and-arrow point. The operative picture is theft.

But when people *choose* to pay their money for something they want— like a Nepalese vacation or ten shares of IBM or an education at Williams—it is hard to argue that *theft* is an appropriate metaphor. Because their choice is voluntary, the consumers control it. If they decide it's too expensive, they can vacation in the Adirondacks or buy ten shares of AT&T or send their favorite daughter to the State University of New York at Albany. Victims of Robin Hood didn't have such choices, and the metaphor invites us to forget that affluent families choosing colleges always do.

Part of what those full-freight students are getting when they choose to buy a Williams education is association with other excellent students as well as a breadth and diversity of classmates. Both the quality of students and their diversity would be lower if everyone had to pay the same price. And quality and diversity are part of the appeal of these places; part of what makes them educationally excellent and desirable. Indeed, it can be argued that making access independent of ability to pay is an important part of the *educational* mission of these colleges. Were they *not* to put into concrete practice this meritocratic principle, much of the curriculum would have a hollow and hypocritical ring. These schools *believe* in the social ethic inherent in having different charges for different students based on their ability to pay; they are *committed,* as an assertion of institutional principle, to admitting the best entering class they can, regardless of family income.

The other error in the Robin Hood analogy is, quite simply, that *every* student in these colleges is getting a gift, the rich and the poor alike. The gift comes from alumni and the endowment—from the (voluntary) generosity of friends and of previous generations. *No current student pays the full costs of his or her education.* A full-price students picks up most of his own room and board expenses, but often less than half of his educational costs. At Williams, the typical example I know best, the total cost per student next year will be $27,000, compared with the $15,666 that even the full-fare student will have to pay. *Every* student at Williams and Stanford and Mt. Holyoke gets much more than he or she pays for. Of course wealthier students get a smaller gift than the less wealthy. But everybody gets the gift.

So, while high-quality private colleges do price discriminate, the Robin Hooding idea is pretty dubious. It doesn't acknowledge the voluntary nature of the choice to go to schools with a dedication to quality, diversity, and therefore need-blind admissions; it doesn't recognize that those policies support an important part of what's educationally attractive at such schools; it doesn't accept the fact that the wealthy, just like the poor, are on the receiving end of the income transfers, rather than being the victims of armed robbery the metaphor would have us see.

Part 4
Institutional Finance

CHAPTER 10

The Effect of Government Financing on the Behavior of Colleges and Universities

Michael S. McPherson and Morton Owen Schapiro

The aim of this chapter is to improve our understanding of the effects of external government financing on the behavior of colleges and universities, focusing on their tuition and fee charges, institution-specific scholarship aid, and instructional spending. The chapter is organized as follows. After a brief discussion of some relevant literature in the first section, we turn in the second section to a description of our data set: a panel of individual college and university financial data for the period 1978–79 to 1985–86.[1] The third section presents an econometric model of college and university finance, and the fourth section analyzes the empirical findings that result. The fifth section concludes.

Relation to Literature

The research reported here fits into the growing but still quite limited empirical literature on the behavior of governmental and not-for-profit institutions. This important subject has recently started receiving considerable systematic attention from economists, legal theorists, and other social scientists.[2] Within higher education, empirical work on institutional behavior has been surprisingly rare. Papers by James (1978) and by Hoenack and Pierro (1986) develop models of the behavioral response of institutional resource allocation to changes in external constraints. The piece by Hoenack and Pierro includes some empirical estimation of the influence of state legislative appropriations on the behavior of a public institution. To our knowledge, no systematic empirical work has been done on the implications of other forms of government spending on institutional behavior. Several studies of student aid do,

A version of this chapter appears in our book *Keeping College Affordable: Government and Educational Opportunity* (Washington, D.C.: Brookings Institution, 1991), chap. 4.

1. The academic year 1985–86 is the latest for which national data are available.
2. See the useful collection of articles assembled in Rose-Ackerman 1986.

however, note the potential importance of these issues (Hearn and Wilford 1985, Finn 1978).

Empirical studies parallel to this study have been performed for policy areas other than higher education, and they have instructive findings. An interesting example is the work on measuring the effect of state and federal grants on the spending patterns of local school districts. Not surprisingly, the results indicate that responses depend on the type of subsidy and the manner in which it is distributed (examples include Tsang and Levin 1983 and Craig and Inman 1982).

Feldstein (1978) examined the effects of federal Title I aid on local district spending. The major question was whether local governments spent all of their Title I grants on additional educational expenditures (as required under the terms of the program) or whether, instead, some of the federal money was used to replace state and local money or even to provide tax relief. While this question relates to elementary and secondary schooling rather than postsecondary education, the analogous issue in higher education is whether federal funds targeted at low-income groups replace institutional support. Feldstein's regression results indicated that an extra dollar of Title I funding augmented total educational spending by seventy-two cents.[3]

Craig and Inman (1982) examine the effects of different types of federal aid on the educational spending of state and local governments. Their results indicate that different types of aid are in fact allocated differently. A dollar of federal aid that is given to local governments but administered through the state ultimately increases local spending by eighty-seven cents. On the other hand, a dollar of federal aid that goes directly to the local government appears to have a zero or even negative impact on total spending on education, indicating substantial substitutability between federal and local educational expenditures.

The relevant literature is not limited to studies of education. Some of the work on the effects of government subsidies on demand and supply in housing (for example, Barnett and Lowry 1979) and health markets (for example, Sloan, Cromwell, and Mitchell 1978) is germane. In each case, response functions are estimated which seek to ascertain the effects of different forms of government expenditures.

In sum, while relatively little work has sought to address the response of higher education institutions to changes in external funding, there are a variety of studies that provide a methodological basis for our work, and which lead us to believe meaningful empirical estimates can be obtained.

---

3. See Craig and Inman 1982, Tsang and Levin 1983, and Gurwitz 1980 for discussion of this work.

The Data

We base our econometric results on a data set reporting financial information on individual colleges and universities. The data set was constructed by merging three federally maintained data sets.[4] One, the Financial Statistics report from the Higher Education General Information Survey (HEGIS), describes the basic financial accounts of all public and private nonprofit postbaccalaureate institutions in the United States, as well as a handful of "proprietary" trade schools that are run for profit. The second, the Fiscal-Operations Report and Application to Participate (FISAP) data base, provides more detailed information on student aid spending, on revenues, and on the aided population at colleges and universities which apply for federal assistance under any of the so-called campus-based programs (direct loans, SEOGs, and college work-study). The third, the HEGIS Enrollment Survey, reports full- and part-time enrollment for all institutions, allowing us to construct estimates of FTE enrollment. We have these merged data sets for all private nonprofit and public colleges and universities for the academic years 1978–79 and 1985–86. The data set has been constructed as a panel, so that only schools with data for both observations years are included. All of our financial variables are calculated on a per FTE student basis and are expressed as the difference in value between the end and the beginning of the period, adjusted for inflation over the period.

The data sets lack two significant pieces of data, which unfortunately are very hard to supplement from other sources: the amount of borrowing undertaken by students at an institution through the federal GSL program and the amount of grant aid provided to an institution's students through state grant programs. With these two exceptions, coverage of the major items of interest is thorough. Painstaking efforts have been made to clean the data set of reporting and recording errors. In addition, we have dropped all proprietary schools along with all private nonprofit two-year colleges from the sample as well as all schools with fewer than 200 undergraduates. The resulting sample contains a total of 1,934 institutions: 896 private four-year colleges and universities, 371 public four-year colleges and universities, and 667 public two-year colleges. Each of these categories of institutions is analyzed separately.

Table 1 provides descriptive statistics for the variables used in the regression analysis. In addition to reporting the changes over the period, which are used in the regressions, Table 1 also reports the 1978–79 values of the financial variables.

---

4. We are grateful to the American Council on Education (ACE) for preparing the merged data set for our use. Laurent Ross of the ACE was very helpful to us in programming and documenting the merge.

TABLE 1. Descriptive Statistics for Regression Analysis

Variable	N	Mean	Standard Deviation	Mean Value for 1978–79	
Private Four-Year Colleges and Universities					
CHINTSCH	896	266.1	374.0	INTSCH	699.0
CHT&F	896	768.3	665.2	T&F	3602.7
CHINSTRUCT	896	250.6	634.3	INSTRUCT	2052.1
CHFEDFINAID	896	9.3	147.8	FEDFINAID	319.5
CHS&LGR&CNT	896	45.8	504.2	S&LGR&CNT	153.5
CHS&LAPP	896	−7.1	113.1	S&LAPP	50.8
CHFEDGR&CNT	896	−73.3	482.2	FEDGR&CNT	399.7
CHENDOW	896	1983.1	5013.4	ENDOW	6802.7
CHINCRES	896	1298.0	4877.2	INCRES	2989.7
CHPERCAP	896	1009.1	659.2	PERCAP	8754.4
ENROLL79	896	1721.1	2307.3		
%CHENROLL	896	5.2	32.2		
Public Four-Year Colleges and Universities					
CHINTSCH	371	28.9	130.4	INTSCH	144.4
CHT&F	371	219.8	224.2	T&F	1009.7
CHINSTRUCT	371	132.0	574.1	INSTRUCT	2256.5
CHFEDFINAID	371	37.9	85.0	FEDFINAID	266.0
CHS&LGR&CNT	371	8.9	178.7	S&LGR&CNT	126.5
CHS&LAPP	371	187.9	1549.0	S&LAPP	3391.2
CHFEDGR&CNT	371	−103.4	477.6	FEDGR&CNT	441.8
CHENDOW	371	78.4	401.1	ENDOW	372.0
CHINCRES	371	−188.6	2244.7	INCRES	737.8
CHPERCAP	371	890.1	660.4	PERCAP	8424.6
ENROLL79	371	7792.0	7343.7		
%CHENROLL	371	8.0	16.6		
Public Two-Year Colleges					
CHINTSCH	667	9.5	118.4	INTSCH	60.1
CHT&F	667	86.2	153.7	T&F	500.3
CHINSTRUCT	667	89.5	472.3	INSTRUCT	1454.1
CHFEDFINAID	667	52.0	99.4	FEDFINAID	221.9
CHS&LGR&CNT	667	28.3	243.5	S&LGR&CNT	106.4
CHS&LAPP	667	120.7	572.8	S&LAPP	2117.6
CHFEDGR&CNT	667	−20.8	287.0	FEDGR&CNT	153.3
CHENDOW	667	20.9	155.0	ENDOW	40.9
CHINCRES	667	−231.5	1201.6	INCRES	245.6
CHPERCAP	667	968.3	641.5	PERCAP	8733.6
ENROLL79	667	2423.5	2292.1		
%CHENROLL	667	11.8	32.2		

The first three variables represent the dependent variables estimated in the equation system reported below. They are (1) the change in scholarship aid per FTE student from institutional resources (CHINTSCH); (2) the change in gross tuition and fees per FTE student received by the institution (CHT&F) (the convention followed by academic institutions is to calculate this amount by assuming that every student pays the sticker or list price; hence, this variable is gross of financial aid); and (3) the change in instructional expenditures (and expenditures for self-supported research) per FTE student (CHINSTRUCT).[5]

The next four variables in the table measure changes over the period in government revenues provided to higher education institutions. These are, first, the change in federal financial aid grants per FTE student (CHFED-FINAID),[6] second, the change in state and local grants and contracts per FTE student (CHS&LGR&CNT), third, the change in state and local appropriations per FTE student (CHS&LAPP), and, finally, the change in federal grants and contracts (exclusive of student aid grants) per FTE student (CHFEDGR&CNT).

In addition to these variables, our analysis includes several variables that control for institutional wealth, for the incomes of potential students, and for possible scale effects. These are the change in institutions' endowment per FTE student (CHENDOW), the change in institutions' income from gifts and endowment earnings (CHINCRES), the change in per capita income in the state where the institution is located (CHPERCAP), the level of FTE enrollment in 1978–79 (ENROLL79), and the percentage change in FTE enrollment over the period (%CHENROLL).

An Econometric Model of College and University Finance

We conceive of the "university" as an institution whose behavior reflects the pursuit of objectives that are valued by various constituencies associated with it.[7] Assume to begin with that the university simply maximizes some given set of objectives subject to an income constraint. Call the set of objectives $\{X_i\}$. Assume that the costs associated with these objectives are additively separable, so that the cost of X_i is $C_i(X_i)$ and the university's budget constraint is

---

5. Unfortunately, the data gathered in the federal survey on instructional expenditures do not permit us to break out these two categories of spending separately.

6. This is the change over the period in the sum of awards to students from the federal Pell grant and SEOG programs. Pell provides awards to qualifying students based on a formula reflecting their family resources and costs of attendance. SEOG funds are supplied to campuses, which have discretion over who among their needy students will receive awards.

7. "University" here refers to colleges and universities.

$$\Sigma\ C_i(X_i) \leq I,$$

where I is the university's income.

If the X_i enter a utility function for the university in which each counts positively with diminishing marginal rates of substitution and if costs rise with higher levels of X_i at a diminishing rate, the university will select optimum levels of activities, X_i^*, with associated cost levels $C_i(X_i^*)$.

Suppose the university has an increase in unrestricted income of amount g. Assuming all activities are "normal," each will increase to a new equilibrium level $X_i^{**} > X_i^*$.

What if, instead, the institution receives revenues in amount g that are targeted to be spent on a particular activity, say X_1? If this increase in "earmarked" funds does not change the cost or utility functions, the university's response will depend on whether $C_i(X_i^{**})$ is greater or less than g. If the earmarked revenues are less than or equal to the amount that would be spent on X_1 from a total income if $I + g$, then the "earmarking" constraint is not binding and the university will spend the added revenues exactly as if they had come as unrestricted income. If, instead, the earmarked revenues exceed $C_i(X_1^{**})$, then the constraint implied by the earmarking becomes binding. The university will then spend g on X_1, and will maximize its utility subject to that constraint and a constraint that its total spending on other activities cannot exceed I. Obviously, this added constraint will result in both more spending on X_1 and a lower "utility" level for the institution than it would attain from an increase in unrestricted income equal to g.

Thus a simple optimizing model of the university would imply perfect "fungibility" of earmarked dollars up to the point where earmarked funds match the amount the university would spend in the absence of such support, and zero fungibility thereafter.

However, we do not believe that this model adequately captures the reality of university decision making. Introducing some reasonable complications to the model modifies these simple and strong conclusions: there are reasons to expect less than perfect fungibility below the level of an activity that would be chosen in the absence of external finance, and more than zero fungibility above that level.

The first complication arises even within the simple maximizing model. Within relatively broadly defined activities, sources of external support are likely to impose constraints that blur the picture of a sharp dividing line after which external support ceases to replace internal spending. Formally, one could say that each broadly defined activity is composed of a number of more narrowly defined activities (e.g., aiding this student versus aiding that student). At any given level of earmarked external support for the broadly defined activity, some of the narrow activities will have been fully funded externally, while others will not. As the overall level of external funding increases, the number of narrow activities that can still "absorb" funding will decrease, so that the degree of fungibility will decline more smoothly than the discontinuous result of the simple model.

Second, recognition of political elements in the allocation of resources within a university suggests less than perfect fungibility. The simple model assumes a unified objective function which "the university" is maximizing. In fact, while there may be broad consensus within a university on what objectives are worth pursuing, it is implausible to suppose that such an institution puts stable and agreed weights on these objectives. The availability of external funding is likely to increase the political influence of a constituency that favors a particular objective. This makes it likely that such a group could "capture" more of the benefits of increased external funding than the simple model implies.

A distinct but related point pertains to the incentives the university provides to those who seek and obtain external funding. Unless gains in external funding are shared with those who obtain them, the incentive to seek such funding will be small. Although in principle such rewards could take the form of direct side payments, it seems more plausible that a successful constituency will be rewarded by letting a larger share of the increased funding remain with that area than strict short-run optimizing would imply.

Finally, we should note that the simple model assumes that the cost functions facing the university are insensitive to changes in external funding. But this obviously depends on the form that the external funding takes. Suppose, for example, that research funding took the form of "matching grants" with, say, half the marginal cost of a research project being provided externally on condition that the rest is provided internally. Such regulation would reduce the marginal cost of research activities and increase the level of research activity the institution would undertake. Such linkages will clearly increase the responsiveness of activity levels to changes in external funding for them, relative to the simple model sketched above.

For purposes of developing our empirical model, we can identify four major kinds of objectives that, we hypothesize, most institutions of higher learning share. These are objectives that can readily be linked to institutions' resource allocation decisions. These objectives are

1. to maintain or improve the quality of education the institution can offer in the future. This objective implies that, ceteris paribus, institutions will prefer a larger endowment, or a higher rate of saving, to a smaller endowment or a lower savings rate.
2. to expand the applicant pool—either with the objective of attaining adequate enrollment (for nonselective institutions) or of increasing

the institution's capacity to select preferred students. This will normally lead institutions to prefer lower tuition to higher tuition (ceteris paribus) and to prefer higher to lower quality of undergraduate instruction.[8]

3. to recruit a socioeconomically diverse population of students. For most institutions, this will imply a desire to increase the number of disadvantaged and minority students, and this will normally lead the institution, ceteris paribus, to prefer a larger to a smaller rate of spending on student aid.

4. to improve the institution's prestige and reputation. Thus, institutions will normally prefer larger amounts of spending on research and on instruction to smaller amounts and will also prefer higher "quality" of service provision more generally.

Our picture then is of a university pursuing such broad goals as these in the context of a variety of constraints. We would expect the weights attached to these goals to be different in different segments of higher education. How will changes in the amount of funds the institution receives for the pursuit of specific purposes—"earmarked funds"—affect the way it allocates its resources?

Our discussion above implies that part of any increase in funds "earmarked" for a particular purpose will be "captured" by the university for other purposes. To the extent that this happens, the impact of the increase in funding will be the same as that of an increase in unrestricted income. We would normally expect, however, that spending on the activity for which the funds were designated will increase more than we would predict from an increase in unrestricted income of equal magnitude, and spending on other activities will therefore increase by a smaller amount. The extent of the difference between the effects of an "earmarked" and an unrestricted increase in revenue is an empirical question, the answer to which may differ from one variable to another.

The dependent variables in the three equations in our model are related to the objectives identified in the preceding section. The three equations with our theoretical expectations about signs are displayed in table 2.

A number of our expected signs follow directly from wealth effects in the theoretical model. Institutions experiencing more rapid increases over the period in state and local appropriations (CHS&LAPP), federal grants and contracts (CHFEDGR&CNT), or state and local grants and contracts

---

8. For some private institutions, higher tuition may be seen as an indicator of higher quality and therefore may make it possible for these institutions to increase their applicant pool by raising tuition. Even for these institutions, however, such constituencies as alumni and trustees are likely to prefer lower tuition to higher.

TABLE 2. Expected Signs for Regression Analysis

	Dependent Variables		
Explanatory Variables	CHINTSCH	CHT&F	CHINSTRUCT
CHFEDFINAID	?	?	+
CHENDOW	+	•••	•••
CHINCRES	•••	−	+
CHS&LAPP	+	−	+
CHFEDGR&CNT	+	−	+
CHS&LGR&CNT	+	−	+
CHPERCAP	−	+	•••
ENROLL79	•••	•••	−
CHENROLL	•••	•••	?
CHT&F	+	•••	+
CHINTSCH	•••	+	•••

(CHS&LGR&CNT) will gain more in institutional wealth and, given the objectives described above, are expected to increase institutionally based scholarship aid more rapidly, to raise tuition and fees more slowly, and to raise instructional expenditures more rapidly than other institutions. Similarly, more rapid growth in endowment (CHENDOW) or more rapid increases in income from gifts and endowment (CHINCRES) should add to the growth in wealth and have the same effects on institutional behavior.[9]

More rapid increases in federal financial aid (CHFEDFINAID) also have a positive wealth effect, which explains the expected positive sign for this variable in the equation for changes in instructional expenditures.[10] However, in explaining changes in tuition and in institution-based aid expenditures,

---

9. We postulate that changes in tuition and fees and instructional expenditures are based on changes in the flow of earnings—that is, when the sum of gifts, interest, and dividends declines from one year to the next, institutions respond by increasing the sticker price and lower instructional expenditures. On the other hand, we assume that changes in the amount of institutional financial aid depend more on changes in the long-run financial situation of an institution as reflected in changes in the stock of wealth rather than changes in year-to-year gifts and earnings. Thus, CHENDOW is included as an independent variable in the CHINTSCH equation while CHINCRES is included as an independent variable in the CHT&F and CHINSTRUCT equations. It should be noted that the high correlation between CHENDOW and CHINCRES implies that they cannot both be included as exogenous variables in a particular equation and that these assumptions are basically consistent with ordinary least-squares regression results.

10. A large positive effect would imply that increases in federal student aid induce institutions to increase their instructional expenditures substantially. This might be viewed as a good thing, if one believes that at the margin society would benefit from more resources being devoted to student instruction. Yet it might be seen as a negative outcome, to the degree that it implies that university expenditures, and hence the cost to the nation of higher education, tend to be pushed up by higher student aid.

changes in federal financial aid have effects additional to the wealth effect. In the case of institution-based aid, this wealth effect may be augmented by the effect of federal aid in making it easier for institutions to attract more lower income students, who may then receive additional institution-based aid.[11] However, these complementary effects may be offset by a tendency for federal aid to substitute for institutional aid spending, tending to counteract the positive effects and leaving the expected sign ambiguous.

The effects of increased federal aid on rates of growth in tuition are similarly ambiguous. Although the wealth effect of more rapid federal aid growth, given the assumed objectives of the institutions, will tend to reduce tuition, some observers have suggested that increased federal aid availability may tend to raise tuitions, as institutions attempt to "capture" more aid through setting a higher sticker price.[12]

State per capita income (CHPERCAP) is included in these equations as an indicator of the makeup of the student population of institutions. Institutions from states where income is growing more rapidly are expected to be able to raise tuition more rapidly while sustaining any given level of demand for enrollment, and given objective (1) above, we expect institutions to attempt to gain added revenue in this way. Thus, we expect a positive effect of CHPERCAP on CHT&F. Similarly, institutions should be able to attain any given level of diversity in the student population at lower cost in terms of institution-based aid if they are in a state where incomes are rising. Thus we expect the sign on CHPERCAP to be negative in the CHINTSCH equation.

Measures of the level and rate of growth on enrollment (ENROLL79 and

---

11. There are actually two forces at work here. First, enrollment demand among lower income students is increased by larger federal student aid awards. (For evidence, see McPherson and Schapiro 1991.) Second, the cost to an institution of recruiting a lower income student (thereby pursuing its objective of promoting diversity) is reduced by the presence of larger amounts of federal student aid.

12. The argument here is that the level of federal financial aid received by an institution may be a function of its tuition level—that raising tuition qualifies an institution's students for more federal aid. This might be seen as analogous to medical insurance arrangements which encourage providers to raise their fees. For an influential statement of this argument by the former secretary of education, see Bennett 1987. Note that to the extent that this is the case, federal financial aid must be seen as an endogenous variable, while our model assumes it is exogenous. In fact, however, current institutional arrangements imply that there is little responsiveness of federal student aid grant levels to tuition levels, at least in private higher education. The two relevant federal programs are SEOG and Pell. Funding levels in the SEOG program have consistently been below the levels at which the "needs" mechanism for awarding incremental dollars kicks in, and award maxima in Pell have been below the student charges of almost all private and many public institutions; in this case it is the family's income rather than the institution's tuition that is the binding constraint in determining the award level. Thus, there are some public institutions, but almost no private institutions, at which Pell award levels are responsive to tuition increases.

%CHENROLL) are included in the equation explaining instructional expenditures in order to capture possible scale or capacity effects. For any given percentage growth in enrollment, the presence of economies of scale would imply that institutions with smaller enrollments at the beginning of the period would experience larger increases in instructional spending than those with larger enrollments; thus the sign on the 1978–79 enrollment level in the CHINSTRUCT equation is expected to be negative.[13] The impact of the percentage growth in enrollment depends on whether institutions have excess capacity; if so, we expect a negative impact of more rapid growth in enrollment on expenditure growth; if not, rising short-run marginal costs should lead to a positive effect.

Finally, two endogenous variables, CHT&F and CHINTSCH, enter as explanatory variables in our equations. In explaining changes in instructional expenditures, we assume that more rapid increases in tuition and fees cause instructional expenditures to rise more rapidly through an income effect; a further effect is that institutions with more rapidly growing tuitions may need to increase their instructional expenditures more rapidly to ensure adequate demand. More rapid increases in tuition and fees are also expected to have a positive effect on the growth of institution-based student aid spending, both through an income effect and because more rapid tuition growth will require more rapid increases in spending on student aid to maintain diversity. There is also a reverse causal effect of increases in growth rates of institution-based student aid on rates of growth of tuition. Given the long-run solvency objective of the university, we expect that more rapid growth in institution-based student aid leads to more rapid growth in tuition.

Empirical Results

We have used two-stage least squares to estimate the model for three samples of institutions: four-year private colleges and universities; four-year public colleges and universities; and two-year public colleges. The results are presented in table 3.

As should be obvious from the above discussion, a central concern of ours is the degree to which government funds affect the finances of institutions of higher learning. These funds can be divided into the following categories:

1. federal financial aid—CHFEDFINAID;
2. direct state and local government support—CHS&LAPP; and
3. government grants and contracts—CHFEDGR&CNT and CHS&LGR&CNT.

---

13. For a review of the literature on economies of scale in higher education, see Brinkman and Leslie 1986.

TABLE 3. Regression Results

	Four-Year Privates ($n=896$)		Four-Year Publics ($n=371$)		Two-Year Publics ($n=667$)	
	Parameter Estimate	Standard Error	Parameter Estimate	Standard Error	Parameter Estimate	Standard Error
Equation 1—CHINTSCH						
INTERCEPT	137.0	35.8[a]	45.2	33.5	−15.8	10.3
CHFEDFINAID	.203	.091[b]	−.154	.097 ⁻	−.006	.092
CHENDOW	.009	.003[a]	.050	.029[c]	−.012	.032
CHS&LAPP	.215	.111[c]	.008	.006	−.008	.013
CHFEDGR&CNT	.108	.027[a]	.040	.014[a]	.076	.018[a]
CHS&LGR&CNT	.057	.024[b]	.063	.040	−.106	.025[a]
CHPERCEP	−.061	.023[a]	.001	.011	−.011	.013
CHT&F	.232	.064[a]	−.061	.156	.489	.195[b]
F value	20.60[a]		2.67[b]		9.54[a]	
Adjusted R^2	.133		.031		.082	
Equation 2—CHT&F						
INTERCEPT	−173.9	138.4	156.5	39.5[a]	25.7	17.2
CHFEDFINAID	−.197	.274	.502	.221[b]	.135	.130
CHINCRES	−.016	.011	−.007	.009	.002	.007
CHS&LAPP	−.861	.297[a]	.010	.012	.027	.017[c]
CHFEDGR&CNT	−.220	.104[b]	−.047	.039	−.099	.055[c]
CHS&LGR&CNT	−.132	.078[c]	−.021	.084	.170	.051[a]
CHPERCAP	.264	.047[a]	−.004	.023	.032	.015[b]
CHINTSCH	2.565	.488[a]	1.388	.681[b]	1.388	.539[b]
F value	14.64[a]		1.01		7.87[a]	
Adjusted R^2	.096		.000		.067	
Equation 3—CHINSTRUCT						
INTERCEPT	−43.8	68.5	−317.2	108.9[a]	49.9	40.7
CHFEDFINAID	−.047	.128	−.240	.343	−.031	.215
CHINCRES	.025	.004[a]	−.038	.014[a]	.054	.012[a]
CHS&LAPP	1.389	.163[a]	.299	.021[a]	.377	.034[a]
CHFEDGR&CNT	.220	.041[a]	.132	.055[b]	.311	.051[a]
CHS&LGR&CNT	−.017	.037	−.310	.146[b]	.377	.069[a]
ENROLL79	.035	.009[a]	−.013	.006[b]	−.003	.007
%CHENROLL	−2.216	.689[a]	2.364	1.691	−1.142	.656[c]
CHT&F	.314	.098[a]	2.237	.617[a]	.299	.488
F value	46.30[a]		37.94[a]		47.74[a]	
Adjusted R^2	.288		.444		.360	

[a]Significant at the .01 level.
[b]Significant at the .05 level.
[c]Significant at the .10 level.

In terms of category (1)—federal financial aid—we find an effect on the change in institutional scholarships for the private sample and, for public four-year institutions, an effect on the change in tuition and fees. Specifically, an increase in federal financial aid of $1 leads to a twenty cent increase in scholarship expenditures from institutional funds for four-year private colleges and universities (hence, federal financial aid and institutional aid are complements rather than substitutes) and an increase in tuition and fees of fifty cents for their public counterparts.[14] We find no effects of changes in federal financial aid on changes in instructional expenditures for any of the samples, on changes in institutional scholarships for either four-year or two-year publics, or on changes in tuition and fees for either four-year privates or two-year publics. The finding that there is no statistically significant relationship between changes in federal financial aid and changes in the "sticker" price at private four-year institutions goes against the "Bennett hypothesis" that higher federal aid induces these institutions to raise tuition.

Unlike federal financial aid, changes in direct state and local educational appropriations lead to changes in instructional expenditures in all three samples. An increase in direct state and local expenditures of $1 leads to increases in instructional expenditures of $1.39, thirty cents, and thirty-eight cents at four-year privates, four-year publics, and two-year publics, respectively. While the first coefficient is unexpectedly high, the general finding that state and local appropriations support instructional expenditures is not surprising. At private four-year institutions, changes in state and local appropriations also translate into increase in scholarship aid: a $1 increase in these appropriations leads to a twenty-two cent increase in institutional scholarships. A $1 increase in state and local appropriations also reduces the increase in tuition and fees at four-year privates by eighty-six cents. The effect on tuition and fees at two-year publics is unexpectedly positive but quite close to zero: a $1 increase in state and local appropriations leads to an increase in tuition and fees of less than three cents.[15]

Turning to the third category of government expenditure variables, government grants and contracts, we find significant effects of changes in federal grants and contracts on changes in institutional scholarships, tuition and fees,

---

14. The F-value for the tuition and fees equation for four-year publics is insignificant. However, when the equation is rerun dropping all right-hand side variables other than CHFED-FINAID and CHINTSCH, the F-value equals 3.38, which is statistically significant at the .05 level. The coefficient of CHFEDFINAID is .377, significant at the .05 level.

15. Putting aside scale effects, all five of the unexpected signs in our regressions were in the public sector regressions—two in the tuition and fee equation for two-year publics, one in the institutional scholarship equation for two-year publics, and two in the instruction equation for four-year publics—where behavior is not always based on institutional discretion (particularly in the case of setting tuition and fees). For the privates, where institutional sovereignty is the governing mechanism, all fifteen of the significant variables with predicted signs based on our theoretical model had the expected sign.

and instruction. A $1 increase in federal grants and contracts leads to increases in institutional scholarships of eleven cents, four cents, and eight cents, and to increases in instructional expenditures of twenty-two cents, thirteen cents, and thirty-one cents at four-year privates, four-year publics, and two-year publics. It leads to a decline in tuition and fees of twenty-two cents at four-year privates and ten cents at two-year publics. This suggests that federal grant and contract awards have substantial fungibility, with a sizable portion of each dollar in grants going to reduce revenues or increase other spending. A $1 increase in state and local grants and contracts at four-year privates increases institutional scholarships by six cents and lowers tuition and fees by thirteen cents. The only significant effect of state and local grants and contracts at four-year publics is an unexpected negative effect on instruction: a $1 increase leads to a thirty-one cent decline in instructional expenditures.[16] On the other hand, a $1 increase in state and local grants and contracts at two-year publics increases instructional expenditures by thirty-eight cents, although it unexpectedly lowers institutional scholarships by eleven cents and raises tuition and fees by seventeen cents.

Besides the results relating to external funding reported above, there are a number of other interesting findings. As expected, changes in state per capita income affect institutional scholarships and tuition and fees—a $1 increase in per capita income lowers growth in institutional scholarships at four-year private institutions by six cents and raises the growth in tuition and fees by twenty-six cents, while increasing tuition and fee growth at two-year publics by three cents. An increase in institutional wealth also leads to an increase in scholarships, with a $1 rise in the market value of the endowment raising scholarships by one cent at four-year privates and five cents at four-year publics. A $1 increase in annual income (INCRES) raises instructional expenditures by three cents at four-year privates and five cents at two-year publics, but unexpectedly leads to a decline in instructional expenditures at four-year publics of four cents. The results relating to the scale effects on instructional expenditures differ among sectors: at four-year publics, the larger the enrollment at the beginning of the period (a higher value of EN-ROLL79), the smaller the increase in instructional expenditures, indicating that there are significant economies of scale in instruction. However, for four-year privates, we find that the larger the enrollment, the larger the increase in these expenditures.[17] Moreover, at both four-year privates and two-year pub-

---

16. However, the causality may go from low instructional expenditures to high levels of state and local grants and contracts. That is, state and local governments may allocate these funds to institutions in which instructional spending is quite low, in an effort to increase these expenditures.

17. We suspect that in private higher education, enrollment levels may be functioning as a proxy for "quality" or expenditure levels per student. There are a great many very small private institutions with low expenditures per student. Thus, our finding may suggest that higher "quality" institutions had more rapid increases in instructional spending over this period.

lics, the larger the percentage increase in enrollment over the period, the smaller the increase in instructional expenditures, which would be consistent with the presence of substantial excess capacity in these sectors at the beginning of the period. Our finding that excess capacity existed in the private sector supports the result of Cohn, Rhine, and Santos (1989) that economies of scale persist for the private sector even at 600 percent of the output means.[18]

Finally, the relationship among the endogenous variables deserves some attention. A $1 increase in tuition and fees raises institutional scholarships by twenty-three cents at four-year privates and forty-nine cents at two-year publics. On the other hand, a $1 increase in institutional scholarships raises tuition and fees by $2.57 at four-year privates and by $1.39 at both four-year and two-year publics. A $1 increase in tuition and fees increases instructional expenditures by thirty-one cents at four-year privates and $2.24 at four-year publics.

Conclusion

Our empirical analysis is certainly subject to the typical concerns about specification error and the like. Nonetheless, we feel that it represents an important first look at a set of questions that have obvious policy implications. Some of the major results that provide insight into the multiple effects of government funds on institutions of higher learning are (1) with regard to federal student aid, we find that, at four-year private institutions, increases in federal student aid expenditures do not induce schools to raise tuition and fees, although increases in federal financial aid lead to higher tuition and fees at four-year public institutions; (2) federal grants and contracts have important effects on tuition and fees, institutional scholarships and instructional expenditures throughout higher education; our results indicate that cutbacks in these revenue sources would lead to higher tuitions at private four-year and public two-year institutions, lower institutional financial aid at four-year privates and both four- and two-year publics, and lower instructional expenditures for all three groups; and (3) increases in state and local appropriations significantly increase instructional spending in all three of the institutional categories we examined.

Understanding these various relationships is important in order to lessen the chances that changes in government policy will have unanticipated, undesirable effects on the educational sector. At the same time, the results suggest

18. Cohn, Rhine, and Santos (1989) examined data for the academic year 1981–82. While they did not distinguish four-year and two-year public institutions, they found that economies of scale in the public sector were exhausted around the output means. Note that their analysis, because it relies on data for a single year, is unable to distinguish between shorter run capacity effects and longer run scale economies.

that some widely discussed negative side effects of federal student aid spending do not exist.

REFERENCES

Barnett and Lowry. "How Housing Allowances Affect Housing Prices." Santa Monica: The Rand Corporation, 1979.

Bennett, William. "Our Greedy Colleges." *New York Times,* Feb. 18, 1987, A27.

Brinkman, Paul T., and Larry L. Leslie. "Economies of Scale in Higher Education: Sixty Years of Research." National Center for Higher Education Management Systems and University of Arizona. Mimeo. 1986.

Cohn, Elchanan, Sherrie L. W. Rhine, and Maria C. Santos. "Institutions of Higher Education as Multi-Product Firms: Economies of Scale and Scope." *The Review of Economics and Statistics* 71 (1989): 284–90.

Craig, Steven G., and Robert P. Inman. "Federal Aid and Public Education: An Empirical Look at the New Fiscal Federalism." *The Review of Economics and Statistics* 64, no. 4 (November 1982): 541–51.

Feldstein, Martin. "Effect of a Differential Add-On Grant; Title I and Local Education Spending." *Journal of Human Resources* 13 (Fall 1978): 443–58.

Finn, Chester E., Jr. *Scholars, Dollars, and Bureaucrats.* Washington, DC: The Brookings Institution, 1978.

Gurwitz, Aaron S. "The Capitalization of School Finance Reform." *Journal of Education Finance* 5 (Winter 1980): 297–319.

Hearn, James C., and Sharon L. Wilford. "A Commitment to Opportunity: The Impact of Federal Student Financial Aid Programs." Unpublished, 1985.

Hoenack, Stephen A., and Daniel J. Pierro. "An Econometric Model of a Public University's Income and Enrollment." Unpublished, 1986.

James, Estelle. "Product Mix and Cost Disaggregation: A Reinterpretation of the Economics of Higher Education." *Journal of Human Resources* 13 (Spring 1978): 157–86.

McPherson, Michael S., and Morton Owen Schapiro. "Does Student Aid Affect College Enrollment? New Evidence on a Persistent Controversy." *American Economic Review* 81 (March 1991): 309–18.

Rose-Ackerman, Susan. *The Economics of Not-for-Profit Institutions.* New York: Oxford University Press, 1986.

Sloan, Frank A., Jerry Cromwell, and Janet B. Mitchell. *Private Physicians and Public Programs.* Washington, DC: Heath, 1978.

Tsang, Mun, and Henry M. Levin. "The Impact of Intergovernmental Grants on Educational Expenditure." *Review of Educational Research* 53, no. 3 (1983): 329–67.

CHAPTER 11

Total College Income: An Economic Overview of Williams College 1956–57 to 1986–87

Gordon C. Winston

The purpose of this chapter is simple and apparently unusual. It is intended to present a global or comprehensive economic description of a college— comprehensive in the sense of providing information above all its economic activities, taken together. The period covered is encompassing, too—the thirty years since 1956–57, like in the companion study of Williams' costs of August 1987.[1] That earlier paper looked at the College's operating budget and how expenditures were divided up. This one looks in the other direction, toward aggregation, bringing together in a coherent description the pieces of our operations that are usually reported separately. It is intended to describe the context—both within the College and over time—in which our current economic decisions are being made.

Management Responsibility Versus Fund Accounting and Donor Sovereignty

The balkanization of accounts—and of responsibilities and functions—is the order of the day in college financial management, and a major effort is needed to bring the parts together. Apparently simple questions like, How much money did the College take in last year? or Is our wealth growing or shrinking? have obscure answers, and more subtle ones like, Are students providing a larger share of the College's revenues than they did thirty years ago? defy answer from easily available data. Indeed, college accounts are such that even

---

Or "Everything You Always Wanted to Know About Williams' Finances But Were Too Intimidated by Fund Accounting to Ask." The study was undertaken with the support of the president's office and with the help of a number of people, including Mike McPherson, Saeed Mughal, Will Reed, Doug Phillips, and Leo McMenemen. Ellen Hazen checked numbers, spelling, and formatting with skill and diligence.

    1. "A Thirty Year Perspective on Williams' Costs: Operating Expenditures, 1955–56 to 1985–86." The study reported here is shifted by a year; it still covers a thirty-year span, but because of data problems in the 1950s, it starts in 1956–57 and goes through 1986–87.

those who constantly deal with them cannot answer such questions with ease and confidence. It is hard to repress a worry that when such basic questions are hard to answer, they tend not to be asked.

But the structure of these accounts—and their obscurity—is no accident. There is a quite deep rationale behind the conventions of the fund accounting required of nonprofit enterprises, one that may be obscured here by my irritation at the barriers to understanding it has thrown up.[2] That rationale rests on a view of nonprofit institutions like colleges as, primarily, vessels through which the wishes of donors are to be passed.[3] Management, in the extreme version of that view (and the tradition of fund accounting), serves donors' ends and has no independent responsibility for the institution. Members of the board are trustees for donor interests, past and present, and among their major functions is that of protecting the interests of donors from those of management.[4]

This concept of donor sovereignty makes sense out of a number of otherwise mysterious traditions of college economics. For one example, important to the present issues, it is reasonable to focus management attention on the operating budget if that is the only part of the institution's economic activities over which management has been given full discretion by the donors. And it makes sense, too, to divide up the accounts into distinct funds, each reflecting a separate donors' purpose.[5]

But the major legacy of fund accounting and a donor-centered economic structure appears to be the failure to put things together, to create and maintain

---

2. Interestingly, the leading textbook on managerial control information for nonprofits appears quite innocent of that understanding, simply promulgating, instead, a set of rigid dicta on what is and what is not permissible, without explanation. Robert N. Anthony and David W. Young, *Management Control in Nonprofit Organizations* (Homewood, IL: Richard D. Irwin, Inc., 1984).

3. "In the absence of [the] implicit regulator [of profits], regulation of the allocation and utilization of financial resources of nonbusiness organizations is often achieved by the imposition of stringent controls . . . legally imposed . . . or . . . imposed through formal action of the governing board . . . [and] also . . . directly . . . by the individuals or groups that contribute such resources . . . the donor. . . . In order to account for these legally imposed, externally imposed, and self-imposed restrictions or limitations on the utilization of their resources, nonbusiness organizations have generally adopted the concepts of fund accounting." Andrew A. Harried, Leroy F. Imdieke, and Ralph E. Smith, *Advanced Accounting,* 3d ed. (New York: John Wiley and Sons, Inc., 1985), 722.

4. Henry B. Hansmann, "The Role of Nonprofit Enterprise," in Susan Rose-Ackerman, *The Economics of Nonprofit Institutions: Studies in Structure and Policy* (New York: Oxford University Press, 1986).

5. "In fund accounting, each fund . . . constitutes a *separate accounting entity* created and maintained for a specific purpose. The inflow and outflow of resources of each fund must be accounted for in such a way that they can be compared with the approved or stipulated resource flows for that fund" [italics in original]. Harried, Imdieke, and Smith, 722.

comprehensive, global accounts that can tell us what is going on in the college as a whole.

In a simpler world, formal accounts may not have been necessary to bring things together; bright people could casually stay informed of the whole of a simple operation. But institutions even as small as Williams have lately become complex enough that with traditional accounting practices, neither the management nor the board of trustees has easy access to the kind of comprehensive information needed to run the place well. Management is discouraged by the philosophy and structure of fund accounting from seeing the whole picture, yet a board made up of very busy people must rely on management for just such information.

The result is that accessible information describing the whole of the College's economic operations simply does not exist. This study was undertaken to see if it could be created—if a set of comprehensive data on our economic performance could be nursed from the fund accounts in the *Treasurer's Reports* over a sufficient piece of the past to give some historical context for what we are doing now.

It worked.

What has been done here, then, is to aggregate information from the various funds to answer three quite basic questions about Williams' operations and how they have changed over thirty years since it was a small, all-male, fraternity-centered college. The questions are,

> What is the *total yearly income* earned by the College, and how has it changed?
> What are the *sources* of that income, and how have they changed? and
> How have we *used* that income?

These questions organize the paper into the three sections that follow.

Total College Income

We start with *college income*. It is a measure of economic income—the total flow of resources into the College in the course of a year. It includes all asset income, income from tuition payments, gifts and grants, earnings from the sale of educational and general services, and income from sales of auxiliary enterprises. It is exhaustive.[6] It is analogous to *total revenue* in Econ 101 or *total income* for a family or the economic definition of income in the litera-

---

6. Actually, there are six sources with an "other" category that accounts for less than half of one percent of income over the period, so it has been ignored.

ture.[7] There appears to be no widely accepted term for this inclusive income measure for a college since it is not typically reported.[8]

College income describes the flow of money to the College from the outside. That is a bit less than college income implicit in the *Treasurer's Report* since fund accounting practice endorses a curious double counting of college-administered student financial aid; it shows up first as tuition income, then as an operating expenditure.[9] Generally, I will stick to actual income, without this double counting.

In current dollars, the actual income of Williams College has increased from some $4.4 million in 1956–57 to just under $97.0 million in 1986–87—an increase of more than 2,000 percent. Eliminating the extraneous effect of inflation by measuring things in constant 1967 dollars—as I will throughout—gives the more accurate picture in figure 1 in which real college income has grown from $5.3 million to $29.0 million. That's still an increase of almost 450 percent in the yearly value of the real resources flowing into the College over thirty years.[10]

---

7. The classic is Henry C. Simons, *Personal Income Taxation: The Definition of Income As a Problem of Fiscal Policy* (Chicago: The University of Chicago Press, 1938). Two departures here from a strict Simons definition of income lie in the treatment of assets; both are necessary because of data limitations. Changes in the value of financial assets are counted as capital gains income, but only when they are realized. A more conceptually pure measure would base the capital gains income on changes in market value, whether realized or not. The more serious departure is the failure to include changes in the value of physical assets as income, so the appreciation or depreciation of buildings, land, books, and paintings escapes our measure of total college income. Both of these departures, it seems reasonable to suppose, tend to understate both college income and its growth.

8. Indeed, a rather querulous argument is advanced by Anthony and Young that nothing like it *should* be reported.

9. So the $5 million or so of financial aid given to Williams' students in 1986–87 shows up on both sides of the books—as an expenditure in the College's operating budget and as income in the College's treasurer's report. The fact of the matter, of course, is that we discount the sticker price of our product, charging some students less tuition than others, on the basis of need. But the income we report is based on the procedural fiction that every enrolled student pays the sticker price in full and then the College hands some of them money in reimbursement, calling it an operating expense. The left hand counts as income what it gets from the right hand. Of course, money for student aid coming from outside the College, like federal funds, legitimately counts as part of income. But only once.

10. The unadjusted income implicit in the treasurer's report, which double counts tuition, overstated actual college income by some 5.3 percent in the first year of the study and by 5.0 percent in the last, so the overall growth rate for college income is not much affected. Things are not quite so dead level in the intervening period, but variations in the distortion are not extreme: overstatements range from a high of 8.7 percent in 1969–70 to a low of 3.8 percent in 1965–66. (Higher distortion percentages, of course, mean that a higher proportion of treasurer's report tuition income is actually aid from Williams.) The distortion in tuition income, considered alone, is larger, of course, ranging from an overstatement of 23 percent in 1983–84 to nearly 40 percent in 1971–72.

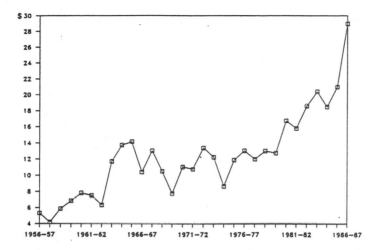

Fig. 1. Total real college income (1967 dollars, in millions)

In figure 2, real college income is adjusted for the changing size of the College over the period: the student body grew from a bit more than a thousand at the beginning of the period to nearly two thousand at the end. That expansion tends to turn the period of stagnant income growth in the late 1960s and 1970s into a period of significant decline. It is worth noting, too, that figure 2 looks a whole lot like the graph of real per student operating costs in our earlier report: the economies of scale by which expansion lowered the costs of educating a student at Williams in the 1970s just as relentlessly lowered much of the income the College received to educate a student. This is an issue we will return to in discussing the sources of income in the next section.

Before we examine its sources, though, it is useful to look a bit closer at what happened to total college income within this thirty-year period: figure 1 makes it clear that growth in total income was not steady, and figure 2 shows that income per student was even more variable.

College income grew—from the beginning to the end of these thirty years—at an impressive real rate of 5.8 percent per year. But table 1 (and figure 3) break that overall growth into annual rates of growth for each of the six five-year subperiods.

The first ten-year period, from the mid-1950s to the mid-1960s, was one of generally quite good growth of college income; for the decade, the annual real rate was nearly 7 percent. Year-to-year changes, though, were all over the map, with some as low as −21 percent (to 1957–58) but others as high as 85

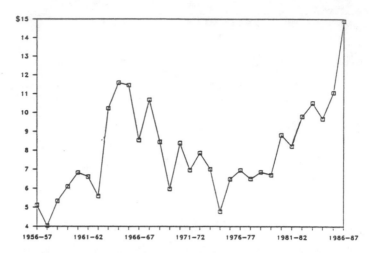

Fig. 2.   Total real college income per student (1967 dollars, in thousands)

percent (to 1963–64). A peak in real college income of $14 million was reached in 1965–66, and that level was not reached again until 1980–81.

But the more important fact in table 1 and figure 3—and the other two figures, if less obviously—is the spectacular and unprecedented growth of the College's total income in the most recent period—since 1981–82. The real, compound, yearly growth rate over the five years through 1986–87 has been almost 13 percent, roughly twice as high as in any previous five-year period within the last three decades. Actual income, still in real terms, increased from a bit under $16 million to nearly $29 million—just short of doubling— in those five years. (In current dollars, the five-year increase was from $44.5 to $97.0 million.)

When this expansion of resources in the 1980s is contrasted with the sombre realities of the preceding fifteen years (1964–65 to 1979–80), during

TABLE 1.   College Income, Annual Growth Rates, Five-Year Averages from 1956–57 to 1981–82 (1967 dollars)

	1956–57	1961–62	1966–67	1971–72	1976–77	1981–82	Whole Thirty Years
Average income (in millions)	$6.0	$10.7	$10.6	$12.0	$13.5	$18.9	$12.5
Average yearly growth	7.3%	6.7%	0.7%	3.9%	3.9%	12.9%	5.8%

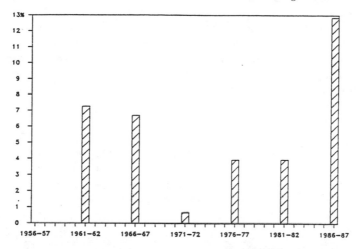

Fig. 3.   Total real college income, annual growth, five-year periods

which the annual real rate of growth of college income was often negative, a powerful part of the College's recent history is evident, one that must certainly have had a strong influence on our present behavior. We have been virtually buried under an avalanche of real resources—of money—after a long, sober time without it. The concerns expressed in our study of Williams' operating costs—that we may currently be losing our ability to control those costs—appear to have their justification in an expanded flow of resources that makes it very hard indeed to discipline spending—and even easy to believe we do not have to.

That study of the operating budget, it may be remembered, showed that its expenditures had been growing, in the period since 1980–81, at a real annual rate of roughly 7 percent with educational and general services (E&G) spending per student close to 8 percent.[11] So the good news in these figures for college income is that we could afford it—that the strong growth in operating costs was more than matched by even stronger growth in college income, a 7 percent growth rate for costs is spartan in the presence of a 13 percent growth rate for income.

But the bad news is that obviously neither of those rates is sustainable. Both costs and income are currently off the charts. So the most important message to be read from this pattern of income growth, I think, is how very unusual are the times in which we find ourselves. No reasonable view of our

11. With slight variations in period, there are many figures being bandied about. Between 1980–81 and 1985–86, real E&G increased by 8 percent, total expenditures by 6.88 percent. Some recent studies have extended the data by a year with, generally, higher rates of growth.

economic history would support the idea that either income or expenditures can be expected to keep on growing like they have in the last five years.[12]

But the immediate questions are two: where have these increased resources come from, and what have we been doing with them? We turn to these in the next two sections.

The Sources of College Income

The College has five sources of income: its assets, gifts and grants, tuition, sales of educational services, and income from auxiliary enterprises. The first three are the major sources of college revenues and are familiar. The fourth, sales of educational services, includes such things as the Center for Development Economics, health fees, and athletic receipts, while auxiliary income is dominated by room and board fees but includes a few other things like summer conference receipts.

Consider the average share of college income generated by each of the five sources over the thirty-year period. Gifts and grants have accounted for roughly a third of our total income, making that the most important single source, over all. Asset income—both investment income and realized capital gains—is next in importance with just under 30 percent of income. Together, gifts and grants and assets account for more than 60 percent of the total. Tuition has provided just over 20 percent of income during these thirty years, while income from auxiliary enterprises has averaged just under 14 percent. Finally, E&G sales have generated about 3 percent.

While something can be said about these shares and how they have changed over time, it is more useful first to turn to a brief discussion of the individual components of income and then come back to put them together.

Asset Income

Asset income includes both investment income—the yearly flow of interest and dividends to the College's portfolio—and the capital gains income (or losses) realized when securities are sold. So it is a total return. Over the thirty years, interest and dividends have represented about two-thirds of asset income and realized gains the rest (interest on student loans is about 0.1 percent of total income). Real asset income grew from $1.9 million in 1956–57 to over $11.3 million in 1986–87.

---

12. It would seem important to begin to think about how we will adjust when the inevitable turnaround comes, but more immediate and probably more important is the need to judge even current spending with far more attention to its reversibility. A study under way at Columbia addresses the global issues of an overextended national economy and their likely impact on higher education. That study might provide a context for our own more parochial efforts.

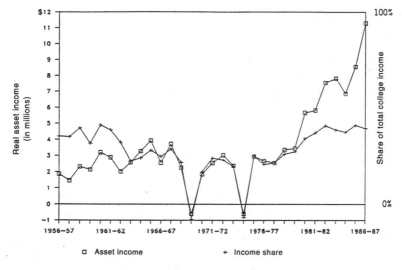

Fig. 4. Asset income, real value and share

Figure 4 shows both the level of real asset income year by year over the thirty years (the squares) and its share in total college income (the x's). The fact that leaps most quickly from figure 4 is probably that in the black years of 1969–70 and 1974–75, asset income was negative: in each of them something over $2.0 million of real investment income was more than offset by nearly $3.0 million of capital losses. But while that and an accompanying operating loss in 1969–70 appear to have been quite effective in signaling the grim times of the 1970s,[13] it is probably more important that during much of the thirty-year period—till the end of the 1970s—the share of assets in college income drifted generally downward and its real value did not increase very much. Figures like $1.9 million in 1956–57 and $2.6 million in 1963–64 look very much like the $1.8 million of 1970–71, the $2.7 million of 1976–77, and the $3.5 million of 1979–80.

Of course, the thundering bull market of the 1980s changed all that. Asset income took off, increasing dramatically in both its share of college income and in its value. Assets provided 17 percent of the College's income in 1970–71, 20 percent in 1976–77, and almost 40 percent ten years later. That powerful surge is reflected in figure 4. Real asset income increased from $3.5 million in 1979–80 to more than $11.3 million in 1986–87, growing by more

---

13. Charlie Foehl wrote in his cover letter to the 1970 treasurer's report, "This is my 20th Report as Treasurer and it unfortunately shows an operating deficit for the first time in 22 years. . . . A trend of increasing costs and inflation outrunning increases in income emphasizes the need for the most careful financial planning." *Williams College Treasurer's Report* (1970).

than a factor of three in seven years. (In current dollars, asset income increased from $8.0 million in 1979–80 to nearly $38 million in 1987–88, a factor of almost five.)

While the annual rate of growth of real asset income was a quite respectable 6.2 percent over the whole of the thirty years, average annual growth rates over five-year subperiods went from 9.2 percent to −2.3 percent to −0.1 percent to 0.9 percent to 16.9 percent to 14.2 percent[14]; that is the dramatically falling and rising pattern reflected in figure 4, and it is another way of describing the grim income picture of the late 1960s and the 1970s in their −2.3 percent, −0.1 percent, and 0.9 percent annual real rates of growth.

Gift and Grant Income

As the most important component of college income over the thirty years lumped together, gift and grant income shows a quite different pattern from asset income—at least until this past year. Gifts and grants accounted for some $2.0 million in real dollars at the beginning of the period and over $9.0 million at the end. But figure 5 makes it clear that those two endpoint numbers obscure more than they reveal. They obscure, most importantly, the fact that 1986–87 was a remarkable year in which gift and grant income more than doubled from even the preceding year. They also obscure the fact that the real value of gifts and grants had, until last year's bonanza,[15] been falling for most of twenty years. After three big years in the early 1960s—in the 175th Anniversary Campaign when it reached levels from $6.6 to $7.3 million— gift and grant income had been as high as $5.0 million during only three years prior to 1986–87. Only a year before—in 1985–86—it was around $4.0 million.

The share of college income provided by gifts was highly variable, but it mirrors this general downward drift. The five-year average share of asset income drops from a high of 42 percent to a low of 23 percent in the most recent period—despite 1986–87's record receipts. The figures for individual years are even more dramatic as gifts and grants provided over 56.3 percent of total college income in 1963–64 and less than 20 percent in 1985–86, the year before the manna rained from heaven.

Real rates of growth of gift and grant income tell much the same story of

---

14. It may seem strange that the annual rate of growth of asset income was higher between 1976–77 and 1981–82 than it was in the Roaring 80s. The explanation, of course, lies in the fairly dismal performance of the mid-1970s, against that base, the kick of the late 1970s and early 1980s generated a high growth rate.

15. Due, in large part, to the gift of some $9 million in paintings to the College Art Museum from Mrs. Prendergast.

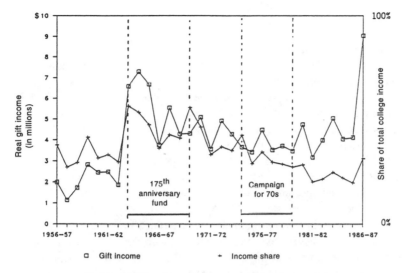

Fig. 5. Gift and grant income, real value and share

generally lackluster performance. Over the whole thirty years, from begin-ning to end, the annual real rate of growth was a respectable 5.2 percent, but annual growth rates for five-year subperiods were 1.5 percent, 8.6 percent, −1.0 percent, 4.7 percent, −6.7 percent, and, finally, a whopping 23.4 percent, due almost entirely to this past year.[16]

It's worth looking at the Alumni Fund separately. Over the thirty years, it has provided about 5 percent of college income, and the trend has been fairly steady. It reached a high share of 7.7 percent in 1969–70, which nicely emphasizes that share can go up because other things have gone down; in this case, asset income went negative in that year. In real terms, the Alumni Fund increased from a bit more than a quarter of a million dollars in 1956–57 to $1.2 million in 1986–87; it has been growing fairly steadily if not dramat-ically since the mid-1970s.[17] Over the thirty years, the real yearly rate of growth was 4.9 percent; in five-year subperiods, annual growth rates of the Alumni Fund pretty much mirrored those of total college income in table 1 with 7.7 percent, 5.5 percent, 3.7 percent, −0.1 percent, 3.6 percent, and 9.1 percent. So the Alumni Fund often leaned against changes in other gift and grant income.

---

16. Between 1981–82 and 1985–86, the yearly growth rate was 6.7 percent.

17. Just as it is useful to calculate costs per student and income per student, it might be useful to figure out the real contributions to the Alumni Fund per living alumnus.

Tuition Income

Compared with the other major sources of income, tuition has been the picture of steadiness, as reflected in figure 6. Starting a bit under $1 million in 1956–57, real tuition income had reached $5.1 million thirty years later, with a yearly growth rate of 5.7 percent. Even the subperiod growth rates reflect the consistency of tuition income with 4.8 percent, 8.5 percent, 4.6 percent, 6.5 percent, 4.2 percent, and 5.5 percent—none is negative, none even falls below 4 percent, and none gets up into double digits, even in the strong period of the early 1960s. Tuition income contributed a fairly consistent share of total college income, as is also evident from figure 6: at the least, it provided more than 15 percent of total income, and at its greatest, a bit less than 25 percent.

But in fact, that very steadiness of tuition income is strange and maybe worrisome. Why didn't tuition income increase much more strongly with the expansion of the College—as it nearly doubled—in the late 1960s and early 1970s? Tuition income is average tuition charge times number of students. Annual rates of tuition income growth during that period were modest, actually below those of the early 60s, despite that after the expansion, almost twice as many students were paying tuition.

Without turning this chapter into a report on tuition and aid policies, it is useful, I think, to look at what happened. To do that, we need the information of table 2. It shows, for the six five-year subperiods, the real rates of growth of actual tuition income, the tuition charge—the sticker price (tuition alone, no room and board or fees)—enrollment, and aid expenditures from the operating budget. The rate of growth of tuition income, of course, is increased by a higher sticker price and higher enrollment and decreased by higher aid expenditures. So table 2 suggests that a great deal of action underlay those relatively constant rates of growth of tuition income, from period to period.

In the first period—from 1956–57 to 1961–62—a strong increase in tuition charge was reinforced by an increase in the student body but offset by a large increase in student aid. The net result of these three pressures was an increase in tuition income just under 5 percent per year—almost a percentage point under the thirty-year average. In the next period, the early 1960s, the same sort of increase in tuition charge was again reinforced by the same sort of growth of the student body, but student aid grew at a markedly lower rate, so the net effect was a much higher rate of growth of tuition income—8.5 percent.

The late 1960s into the early 1970s saw the first of the significant enrollment expansions. But that big increase in the number of dues-paying students was offset both by a meagre increase in the tuition charge—at 0.9 percent, the lowest rate in the thirty years—and by a big increase in the aid budget—at

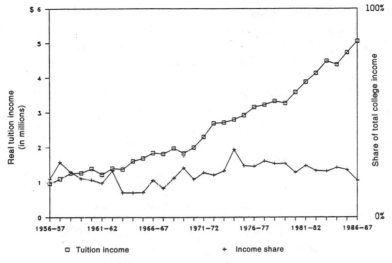

Fig. 6.   Actual tuition income, real value and share

10.2 percent, the highest rate of increase in the thirty years. The result was an annual increase in tuition income of only 4.6 percent. In the early 1970s—to 1976–77—continued expansion of the student body joined with a modest increase in the tuition charge and a striking decline in the growth of financial aid. So in that period a larger student body drove the rate of growth of tuition income up to 6.5 percent.

In the mid-1970s to mid-1980s, the expansion of the College has clearly been a thing of the past; in neither subperiod does annual enrollment growth get above half a percent. But from 1976–77 to 1981–82, a slight decline in

TABLE 2.   Tuition Income, Annual Growth Rates, Five-Year Subperiods (1967 dollars)

	1956–57 to 1961–62	1961–62 to 1966–67	1966–67 to 1971–72	1971–72 to 1976–77	1976–77 to 1981–82	1981–82 to 1986–87	Whole Thirty Years
Tuition income	4.8%	8.5%	4.6%	6.5%	4.2%	5.5%	5.7%
Tuition charge[a]	6.6	6.5	0.9	2.3	3.0	5.6	4.1
Size[b]	1.9	1.4	4.9	4.0	0.5	0.2	2.1
Aid	9.2	5.2	10.2	1.0	−0.1	8.7	5.6

[a]Tuition only.
[b]Enrollment, from the operating budget.

financial aid and an increase in the tuition charge serve to increase tuition income modestly—by 4.2 percent a year—while from 1981–82 to 1986–87, larger increases in both tuition charge and financial aid bring the rate of growth of tuition income up to 5.5 percent.

So what we see in the relatively steady growth of tuition income and its relatively constant share is the result of a lot of differences in tuition charge,[18] enrollment growth,[19] and aid policies that, together, tended to cancel each other out. While these are all to a considerable extent policy variables, I think it is important to recognize that the apparent stability of tuition income was the result of considerable instability in its underlying parts that, by and large, canceled out rather than amplified their differences. The point is that we would not want to count on the future stability of this important component of income unless we had reason to expect the stability of charges, numbers, and aid or offsetting changes.

Auxiliary Income

Unlike tuition income, auxiliary income does reflect the major changes taking place in the school. Figure 7 shows a striking increase in both the real value of auxiliary income and its share in college income during, roughly, the early 1960s to the early 1970s. That rise is both preceded and followed by fairly flat levels of auxiliary income. What was happening, of course, is that auxiliary income went up sharply, first, because the College took over the feeding and housing functions that had previously been the purview of the fraternities and, second, because of the expansion with coeducation. So real auxiliary income was under $300,000 in 1956–57 and a bit under $3.0 million in 1986–87 for an annual real growth rate of nearly 8 percent over the thirty years, the highest of any income component. But the very concentrated timing of that growth is evident in the five-year subperiod growth rates that go from 18.1 percent and 18.2 percent in the fraternity decade, then settle down to 5.9 percent and 2.8 percent in the expansion decade, and finally to 0.04 percent and 3.4 percent most recently. It is clear that some of the more recent growth is due to newly expanded enterprises, like summer conferences, rather than the more tradi-

---

18. Data that compare Williams' tuition (and room and board and fees) charges with those of Harvard, Yale, MIT, and Wesleyan over a fifty-year period, since 1936–37, show that 1970–71 marks the beginning of a period during which Williams' charges fell distinctly below all the others, a period that is still with us. Prior to that time, Williams' charges were often on the low side of the pack, but not typically at the bottom: Wesleyan was lower in the 1930s, and again in the 1950s; MIT was lower in the mid-1960s; Harvard and Yale were lower in the 1940s.

19. It came as a surprise to me that there are three, not two, distinct patterns of enrollment growth over these thirty years: the first decade with a nontrivial upward drift in size, the second decade of conscious expansion and coeducation, and the most recent decade of virtually stationary size.

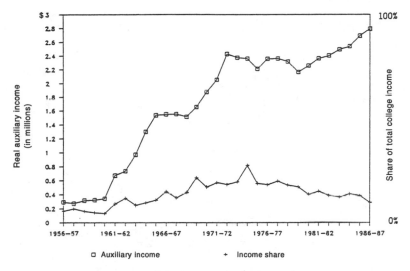

Fig. 7. Auxiliary income, real value and share

tional feeding and housing function, but this is an issue I have not closely examined.

It is worth noting that the extended, fifty-year series on tuition, fees, and room and board charges at Harvard, Yale, MIT, Wesleyan, and Williams shows that room and board charges have been virtually constant in real terms over that long span, a fact that makes sense since we are deflating current values with the consumer price index, which reflects things like food and housing and not things like professors and laboratories. (It does, however, give some credence to the argument that colleges have typically been reluctant to raise charges except when pushed to do so by real cost increases. But that is a different issue.)

Sales of Educational and General Services

This final income category is sufficiently small that its growth rates can be impressive—like a positive 21.4 percent between 1961–62 and 1966–67 or a negative 16 percent between 1966–67 and 1971–72—and not mean a great deal for college income. Though E&G sales started a bit below $200,000 and got to a bit more than $700,000 most recently, figure 8 shows a high degree of variability and, until the late 1970s, no particular trend in level. Its share of college income has been pretty close to dead level for fifteen years and its overall real rate of growth the lowest of any income component at 4.5 percent a year.

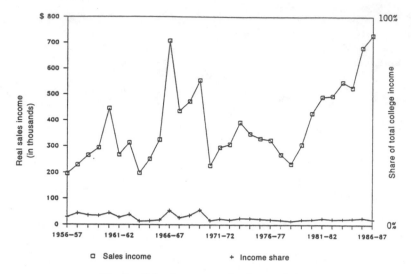

Fig. 8. Sales income, real value and share

The Sources of College Income Together

A discussion of the individual components of college income leads to the more basic question, how have these various sources affected total college income over the thirty years of our data? And what can we expect for the future in light of this history?

There appears to be a simple and rather basic answer to the first of these. The tides are moderate when the sun and the moon pull in different directions; the extremes of the Spring tides come only when they reinforce each other. And like the tides, total college income grew smoothly when movements in the big four income sources—assets, gifts and grants, tuition, and auxiliary income—offset each other, but when their often-considerable variations reinforced each other, swings in total college income were extreme. Underlying is that the major components of income have often been quite variable. Except for a couple of periods, their variations appear to have had some independence.

That being the case, the answer to the second question—what this tells us about the future—seems also to be clear: we can expect continued volatility in total college income with high highs and low lows coming only with an atypical coincidence of movements of its parts.

It is worth looking more closely at the way these pieces have fit together then, period by period over the thirty years. In table 3, the annual real growth rates for the five components and total college income are shown for each of the five-year subperiods. In these the interaction among the components of income is quite evident.

Look at the first period, from 1956–57 to 1961–62. Gift and tuition income grew moderately—a bit below their thirty-year average—but asset income growth was powerful—half again its thirty-year average—and auxiliary income grew at even higher annual rates. The result was a strong growth in college income. In the next period, to 1966–67, the rate of growth of asset income fell by almost twelve percentage points to be large and negative, but the growth of both gift and tuition income nearly doubled while auxiliary income continued to expand at its very high rate. The result of all this was a negligible drop in the rate of growth of college income—by about half a percentage point.

But then the moon and the sun got in phase between 1966–67 and 1971–72, with dismal results. Asset income growth actually improved a bit—going from large and negative to small and negative is an improvement—but the growth of gift income declined, and tuition income, ever steady (because its own variations cancelled out), went back to earlier rates of growth while auxiliary income increased at a less immodest rate than in the preceding decade. All this added up to near paralysis of college income with the lowest annual growth rate of any five-year period.

The early 1970s saw improvement from awful to mediocre in the growth of asset income and from awful to a bit below average for gift income, while the growth rate for tuition income increased by nearly half and that for auxiliary income fell by half. All these, together, produced a low but decent growth rate for college income.

In the next five years, to 1981–82, things changed radically in each of its components, but the rate of growth of college income was exactly the same as in the period before—to one decimal place. The growth rate of asset income went from near zero to 17 percent a year, gift income shrank by almost seven percentage points a year, tuition income grew at modest rates, and auxiliary

TABLE 3. College Income, Real Annual Growth Rates, Five-Year Subperiods

	1956–57 to 1961–62	1961–62 to 1966–67	1966–67 to 1971–72	1971–72 to 1976–77	1976–77 to 1981–82	1981–82 to 1986–87	Whole Thirty Years
Assets	9.2%	−2.3%	−0.1%	1.0%	17.0%	14.2%	6.2%
Gifts	4.5	8.6	−1.0	4.7	−6.7	23.3	5.2
Tuition	4.8	8.5	4.6	6.5	4.2	5.5	5.7
E&G sales	6.5	21.4	−16.0	1.8	8.7	8.2	4.5
Auxiliary sales	18.1	18.2	5.8	2.8	0.0	3.4	7.8
College income	7.3	6.7	0.7	3.9	3.9	12.9	5.8

income was stagnant. Yet the growth rate of total college income remained the same.

Which brings us to the mid-1980s. Like the late 1960s, the early 1980s have found the sun and the moon in phase, but this time they are producing very high tides of college income growth rather than low ones. Very very high rates of growth of asset and gift income have combined with so-so growth of tuition income and below average growth of auxiliary income to give us the highest income growth rates, by far, in the thirty years—nearly double those of the strongest earlier period and more than double the thirty-year average.

It is interesting, I think, how the importance of the phasing of income components shows up in comparing the periods of lowest and highest growth of college income. What distinguishes them is only the strikingly different behavior of asset and gift income. In both periods, they move together, but they went from negative to huge positive rates of growth. The growth rate for tuition income, on the other hand, went up by less than a percentage point, and that for auxiliary income went down by two.

What is wrong with my tide analogy, of course, is that we can buy tide tables to tell us when the moon and sun are going to be in phase, but we have only a bit of history and a lot of guessing to tell us when the components of college income will next be in phase. We can be sure, though, that they will go in and out of phase, with large impact on college income, for better and for worse.

Economies of Scale—the Dark Side

In writing on higher education, much is made of the fact that a larger student body allows fixed costs to be spread over more people, reducing the average cost of educating a student. These are economies of scale. So Williams' expansion in the late 1960s and early 1970s reduced operating costs per student from $6,570 in 1969–70 to $5,190 in 1974–75; only in 1984 did per-student costs rise above their 1969 level in real terms.

But college income figures reveal another side of that same coin. Colleges, unlike the business firms for whom the idea of economies of scale was initially formulated, have not only fixed *costs* that do not change with the number of students, they also have fixed *income*—in the form of asset and gift and grant income—that does not change with the number of students. So there are income *dis*economies of scale along with the cost economies of scale; expanding the size of the College reduced costs per student and income per student simultaneously.

Figures 9 and 10 show the effect of that expansion. Figure 9 shows the income diseconomies of scale. Fixed income per student—asset income and income from gifts and grants—falls sharply with the growing student body,

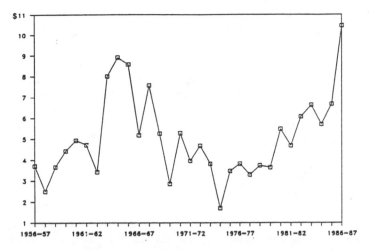

Fig. 9. Fixed college income per student, asset and gift-grant income (1967 dollars, in thousands)

from an average of $10,496 over the five years from 1962–63 to 1967–68 to an average of $6,631 over the five years after the expansion was pretty much complete, from 1974–75 to 1979–80. Lots more is going on in these figures than just expansion—the 175th anniversary campaign and a lousy stock market—but the fact remains that not until 1986–87, with its exuberant asset

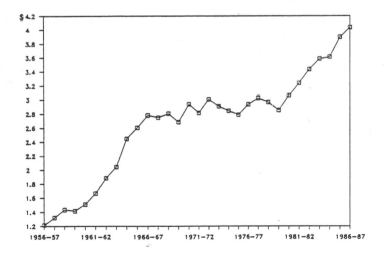

Fig. 10. Variable college income per student, tuition and auxiliary income (1967 dollars, in thousands)

and gift income, did fixed income per student reach its preexpansion levels. It seems unlikely that it will stay there. It is worth noting, again, that these fixed components of income provide Williams with more than 60 percent of total college income.

The variable income per student of figure 10—tuition and auxiliary income—shows a much smoother pattern with none of those diseconomies of income scale. There, despite the slowdown in tuition charges in the 1970s, variable income per student grew throughout the period, even if at moderate rates during the depression of the 1970s.

Growing Tuition Dependency and Other Such Ratios

Aside from their graphic demonstration of a side of economies of scale for colleges that is usually neglected, these data shed some light on the question of increasing tuition dependency and, more generally, on the potential pitfalls of such ratio analyses. Growing tuition dependency describes a concern frequently voiced but not often, to my knowledge, carefully analyzed. It asserts that private colleges need to worry because they are, over time, becoming more and more dependent on tuition as a source of income; in other words, they are being less adequately supported by nontuition income. In the simplest—and usual—version, that assertion is supported by a comparison of total tuition income and the revenue side of the operating budget.

But that is much too simple. The operating budget is only one of the uses of college income, and sometimes a minority use, as the next section will emphasize. More importantly, the allocation of college income to the operating budget is within the discretion of the board of trustees (with some mild restrictions, usually not seriously reducing fungibility), so the fact that tuition makes up a larger proportion of operating budget revenues is not as significant as it might seem to be—it is certainly not the necessary result of uncontrollable outside forces, since the trustees control the denominator. An increase in tuition's role in the operating budget, then, could be evidence of a decline in nontuition sources of income, but it might instead be evidence of an increase in savings from college income so that less, in total, is going to the operating budget or—clearly relevant to Williams—a decision to expand the student body that brought diseconomies of income scale, diluting fixed income sources while leaving per-student variable income, like tuition income, unaffected.

At Williams, a growing tuition dependency does indeed show up in looking at the last twenty years of the operating budget (especially when the double counting of student aid is not eliminated). Figure 11 describes tuition

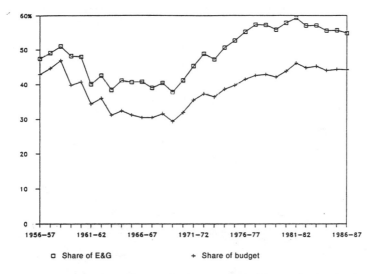

Fig. 11. Tuition dependency—budget, gross tuition and gross budget

income as a proportion of operating revenues, straight from budget figures.[20] For the twelve years from 1969–70 to 1981–82, the share of the operating budget that was covered by tuition increased almost without interruption from a low of just under 30 percent to a high of over 46 percent. But even within the scope of figure 11, that is a selective description both because the period of increasing tuition dependency was preceded by ten years of significantly decreasing tuition dependency and because it was followed by five years more of moderate reversal of that trend. The pattern is the same for the total operating budget and for E&G alone.

Figure 12 takes the broader view of tuition dependency—as something happening *to* us—by picturing the contribution of tuition income to total college income. That gets rid of the effect of the trustees' discretionary allocation of college income to operating revenues; how much they spend and how much they save does not affect this representation of tuition dependency.

The top line shows actual tuition income as a percent of college income, repeating on a larger scale the share line from figure 6. This percentage is

---

20. I actually used operating expenditures for figure 13, since those data are right handy and the College never ran a significantly imbalanced operating budget. Since no adjustment was made for the double counting of student aid, tuition income will look more important than it is. (If actual tuition income were $5 million and aid payments were $1.5 in an operating budget of $10 million, the share of tuition would show up as 65 percent though it was actually 50 percent. These figures are close to Williams' constant dollar figures.)

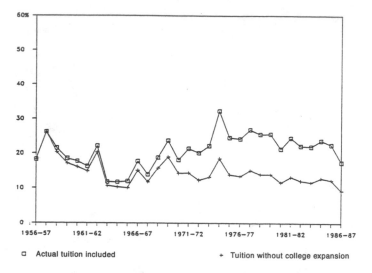

Fig. 12. **Tuition dependency—income, with and without college expansion**

simply total tuition income as a proportion of total college income, so growing dependency on tuition would show up here. It is hard to see any clear trend; broadly, tuition dependency went down, and it went up, and it went down. Tuition started as 18 percent of college income in 1956–57, then jumped immediately to over 26 percent, then fell to about 10 percent, when gifts and grants were very high, then it returned to the low 20 percent range during the depressed 1970s and into the 1980s and wound up at 17.5 percent at the end, falling largely because of the big increase in asset and gift income. So it is hard to see evidence here of a trend toward the College's growing dependency on tuition as an income source.

But more to the point of distinguishing what is happening *to* us—as against what we have chosen to do to ourselves—is the other, lower, line in figure 12. It shows the share that tuition income would have represented in College income if Williams had not chosen to expand, thereby diluting the contribution of fixed income and increasing the share of variable income. It is clear that we'd have seen a strongly reduced tuition dependency, had we not chosen to increase the size of the College. Had we held enrollments at the 1956–57 figure of 1,038, tuition would have made up a smaller and smaller share of total income. The average share of tuition in college income would have fallen from 16.3 percent in the first decade to 14.2 percent in the second decade and to 12.7 percent in the last.

So it is hard to worry about a growing tuition dependency as a hostile trend affecting the College. There is evidence that we have chosen both to dilute our fixed income with a larger student body and to increase savings, allocating a smaller part of our total income to the operating budget and a larger part to accumulating assets and buildings. That takes us to the next question—the uses of college income—but it also justifies a parting shot on this one: Beware simple "ratio analysis" of college finances unless unusual thought has gone into interpreting those ratios with attention to their numerators and their denominators—and their hidden assumptions about managerial discretion.

The Uses of College Income

Two things can be done with income: it can be spent or it can be saved. That is as true for a college as it is for a family or a business or a nation. Figure 13 shows Williams' total college income over the thirty years (duplicating the stuff of figure 1) and our total spending out of that income. The area between the two lines shows total saving. Over the whole of the period, the College spent roughly 65 percent of the money it took in and saved about 35 percent. Annual saving rates, as a percent of college income, varied widely over the thirty years, from a high of 55 percent at one point during the 175th Anniversary Campaign to a low low of −1.4 percent in the grim year of 1969–70. Saving rates averaged over five-year subperiods show the now familiar pattern: high between 1956–57 and 1966–67 (over 42 percent in the first five years and 43 percent in the next period), low between 1966–67 and 1976–77 (25 percent in the first five years and 23 percent in the next), and high in the last decade (34 percent in the first five years and 43 percent most recently). At 51.8 percent, the saving rate for 1986–87 was fourth highest in the thirty years.

Spending

Our earlier study of costs over these thirty years provided enough detail about the College's spending that not much needs to be added here. A couple of useful comments, though, can be made from the broader perspective of these data. One is that most, but not all, spending shows up in the operating budget; some spending, like ongoing museum projects and the president's discretionary funds, appears in the treasurer's report but not in the operating budget. In

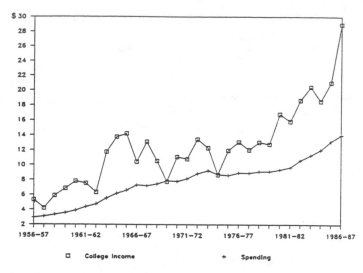

Fig. 13. Total college income, spending and saving (1967 dollars, in millions)

the late 1980s, the amounts were very small.[21] In addition, interest on the Higher Education Financing Administration (HEFA) loans, spending for the capital campaign, and portfolio management costs are expenditures additional to those in the budget: starting with some $300,000 in 1977–78, the HEFA interest costs have grown to $1.3 million in 1986–87.[22] The operating budget captured all spending reported in the treasurer's report in only ten of the thirty years covered, and with the more systematic use of nonoperating budget expenditures, about 5 percent of total spending does not now enter the budget.

Saving—Financial and Physical

Figure 14 shows real College saving over the period. It makes explicit what was only implicit in the vertical distance between the spending and income lines in figure 13. And figure 15 shows saving relative to total college income. We have already commented on total savings rates and their variation over the

---

21. Some spending, however, has appeared in the treasurer's report that was not really spending but was reduction in income, notably a capital loss of some $4.1 million in 1974–75 and (much) smaller amounts in the years on either side. For this study, I have simply moved those entries into (negative) asset income with the other capital loss incurred in 1969–70 and reported as such.

22. Since the HEFA activity earns money for the College through interest arbitrage—simultaneously borrowing and lending at interest rate differentials—this money, too, should arguably show up as a reduction in asset income. I have not treated it that way.

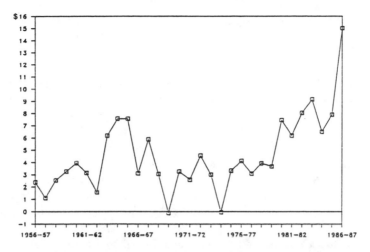

Fig. 14.   Total college saving (1967 dollars, in millions)

period, variations amply evident in figures 14 and 15, so we can turn here to the question of the form that saving has taken: how much of each year's saving was put into financial assets and how much into physical assets.

Over the whole period, total real saving was about $145 million. Of that, some $97 million took the form of financial saving, and about $48 million was

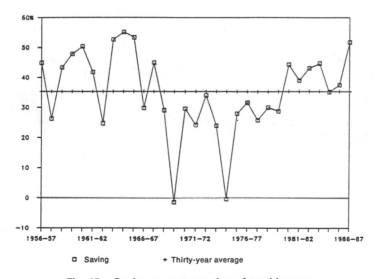

□ Saving   + Thirty-year average

Fig. 15.   Saving as a proportion of total income

in new physical assets.[23] So for that considerable chunk of history, financial saving accounted for two-thirds and saving through new buildings and other physical assets accounted for one-third. I do not think I would have expected that balance.

On the other hand, figure 16 shows the distribution between financial and physical savings over the whole period. It makes sense that financial savings (and losses) should be more volatile than saving in a physical form; it is hard to turn building programs on and off, and, more important, it is usually foolish to liquidate physical assets when there are temporary reversals, as in the 1970s. So financial asset accumulation takes up the slack.

What I get out of figure 16 is that over much of the period financial and physical saving went up and down; the physical expansion of the College with coeducation is clear in the 1970s along with the problems of capital losses in that decade. But starting in the mid-1970s, there appears to have been an effort both to increase the rate of saving and, for a time at least, to devote more of it to rebuilding financial assets with a reduction in building and an increase in financial accumulation. Then starting with the early 1980s and accelerating up to the late 1980s, there is a building boom of historic proportion with much of saving going into bricks and mortar rather than the endowment: the balance between them, of course, is maintained by last year's very large increases in income, hence total saving.

These figures, I think, raise important questions about the rationale—the policy—behind the allocation of saving between (crudely) endowment and buildings. And there is the underlying question Hansmann and Massy have recently asked, "Why do nonprofit institutions save at all?" It is a question I sense can usefully be addressed for Williams and should be. Pending a careful examination, financial saving can be justified as necessary to reestablish Williams' historical level of endowment or net worth per student, which has fallen, in constant dollars, from roughly $60,000 in 1968 to a low of $28,650 in 1980 and back to some $42,800 in 1986. Or it can be understood more rigorously if we estimate the endowment required to maintain the quality of our education with future cost growth and inflation in a Stanford-type equilibrium model.

But the other question these figures raise is that of borrowing. Our debt is now approaching $50 million, making our net worth a decreasing proportion of the endowment. *The endowment* does not have the same meaning for

---

23. There is about $4 million of accumulated error in these thirty-year figures. Since the total saving estimate was done from yearly flows and the allocation of that total between financial and physical asset acquisitions was independently done by differencing stock values, year to year, I find it quite reassuring that the two approaches are off by only about 3 percent. I hope others do, too.

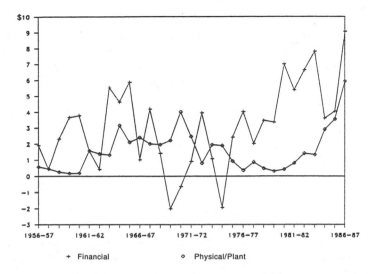

Fig. 16. The distribution of real savings, financial and physical assets (1967 dollars, in millions)

colleges that it used to, a fact that seems not to be widely recognized. We are conditioned by history to think of the endowment as *unencumbered* wealth, so a measure of a college's endowment is a measure of its net wealth. That has changed as colleges have taken on significant amounts of debt: gross endowments are increasingly offset by debt. In crude terms, for Williams, our endowment of about $250 million is reduced by roughly a fifth by $50 million in debt to an actual net endowment of about $200 million. Clearly, concentration on gross endowment figures is seriously and increasingly misleading, giving us (and donors) an inflated view of our wealth. Failure to recognize this fact would add about $10,000 to endowment per student described above. These are not issues to be addressed casually in a report like this; they appear to warrant considerably more focused thought and study.

Finally, the allocation of our saving between financial and physical capital, like the determination of the level of financial saving, might also benefit from closer study. Most striking is the fact, embedded in college accounting conventions, that transferring a dollar from financial to physical assets—or choosing to save it in a new building rather than in increased financial assets—carries three often important costs: (1) income is earned on financial but not on physical assets; (2) operating costs are incurred on physical but not on financial assets; and (3) in the highly cyclical, boom and bust environment in which colleges operate, saving in the form of buildings is not easily reversible, either for liquidity or for reallocation to another purpose.[24] A more complete and realistic system of accounts—in which the value of capital services, like the value of labor services of administrators and faculty, was included in calculating the costs of a Williams education—would recognize the first two of these. It would still remain that saving in the form of physical asset accumulation carries an irreversibility that may prove to be a considerable problem in a more austere economic environment. For that reason, the recent building trend in figure 16 warrants attention. Of course, saving in any form better serves the future than not saving at all.

Conclusion

This chapter provides a basis for the comprehensive or global accounts of a college's economic activity that are needed to overcome the restrictions on perspective and information imposed by fund accounting. Conventional accounting organizes information to protect the interests of donors; these college income accounts organize the same information to give management—the administration and trustees—an overview of the economic operations of the College. So these accounts complement conventional fund accounting, embedding a broader view of managerial responsibility.

The economic information on Williams that is reported here should provide an essential sense of context in which to judge current and future economic decisions. That context has two dimensions: in one, the separate pieces of our operation—capital budget, endowment, various income sources, operating budget, and so on—are put together to see how they fit and how they interact; in the other, present and prospective decisions are put in a long enough historical setting to give us some perspective on change and stability—and warnings of impending change.

Of course, the proof of this particular pudding will be in the use of these accounts. They have yet to be made simple and accessible enough that they can serve the needs of busy people, and to do that they will have to be kept up, regularly updated with the most recent information we can get and need to frame current operations. The essential test, then, of this view of the College will be whether it is of use to those making our basic economic decisions, whether it will help guide more thoughtful and informed policies.

---

24. Steve Lewis has argued that building costs rise faster than inflation, making saving in the form of appreciating buildings a better form than saving in financial assets. I am curious one day to check that intuition out.

CHAPTER 12

The Necessary Revolution in Financial Accounting

Gordon C. Winston

The financial accounts of a college or university do not report economic information for the institution as a whole, as one would expect. Instead, the college is divided up into separate activities, and a separate set of financial accounts—income statement and balance sheet—is reported for each of those activities. Each is treated as if it were a separate firm (Garner 1991). Often complex loans and transfers between those firms are recorded in each set of accounts. The system is called fund accounting. Eight or nine fund accounts and their interwoven transfers typically make up the annual financial statement for even a small and simple college.

Fund accounts have come to remind one of the old saw about the weather—that everyone complains but no one does anything about it.[1] This chapter describes the results of a five-year effort to organize the basic economic information about a college's performance in a different and more useful way. The result is a set of global accounts that present an *encompassing*—all-inclusive, complete, integrated—view of a college's eco-

Reprinted from *Planning for Higher Education* 20, no. 4 (1992): 1–16. Reprinted by permission of the Society for College and University Planning. The structure of this analysis was developed between 1986 and 1988 and given an important shot of practicality during my stint as provost at Williams from 1988 to 1990. The support of the Andrew W. Mellon Foundation through its support, in turn, of the Williams Project on the Economics of Higher Education is gratefully acknowledged. William Bowen, Shaun Buckler, Keith Finan, George Goethals, David Healy, Robinson Hollister, George Keller, Duncan Mann, Charles Mott, Saeed Mughal, Will Reed, Joseph Rice, Morton Schapiro, David Schulte, and Winthrop Wassenar gave me valuable insights into these issues with considerable improvement in the quality of the analysis and understanding. I am especially indebted to Harold Bierman, Roger Bolton, David Booth, Anne MacEachern, and Michael McPherson. Needless to say, I did not take all of their good advice.

1. That is not quite accurate. Almost twenty years ago, Bierman and Hofstedt showed how misleading conventional budget deficits can be, using an analysis similar in some ways to that of this paper. Their effort got them an Andy Rooney segment on CBS, a front-page *Wall Street Journal* article titled "Ten Eastern Colleges Accused of Crying Wolf in Reporting Deficits: Two Cornell Accounting Profs Contend the Schools Conceal Gains in 'Financial Condition,'" and strenuous objections from comptrollers and presidents. But there has been little lasting effect.

nomic activities and status. It is the kind of information essential to the governance of the college, the kind the board of trustees, the faculty oversight committee, and the top administrators need. It describes the economic effects of a year's activities and most specifically their effect on the college's real wealth. The structure of the global accounts is the antithesis of that of the fund accounts that *divides* a college into a set of *discrete*—self-contained, balkanized—accounting entities. Global accounts bring information about the whole of the college together. Their aim is to be accurate, clear, and accessible to those who are not steeped in fund accounting.

Fund Accounts

Fund accounting has a long and honorable tradition of service to government and nonprofit institutions, and there are still important questions that only fund accounts—or something like them—can answer. The question addressed in this chapter is the inadequacy of fund accounts to provide the sole or primary way to frame economic information for colleges and universities. The main problems with using fund accounts as the primary way of describing the economic performance of colleges and universities appear to be the following (which are clearly related and all derive from the balkanization of the college's activities):

1. Fund accounts obscure an overall, global understanding of an institution's economic performance.
2. Fund accounts are hard to read and understand—*inaccessible* without a significant investment of time—with their mass of detailed information repeated separately for each fund and the often complex transfers and interactions among funds.
3. One result of balkanization and inaccessibility is a focus of attention on understandable information even though it is partial and may be marginally relevant or even misleading, like operating budget deficits, endowment wealth, or an endowment payout rate. The operating budget often leaves out a third or more of all current economic activity, budget deficits or surpluses are easily manipulated, and the endowment (and quasi-endowment) is only a fraction of total wealth in even the best endowed schools.[2]
4. A worrisome result would appear to be an inherent temptation— usually resisted but always present—to present misleading information. It may happen unintentionally, but funds are potential shells that invite shell games because their complexity induces some parts of the accounts to be ignored while other parts are given unwarranted attention. In moving $5 million of current spending off the operating

---

2. Winston 1988.

budget in the 1980s, for instance, Williams markedly reduced the apparent, but not the actual, growth of its operating expenditures; Carleton reported large current expenditures in their endowment fund instead of the current fund; Swarthmore noted its forty years of exactly balanced operating budgets,[3] apparently achieved by transferring to the budget, after the fact, whatever was needed to cover operating expenses; MIT and Harvard followed the same convention in the 1970s (Bierman and Hofstedt 1973).

5. It is important for the broader understanding of higher education that fund accounting reduces comparability among schools and even for a single school over time.

The original rationale for fund accounts in colleges was that they made it easier to monitor performance in specific areas supported by outside agents, by donors or governments who gave funds to the college for restricted purposes and needed to know if those purposes were being well served and managed.[4] But while that stewardship role remains, it does not justify the use of fund accounts as the primary way of organizing economic information. Efforts to make fund accounting serve purposes of both stewardship and governance—by using ratio analysis, for instance (Chabotar 1989)—have been only partly successful since they retain the shortcomings of fund account data. On the other hand, global accounts that define the context and inform the governance of a college will always need to be complemented by subaccounts, fitted within that inclusive global reporting, that deal with the more detailed information essential to management and that identify restrictions on the use of funds.

Global Accounts

The basic structure of the global accounts is simple. For a year's economic activity, three elemental economic facts are reported.

1. How much the college took in, in total, from all sources
2. What it did with that money
3. The effect of these activities on the institution's real wealth

---

3. "The 1986–87 fiscal year was the fortieth consecutive year in which the College operated with a balanced budget" (Swarthmore College 1987, 17).

4. "In the absence of [the] implicit regulator [of profits], regulation of the allocation and utilization of financial resources of nonbusiness organizations is often achieved by the imposition of stringent controls . . . legally imposed . . . or . . . imposed through formal action of the governing board . . . [and] also . . . directly . . . by the individual or groups that contribute such resources . . . the donor. . . . In order to account for these legally imposed, externally imposed, and self-imposed restrictions or limitations . . . nonbusiness organizations have generally adopted the concepts of fund accounting" (Harried, Imdieke, and Smith 1985, 722).

That is the essential framework of global accounts.[5] What is centrally important is that they completely encompass the institution's activities: no flow or
claim between the college and an outside agent—of income, expenditure,
saving, assets, or liabilities—should be left out. And no financial flows or
claims simply between funds should be included.

The hope in constructing global accounts, initially, was that they would
only reorganize the economic information already reported in the fund accounts. Global accounts were derived from audited, published information,
largely by combining fund activities and eliminating double counting among
them (Winston 1988). And that worked, at first. Indeed, a major question was
whether the approach that generated global accounts from Williams' published fund accounts would work, too, for other schools, a question that was
answered when Duncan Mann and I were able to create global accounts for
Wellesley, Carleton, Swarthmore, and, for contrast, the State University system of New York (Winston and Mann in preparation). The result was an
accounting of the year's total income, total current spending, and total real
financial saving—the change in financial wealth.

But not all wealth. It has become increasingly clear that global accounts
that simply reorganize existing information create a useful set of global financial records that monitor real financial wealth, but they share the shortcoming
of the fund accounts in being inadequate to the incorporation of physical
capital wealth. Neither one can account for all of an institution's wealth: at
Williams, for example, they ignore more than half of its $645 million of net
worth.

So the set of genuinely global accounts presented here, while still heavily
dependent on a reorganization of published information, augments those data
with a more realistic treatment of land, plant, and equipment (a treatment very
much in the spirit of the current literature on capital planning in colleges
(Dunn 1989; Probasco 1991)). For some potential users, these full global
accounts may go too far; not everyone is ready to monitor all of his or her
institution's wealth. One can retreat to the halfway house of global financial
accounts, a system that is no worse then conventional accounting in its neglect
of capital wealth and is a whole lot better in dealing with the other problems of
fund accounting noted above. So considerable improvement lies in using the
global financial accounts, even if they are importantly incomplete. (Table 1 is
repeated in appendix A as table 1-A to show the same college in the abbreviated form of a global financial account, but the rest of the text will deal with
the fully global accounts that include all institutional wealth.)

In a significant and encouraging recent development, Harvard's new

---

5. It is also the underlying framework—often honored in the breach—of the familiar
income statement and balance sheet.

annual *Financial Report* treats the physical capital stock much as described below, even though that increased realism raised their reported operating expenses by $77 million and gave them a $42 million budget deficit (Harvard University 1992). Harvard's decision not only reduces the risk to other schools of adopting these innovations in reporting economic information, but it indicates another way for an institution to move *toward* fully global accounts without embracing them all at once.

A caveat before describing the global accounts in detail. Their application is more immediately appropriate to most private than to most public institutions. The reason, of course, is the often Byzantine arrangements of responsibility, ownership, and governance that have grown up between public colleges and state and local agencies, arrangements that can affect, inter alia, the ownership of the school's capital stock, responsibility for tuition levels, salaries and fringe benefits, and even control over the use of any endowment wealth. So the scope of responsibility and control may sometimes be very different from that implied by these accounts. It remains, however, that global accounts or something quite like them are essential to public institutions if anyone is to know the real costs of public education and the effects of a state's policies on its educational wealth.

How the elements of global accounts work to form a coherent system of information will be clearer if they are embedded in a concrete example, so two years' data are presented in table 1.[6] Consider the components in turn.

College Income

The income elements in table 1 are fairly straightforward at a small school, but a few comments are useful, nonetheless. The list of income sources is exhaustive: all income flowing into the college during the year is included, whether it comes from students,[7] donors, government, borrowers of the college's wealth, or purchasers of services from the college. Gift and grant income in table 1 is separated according to donors' wishes to recognize that part of gift income is intended to expand the college's wealth and that that part is potentially different from gifts that donors intend should be used at the discretion of the college. Asset earnings include interest, dividends, and

---

6. These are similar to historical data from Williams' published sources, so no legal issues are raised by their use here. In the description of an economic plan below, pains are taken to present transparently unrealistic and uninformative planning parameters to illustrate only the structure of the plan and nothing of Williams' expectations or intentions.

7. Tuition and fee income in these accounts is gross. An alternative would leave institutional student aid out of both income and expenditures and report as income only net tuition and fees.

TABLE 1. Global Accounts

	1989–1990	1990–1991
1. College income		
Tuition and fees	$29,262,691	$32,543,540
Gifts and grants		
To endowment	7,066,669	8,744,806
To plant	1,016,397	713,124
All other	12,664,824	13,951,045
Asset income		
Interest and dividends	17,039,521	15,859,257
Appreciation	18,582,670	6,873,486
Sales, services, and other	1,950,970	2,724,059
Auxiliary income	11,599,559	11,862,813
Total college income	99,183,301	93,272,130
2. Current expenditures		
Operating budget expenditures	62,425,303	66,924,329
Other current expenditures	6,304,914	5,634,728
Less current account maintenance	703,276	642,167
Total current expenditures	68,026,941	71,916,890
3. Additions to capital stock		
Investment in new plant	9,334,326	2,310,285
Less deferred maintenance		
Real depreciation	7,500,000	8,097,195
Less maintenance spending		
In current account	703,276	642,167
In plant fund	3,477,560	4,639,692
Total deferred maintenance	3,319,164	2,815,336
Total additions to capital	6,015,162	(505,051)
4. Operating costs		
Current expenditures	68,026,941	71,916,890
Real depreciation	7,500,000	8,097,195
Total operating costs	75,526,941	80,014,085
5. Wealth end of year		
Financial wealth		
Assets	346,203,972	358,726,081
Less liabilities	50,596,648	49,355,661
Net financial wealth	295,607,324	309,370,420
[Endowment value]	[333,553,551]	[341,572,081]
Physical capital wealth		
Replacement value	323,887,799	341,438,861
Less accumulated deferred maintenance	3,319,164	6,290,686
Net physical wealth	320,568,635	335,148,175
Net worth	616,175,959	644,518,595

capital gains or losses (whether realized or not).[8] Auxiliary income, in a small liberal arts college, consists largely of student charges for room and board; for a university, that line would be both larger and more complicated, as would sales, services, and other, the catchall income line here.

Current Expenditures

Current expenditures in the global accounts is both a more and a less inclusive category than spending from the current fund, in fund accounting: it includes all current expenditures, and it excludes maintenance spending. Current expenditures are included whether they appear within the operating budget or elsewhere in the current fund, the capital budget, the endowment fund, or somewhere else in the fund accounts. So in a global accounting, there is no opportunity to reduce the apparent level or growth of current expenditures by shifting some of them from a closely monitored area like the operating budget to a less scrutinized part of the accounts, like off-budget current fund or endowment fund spending. Spending on the maintenance of the plant and equipment is excluded because it is not a current expenditure: it is spending that buys a durable good—the restoration, renovation, and adaptation[9] of the physical plant.[10]

Additions to the Capital Stock

Predictably, the greatest departure from conventional reporting comes in the global accounts' treatment of the physical capital stock, since that aspect of college management and college wealth is so effectively neglected in fund accounting. The purpose of global accounting of the capital stock is to report its real value and record the effects of the year's activities on that value. It serves, too, to inform a more accurate measure of the college's operating costs that recognizes both current spending and real depreciation of the college's physical wealth.

Additions to the capital stock are simply the year's gross investment in

---

8. While this is logically necessary because Williams accounts its financial assets at market value, it would be desirable even if they did not.

9. *Adaption* refers to action to offset depreciation due to *obsolescence,* in the trilogy described long ago by Terborg. The other sources are depreciation due to *use* and depreciation due to the *elements*—these would be addressed by *renovation* spending as used here.

10. Under present practice, some of renovation and adaptation is embedded in current spending, but the largest part of renovation and adaption spending typically appears as capital spending (labeled *investment in plant*), so only a relatively small adjustment to reported current spending is usually needed to purge total current expenditures of what is more accurately capital spending. At Williams, the maintenance part of current expenditures was only $703,000 in 1989–90 and $642,000 in 1990–91.

new plant less any value lost through deterioration of the capital stock—the year's deferred maintenance. Investment in new plant is uncomplicated: it includes all additions and acquisitions of new land, plant, and equipment that will augment the capital stock. Deferred maintenance describes how much of the year's real depreciation of the capital stock was not repaired or renovated—by how much the physical plant was allowed to deteriorate over the year.[11] Given depreciation, repairs and renovation reduce deferred maintenance. Deferred maintenance is not a money expenditure, per se, of course, but it is an expenditure of part of the capital stock—consequent on time and its use in production—and therefore a very real cost of the year's operations. The recognition of deferred maintenance is essential if the full effect of the year's activities on the value of the college's wealth are to be reported.

Real depreciation is an estimate of the potential amount of capital stock worn out or used up in the course of the year's operations—the amount it would have depreciated had there been no repairs, renovation, or adaption. The emphasis on *real* depreciation is intended to distinguish this estimate of *actual* decline in the value of a capital stock over the course of the year, due to time and its use, from the more familiar but quite different matter of income tax liability in a for-profit firm: for many, that is what depreciation has come to mean, both in accounting and the public mind. In the global accounts, it is pure economic depreciation.

Finally, maintenance spending, as noted above, is much the same as investment in new plant—it increases the value of durable capital through renovation and adaption—so it is treated the same in the global accounts. To the small amount of such spending found in the current account is added that portion of a conventional investment in plant entry that in fact pays for renovation and adaption.

In table 1, real depreciation was estimated as 2.5 percent of the $324 million capital stock with which 1990–91 started, or $8.1 million.[12] But since that was offset in 1990–91 by an estimated $4.6 million of maintenance spending from the capital budget and another $.64 million from the operating

---

11. *Deferred maintenance* is often used to describe the accumulated result of past failure to spend enough on maintenance to offset real depreciation. It reduces the value of a stock variable. Here we use the phrase, too, to describe a flow—the extent to which this year's maintenance spending failed to offset this year's depreciation. As usual, this year's flow is an increment to the previously accumulated stock. Note that there is nothing necessarily pejorative about deferred maintenance: it often is advisable to let physical capital depreciate.

12. The 2.5 percent is a conservative estimate. Economists (Schultz 1960; O'Neill 1971) have put it at 2 percent of the replacement value of plant and equipment per year, but estimates more carefully done by university capital planners get 1.5–2.5 percent for renovation and another .5–1.5 percent for adaption (Dunn 1989). So the 2.5 percent used in the text and tables appears to be a conservative estimate of total depreciation and therefore of the spending needed to eliminate all deferred maintenance.

budget, deferred maintenance for the year is estimated, with rounding, as $2.8 million.[13] If current spending on maintenance had been $8.1 million for the year, deferred maintenance would, of course, have been zero.

Additions to the capital stock are the net result of all this: investment in new plant is augmented by maintenance spending and reduced by depreciation. Additions to the capital stock will be positive when new plant and maintenance, together, are larger than real depreciation and negative when they are overwhelmed by the year's depreciation.

Operating Costs

In the global accounts, the year's total real operating costs are reported directly. To total current expenditures is added the year's depreciation of physical plant. So both forms of current spending are recognized as operating costs: current expenditures of the usual sort (less maintenance spending) and current spending of the capital stock through depreciation. Together, these describe the costs of the year's operations.[14]

Wealth: Assets and Liabilities

Assets and liabilities, together, describe the state of a college's wealth at the end of each year. They are the college's stock variables. Two aspects of the reporting of assets in global accounts should be noted. One is de-emphasis of the college's endowment: it shows up in table 1 as a parenthetical notation sandwiched into the list of assets and liabilities that make up the college's wealth. The reason for this dismissive treatment is, simply, that the endowment has come erroneously to be seen as synonymous with total financial wealth. While that was nearly true when colleges had very few nonendow-

---

13. An important departure from the facilities planning literature lies in the fact that the global accounts identify the year's deferred maintenance without implying that it must therefore be prevented; the *recognition* of the cost of real depreciation is not the same thing as *funding* it. See Dunn 1989 or Probasco 1991.

14. An issue lurks under the surface here: it is the classic neglect of the opportunity cost of capital as a real cost of production in colleges and universities (and nonprofits in general). So it is inaccurate to call total current costs *total* when they leave out, in the case of Williams, roughly $30 million a year of real costs of production—half again as much as is typically reported (Winston 1991). Two facts might recommend that we continue to leave them out, however: (1) the global accounts are concerned with the total flows of income and spending by the institution from and to outside agents, so it may be permissible to neglect a real cost of production that is paid, by virtue of the college's ownership of its capital stock, back to itself as imputed income, even though the resulting accounts seriously distort the *costs* of production; and (2) it may be strategically unwise to try to persuade people of the good sense of both the global accounts and an accounting of capital costs at the same time, though a more courageous effort would take on both at once.

ment financial assets and, importantly, very little debt aside from some stray accounts payable, it is not true for many colleges now. Again, Williams' numbers are instructive. In 1989, its endowment had a market value of some $307 million, but the college also had another $22 million in nonendowment assets[15] for total financial assets of $329 million (Williams College 1991). But those assets were encumbered by some $51 million in debt. So the global accounts report net financial wealth of $278 million—total financial assets less total liabilities—as the appropriate measure of the college's financial wealth. In 1990, the endowment was up to $334 million but net financial wealth only to $296 million.

The other important differences in global accounts' wealth reporting are that physical capital assets—land and plant and equipment—are (1) accounted for in current replacement values rather than in the book values that the college originally paid for them and (2) adjusted for accumulated deferred maintenance. At Williams, which is an old school, one major instructional building with seven large classrooms and 13,000 square feet has a book value of less than $50,000 and one faculty residence, not large but pleasant, is valued at $850 (Williams College 1991). Most other campuses would offer similar examples of the distortions inherent in using book values. So while the estimates of replacement values inevitably involve some guesswork, they are clearly a whole lot closer to the truth than are historical values. Accumulated deferred maintenance is treated as an offset against the replacement value of the physical assets, leaving net physical wealth as the measure of value of the capital stock. Table 1 assumes that there was no deferred maintenance before 1989–90, so there is little immediate difference between capital assets and net physical wealth; but table 4 below shows that over a long period, deferred maintenance will significantly reduce the college's net physical wealth— Yale's current pressing problem (*New York Times*, February 3, 1992).

Because financial and physical assets and liabilities are measured in the same current value terms, they can be added together to report the college's total wealth, its total net worth. We are adding apples and apples. For many purposes, it is essential to distinguish between these two forms of wealth (and savings), but for others, it is useful to recognize total wealth, regardless of its form. In table 1, reporting a total 1991 wealth of $645 million tells a very different and more complete story than either reporting an endowment of $342 million or financial wealth of $309 million.

---

15. Though they may differ from endowment assets in other ways, the defining characteristic of these financial assets is that they are "owned," within the college, by a fund other than the endowment fund.

Savings and Wealth: Flow-Stock Relationships

The usual tautological accounting relationships between economic flows and stocks apply to global accounts: *savings* is the difference between income and spending over the period; any change in wealth between two dates equals and must be due to savings over that period; net worth (wealth) at the beginning of a period plus income minus spending has to equal net worth at the end of the period. Of course, real depreciation must be added to current expenditures to account fully for the year's total spending. This done, the stock-flow identity holds for total savings and wealth (net worth) as well as for financial and physical savings and wealth separately. It is just as relevant to global accounts as it is to one's checking account.[16]

Operating and Capital Budgets

Operating and capital budgets are embedded in the global accounts, serving their managerial and planning functions but firmly in the context of the college's overall activities. So total operating expenditures, the bottom line in an operating budget like that of table 2, appears in the global accounts as a component of current spending (the largest). The effect, then, of operating budget performance on the college's wealth is incorporated immediately and directly. Though it is not made explicit here, the same is true for a capital budget that is mapped directly into the global accounts in the form of either new investment or as current spending on renovation and adaption.

---

16. But with one awkwardness caused by the use of current market or replacement values for physical capital wealth in an inflationary environment. It lies in the need for an inflation adjustment to the value of the physical capital stock from year to year that does not (as would be strictly appropriate) appear here as nominal income. Strict adherence to the tautology would have to report the gain in physical asset value due to inflation as income (a physical capital gain) and then assign all of that income to savings, thereby justifying the increase in the nominal value of the capital stock. But since that portion of income is always saved and serves only to keep the replacement value of the capital stock in current dollars, the better choice seems to be to introduce an apparent violation of the stock-flow tautology rather than insert a large piece of funny money income explicitly into the body of the accounts. So the replacement value of physical capital reflects inflation within each year as well as showing the effect of net investment. As presented in table 1, then, the tautology applies directly to financial savings and wealth but not to physical capital or total savings and wealth, unless inflation-induced physical capital gains income is included. (For the reader who would like to confirm this relationship, the replacement value of the capital stock was $300,000,000 in 1989 while the inflation rate was (rounded) 4.85 percent over 1989–90 and 4.71 percent over 1990–91, so the inflation adjustments in replacement value are $14,553,473 and $15,240,777 in 1989–90 and 1990–91, respectively. With these, net physical wealth and net worth at the beginning of each period plus savings and inflation adjustment will equal net physical wealth and net worth at the end of the period.)

TABLE 2.   Global Accounts: Current Expenditure Component

	1989–90	1990–91
Operating budget		
Salary pools		
Faculty	$10,194,014	$11,415,331
Administrative/Prof	6,029,465	6,315,789
Weekly	11,568,273	12,101,430
Total salary pools	27,791,752	29,832,550
Fringe benefits	7,258,226	7,816,225
Financial aid	6,517,892	7,719,186
Other restricted spending	2,720,321	3,505,429
Managers' budgets	18,137,112	18,050,939
Total operating budget expenses	62,425,303	66,924,329
Other current expenditures	6,304,914	5,634,728
Less maintenance spending in current account	703,276	642,167
Total current expenditures	68,026,941	71,916,890

Note that while operating *expenditures* are reported in a line in the global accounts, operating *revenues* do not appear. The reason is, simply, that a college's decision on how much of its total income to allocate to an operating budget as revenue is an internal and essentially arbitrary one. That decision may be influenced by some accumulated tradition—tuition and fees, for instance, may all go to the operating budget while only some gifts and a formulaic portion of asset income do—but a college can, by assignment and transfer of its income to and from the budget, make a budget deficit or surplus virtually anything it wants to be including, Swarthmore and others have shown, always exactly zero.[17] Clarity is served, then, by focusing the global accounts on *spending* in the operating budget—or more broadly, on all current spending—as it encompasses an important set of activities in the college's educational enterprise. Attention to the arbitrary assignment of operating budget *revenues*—the result of shifting money between pockets—and the consequent budget deficits or surpluses can be replaced by attention to real

17. In addition to Bierman and Hofstedt's brief fame for showing that budget deficits are often highly misleading—when MIT reported a $5 million deficit, they actually saved $100 million; Princeton's reported $1.5 million deficit went with $151 million in savings; and Harvard's $1.4 million deficit coincided with $314 million in savings, inter alia—a number of others have tried to sound the same warning. William Nordhaus, economist and provost at Yale from 1986 to 1988, for instance, cautioned against relying on operating budget deficits and surpluses because "actions are generally taken to produce a balanced budget" (Nordhaus 1989, 10).

current spending and to actual performance relative to an approved spending plan.[18]

Using Global Accounts

The global accounts structure was first used to organize a historical review of Williams' economic behavior to provide a descriptive context for evaluating present and future performance (Winston 1988). It was done at the height of the public criticisms of cost growth in higher education when it was deemed wise to know how present performance compared with the past. We were able to generate long data series[19] on income levels and changes in its composition; on spending, its composition, and real rates of growth; and on real saving and its distribution between financial and physical capital wealth. The result provided a foundation for economic policies.

But the broader significance of global accounts appears to lie in their ability to describe, monitor, and evaluate a college's current economic performance and in the structure they give to economic planning.

Monitoring and Evaluating Economic Performance

The global accounts do not force any specific criteria of performance evaluation on a college except implicitly in describing the totality of the school's economic activity, but they do make it especially easy to monitor the effects on its real wealth on the college's behavior and the economic circumstances it operates in: the difference between income and current spending is savings (or dissavings), and that, dollar for dollar, increases (or decreases) wealth. And global accounts make it easy to break that down to monitor, separately, the effects of college behavior on financial wealth and on physical capital wealth. There are good reasons why a governing board might consider a dollar saved in a liquid financial asset to be very different from a dollar saved in constructing or renovating a building; both are savings, but their different forms carry quite different implications for future flexibility, costs, returns, and perfor-

---

18. Operating revenues are structurally a lot like a child's allowance—the part of family income the parents assign for the child to spend. Whether or not the child can get by on, or even save from, the allowance is not an uninteresting question or one always viewed with dispassion. But it would be a mistake of some significance if the parents (or their creditors) were to represent the child's deficit or surplus on the child's allowance as a measure of the family's economic fortunes for the week. So, in the context of higher education, a number of Princeton faculty members were vocally unimpressed with the university's recent and much publicized operating budget deficits, convinced that there had to be more going on there than met the eye (Lyall 1989). Global accounts make it clear that there was.

19. Initially, for the thirty years since Williams was a small, all-male, fraternity-centered college.

mance. Even at the level of total savings, a board may think it wise to maintain real wealth or to increase it or to spend some of it down.[20] Or it may prefer only to monitor real wealth or income or spending or their components, rather than to define explicit policies in those respects. These are all decisions on which the structure of the global accounts is agnostic.

Using data from table 1, table 3 illustrates one sort of evaluative summary that global accounts can produce to describe, in the broadest terms, a college's performance for a year.[21] Other summary data could be generated, but these are especially useful in informing broad questions of strategy and governance.

The first line of table 3—savings, or the gain or loss of real wealth—is, in a sense, the bottom line of the global accounts. It describes the change in total real wealth that results from the college's activities for the year, recognizing all its sources of income, all its expenditures on current account and new capital and maintenance, all the depreciation of its physical capital stock, and the contrary effects of inflation in eroding the real value of its financial wealth while increasing the nominal value of its physical wealth. In this fundamental measure, the fortunes of the college illustrated in table 3 declined by some $11 million between 1989–90 and 1990–91, from real savings of $10.2 million to real dissavings of $.7 million.

The next four lines of table 3 address two of the many questions that might be asked about the year's total real savings. The first two lines describe the distribution of total real savings between financial and physical wealth. Physical wealth fared better than did financial wealth in 1989–90 but had a slightly larger decline in 1990–91. The next two lines ask what would have happened to savings without the gifts that were targeted to increase wealth. Some of the increase in wealth on line 1 was the result of the explicit intentions of donors who gave the college money for the purpose of increasing its wealth, so that component might well be separated out from any change in wealth, savings, that was due, instead, to the college's decisions and external circumstances during the year. Without the gifts to wealth (to endowment and plant) of $8 and $9 million in the two years, the college would have saved in other ways some $2.1 million in the good year and lost a bit more than $10 million in the bad one. Again, governing boards would differ in their evaluation of these facts: had the school's performance led to neither savings nor dissavings in those years, that might be considered good work by a board

---

20. The four alternative objectives that Dunn described for endowment wealth are relevant in this broader context of total wealth: (1) protect its nominal value, (2) protect its purchasing power—its real value, (3) have wealth grow as fast as operating expenses, or (4) increase wealth per student as fast as that of competing or peer institutions (Dunn 1991, 34–35).

21. The details of getting from table 1 to table 3 are included in the table in appendix B.

TABLE 3.   Global Accounts Summary

	1989–90	1990–91
1. Savings—Gain (or loss) of total real wealth	$10,171,785	($651,954)
Gain (or loss) of real financial wealth	$4,156,623	($146,923)
Gain (or loss) of real physical wealth	$6,015,162	($505,051)
Gifts to increase real wealth	$8,083,066	$9,457,930
Savings to increase real wealth	$2,088,719	($10,109,904)
2. Income	$99,183,301	$93,272,130
Real growth rate	−3.26%	−10.19%
3. Spending		
Operating costs	$75,526,941	$80,014,085
Deferred maintenance	$3,319,164	$2,815,336
Investment in new plant	$9,334,326	$2,310,285
Real growth rates:		
Operating costs	4.51%	1.18%
Deferred maintenance	36.27%	−18.99%
Investment in new plant	4.35%	−76.36%
4. Savings—Gain (or loss) of total real wealth, using		
smoothed asset income	$7,276,151	$8,600,747

interested in real wealth maintenance while it would be considered poor performance by a board that wanted, say, to catch up to Amherst or Swarthmore in wealth per student. So again, the global accounts are agnostic on policy aims.

College income is reported next in table 3 in current dollars while its growth is reported in real terms, adjusted for inflation; together they monitor the flow of total resources into the school over the year.

Direct monitoring of costs and spending levels and their real growth, as presented in the third section of table 3, is a response to the criticisms of higher education in the 1980s and the conviction that real spending growth should be watched closely, both in detailed categories and broadly. Operating costs include both current expenditures and real depreciation as reported in table 1. The year's deferred maintenance is reported as a separate line because of its usual neglect and its potential for causing serious long-term mischief. A board might adopt the policy that deferred maintenance should always be zero (giving top priority to protection of physical plant, whatever it costs in other objectives), or it might feel that deferred maintenance is simply one important aspect of performance that needs to be monitored attentively—a board might conclude that deferring maintenance, like any other reduction in savings, can sometimes provide money to do other, more important, things. Again, global accounts inform policy by defining required maintenance spending and showing the cost of not doing it. Investment in new plant describes only spending for new physical capital.

The last section of table 3 addresses an evaluation problem for well-endowed schools that report their financial assets at market values and thereby incur potentially large variations in reported income through capital gains and losses caused by market fluctuations: year-to-year comparisons of global performance will be hard to interpret if major changes in asset market value have dominated the numbers. So in this last section of the table, the effect of the year's activities on the college's wealth are reexamined using a five-year moving average of asset income instead of actual asset income for each year: that smooths out the volatile element while still reflecting its underlying changes in a subdued form. These data for 1989–90 and 1990–91 illustrate the effect nicely. Between the two years, the school's capital gains income fell by almost $12 million, so much of the striking difference in the effects of performance on real wealth between the two years was due to that sharp (and uncontrollable) decline in income and not, as it might first appear, to the way the college was run in the latter year. Indeed, the effect of operations on real wealth was, with smoothed income, better in the second year: without that abrupt decline in asset income, reductions in deferred maintenance and the growth of current spending would have increased savings by $1.3 million in 1990–91.

The Global Economic Plan

Global accounts easily provide the framework for an economic planning model that has the same inclusive scope and the same ability to integrate detailed management subplans while showing the global economic implications of the school's intended behavior and anticipated circumstances. Tables 4 to 6 illustrate such a model. Table 4 is a basic global economic plan; table 5 is a subaccount giving more detail on planned current spending, the operating budget; and table 6 gives the sort of evaluative summary data just described, here extended to include anticipated future performance over the period of the plan. All values are in 1992 dollars with an assumed 5 percent inflation rate, and past accumulation of deferred maintenance is arbitrarily set at zero at the beginning of 1989–90. All planned and projected values are rounded.

Two years of historical performance data—1989–90 and 1990–91—are the starting point for projections of both anticipated circumstances (inflation, asset market conditions, etc.) and planned college behavior (staffing, salaries, tuitions, resource allocation, etc.). The heart of a planning process is, of course, the thoughtful specification of these planning parameters—projections of future intentions, plans, and expectations. But in terms of the plan *structure* that is at issue here, after the college has decided on those

planning parameters—how it wants and expects the components of the accounts to change in the future—a global economic plan will show the effects
of that behavior on the college's real wealth over the period of the plan. It is,
then, a consistency-and-implications model: the pieces have to fit together
over any year, and they have to fit together from one period to the next,
satisfying the truism that wealth at the beginning of the period plus income
less spending has to equal wealth at the end of the period; each period's
performance is anchored in the past year's and the projections are anchored in
the most recent history. The result is neither an optimization model nor an
equilibrium model. It can be made into a long-run financial equilibrium model
if a constant rate of growth of wealth is imposed, but that remains an option
and not a characteristic. It is hoped that its more modest logical structure may
well be of greater practical value than the more abstract alternatives in actual
planning, administration, and governance. The global plan takes the concrete
form of a Lotus spreadsheet that is easy to use to ask, repeatedly, the question,
What will be the economic implications of the following behavior, now and in
the future?

The data in tables 4 through 6 are based on tables 1 through 3, but it is
important that they carry no implication about future plans or projections for
any actual school. They are illustrative only of the structure of the economic
plan. To make that very clear, planning parameter values in these tables have
been entered as caricatures—most either as the constant rate of growth of 6
percent (nominal) or as a constant nominal quantity[22]—with the hope that that
high level of artificiality will make it starkly clear that these tables deal only
with model structure and no privileged information is conveyed.

A cost of that artificiality, though, is that the numbers in these tables are
less revealing of an actual planning exercise than they would be with more
realistic parameter values. Nonetheless, they show that if a college, starting
with the historical performance described in the first two columns, were to
plan its spending and anticipate income as described by these rates and levels,
it would wind up as described in the last four columns: it would see increasing
yearly dissavings, the loss of more real financial wealth than physical wealth,
an increased underlying dissavings that is hidden in part by gifts intended to
increase wealth, real income growth hovering around zero with real operating
costs that are increasing modestly, declining real new investment, and declining but still positive real deferred maintenance. If that pattern of behavior (and
circumstances) continued until the academic year 2001–2, the college would

---

22. In practice, three kinds of parameter values might be used to describe plans and
projections: (1) rates of growth (constant or changing from one year to the next), (2) levels
(constant in real or nominal terms or changing over time), and (3) functionally dependent
parameters reflecting things like the way institutional need-based financial aid expenses depend
on tuition decisions.

TABLE 4. Global Economic Plan (current dollars, inflation rate 5%)

	1989–90	1990–91	Plan Parameters	Planned 1991–92	Planned 1992–93	Planned 1993–94	Projected 2001–02
1. College income							
Tuition and fees	$ 29,262,691	$ 32,543,540	6.0%	$ 34,500,000	$ 36,600,000	$ 38,800,000	$ 61,800,000
Gifts and grants							
To endowment	7,066,669	8,744,806	$9M	9,000,000	9,000,000	9,000,000	9,000,000
To plant	1,016,397	713,124	$1M	1,000,000	1,000,000	1,000,000	1,000,000
All other	12,664,824	13,951,045	$14M	14,000,000	14,000,000	14,000,000	14,000,000
Asset income							
Interest and dividends	17,039,521	15,859,257	6.0%	16,800,000	17,800,000	18,900,000	30,100,000
Appreciation	18,582,670	6,873,486	6.0%	7,300,000	7,700,000	8,200,000	13,000,000
Sales, services, and other	1,950,970	2,724,059	6.0%	2,900,000	3,100,000	3,200,000	5,200,000
Auxiliary income	11,599,559	11,862,813	6.0%	12,600,000	13,300,000	14,100,000	22,500,000
Total college income	99,183,301	93,272,130		98,100,000	102,500,000	107,200,000	156,600,000
2. Current expenditures							
Operating budget expenditures	62,425,303	66,924,329	On Table 5	70,900,000	75,200,000	79,700,000	127,000,000
Other current expenditures	6,304,914	5,634,728	On Table 5	6,000,000	6,300,000	6,700,000	10,700,000
Less current account maintenance	703,276	642,167	$650,00	650,000	650,000	650,000	650,000
Total current expenditures	68,026,941	71,916,890		76,300,000	80,900,000	85,800,000	137,100,000

3. Additions to capital stock							
Investment in new plant	9,334,326	2,310,285	$7 M constant	2,100,000	2,100,000	2,200,000	2,600,000
Less deferred maintenance							
Real depreciation	7,500,000	8,097,195	2.5% K-stock	8,500,000	9,000,000	9,500,000	14,600,000
less maintenance spending:							
In Current Account	703,276	642,167	$650,000	650,000	650,000	650,000	650,000
In Plant Fund	3,477,560	4,639,692	6.0%	4,900,000	5,200,000	5,500,000	8,800,000
Total deferred maintenance	3,319,164	2,815,336		2,950,000	3,150,000	3,350,000	5,150,000
Total additions to capital	6,015,162	(505,051)		(850,000)	(1,050,000)	(1,150,000)	(2,550,000)
4. Operating costs:							
Current expenditures	68,026,941	71,916,890	As above	76,300,000	80,900,000	85,800,000	137,100,000
Real depreciation	7,500,000	8,097,195	As above	8,500,000	9,000,000	9,500,000	14,600,000
Total operating costs	75,526,941	80,014,085		84,800,000	89,900,000	95,300,000	151,700,000
5. Wealth end of year							
Financial wealth							
Assets	346,203,972	358,726,081		373,500,000	387,100,000	400,200,000	481,100,000
Less liabilities	50,596,648	49,355,661	$50M	50,000,000	50,000,000	50,000,000	50,000,000
Net financial wealth	295,607,324	309,370,420		323,500,000	337,100,000	350,200,000	431,100,000
[Endowment value]	[333,553,551]	[341,572,081]	$350M	[350,000,000]	[350,000,000]	[350,000,000]	[350,000,000]
Physical capital wealth							
Replacement value	323,887,799	341,438,861		360,600,000	380,800,000	402,000,000	617,000,000
Less accumulated deferred maintenance	3,319,164	6,290,686		9,600,000	13,200,000	17,200,000	66,200,000
Net physical wealth	320,568,635	335,148,175		351,000,000	367,600,000	384,800,000	550,800,000
Net worth	616,175,959	664,518,515		674,500,000	704,700,000	735,000,000	981,900,000

TABLE 5. Global Economic Plan: Current Expenditure Component

	1989–90	1990–91	Plan Parameters	1991–92	1992–93	1993–94	2001–02
Operating budget							
Salary pools							
Faculty	$10,194,014	$11,415,331	6.0%	$12,100,000	$12,800,000	$13,600,000	$21,700,000
Administrative and professional	6,029,465	6,315,789	6.0%	6,700,000	7,100,000	7,500,000	12,000,000
Weekly	11,568,273	12,101,430	6.0%	12,800,000	13,600,000	14,400,000	23,000,000
Total salary pools	27,791,752	29,832,550		31,600,000	33,500,000	35,500,000	56,600,000
Fringe benefits	7,258,226	7,816,225	6.0%	8,300,000	8,800,000	9,300,000	14,800,000
Financial aid	6,517,892	7,719,186	6.0%	8,200,000	8,700,000	9,200,000	14,700,000
Other restricted spending	2,720,321	3,505,429	6.0%	3,700,000	3,900,000	4,200,000	6,700,000
Managers' budgets	18,137,112	18,050,939	6.0%	19,100,000	20,300,000	21,500,000	34,300,000
Total operating budget expenses	62,425,303	66,924,329		70,900,000	75,200,000	79,700,000	127,000,000
Other current expenditures	6,304,914	5,634,728	6.0%	6,000,000	6,300,000	6,700,000	10,700,000
Less maintenance spending in current account	703,276	642,167	$650,000	650,000	650,000	650,000	650,000
Total current expenditures	68,026,941	71,916,890		76,300,000	80,900,000	85,800,000	137,100,000

TABLE 6. Global Economic Plan: Summary (current dollars, inflation rate 5 percent)

	1989–90	1990–91	Plan Parameters	1991–92	1992–93	1993–94	2001–02
1. Savings—gain (or loss) of total real wealth	$10,171,785	($651,974)		($2,200,000)	($3,600,000)	($4,900,000)	($16,300,000)
Gain (or loss) of real financial wealth	$4,156,623	($146,923)		($1,300,000)	($2,600,000)	($3,800,000)	($13,700,000)
Gain (or loss) of real physical wealth	$6,015,162	($505,051)		($900,000)	($1,000,000)	($1,200,000)	($2,600,000)
Gifts to increase real wealth	$8,083,066	$9,457,930	Details	$10,000,000	$10,000,000	$10,000,000	$10,000,000
Savings to increase real wealth	$2,088,719	($10,109,904)		($12,200,000)	($13,600,000)	($14,900,000)	($26,300,000)
2. Income	$99,183,301	$93,272,130	on	$98,100,000	$102,500,000	$107,200,000	$156,600,000
Real growth rate	-3.26%	-10.19%	tables	0.12%	-0.45%	-0.39%	0.03%
3. Spending							
Operating costs	$75,526,341	$80,014,085		$84,800,000	$89,900,000	$95,300,000	$151,700,000
Deferred maintenance	$3,319,164	$2,815,336		$3,000,000	$3,200,000	$3,300,000	$5,200,000
Investment in new plant	$9,334,326	$2,310,285	4	$2,100,000	$2,100,000	$2,200,000	$2,600,000
Real growth rates							
Operating costs	4.51%	1.18%	and	0.93%	0.96%	0.95%	0.93%
Deferred maintenance	36.27%	-18.99%		0.40%	1.13%	1.02%	0.26%
Investment in new plant	4.35%	-76.36%	5	-14.18%	-2.25%	-2.32%	-3.10%
4. Savings—Gain (or loss) of total real wealth (using smoothed asset income)	$7,276,151	$8,660,747		$2,600,000	$4,000,000	($2,000,000)	($17,100,000)
5. Accumulated deferred maintenance	$3,319,164	$6,290,686		$9,600,000	$13,200,000	$17,200,000	$66,200,000

find itself dissaving at an annual real rate of $16 million, despite $10 million a
year in gifts intended to increase its wealth. Most of that dissavings would
take the form of drawing down financial assets, but there would still be an
accumulated deferred maintenance of some $66 million or a bit less than 10
percent of its capital stock (all in 2002 dollars). A governing board, looking at
these results, would have to conclude that the projected behavior under the
projected circumstances is not sustainable. The elimination of asset income
volatility makes a significant difference in the evaluation of short-run performance, but, predictably, it has a declining effect on the evaluation of smoothly
projected future performance. So the plan reveals that something more fundamental than asset income volatility is producing unsustainable results.

Given the artificiality of these numbers, the results of these plan projections probably do not deserve much more discussion, but they should serve to
give a sense of the kind of strategic information that is generated by the global
plan: it is, most generally, a description of the future resource implications of
the behavior and circumstances envisioned by the college.

Premises and Promise

The premise of the global accounts has been that a college's administration or
governing board *wants* to have meaningful and accessible economic information about the college's performance, but that may sometimes be naive. That
the operating budget can be a political document is often acknowledged and
usually described as regrettable, but it is also of considerable value in avoiding questions and discussions that might be time consuming, tedious, and
challenging to administrative decisions. The fact that fund accounts can selectively hide or reveal transactions is often convenient. So is the emphasis on
endowment wealth, as though there were no other kind of financial assets and
no offsetting debt. And so on. But the difficulty with the manipulation of
economic information or selective optimism in its reporting is the old one that
plagues any departure from scrupulous efforts to report the economic facts:
that the first victim of distorted economic information is often the author of
those distortions. It is simply hard to manage a place if you do not know what
is going on. This is a lesson learned and relearned in contexts ranging from
the Soviet planned economy to the current gyrations of state and city budgets
in New York. Unfortunately, as the government parallel suggests, governors
and mayors change and so do college administrations, increasing the temptation those transients face to keep their economic numbers looking good and let
the sober facts show up eventually "but not on my watch."

But more positively, and more importantly, global accounts appear to
represent a marked improvement over fund accounting both in informing the
long-run policy issues that confront colleges and universities and in monitoring their most basic economic performance. The information these accounts

present has proven to be the sort that induces and encourages the discussion of strategic fundamentals, of issues that are basic to the governance of the institution, issues that take the form of the question, If we keep on doing what we are doing, or what we are planning to do next year, what will happen to our economic wealth? Such elemental questions are not so readily induced or addressed by the kind of economic information now readily available to colleges and universities.

Global accounts describe the effect of a year's activities, actual or planned, on all of the college's real wealth, on the distribution of that wealth between financial and physical assets, on deferred maintenance, and on levels and real growth of income from its various sources and of spending on its various objectives, this in an environment of inflation with its opposing effects on the values of financial and physical wealth. Global accounts describe the whole of an institution; their data are designed to avoid omissions and partial truths, to be clear and accessible, and to direct attention to the most basic economic implications of a college's behavior.

APPENDIX A

TABLE 1-A. Global Financial Accounts

	1989–90	1990–91
1. College income		
Tuition and fees	$ 29,262,691	$ 32,543,540
Gifts and grants		
To endowment	7,066,669	8,744,806
To plant	1,016,397	713,124
All other	12,664,824	13,951,045
Asset income		
Interest and dividends	17,039,521	15,859,257
Appreciation	18,582,670	6,873,486
Sales, services, and other	1,950,970	2,724,059
Auxiliary income	11,599,559	11,862,813
Total college income	99,183,301	93,272,130
2. Current expenditures		
Operating budget expenditures	62,425,303	66,924,329
Other current expenditures	6,304,914	5,634,728
Less current account maintenance	703,276	642,167
Total current expenditures	68,026,941	71,916,890
3. Capital expenditures		
Investment in new plant	9,334,326	2,310,285
Maintenance in current account	703,276	642,167
Maintenance in plant fund	3,477,560	4,639,692
Total additions to capital	13,515,162	7,592,144

(Continued)

TABLE 1-A.—_Continued_

	1989–90	1990–91
4. Financial wealth end of year		
Assets	346,203,972	358,726,081
[Endowment value]	[333,553,551]	[341,572,081]
Less liabilities	50,596,648	49,355,661
Net financial wealth	295,607,324	309,370,420
5. Financial savings		
Total financial savings	17,641,198	13,763,096
Breakeven savings (inflation offset)	13,484,575	13,910,019
Real financial savings	4,156,623	(146,923)
Real net of gifts to endowment	(2,910,046)	(8,891,729)

APPENDIX B

Performance Calculations

	1989–90	1990–91
Savings—gain (or loss) of real wealth	$10,171,785	($651,974)
Total real savings: $Y-X-[hK^*(t-1)-(mc+mk)]+iK^*(t-1)$	$38,209,833	$28,498,822
Breakeven savings: $iNFW(t-1)+iK^*(t-1)$	$28,038,048	$29,150,796
Gain (or loss) of real financial wealth—Real savings	$4,156,623	($146,923)
Total financial savings $Y-X-K$	$17,641,198	$13,763,096
Breakeven savings (inflation offset) $i(NFW)(t-1)$	$13,484,575	$13,910,019
Gain (or loss) of physical wealth—Real savings	$6,015,162	($505,051)
Total physical capital savings: $K-[hK^*(t-1)-(mc+mk)]+iK^*(t-1)$	$20,568,635	$14,735,726
Breakeven savings (inflation offset): $iK^*(t-1)$	$14,553,473	$15,240,777
Composition of savings		
Financial savings	41%	23%
Physical savings	59%	77%
With smoothed asset income		
Savings—gain (or loss) of total real wealth, smoothed	$7,276,151	$ 8,600,747
Total savings	$35,314,199	$37,751,543
Gain (or loss) of real financial wealth	$1,260,989	$ 9,105,798
Total financial savings, smoothed	$14,745,564	$23,015,817
Spending		
Deferred maintenance: $hK^*(t-1)-(mc+mk)$	$3,319,164	$ 2,815,336
Real yearly growth	36.27%	-18.99%
Current expenditures: $X-(mc+mk)$	$68,026,941	$71,916,890
Real yearly growth	4.72%	0.97%
Operating costs: $X-(mc+mk)+hK^*(t-1)$	$75,526,941	$80,014,085
Real yearly growth	4.51%	1.18%
Investment in new plant	$9,334,326	$ 2,310,285
Real yearly growth	4.35%	-76.36%

Note: K = new investment; K^* = replacement value of capital stock; h = depreciation rate; mc and mk = maintenance spending in current and capital-budget, respectively (both included in X); i = inflation rate; Y = income; X = (current expenditures + mc + mk); $(t-1)$ = end of previous period.

REFERENCES

Bierman, Harold Jr., and Thomas R. Hofstedt. "University Accounting (Alternative Measures of Ivy League Deficits)." *Non-Profit Report,* May 1973, 14–23.

Chabotar, Kent John. "Financial Ratio Analysis Comes to Nonprofits." *Journal of Higher Education* 60, no. 2 (March/April 1989), 188–208.

Dunn, John A., Jr. *Financial Planning Guidelines for Facilities Renewal and Adaption.* Ann Arbor: The Society for College and University Planning, 1989.

Dunn, John A., Jr. "How Colleges Should Handle Their Endowment." *Planning for Higher Education* 19, no. 3 (Spring 1991).

Garner, C. William. *Accounting and Budgeting in Public and Nonprofit Organizations.* San Francisco: Jossey-Bass Publishers, 1991, chapter 2 ("The Role of Funds").

Harried, Andrew A., Leroy F. Imdieke, and Ralph E. Smith. *Advanced Accounting.* 3d ed. New York: John Wiley and Sons, Inc., 1985.

Harvard University. *Financial Report to the Board of Overseers of Harvard College.* Cambridge, MA: Harvard University, 1992.

Lyall, Sarah. "Strife over Style and Substance Tests Princeton's Leader." *New York Times,* December 4, 1989, B1.

Nordhaus, William. "Evaluating the Risks for Specific Institutions." Yale University, March 14, 1989.

O'Neill, June. *Resource Use in Higher Education: Trends in Output and Inputs, 1930 to 1967.* A Technical Report Sponsored by the Carnegie Commission on Higher Education. Berkeley: The Carnegie Commission on Higher Education, 1971.

Probasco, Jack. "Crumbling Campuses: What Are the Real Costs?" *Business Officer* 25, no. 5 (November 1991), 48–51.

Schultz, Theodore W. "Capital Formation by Education." *Journal of Political Economy* 68, no. 6 (December 1960): 571–83.

Swarthmore College. "The Treasurer's Report 1986–87." In *The President's Report, 1986–87.* Swarthmore: Swarthmore College, 1987.

Williams College. "The Treasurer's Report 1990–91." Williamstown, MA: Williams College, 1991.

Winston, Gordon C. "Total College Income: An Economic Overview of Williams College, 1956–57 to 1986–87." Williams College, April 10, 1988.

———. "Why Are Capital Costs Ignored by Colleges and Universities and What Are the Prospects for Change?" Williams Project on the Economics of Higher Education, Discussion Paper No. 14. July 1991.

Winston, Gordon C., and Duncan Mann. *Global Accounts: Reorganizing Economic Information for Colleges and Universities.* Unpublished.

CHAPTER 13

Why Are Capital Costs Ignored by Nonprofit Organizations and What Are the Prospects for Change?

Gordon C. Winston

An important part of the cost of an education in U.S. colleges and universities is ignored in the economic information policymakers, the public, and the colleges themselves use. They try to understand and manage the educational enterprise with only crude and incomplete information about the costs of the plant and equipment services used in education. At Williams, as a convenient if extreme example, the cost of producing a year of education for a student in 1991 appears to be $33,600, but accounting for the use of capital, it is a bit more than $51,000. Put differently, leaving some $18,000 of capital costs[1] out of the calculation of the educational cost of a year at Williams has the same effect, almost to the dollar, as would leaving out all personnel costs—the total costs of the faculty, administration, and hourly workers, including their fringe benefits ($18,051 per student).

The distorted view of actual costs that comes from neglecting capital at a school like Williams is especially severe because, oddly, the degree of neglect and distortion depends primarily not on how much capital a school uses in its activities but on the accident of how it pays for that plant and equipment. Williams' costs are understated a great deal because the school owns its capital stock outright. If Williams were to sell its campus to a private real estate entrepreneur, lock, stock and barrel, and rent it back at a competitive rate, its apparent current costs per student would rise by almost 60 percent and reflect its true costs. But of course nothing real would be changed, economically. So inconsistency in the treatment of capital costs among schools com-

Reprinted with permission of *Business Officer* magazine. Copyright 1993 National Association of College and University Business Officers. Collin Roche contributed helpful research assistance to this project.

1. A $300,000,000 plant at 10 percent interest rate and 2 percent depreciation spread over 2,000 students. This figure is conservative; total return on endowment has been 12 percent in the recent past, and the plant size is probably understated.

pounds the problems of their understatement, per se, since it becomes impossible to compare educational costs meaningfully except among schools that have very similar financial arrangements in using their plant and equipment.

None of this is news, of course, to economists. In his early work on the costs of higher education, Schultz (1960) explicitly corrected for the absence of capital cost data, and it became routine in studies of educational costs to estimate and add in imputed capital costs (see O'Neil 1971; James 1978; etc.).

But that still leaves the questions in the title of this note: Why don't nonprofit enterprises explicitly and routinely recognize the considerable cost (and contribution to production) of their physical capital stocks, and what, after all this time during which the distortion has been recognized, is likely to come of it?

Why Don't Nonprofits Recognize Capital Costs?

Intermediate microeconomic theory—as taught to undergraduates and in the nation's MBA programs—provides an effective way to organize an understanding of the role and costs of capital in higher education. The theory of the firm distills out the essential elements of technology, costs, and prices that characterize production processes, including those of colleges and universities. It is easy to misapply the economic model of the for-profit firm, to be glib and careless in transferring it to nonprofit activities, but used with modesty and care, it can serve many purposes well.

The Tradition: Capital Costs in the For-Profit Firm

The past couple of decades have seen significant clarification of the theory of productive capital in for-profit firms with the work of Haavelmo (1960) and Jorgenson and Grilliches (1967) and, with particular respect to capital utilization, my own efforts of a few years ago (1982). Capital costs are conceptually slippery for two related reasons: because a firm's capital stocks are *durable*, purchased in one period for use well into the future, and because capital services enter the production process *from within* the firm, unlike the typical flow of current inputs to production that are purchased from outside agents. A firm typically buys a year's labor services and fuel and raw materials from outside suppliers, but it gets the complementary flow of capital services from the durable buildings and machinery that it owns itself. Those characteristics generate no special conundrums in modeling the production process, but they do create problems in measuring capital costs and responding to them.

The costs of using plant and equipment that the firm already owns have, broadly, two dimensions.[2] The first is the value of the capital stock used in production: the number of machines, K, in a stylized example, times the price paid, P_m, for each machine[3] measures the value of the firm's capital stock, P_mK. The other dimension of capital cost recognizes its durability and the fact that it wears out (depreciates) over time and use.

Scarce resources are tied up in capital assets (machines and classrooms and libraries and lab equipment) for a long time. The owner of those capital assets forgoes income since those resources would have been earning interest income if they had been invested, instead, in financial assets. The cost of lost earnings—the opportunity cost of owning long-lived plant and equipment instead of financial assets—is usually the largest cost of using capital in production. If, for instance, the interest rate is 10 percent per year, the yearly opportunity cost of a plant worth $1,000,000 is $100,000.[4]

Real deterioration or depreciation is the other and typically smaller component of capital cost—when the capital stock is used in production, it is partially worn out, and that, too, is a cost of using capital. With 2 percent real depreciation each year, a $1,000,000 plant loses $20,000 of its value through wear and tear.[5]

Putting depreciation and opportunity cost together, the total cost of using K of capital in production for a year will be $(r + d)P_mK$. With 2 percent depreciation and a 10 percent rate of interest, the cost of the $1,000,000 plant is $120,000 a year. That is the full, economic cost of using capital services in production. It is the user cost or rental rate of capital, the price that would have to be charged to rent a unit of capital for a year in a highly competitive environment.

Transplanting Capital Costs

That specification of capital costs is quite universal; it describes the economic costs of using capital in production whether in a for-profit or a nonprofit

---

2. A third dimension that is not of immediate relevance to this discussion is the utilization of a capital stock, most simply the proportion of the total 8,760 hours a year it is used in production. However, that issue does motivate some collegiate schemes like Dartmouth's trimester system and the extensive use of campuses in attractive settings like Williams' for summer conferences.

3. This figure raises a familiar but sticky issue since most accounting records will show the historical costs of capital—its value at the prices originally paid—but what is relevant is replacement or market cost—what the capital is worth now.

4. With an interest rate of r, the opportunity cost of using P_mK of capital in production is rP_mK per year.

5. With a depreciation rate of d, the cost of depreciation is dP_mK per year.

enterprise.[6] So it effectively structures the understanding of total capital cost in colleges and universities.

But accounting for those capital costs in a nonprofit firm hits a serious snag. Accounting traditions were developed primarily for for-profit firms and applied to nonprofits like colleges and universities only secondarily. What makes sense for a nonprofit firm, in this case, seems quite strange in the for-profit tradition: intuition, nurtured by for-profits, makes it very awkward to do the right thing about capital costs in nonprofit firms. Furthermore, part of capital costs—depreciation, the smaller part—is recognized more easily and often in nonprofit accounts,[7] while the larger part—opportunity cost—continues to cause problems.

The hitch comes from the fact that in western capitalist economies, the distinctly different roles of (1) the owner of the productive capital stock and (2) the entrepreneur or organizer of the firm have been merged in the private archetypal firm so their functionally quite different rewards—the costs of capital services and the profits that reward entrepreneurial risk—have been mixed up too. The ownership of capital carries with it rights and responsibilities—and rewards—of management. In the typical for-profit firm like that presented in Economics 101, these roles are joined in a single owner (or a group of stockholder-owners), so Econ 101 instructors routinely insist that their students disentangle these two things. The accounting profits an owner-entrepreneur earns are shown to be an amalgam of, on the one hand, payments to the owner for the use of his capital—$(r + d)P_mK$—and, on the other hand, any additional or economic profits the owner-entrepreneur might earn as an entrepreneur—residual payment for the entrepreneur's organizing-managing-risk-taking function. It is unlikely that that distinction lasts in the minds of the students much beyond the final exam, but the effort at clarity satisfies the instructor.

But if capital costs are mixed in with entrepreneurial profits in the accounting concepts of the private, for-profit firm, what happens to capital costs when those accounting concepts are transplanted to nonprofit firms? The answer has been that they have largely disappeared along with the accounting profits of which they were part. No accounting conventions exist to report the costs of capital separately from entrepreneurial profits because separation was not needed in the capitalist for-profit firm. The owner got the residual: economic profits, capital costs, and all.

---

6. Despite some caveats based on restricted funds.

7. Though it falls short of full accounting of depreciation, an effort is made by nonprofit hospitals, private foundations and others, and a similar (and similarly inadequate) depreciation accounting has been mandated, as discussed below, for colleges and universities starting this year (FASB 1987).

With no way to recognize the opportunity cost of owned productive capital in its own right, even mixed in with profits, the treatment of capital costs in college and university accounting has depended on the accident of its financing. Specifically,

> if *capital is not owned* by the school but is *rented* from outside agents, its full cost, $(r + d)P_mK$, will be recognized as a cost of production because it is explicitly paid to an outside agent;
>
> if *capital is owned* by the school but is *financed by borrowing*, its opportunity cost will be recognized because interest costs, rP_mK, are, again, explicitly paid to an agent outside the institution; the depreciation component of its capital costs, dP_mK, need not be recognized; and
>
> if *capital is owned* by the school but was *purchased from its own funds*, neither its depreciation nor its opportunity costs will be recognized as a current cost: $(r + d)P_mK = 0$ (this is why the Williams illustration in the introduction is an extreme case of cost distortion).

But if the theory of the for-profit firm, with its implied accounting logic and the accumulated weight of tradition, has eliminated most of capital costs from the economics of production in nonprofit firms, it also provides the conceptual structure through which to put them back.

Capital Costs in a Nonprofit Firm

A nonprofit firm has three relevant characteristics that differentiate it from the for-profit firm and tangle any simple effort to transplant the logic of for-profit accounts to nonprofit firms. They are important to why a nonprofit is a nonprofit.

First, the nonprofit firm has no owners (entrepreneurial or stockholder), either inside or outside, separable from the firm itself; no one who has, in capitalist tradition, invested in the capital stock and therefore become entitled to be paid its returns. This point underlies the "nondistributional constraint" that Hansmann (1986) saw as distinguishing nonprofit from for-profit firms: nonprofits can and do earn profits, but they cannot distribute them to anyone.

Second, the nonprofit firm usually earns negative economic profits when those are defined as they are for the typical for-profit firm, as proceeds from the sale of its products less the costs of their production: total revenues minus total costs, like in Econ 101. In colleges and universities, the sticker price (tuition) is typically a good deal less than the average cost of production; each student-customer is subsidized: with a total charge of $20,760, Williams students got a subsidy of at least $29,000 in 1991.

But third, the nonprofit firm very often does earn profits; it can run at a conventional loss but accumulate regular surpluses because its sales revenues are augmented by other nonproduct sources of income—notably gifts, endowment earnings, and indirect cost recovery—so that its total or global income exceeds total expenditures. These sources of income are, of course, absent from the typical for-profit firm.[8]

So for a nonprofit firm, accounting logic stymies the incorporation of capital costs in three ways: (1) there normally is no conventional profit to act as a carrier for the cost of capital services; (2) though there often are positive global profits, they cannot legally be distributed outside the firm; but (3) the capital stock is owned by the firm itself, so any explicit payment of capital service costs will involve the disconcerting practice of the firm's making payments to itself, increasing both its expenditures and its income, the one as a cost of its production and the other as a return on its invested wealth.

Despite the Looking Glass nature of the accounting procedures by which a nonprofit firm can accurately reflect the cost of capital services, how it should be done seems clear. To recognize the opportunity cost of capital, the nonprofit firm would estimate the current value of its physical capital stock, P_mK; it would estimate yearly earnings lost by diverting that wealth from financial investments, r; and it would include the resulting opportunity costs of capital, rP_mK, in both its current production costs and its asset income. To recognize depreciation costs, it would estimate yearly real depreciation, dP_mK, and add to current production costs any excess over current maintenance spending.

What may be jarring about the treatment of capital costs is the addition of the same, imputed, opportunity cost to both spending and income. Why not, it is reasonable to ask, leave things alone? If the neglect of these capital costs misstates the income and expenditures of a nonprofit firm by equal amounts, the bottom line, their difference, will not be affected.

But that is a question framed for the for-profit firm where the bottom line is profits, literally the difference between income and expenditures. Of greater relevance for the nonprofit firm is the composition of costs and income. Where do the resources to pay for education come from, for instance, and where do they go? What is the total cost of education? How and how well are various resources used in producing education? Do the inevitable trade-offs between the use of capital and noncapital resources—computers and teachers, for instance—reflect their costs to the institution? To society? These are questions that simply cannot be answered without an accounting of capital costs. They are far different from questions about profit levels.

But even the procedure that would accurately measure the opportunity costs of capital is not as unconventional as it might appear. Rental income from owner-occupied houses is routinely estimated and imputed to home

---

8. For a more detailed discussion, see Winston 1991.

owners as both income and expenditures in the national income accounts. That convention involves the same thing for the same reason: to capture the value of an economically meaningful flow of capital services that are hidden within the accounting-ownership unit. So we impute the value of that flow of capital services. The same entity both spends and receives the imputed flow; it spends as a *user* of capital services and receives as an *owner* of the capital stock. Samuelson and Nordhaus put it this way:[9]

> *Rent* income of persons [in the national accounts] includes rents received by landlords. In addition, if you own your own house, you are treated as *paying rent to yourself.* This is a so-called imputed item and makes sense if we really want to measure the housing services the American people are enjoying and do not want the estimate to change when people decide to own a home rather than renting it. This imputed item has to be estimated, since people do not report rental receipts on their own homes. (1989, 115)

What Are the Prospects for Change?

Which leads to the second question in the title: how likely is it that there will, in the future, be something more than repeatedly ad hoc recognition and incorporation of the costs of capital services in studies of higher education? What are the chances, in other words, that the kinds of procedures needed to measure and report capital service costs will be incorporated into the routine economic information generated by and for colleges and universities?

One can only speculate, of course, but speculation leads me to doubt that the recognition of the capital costs will become widespread in the accounts of institutions of higher education. The imputation of income seems too much of a departure from the conventions of for-profit firms, and those firms provide the framing that practical people, like trustees, accountants, and auditors, will use to define what is sensible. The reasons, rehearsed here, why for-profit accounting conventions do not serve nonprofit firms well are a bit arcane, dealing with grand issues like the traditions of western capitalism, and it is unreasonable to expect that they will be widely appreciated by those outside of nonprofit firms themselves. And those inside may well be so accustomed to neglecting capital costs that few can be expected to find these suggestions anything but baffling. Their appeal is not increased, either, by the fact that the most important of capital costs leave the bottom line unchanged—that it is, for a nonprofit firm, a less than relevant bottom line may escape notice.

Nor does the recent mandate from the Financial Accounting Standards

---

9. A more official statement is found in U.S. Department of Commerce 1987, 2.

Board (FASB, the official arbiter of accounting practices) that nonprofit organizations report depreciation costs turn out to be as encouraging as it first appears. Despite the clarity with which they recognize the problem ("Omitting depreciation produces results that do not reflect all costs of services provided." FASB 1987, 13), their new standards will not alter the reported operating budgets, educational and general spending, or current fund spending on the basis of which the costs of higher education will usually be judged: instead, the depreciation costs that FASB requires will be hidden away as an obscure accounting adjustment to plant fund balances. Nor does the board give any guidance on how to measure depreciation, leaving the method up to the individual institution with only the requirement that it be based on historical asset costs and that it be made explicit.[10] It appears that when all colleges are in full compliance with the FASB depreciation reporting requirement, it will still be just as necessary as it is now to estimate and impute both the depreciation and opportunity costs of capital if one wants to know the costs of higher education.[11]

The final reason for pessimism is, simply, that large dollar figures are involved for colleges that own their own capital stocks. The recognition of capital costs in reported financial data, however accurate it might be, would increase the measured costs of higher education markedly; the 60 percent increase in Williams' costs is not extreme for a wealthy private institution. In itself, therefore, the very importance of capital costs in higher education will discourage their recognition as that makes it politically so unattractive to administrators.

But, of course, the fact will remain. Those real capital costs *are* being incurred in the production of higher education at the same time that colleges *are* earning implicit returns on their capital stocks. And decisions *are* being made about the efficient use of capital and other resources, and schools' efficiency *is* being judged. And all of this is done in the absence of explicit information about the very considerable costs of capital.

---

10. They acknowledge that using historical values for capital assets creates inherent inaccuracies, but since that problem plagues all capital asset valuation—of for-profit and nonprofit alike—they sensibly argue that the nonprofit context is not an appropriate one in which to take that issue on.

11. It is significant that neither the FASB discussion of depreciation nor the much longer analysis done for the National Association of College and University Business Officers by Collins and Forrester (1988) has even a passing reference to the larger part of capital service costs represented by their opportunity costs.

REFERENCES

Collins, Stephen J., and Robert T. Forrester. *Recognition of Depreciation by Not-for-profit Institutions.* (Washington: the National Association of College and University Business Officers, 1988).

Financial Accounting Standards Board. "Statement of Financial Accounting Standards No. 93: Recognition of Depreciation by Not-for-Profit Organizations." *Financial Accounting Series, No. 047.* (Stamford: FASB, 1987).

Haavelmo, Trygve. *A Study in the Theory of Investment.* (Chicago: The University of Chicago Press, 1960).

Hansmann, Henry. "The Role of Nonprofit Enterprise," Chapter 3 in Susan Rose-Ackerman, ed. *The Economics of Nonprofit Institutions.* (New York: Oxford University Press, 1986).

James, Estelle. "Product Mix and Cost Disaggregation: A Reinterpretation of the Economics of Higher Education." *The Journal of Human Resources,* Vol XII, No. 2, 1978.

Jorgenson, D. W., and Z. Griliches. "The Expansion of Productivity Change." *Review of Economic Studies,* Vol 34, 1967, 249–83.

O'Neill, June. *Resource Use in Higher Education: Trends in Output and Inputs, 1930 to 1967.* A Technical Report Sponsored by the Carnegie Commission on Higher Education. (Berkeley: The Carnegie Commission on Higher Education, 1971).

Samuelson, Paul A. and William D. Nordhaus. *Economics.* 13th ed. (New York: McGraw-Hill Book Company, 1989).

Schultz, Theodore W. "Capital Formation by Education," *Journal of Political Economy,* Vol 68, No. 6 (December, 1960), 571–83.

U.S. Department of Commerce. Bureau of Economic Analysis. "GNP: An Overview of Source Data and Estimating Methods." *Methodology Papers: U.S. National Income and Product Accounts.* Washington, D.C.: GPO, 1987.

Winston, Gordon C. *The Timing of Economic Activities: Firms, Households, and Markets in Time-specific Analysis.* (New York: Cambridge University Press, 1982).

———. "Maintaining a College's Wealth: Endowment Spending Rules, Plant and Equipment, and Global Accounts," Williams College, January 1991.

Part 5
Conclusion

CHAPTER 14

The Next Frontier in Higher Education Economics

Michael S. McPherson, Morton Owen Schapiro, and Gordon C. Winston

What problems will higher education present to economists and policy analysts in the years ahead? What insights in addressing higher education's emerging problems can be gleaned from the studies presented here?

It is not unreasonable to see higher education as having arrived at the end of an era of unprecedented growth and transformation. From the enrollment boom that followed the introduction of the World War II GI Bill through the enormous expansion of open-access community colleges in the 1960s and 1970s, higher education has grown explosively and extended its range of missions and its clientele enormously. The growth of funding and enrollment, fed by rapidly expanding federal and state higher education budgets in the 1960s and 1970s, slowed considerably in the 1980s. Indeed, the analysis in chapter 2 makes clear that the funding crisis that now besets many public higher education systems was beginning to take hold in the late 1980s, as state appropriations for higher education began to lag behind the growth in higher education costs.

It is hard to imagine that higher education will regain the kind of unqualified and exuberant support it enjoyed during much of the post–World War II era any time soon. The federal budget is constrained by the pressing demands of the deficit and a public that remains reluctant to pay enough taxes to finance the services it demands. State governments are hard pressed by public health responsibilities and the need to invest in public infrastructure and elementary and secondary education, while they continue to struggle with a tax revolt of their own. At the same time, the enormous prestige and respect commanded by higher education has been considerably tarnished in recent years. Public attitudes toward and willingness to spend for higher education may well improve from their recent low point, but right now they have a long way to go.

With public revenue sources strained, both private and state-run colleges and universities are increasingly forced to turn to tuition payments from students and parents to finance their enterprise. Meanwhile, these paying customers (like those other paying customers in the statehouse and on Capitol Hill) increasingly want to know just what they are buying. As a result, institutions are becoming increasingly vocal about the need to search for productivity gains and the urgency of improving undergraduate teaching. Talking about these matters is not very hard—talk, after all, is the academy's clearest comparative advantage; on the question of how far universities and colleges will go to "walk the talk," the jury is still out.

Can institutions that are seeking to use resources more efficiently and to get faculty to take teaching more seriously get help from economists? Our answer is a qualified yes. Yes, because we are, after all, economists, and ones who have been heartened to discover through experience that persistent work on higher education issues can yield useful economic insights. But our enthusiasm for economics is qualified by our awareness of what a peculiar beast higher education is. Standard economist's recipes are as likely to mislead as to inform. The right kind of economics for higher education must combine analytical clarity with a considerable knowledge of and respect for the special purposes and the unique institutional realities of the higher education enterprise.

A few examples, drawn in part from the essays presented here, may help make the point.

1. Academic tenure is an affront to the economist's penchant for marginal productivity pricing of inputs and free markets for labor. This conviction of economists has been dealt a blow on a global scale by the conspicuous success of the Japanese economy, whose tradition of lifetime employment and deep suspicion of worker mobility as a sign of disloyalty are much at odds with the ideal of competitive labor markets. But we have argued (in chapter 5) that closer to home, in higher education, some peculiar features of academic work (the importance of peer evaluation, the emphasis on relatively narrow specialization, the difficulty of measuring the quality of work performance) may well make academic tenure a quite suitable form of labor contract for these special circumstances.

2. Economists condemn collusion and all other evidences of monopoly power. Justice Department economists led the charge to condemn collegiate agreements on financial aid awards and practices as violations of the antitrust laws. Yet, as we have had occasion to argue in several essays in this volume, cooperation among institutions to target financial aid on needy students is quite desirable both from the standpoint of efficient use of scarce aid dollars and as a matter of social equity. There are many other areas beyond financial aid where the case is plausible that more cooperation among higher education institutions would serve society better. Presenting a clear picture to high schools of what is expected by way of preparation for college is a simple example. The sharing of expensive and underused resources,

from library books to classrooms and computers, may be another such area. Both the market for students and the market for public support encourage individual institutions to stand on their own and to emphasize their unique identities and distinctive qualities. Much good plainly comes from this competitive spirit; yet it may also cost the system efficiencies and opportunities that are well worth exploring, especially in the strained circumstances of the 1990s.

3. In an argument that at least gestured toward the theory of economic incentives, William Bennett and other commentators asserted in the 1980s that more generous student aid funding would simply induce schools—especially private schools—to raise tuition. Rather than helping the needy, student aid spending hurt everybody by feeding college cost inflation. Coming as it did in an era when medical cost inflation was clearly being fed by exactly this kind of mechanism—with government copayments blunting the incentives of hospitals, doctors, and patients to economize— this analysis quickly developed momentum and soon achieved the enviable status of being repeated often enough to be supposed true. However, a detailed look at the institutional incentives actually set up by the student aid system reveals a crucial difference between higher education and medicine. The copayment system under which most medical care was provided in the 1970s and 1980s was such that a doctor or hospital could, in most cases, get a bigger government payment by raising prices. This key feedback mechanism in generating cost inflation has, however, been largely missing in higher education, because the amounts of federal student aid most students receive are limited by their family resources or statutory maxima, rather than by institutional prices. The automatic escalator built into the medical care reimbursement system just is not there in federal student aid policy. It then becomes an empirical question whether higher student aid tends to cause higher tuition. As we show in chapter 10, the best evidence we could find on this question suggests that there is no tendency for increases in federal student aid to cause increases in private college tuition.

Take these as cautionary tales: a theory that seems to work well when applied to General Motors or the wheat market may be far off the mark when applied to higher education. But we do not want to rest content with paradox mongering, or to imply that standard economic analysis can be put aside in studying colleges and universities. Indeed, our analysis of each of the three examples just recited draws heavily on insights from economics—the economics of information and relational exchange in the case of tenure, the analysis of the Prisoner's Dilemma in the case of student aid agreements (see chapter 4), and multiple regression analysis in the case of the student aid-tuition link.

Moreover, often as not, economic intuitions are confirmed rather than overturned following a careful look at the evidence on a higher education issue: giving poor people more student aid does make them more likely to go to college (chapter 8); organizing college accounts around economic principles does give a more coherent picture of a college's resources and opportunities (chapter 12); theory and evidence both confirm that colleges that charge more tend to devote more resources to providing a quality education (chapters 2 and 4).

The economist's "lore of nicely calculated less and more" may well play a larger role in both public and institutional decision-making about higher education in the decades ahead. Notions of productivity improvement and cost saving that sound sacrilegious to many faculty will be increasingly hard to avoid in deliberations about the choices facing colleges and universities. The challenge for those of us who aim to marry economic analysis to higher education policy is to preserve the insights of economics while respecting the ways in which the special purposes of colleges and universities demand analyses that confound simplistic economic views.

Index

321

Minority students (*continued*)
impact of financial aid on enrollment, 146–47, 188, 196, 210
impact of net cost on enrollment, 207–9
indirect effects of federal aid on enrollment, 157–58
motivations for promoting ethnic and racial diversity, 90
Mitchell, Janet B., 236, 250
Mori, B. M., 227
Mortensen, Tom, 157
Mosteller, Frederick, 63
Mott, Charles, 279n
Mt. Holyoke, 230
Moynihan, Daniel P., 63
Mughal, Saeed, 251n, 279n
Murnane, Richard J., 58n, 65
Murphy, James L., 50n, 53n, 66

Nadiri, M. Ishaq, 42n, 65
NAICU, 185
NASSGP/NCHELP Research Conference, 164, 185
National Academy of Science, 68, 130
National Association of College and University Business Officers, 305n, 312n, 313
National Center for Higher Education Management Systems 48, 62
National Commission on Excellence in Education 39n, 65
National Commission on Student Financial Assistance, 164
National Defense (renamed Direct) Student Loan program, 150, 178n, 199, 205
National Direct Student Loan (NDSL) program, 144n, 180, 200
National Endowment for the Humanities 60
National Governors Association 38, 65
National Institute of Education 59, 67
National Merit Scholarship Corporation, 227

National Student Loan Bank, proposals for, 175, 180–82, 185
NBER (National Bureau of Economic Research), 62, 64, 130, 131
NELS88 (National Educational Longitudinal Survey of 1988) data, 225
Nelson, Philip, 81, 82
Nelson, Richard R., 41n, 42n, 43n, 58n, 65, 166, 180, 181, 185
Neuberger, E., 119n, 131
Newman, F., 191n, 227
Niemi, Richard, 43n, 65
NLS72 (National Longitudinal Survey of the High School Class of 1972) data, 193n, 196
Noell, J., 188, 196, 228
Nordhaus, William D., 290n, 303, 313
Northeast Missouri State University, 40, 45, 46, 49, 65
NPSAS (National Postsecondary Student Assistance Survey) data, 214

Obsolescence, defined, 285n
Office of Education. *See* Department of Education
Oi, Walter, 129, 131
Okun, Arthur, 111, 112, 122n, 131
O'Malley, Michael P., 187n
O'Neill, Joseph P., 47n, 65
O'Neill, June, 54n, 65, 286n, 303, 306, 313

Pace, Robert, 38n, 45n, 48n, 65
Parent Loan for Undergraduate Students (PLUS) program, 200
Pascal, 122
Pascarella, E. T., 47n, 66
Pavitt, Keith, 42n, 66
Pell grants. *See also* Federal student aid; Lower-income students; Middle-income students; Students; enrollment, institutional choice; Upper-income students
award amounts, per FTE, 144–46
easing of income restrictions, 144